"This is a heart-warming, gentle read of profundity. *Ike,* the dog and the story, are a study in perspective and uncomplicated clarity that guides the reader through lessons of friendship, family, redemption, forgiveness, determination, laughter, and all that make a life whole. *Ike,* with his unconditional loyalty and old soul wisdom, offers the beacon of light and hope that illuminates the path from the wreckage of Jason's Olympic dreams through healing, understanding, and love in all its beauty. You will laugh, cry, and cheer as Jason discovers and carves his path forward in life. This story is uplifting, honest, funny, and meaningful. Enjoy the read."

— Ellen Smoor Foster, Ph.D., Author

"There's something wonderful and beneficial about living with a creature that unwaveringly loves you. It's something that has been studied. It's measurable. But we don't get a dog to become a better human. The story of *Ike* and Jason however, is exactly that. I found it to be powerful, captivating, and truly lovely. It's a story that people will relate to on different levels, as I did. Those of us who have lived with dogs will connect immediately with certain aspects, but it might be an even more important book for those who have not."

— Duff Gibson, Olympic Champion, Author

"*Ike* is a true story of unconditional love between a man and his dog—a love which inspired courage, vulnerability, and ultimately a transformational awakening in the heart of the author himself. This is a story with a profound message for people of all ages."

— Peter McCoppin, International Orchestral Conductor, National Host/Broadcaster, Executive Coach

"*Ike* hits you in places you don't expect, scenes lodge in your mind when you put the book down, keep you reflecting and draw you back in to see what's coming next. *Ike* provides a powerful perspective on us as humans that charms you one minute and challenges you the next."

— Cath Bishop, Olympic Silver Medalists, former Diplomat, Author, Consultant/Coach.

IKE

the dog who saved a human

JASON DORLAND

TSPA The Self Publishing Agency, Inc.

Jason Dorland

Ike

TSPA The Self Publishing Agency, Inc.

First Edition

Softcover ISBN: 978-1-7387084-1-3
Hardcover ISBN: 978-1-7387084-0-6
Electronic ISBN: 978-1-7387084-2-0

Editor | Tara McGuire
Cover & Book Design | Kristy Twellmann Hill

Publishing Support | TSPA The Self Publishing Agency, Inc.

Dedicated to the most unselfishly loving soul that I've ever known. Thank you, Ike, for teaching me how to cherish each day and live life to its fullest. How not to get too worked up about the small stuff. And, ultimately, how to more fully love others, and me.

Thank you, Robyn, for everything, and for being the best mom any golden retriever could ever wish for.

Mataya, be who you are, and your animals will naturally embrace, love, and trust you.

And, Mom and Dad, thanks, for teaching me the value of having dogs in our lives.

preface

Before we get started, let me explain something to you; I'm telling this story—me, Ike—yes, the dog! So, if you've never sat down and had a dog tell you a story before, that's about to change. Don't worry, I won't bite, as they say.

Furthermore, if you have ever gone through the process of choosing a dog, you're probably aware of the expression, "Let the dog choose you." Like most expressions, cliché as they may first appear, the reason they become commonplace is that they're true—this one in particular. Believe what you may, you don't choose your dog—we choose you. Long before you've even had the thought of bringing one of us into your life, the wheels of the universe have been put in motion.

Following the belief that people come into your life when you most need them, the same is true of dogs; we're more than just a cute ball of fur with sweet-smelling puppy-breath—we're teachers. We show up and enable the life lessons your spirit is yearning for. Like this story, for example; it's about the human that I chose.

And one last thing, to make it easier for you: when I'm sharing a thought, *I indicate that with italics.* When I'm speaking with another animal, *"I put quotations around it."*

Enjoy...

i'm ike

It felt cool for early summer. Spitting rain from the low-hanging clouds didn't help. Behind our home, on a fragrant bed of freshly cut cedar bows, I lay waiting, motionless. Every small drop that landed gently on my weary and aching body reminded me that I was still here, alive for another brief moment.

My fur was coarse and dry; the result of a body ravaged by disease. My mouth tasted like rot. I'm sure it smelled worse. My breathing was shallow and wheezy. I was so thin, I could feel my heart lightly thumping against my rib cage. My old heart was tired and fading, completely spent from a lifetime of incessantly pursuing fun and play. I was a golden retriever—it's what we did. And, I took it as a good sign; I was crossing life's finish line having given life my all. I was grateful to have travelled the path I did.

Soon, however, with my vet's help, I would leave this physical world and my loving humans who now knelt teary-eyed beside me. They had been incredibly good to me. I loved them dearly, as they did me. I was sad to go and I would miss them terribly. We had lived together, the life we were meant to, and now it was time for me to leave.

I wasn't afraid of dying; dogs never are. It's a part of life. We come into this world full of possibilities, and leave when those possibilities have been exhausted.

Opening my eyes one last time, I could see my humans, Jason and Robyn, beside me. They looked sad, Jason especially. Maybe even a little scared. I wanted to tell them that I was going to be okay. That *they* were going to be okay. That soon their sadness would be replaced by wonderful memories of our life together. Memories that would evoke smiles and laughter anytime they wanted.

Reflecting on those memories in my final moments filled my waning heart. It had been quite a journey. I had no regrets—I had chosen well.

So, before I go, come with me and let's go back to when it all began many years ago.

I came sliding into this world with seven other pups just like me. While my mom dragged her wet, scratchy tongue over my slimy body, I wiggled and cooed, trying eagerly to get closer to her belly and that warm, delicious milk.

Eventually, with all eight of us cleaned and latched on, she closed her eyes and tried to rest. We later found out that our mom was an exceptional breeding dog. She was gentle and patient. Our dad, a strong, handsome golden himself, was bright and obedient. He, too, had produced some standout pups. Their meeting had been brief and purposeful.

If you haven't guessed, my name is Ike; I'm one of the eight pups. My brothers are Ivan, Ivor, Indie, Ian, and Ishtar and my sisters, Iona and Ivy. Our names all start with "I" for a reason. It's how they track pups like us whom they bred to do what we do.

As siblings went, we got along just fine. There were the occasional flare-ups. But nothing a few sharp puppy teeth couldn't sort out.

Our humans were Roberta and Hugh. Not the chattiest couple you could imagine, but they were kind and patient. We were lucky to have them.

Our training would take about a year and a half; our mom called it bootcamp. Not exactly inviting. Then, we'd be rehomed with someone who needed a dog to be their eyes. Yup, we were all going to be guide dogs for the blind.

Once we moved in with our blind humans and they trusted us, we'd begin our new lives together, leading and keeping them safe throughout their day. It was a big deal. I mean, there was so much we had to know, and so much we could screw up. That's why not all of us would make the grade. Some of us would fail. And for plenty of reasons. Too big. Too strong. Too friendly. Too easily distracted. Actually, too anything and you were likely outta there.

Think about it—we had to walk a human who couldn't see anything across busy streets with cars and buses zooming by. If we weren't perfect, that could mean lights out—for both of us.

Until that day arrived, life was all about getting bigger and having fun. I loved this part. Me and my siblings just hanging out with Mom in our big backyard, playing and wrestling. I could chew on a rubber bone, chase balls, eat food anytime, and have my belly rubbed by Roberta. I learned to pee and poo on command in a special place behind the garage, and then have one of our humans, usually Hugh, clean it up—now that's commitment. And, best of all, I could curl up against Mom's warm tummy and take a nap any time I wanted. Boy-oh-boy, life couldn't have gotten much better.

After this brief stint of paradise, however, I had to leave my family, and Roberta and Hugh, to move in with a different human. One I didn't even know. Then, I'd continued to grow and develop the social skills needed to help take care of my next forever human—the one who couldn't see. Phew, things were happening way too fast.

While nursing one evening, I listened in on Roberta and Hugh discussing potential "Puppy Walkers," or PWs, as they called them. That was the fancy term for humans who invited a sweet-smelling ball of golden fuzz into their house—a ball of fuzz that was curious, playful, adorable, full of energy, mischievous at times, and a little nervous too.

These PWs had a pretty easy job: I mean, food, safety and exercise. Not exactly plate tectonics, right? Do all three and they qualified. Train us according to the guide-dog rulebook and get us out into the big busy world once in a while, and the PWs were considered rockstars.

The checklist was simple, but the amount of work it would take wasn't. True, the feeding and exercise part was pretty straightforward. The rulebook, however, could be a challenge.

This was the deal: while on leash, we had to walk on our human's left-hand side—always. We couldn't pull on the leash—ever. We were supposed to walk just ahead of our humans while ignoring everything else—and I mean everything. Including cute little kids wanting to share their fishy crackers.

Yup. I would eventually learn to stand and wait quietly at street corners until I was told to walk. Chasing sticks and tennis balls—hardly ever. Tug o' war—not a chance. And, worst of all, no chasing squirrels or cats. Are you kidding me?! I mean, half of my name is "retriever." Teaching us to ignore our instincts was like telling a fish they couldn't swim.

And the worst part about some of the walks: I'd have to wear these cheap guide dog jackets. Yup, some ugly flap of polyester looped around my neck and chest that scratched and choked me—I hated that thing. Any time we were out in public—going out to restaurants, shopping in malls, or riding the bus—I had to wear it. Yuck.

And then, just when I thought it couldn't get any worse: no sleeping on any furniture or beds—at first I thought it was a typo. We also had to travel in the passenger footwell of cars—no hanging out the window with our ears and tongues flapping in the wind like you see in the movies. We could play, but we had to be...I think "reserved" was the word in the booklet—it basically meant, "no fun allowed!" If we got too excited about anything we had to be called back under control. First-world doggie-problems, I suppose, but those rules could sure get tiresome.

For me, the hardest part was knowing that we'd be leaving our PWs in less than a year. I'd often hear humans say, "Oh, I could never do that, I'd get too attached to the dog!" But what about us? You think we didn't get attached? If I had a tennis ball for every time I heard that, I'd be set.

As Roberta and Hugh ran through the list, this guy named Jason caught my attention. They described him as young and active, someone who loved the outdoors—just like me. He was also hoping to attend some local art school. Roberta was worried. She said being a student and taking care of one of us might be a lot to ask. Me, I couldn't care less. I didn't even know what an art school was. Besides, it was the active and outdoors part that I honed in on.

"I've been thinking; I'm going to pick that young guy, Jason," I quietly shared with Ivor as we both dozed, waiting for the choosing ritual to begin. *"It could be fun!"*

"What? Why would you do that? He's just one person—that's boring," said Indie as he yawned and stretched. Indie was the biggest of the litter. He liked to play alpha and we pretty much just let him. We only had a few more weeks—most of us couldn't be bothered.

"Yah, Ike, you're looking at a year of major boredom and loneliness if you go with that guy," added Ivan.

Now the whole gang was waking up and beginning to chime in. Obviously, who we chose as our PW was a really big deal. But, in this case, no one wanted Jason.

"What are you talking about? So what, the guy's not married. It doesn't make him a criminal," I countered.

"Why not go with a family? You get lots more humans to play with and keep you company. We've only got a year, you know. You might as well stack the odds in your favour," said a now more insistent Indie.

"The guy loves the outdoors. He runs and hikes. Swims. Goes camping. Did you not hear that?"

"He's also going to art school, Ike. Did you not hear that?" replied Indie.

"So? We don't even know what that means?" I replied.

"Don't have to—it just sounds boring!"

"Let him choose the student, Indie" said Ishtar. *"Besides, it makes it easier for us—it means none of us have to!"* My brothers laughed.

"I think that's a great choice, Ike." Iona had heard enough. Although not the biggest of the litter, she was strong-willed and stood her ground when she chose to. *"If it's what you want, don't listen to them. I think you just have to trust your gut with this."*

I smiled at her, acknowledging that she had come to my rescue.

"Whatever—I think you're both crazy," said Indie, dismissing us while pushing Ivor with his outstretched paw in an attempt to start another wrestling match.

One by one, families arrived at Roberta and Hugh's house and came into the pantry off the kitchen, where we spent our time indoors. There were three small windows and a door to the backyard. We were surrounded by shelves and cupboards stocked with food and other stuff. A temporary gate kept us from escaping to the rest of the home. The room was big enough. We had everything we needed—water bowls, food bowls and a place to sleep with Mom. Oh, and newspaper—there was newspaper everywhere.

Indie and Ivy had already claimed their future temporary humans. Jason was the third PW to arrive.

"Boy-oh-boy—he's way taller than all of the others," I said as he walked through the door.

Jason towered over Roberta while the two of them watched us wrestle and play without saying a word.

"They're pretty cute," he eventually said.

"Yes, there's nothing quite as adorable as a golden retriever puppy—except maybe eight of them."

While curiously looking us over, he came closer. "How does anyone choose? I mean, is there something I should look for?"

The wrestling stopped. We all stood up and returned his curious gaze.

"Well, they say you should let them choose you," said Roberta. "I don't know if that's entirely true. But it's what everyone who comes here seems to believe."

"What, so just get inside behind the gate and see who comes up to me first?"

He's a novice, alright.

As soon as Jason stepped one foot inside our pen, the entire gang was upon him. He knelt down and experienced a golden retriever puppy ambush.

"Wow—these guys are full of beans!" All eight of us reached for his face and a quick lick. "Can I take all of them?"

"Ah, that was kinda cute," said Iona. *"I think he'll be perfect for you, Ike."*

I finished sizing this guy up. *"Okay, everyone, time to look uninterested. This one's mine. Ivor, Ishtar, hit the road."*

As the others moved their wrestling match back to the centre of our pen, I remained standing alone in front of my young student.

"Hmm. This guy seems interested? I think your advice worked, Roberta."

"Apparently, it did. His name is Ike. If you're settled on that one, I can claim him as spoken for."

Jason paused for a moment and stared into my eyes. “Hmmm, Ike.” He scratched under my chin. “Can I pick him up?”

“Of course. Just make sure you support his hind legs. Their ligaments haven’t set yet at this age.”

We stared at one another as he held me inches from his nose. Jason felt different from the others who had come by earlier in the day. I was too young to appreciate it at the time, but eventually I would learn that what I was feeling from him was a sense of being lost. Not physically, but instead as if he was adrift in angry, turbulent waters and didn’t know where or how to get out, or even swim.

As much as what attracted me to Jason was the lifestyle that I knew I would inherit, I remember thinking in that moment that somehow I wanted to help. One way or another, I was going to help.

“He’s something else. And, he’s big, too—he’s heavier than I thought.” As his nose passed mine, he shared something the previous couples hadn’t. “Mmm, puppy breath—I love the smell of his breath.”

“Really? Not everyone feels that way.”

“I love it. If I could bottle this stuff, I bet I’d make a fortune.”

Roberta let out a loud laugh as she checked the box beside my name, meaning I’d be going with Jason.

“What’s with the paint on his fur?” Jason asked.

“Oh, that’s just nail polish. We use it to tell them apart.”

“Well, I won’t need that marking—this guy’s the most handsome one in here by far.”

“Ha—take that, Indie.” I said. *“This guy knows a real looker when he sees one!”*

After one more sniff, Jason put me down and stepped out behind the gate to join Roberta. I returned to my siblings and the tussle that was now losing steam. As I bit into the ear of my brother, Ivan, in the hopes of reigniting another round of body slams and lip bites, the others slowly lost interest and began to nod off to sleep.

"Come on. You've got to be kidding—you're all tired? We just started!" I said in a last-ditch attempt to inspire some more carnage.

"No way, Ike. I'm beat," said a drowsy Ishtar.

"Yah, time for another nap," confirmed Ivor.

"Lightweights," I said in disgust, standing amidst a pile of sleeping golden fur.

"Look at him standing there—he's not ready to quit! Oh-oh, I think I just picked the scrappiest one of the bunch. He's sure got some spirit," I heard Jason say as Roberta closed the door behind them.

my new home

For the next two weeks, our routine stayed pretty much the same. Eat, play, sleep—lots of sleeping. We were expanding every which way. Much to our disapproval, “milkies” had been replaced by puppy food from a bag Roberta referred to as “brekky” or “din-dins.”

We were only allowed to nurse first thing each morning and in the evening before we fell asleep. Any other time was now forbidden. If we bothered Mom for a feed, Roberta would chase us off.

Finally, departure day arrived. The morning was unusually quiet—no wrestling, no body-slams, no biting, just quiet. Our mom was out for a long walk with Hugh, preparing her for life after we were gone. We had all said our goodbyes beforehand. I couldn’t imagine this got any easier. In eight short weeks she had kept us clean, fed, warm, safe, and done her best to teach us what we needed to know before we left. What moms do, I guess. Sure, we were her third litter, but I could tell she was sad. Regardless of whether or not this was her ”job,” we could all feel how much she loved us. I sure was going to miss her.

Roberta as well. She’d been the best human mom I could’ve asked for. We knew she was a volunteer and had provided many a guide-dog pup with a great start in life—but I imagined this day was the hardest of all. Roberta wasn't the type to get down on the floor and cuddle with us. It was probably more about self-preservation than anything. However, like our mom, we could feel her love anytime she was close by. That meant everything to us.

There were only four of us left when Jason showed up just before lunchtime. "I can't get over how much he's grown in two weeks!"

Roberta scooped me up. "Now, do you have everything?" she asked as they walked towards Jason's car. "I gave you his jacket, collar, and leash, as well as a bag of puppy food. I'll be around regularly to check in and see how you're doing. If you run out of food, I'll always have some with me. Remember, if you need anything—no matter what time of day—just call me. Okay? You'll do just fine, Jason. Have fun with Ike—he's a special little guy. A lot of spunk, but he's a wise soul too."

Roberta leaned in close to my face. "You be good, now, Ike. I'll see you again soon. And take good care of Jason," she said with a wink. She gave me a final kiss on my forehead before passing me over to Jason, who quickly plunked me into his car.

"I won't let you down, Roberta. He'll be the best guide-dog pup you've ever seen." They shook hands one last time before he climbed in and we drove away.

Sitting on the floor, as prescribed, I looked up at my new temporary human.

This is really happening—I'm leaving my family forever.

For a moment, I felt nauseous. And it wasn't just the floor moving beneath me as we sped away. I was truly on my own. Had I made the right choice? Was art school as boring as Indie said?

Take it easy, Ike—you're going to be just fine.

After finally settling down, I decided that looking out the window would be a good thing to do. When I attempted to climb onto the seat,

Jason wasted little time in responding. "Nope—sorry, little guy—Roberta made the rules pretty clear. You stay put," and he pushed me off the seat. I wasn't giving up that easily. I made one more attempt but was met with stern resistance and tumbled back to the floor.

Boy-oh-boy, this guy's all business. I conceded and curled up.

With the constant vibration and the gentle rocking, it wasn't long before I was fast asleep.

"Come on, Ike—time to meet your new roommates." I awoke to Jason lifting me out of the car.

They both smiled as we approached. "Ike, meet Pat and Trev—they're not quite as furry as you, but you'll find them just as much fun!"

"Hello, Ike," said Trev, as he reached out and stroked my ears. "Looks as though you just woke up? Poor little fella!" He wasn't as tall as Jason, but he had a warm voice like Hugh's. His hair colour was similar to my fur. And his eyes were bright when he smiled. "He's pretty cute, Jase."

"Well, look at this handsome little boy—how's it goin' Ike? Welcome!" said the other roommate, Pat, as he scratched the underside of my chin. His eyes were sparkly and welcoming. Pat actually looked like Jason. Except Jason's nose was bigger and his chin longer. They were both lean and fit looking and, when they smiled, they reminded me of Ivor and Ivan—mischievous. I imagined them as perfect for wrestling. I *was* going to be just fine.

No sooner had those introductions finished than the neighbourhood kids came running over to meet me.

Jason put me down on the grass and stepped back. Like excited bees around fresh pollen, the buzzing children clamoured for my attention, grabbing for their turn to hold me.

Not my idea of fun—I'm outta here!

I broke loose and ran. Randomly changing direction for no other reason than it felt good, I darted in and out of the young kids' legs as they tried to catch me. Their excitement fuelled mine, and we engaged in a mad dash around the front yard.

Their parents, along with my new roommates, laughed and cheered, encouraging the impromptu game of chase. At that stage of my life, my energy, wild as it could be, didn't last long. I collapsed into a chubby ball of panting fur. The kids soon followed—rolling on the grass, exhausted, with their legs and arms flailing in the air.

It was time for a drink of water. As if he had read my mind, Jason appeared with an old and dented stainless steel mixing bowl filled with what I wanted. He placed the bowl on the ground. Ice cubes clinked against the sides as I lapped up the cold water as fast as I could. With my front legs extended out on either side of the bowl and my hind legs outstretched in the opposite direction, the cool grass felt good against my growing belly. However, it didn't take long for that belly to feel as though I'd swallowed a fishbowl. Unable to drink another drop, I raised my left paw and dropped it into the remaining water, tipping the bowl and splashing myself in the face. Not only did that cool water feel good, it provided a moment of levity as the humans laughed at my antics.

Later that evening, just before bed, Jason carried me out the kitchen door, onto the deck, and down the outside stairs that led to the backyard and what would become my playground, and bathroom, for the next year or so. Roberta's instructions were clear; if during the first 48 hours he only took me outside to "go busy," as she called it, I'd be house-trained in no time. And, just as she'd suggested, I got plopped down onto the grass while Jason stood there watching and repeating, "Go busy, Ike. Go busy!"

Goodness me, he's a quick study—just like Roberta told him.

Learning to go to the bathroom on command, behaving on a leash, coming when called, sitting and staying put, waiting for the "Okay" command to begin my meals; it was all part of the deal. Although a year sounded like a long time, Roberta had emphasized over and over to Jason the importance of getting started—we had a lot of work to cover.

Trev and Pat, each with a can of beer, soon joined us out back, while Jason continued to encourage me to do my thing.

"He's quite a good lookin' pup, Jase," said Trev, as he and Pat took a seat at the picnic table.

"Come on, Ike. Go busy! What are you waiting for?" Jason anxiously watched over me while I took a moment to discover my new backyard.

After an audible swig, Pat asked, "I think it's great what you're doing, Jase. I'd be lying if I said I wasn't looking forward to the next year with a dog in the house—really. But, how on earth are you going to give him back come springtime? I can't see how you're not going to get attached to that cute little face."

There, told you—another tennis ball for me—always about the human, never the dog.

Without looking up, Jason answered, "Easy—I've got a plan."

Jason's roommates looked at each other. "We're all ears!"

"The way I see it, Ike's a different dog—a working dog. And, he's going to be someone's eyes someday. So, I want to prepare the best guide-dog pup they've ever seen. I gave Roberta my word!"

"Okay—so, what's your plan?" asked Trev.

"I'm going to keep this relationship like a job. All business."

I stopped sniffing and looked up at Jason.

"What are you looking at? Take a pee, for God's sake. Come on, go busy, Ike! Quit stalling. This is taking way too long."

Pat and Trev looked at each other again.

After a moment, Pat offered the obvious. "Jason, you realize he's a living, breathing dog, right—not a widget?" Jason continued watching me like a hawk. "There's no podium presentation when you're done with him." Trev elbowed Pat who paused for a moment before continuing. "Look, I'm not going to tell you how to take care of him.

But, I think this "all business" thing is going to blow up at some point—you're going to become emotionally attached to that little guy."

"Maybe," acknowledged Jason.

Then more awkward silence.

"What if Pat and I teach Ike all the wrong things?" Trev looked at Pat with a misbehaved smile. "You know, chase the neighbours' cat, lay on the couch, crap on the sidewalk, hump everyone's leg when company comes to visit. Stuff like that?"

Pat choked on his beer as he quickly got up from the table. They all laughed. "What? I'm just trying to help. I heard that if these guide-dog pups fail, the temporary owners get to keep them."

"No, not happening, Trev! I can't keep Ike—not a chance. The only way this one-year deal works is if I have that little guide dog jacket that came with him. It's my ticket for taking him to school, getting on planes, all of it. Without that jacket, Ike's home alone all day—I wouldn't do that to him. Besides, while I'm in school, there's no way I can afford the vet bills, the food—none of it. With this arrangement, all that stuff is covered. Appreciate the sentiment, Trev, but it's better if Ike moves on from here in May. Believe me."

Pat sat down again at the table. "Where do you think of this stuff, Trev? You're such a prairie dog—spelt D-A-W-G!"

Trev looked at Pat and raised his lip. "Grrrrrrrrr. Ruff!" They all laughed, again.

I was done sniffing around. Time to do what we had come out here for.

"Good boy, Ike. Good busy!" Jason said with relief. "Okay, I'm going to take him back upstairs." Jason picked me up and made his way to the stairs, leaving Pat and Trev to finish their drinks.

My new home was decent. Nothing fancy like what I had seen beyond the gate at Roberta and Hugh's. But, it would do. Jason's room was actually a dining room. He'd set up my crate beside his bed, which he called his "crappy old futon."

There were no curtains, and none of his furniture matched, either. I wasn't too fussed—I didn't choose him for his fashion sense. Besides, he and his roommates seemed like good humans.

"This is where you sleep, Ike." Jason pointed to the crate. "Roberta said it's important that you get used to sleeping in it starting with the first night."

Of course, she did.

"I bought some foam and old blankets. You should be okay in there. Oh, and I found this old-fashioned clock too. Roberta said, wrapped in a t-shirt, it mimics the sound of your mom's heartbeat. It's supposed to help you sleep. I guess we'll find out."

I sat down on the cool hard wooden floor and looked up at Jason, who was now sitting on his bed looking down at me. I could feel his worry. Perhaps, wondering about what Pat had said a moment ago. I'll admit, the "all business" part surprised me. I figured he'd crack in a few months, anyway. Are you kidding me? I was a golden retriever—he didn't stand a chance.

Stepping into the crate, it was hard not to appreciate how much Jason was trying. The ticking clock idea was a nice gesture, but, as he likely wouldn't understand, it wasn't just the sound of our mom I'd miss; it was her smell, warmth, and caring spirit. Simply knowing that the dog that had brought me into this world was right beside me—my protector.

"Okay, Ike, I'm going to brush my teeth—back in a sec."

Now was my chance. I figured I'd give Jason's bed a try. Crappy or not, it looked more comfortable than my crate and old foam. But no matter how many times I tried, I could only get my front paws to the edge of his mattress.

"Hey—no, no, no. That's not happening, buddy. In here, little guy." Jason had returned to the room and startled me mid-air on my third and last attempt. He quickly grabbed my collar and led me back into my crate. "Roberta said to start with just the bottom-half. Until you're used to it. I'll add the top-half later on. I'll be right beside you. Trust me, it's no big deal, Ike. Just lay down and go to sleep, little fella. Okay?"

No big deal? When was the last time you slept alone in a plastic box on a bunch of old smelly blankets?

Begrudgingly, I moved to the back of the crate, laid down, and buried my nose in my tail. I thought about my mom and my siblings, wondering if they were managing the same as I was, missing me like I was missing them. Their company, warmth, security—their touch. It had been a long first day. I closed my eyes, having resigned myself to sleep.

The next morning, I felt my crate gently move as Jason slowly got up out of bed and made his way to the kitchen. I lay in my crate a while longer. My first night sleeping alone had been restless—this was going to take some getting used to.

I grew curious as I heard Pat and Trev join him to make their breakfast.

"How'd he do?" asked Pat in a soft voice.

"Did he poo and pee all over your bed?" added Trev.

"I didn't hear a peep! I was expecting to get woken up a bunch of times. But, he's still crashed," answered Jason.

"Did you check if he's breathing?" Trev said with a laugh.

"Yes—he's breathing, thank you very much," answered Jason. "I guess he's just tired. I mean, a new home, leaving your mom, brothers, and sisters. I guess that could be hard for a pup—I don't know, do they have thoughts like that?"

Do they have those thoughts? Goodness me.

I got up and walked into the kitchen. My new roommates sat at the counter, looking out the window. The back half of me wagged as I investigated the new space. *Hmmm, where to pee? Right here seems as good a place as any!*

Just as I splayed my hind legs, lowered my belly, and began to release a night's worth of urine, Jason turned around.

"NO! IKE, STOP!" He quickly lunged toward me. I cowered as Jason swooped me up. Still peeing, my steady stream followed the trajectory of his spinning motion towards the kitchen door and out onto the porch steps.

Landing on the grass with a thud, I looked up at my frazzled human. He was mad.

"Come on, Ike. You have to wait until I get you down here before you pee. You can't just go to the bathroom anywhere you want!"

I slowly meandered around the backyard, searching for the best spot to finish up while Jason stood with his arms crossed, "This is where you go busy, Ike!"

With my business finally done, Jason picked me up and climbed the stairs. According to Roberta, I was too young and small to climb them alone. She said it was too much strain on my ligaments. I remember the first time I did—it felt like I was flying!

In the kitchen, Pat was still cleaning the floor, and the walls.

"Did he get the walls? Really," asked Jason as he plopped me down on the kitchen floor.

"He sure did," answered Pat. "No big deal. It's going to take some time, Jase."

"That's my fault. I guess I need to wake him up and take him straight out. Roberta said that if I get him out as soon as he wakes up and after every meal, he'll figure things out more quickly. Sorry about that."

"Jason, he's a puppy. It's going to happen. Even your soon-to-be award-winning dog might make the odd mistake."

Then Trev piped up, "So what does this little guy eat, anyway? And, more importantly, what's he going to eat from? It better not be one of our cereal bowls!"

"That huge bag of puppy food at the foot of my bed. As for his bowl, my mom mailed out some dog dish she bought. But, I haven't unwrapped it yet." Jason stepped into our room and returned with a white ceramic bowl with the words "Top Dog" painted on the side.

"Holy crap—no pressure, Ike," laughed Trev.

Puppy food was no milkies, but I was growing used to it. After devouring my first meal, Jason picked me up immediately and took me to the backyard to "go busy" once more.

My next few days followed that simple routine; eat, sleep, poop, pee, repeat. Thankfully, with some playtime mixed in as well. And just like Roberta said, it was working—I was becoming house trained. Yes, I still had some accidents, and yes, Jason still got mad every time. But there was hope.

As for his bed, Jason didn't budge. I gave up trying. I could tell he was going to stick to the rules laid out by Roberta no matter what. Boy-oh-boy, he had a stubborn streak.

My favourite time of the day for sure was after dinner when the three of them would sit outside on the picnic table and visit. After I fertilized the lawn, Jason would hold me on his lap, where I would fall asleep. It was as close as I got to the safety of my mom. The warmth of his legs. The fresh evening air. My full belly. The murmur of their conversation. All of it—it was soothing and I savoured that feeling.

Jason was firm with me, but so was my mom. She didn't waste a moment when laying down the law if she had to. I remember one evening before bed when we began to wrestle. We were yelping and nipping at one another, making our usual racket. Well, this one time, our mom wasn't having it. She was tired and wanted to sleep. All it took was one loud bark to get our attention, followed by a low growl and a raised lip. You've never seen eight puppies lay down and curl up faster than we did that night.

I also knew that the guide dog book was full of rules that weren't fun and it was Jason's job to follow them. Despite that, there were times when he seemed different—softer, even. At night when I was falling asleep, Jason would reach over the side of the crate and rest his hand on me. And, before bed, if he was wearing a t-shirt, he would take it off and place it beside me. Sure, they were little things, but I could feel he was trying.

I wasn't regretting my choice. Jason was keeping his promise to Roberta and I was well cared for, I couldn't argue that. But the prospect of spending lots of time outdoors is what initially attracted me to him, and that had yet to happen—I was sure ready for some outdoor fun!

As if he'd read my mind, the next day my wish was granted.

The piercing ring of the kitchen phone woke me up. Followed by Trev's pounding feet as he dashed to answer it.

There was a light tap on our bedroom door. I raised my head. "Jase, you asleep?"

"Not anymore... What's up?"

"That was Colin," answered Trev. "He's taking his boat out for a spin today and was wondering if we wanted to join him. What do you think?"

"What about Ike?"

"Colin said he'd be more than welcome. You think about it. I'm going to get some breakfast started."

Jason stretched and rolled over, closer to the edge of his bed. I returned his gaze with a head tilt. "What do you think, Ike?" Jason's scratchy low morning voice rumbled. "Ready for an adventure today? It's a boat ride."

I had no idea what a boat was, but, at this point, I was up for anything. My tail whacked against the inside of the crate. I stood on my hind legs, my face reaching for his.

"I will consider that a yes." Jason pulled back before I could catch him with my tongue. "Trev—it's a yes from us!"

"Awesome! Let's get going, then. It's looking like a beautiful Sunday morning."

After breakfast and my morning routine, we climbed into the car. I was full of excitement. We were doing something other than hanging around the house.

With Trev in the passenger seat and me at his feet, we drove through the streets of Vancouver. I'm not sure I could've landed in a better or more beautiful city. This was my first time going through downtown, Stanley Park, and over the Lions Gate Bridge. We eventually arrived at the marina in Horseshoe Bay, where Colin was waiting.

"So this is the famous Ike," said Colin, leaning through the window to pet my head.

"Yup, this is the Ikester," answered Trev. "Isn't he the cutest little puppy you've ever seen?" Trev had pulled me up from the floor mat and onto his lap to give Colin better access.

"He sure is! You must be thrilled with him, Jason. He's quite a looker." Colin scratched me under my chin.

"That's what everyone keeps telling me—I just don't want it to go to his head!"

Once onboard, we untied from the dock and slowly made our way out of the marina. A massive white boat was arriving at another dock. "That's a ferry boat, Ike. It has a bunch of cars and people onboard. We'll be taking one of those when we go camping in a month or so."

Camping—now we're talking!

Then it made a huge sound, so loud it startled me. Jason quickly pressed his hands over my ears while this strange, long, chest-rattling sound wrung out over the water and up the mountains behind us. "Sorry, Ike. I should've warned you."

We motored at a steady pace while Colin, Trev, and Jason took in the sights of the Coastal Mountains jutting out of the water and soaring way up into the sky. "That's Black Mountain, Ike—we'll go up there one day," said Jason as he pointed to the top.

More exciting news—now this is a good day!

Further away from the ferry terminal, gigantic fancy homes dotted the rocky shoreline. "I think Indie's in one of those places, Ike."

Trev laughed. "Sorry, little fella—I'm afraid you lost the lottery with us."

Colin laughed as well.

Heading for the open water, Colin yelled, "Hold on—the Georgia Strait can get rough!" With that warning, he fired up the willing engine responding with a roar[1] and the bow of our boat lifted like a bird taking flight. No longer protected by the bay, we began to bounce—a little at first and then a lot as we crashed through the rough chop of the open sea.

Along with the increase in speed, a cool but growing-colder wind now blew over us. Even the midday sun was hard-pressed to ward off the chill that was beginning to take hold. We ventured into more significant and less forgiving waves. Our bouncing intensified. With each crash, our boat shook. Spray shot out from both sides as we slapped against the jagged veneer of the water. I was no longer having fun.

However, Colin, Trev, and Jason clearly were. With each wave came a new thrill. And an approving yell that only encouraged Colin to seek out the bigger waves.

"Is Ike okay?" yelled Trev.

1 Neil Peart, Lyricist for RUSH. Song—Red Barchetta, Album—Moving Pictures, 1981.

Jason reached down to see how I was doing. “I think so. He’s getting a little wet and bounced around, but it looks like he’s managing.”

Managing? I’m freezing cold, terrified, and on the verge of throwing up!

“Hold up, Colin!” yelled Jason.

“Hey, buddy. You okay?” Jason looked into my eyes. “Ahh, shit. He looks frightened. Here, come on up—I gotcha, Ike—don’t worry, it’s okay. I’ve got you, bud.” He unzipped his waterproof jacket and slipped me inside against his warm sweater. “I can feel him shaking,” Jason said. “And, he’s whimpering a little bit too.”

“Sorry about that. I shouldn’t have gone so fast through those waves,” said Colin.

“No worries. Ike’ll be just fine.” Jason rubbed my back from the outside of his jacket. “But, maybe we could go a little slower heading home?”

Warm and safe in Jason’s arms, I was asleep in no time.

After a short nap, I squirmed and stretched and eventually poked my head out from the jacket. We were moving much slower. *This I can handle.* Jason placed me back onto the bottom of the boat. However, I was too short to see anything. Still holding onto my collar, Jason let me venture up onto the bow section. It was perfect. Now I could see everything.

“He doesn’t seem too worse for wear,” said Colin.

“Nope—not at all. I’d say he’s loving his first adventure from home!” said Jason as he pulled me onto his lap.

“Trev, pass me Jason’s camera.” Colin raised it to his face. I stared intently. “There, now you have mementos of Ike’s first day at sea!”

“My mom and dad have been asking for some pictures. These’ll be perfect—thanks.”

“Did you see the look on him, Colin?” asked Trev. “Ike was posing—like he knew what was going on. Crazy!”

"I sure did. That's one regal-looking pup, Jason—I don't think I've ever seen a more striking dog!"

"He'll need more than looks if he's going to be someone's eyes. This boy's going to have to be hardworking, smart, and obedient as well. We're working on that! Aren't we, Ike?"

Jason placed me back on the bow. I rolled slightly left, stretched out, and watched Colin manoeuvre the boat back to the marina. The ride hadn't started out too well, but this part—this part I liked!

Colin barked some orders. "Trev, you jump onto the dock, and I'll throw you the stern line. Jason, if you can make sure we don't hit too hard on the port side, that'd be great."

We gently bumped the dock. Trev tied us up while Colin turned off the engine. I didn't want to leave.

"Look at him—what a little prince. Do you want us to give you some more time in the sun, Ike? Maybe bring back some takeout?" Jason said, smiling at me.

Colin and Trev responded with agreeable laughter.

The humans walked away down the dock toward the car. I decided it was finally time to join them. With a long downward-dog stretch, I stood at the edge of the boat. The gap between me and the dock was too big to leap. I barked. Jason turned.

"You talking to me?" he asked.

I sure am!

Trev and Colin turned, waiting for my next move.

"If you jump from there, you're getting wet, buddy," said Jason. "Go to the side of the boat—you can jump that," Jason laughed and headed back toward me.

At this stage, water was still a new concept for me. It looked solid. Why would I go to the side when moving straight ahead seemed like a much shorter path?

"IKE—STOP!"

Too late, I fell through and into the dark, murky matter beneath me. I couldn't see clearly or feel the ground at my feet. *Goodness me, what just happened?* I began to panic. I kicked and squirmed, struggling to return to the solid floor of the boat from where I had just stepped. I tried to breathe. Water entered my mouth like a cold, flooding mass. *This doesn't seem right.* Something was horribly wrong here.

Before I could try to breathe again, I felt my neck squeeze as something grabbed me from behind. Before I knew it, I was on the dock. I gagged and coughed, then choked and threw-up salty water onto the wooden planks.

"Jesus, Ike. What the hell was that?" said Jason, watching me closely.

"Ike, you big goofball, what were you thinking?" Trev had rushed over and knelt beside Jason. "Do you think he's okay?"

"He seems okay. I mean—he's breathing."

Jason reached into his backpack, pulled out a towel, and wrapped me from head to toe. Standing up, he cradled me in his long arms while drying my soaking wet fur.

Colin quickly reached for the camera and began snapping pictures again. The three of them started laughing uncontrollably—giddy, even. Perhaps shocked by what might have happened and thankfully hadn't. Losing me on my first day out of the house would've made for an unwanted phone call to Roberta, for sure.

I was alive and quietly revelling in that fact. At that point, I'd had enough of my first day of adventure. I wanted to be safely back in our tiny home with my new roommates, curled up on those smelly old blankets in my hard plastic crate.

life as a student

"Ike, wake up. Wake up, little guy." Jason rocked me back and forth until I slowly opened my eyes. I lifted my head and wagged my tail. Startled, I turned around quickly to see what was making the loud thumping sound. *It's me.* I stopped and looked back at Jason. He smiled.

"Hey, crazy dog—how are you feeling? That was quite an adventure for you yesterday. Nice move stepping into the water. Man, you scared us!" Jason rubbed the top of my head with his long fingers, messing up my short fur. "Well, Ike, you won't be sleeping in anymore. Summer classes start today and that means you're comin' with me. Don't worry, you're going to like it. Lots of new people and things to explore."

We were steadily perfecting our morning routine. My house training was coming along too. Good thing; Jason liked everything to run like clockwork.

With his books and our lunch fitted neatly into his panniers, he grabbed his backpack and stuffed a towel into the bottom.

"This oughta work." He picked me up. "You get to ride in this cozy little spot—right in here."

Jason gently placed me into his backpack and zipped up both sides. Then he grabbed a shoelace and tied the zippers together. "There—you should be pretty safe like that. Just don't move around. Okay, bud?"

As we walked out of our bedroom, Trev and Pat came over to say goodbye.

"See ya, Ike—you look adorable in there! Jase, man, he's going to be such a chick-magnet on that campus," said Trev enthusiastically. "I can't imagine what all of the girls will say when they see his cute little head popping out. It's perfect!"

"Well played, my friend." Pat smiled.

"What? I didn't get this dog to meet women—believe me. Have you two noticed how much work he is?" replied Jason with a laugh.

"Have a great first day at school, Ike! Take good care of your dad, and make sure he has breath mints and his little black address book at the ready," yelled Trev as he and Pat let out a big laugh and closed the door behind us.

Slowly down the stairs and onto Jason's bike, and we were away.

At first, it was kinda fun. We made our way up and down the streets of my new neighbourhood. Jason's backpack rocked gently back and forth on the way to his school. I enjoyed the soothing motion of the ride while taking in the sights. There was a big park with massive trees not too far from our home.

"We'll come here soon, Ike. Don't worry."

I knew we lived in Dunbar. I had heard Jason mention it a few times. Given the size of the trees in all of the humans' front yards, I gathered this neighbourhood had been around for a while.

After a few minutes, we turned onto a wider street that appeared to go on forever. Once Jason had straightened his course, he began to pump his legs faster and harder. "Hold on, Ike—we're going to speed up a little bit here. You'll be fine."

That's what you said yesterday!

As we went faster and the cars sped by us, I began to whimper and cry. The gentle meandering ride through our neighbourhood had become scary.

"Ike, it's okay. You're safe in there. Just hold on. We won't be too much longer."

I pulled my head in through the hole and curled up on the towel. The traffic sounds were now muffled and, for the moment, allowed me to relax enough to survive the rest of our trip.

After what seemed like an eternity, we began to slow down. Soon a sharp turn to the right indicated we were off the main road. I popped my head through the opening again to see where we were. The speeding cars had been replaced with humans—lots and lots of humans—all walking in the same direction carrying similar backpacks to the one I was in. Jason slowly wove his way along the road until he got off his bike and then walked while holding the handlebars with his right hand.

I looked back and caught the eye of a female human walking behind us with her friend. They were both short. *Actually, most humans look short from up here—I sure chose a tall human!* She spoke softly with her friend and kept the same pace as everyone else. "Oh my goodness, look," she said, getting louder with each word. "Look at that puppy—he's soooo cute!" She elbowed her friend.

Without any hesitation, she moved closer toward us and began scratching the underside of my chin. "Hi, little cutie—what's your name?"

Jason abruptly stopped walking and spun around quickly. "Excuse me?"

The woman bumped into us. "Oh, I'm sorry. I just wanted to say hello to your cute puppy. What's her name?"

"Umm, his name is Ike," replied Jason, awkwardly looking over his shoulder, trying to face the young woman.

"Ike? That's a different name." She continued petting my ears. "Hello, Ike—you're handsome." Her friend had now joined in and was scratching my neck. I didn't realize it was normal for other humans to just walk up and scratch other humans' dogs—but I wasn't complaining.

"Ya, I didn't name him," explained Jason. "He's a puppy in training to be a guide dog. He's from an I-litter. Which means that all of his siblings..."

"So, he's going to be a guide dog someday?" she asked without waiting for Jason to finish. "Oh, Ike—that's so good of you!"

"Well, he's got a long way to go. But that's why I have him. I'm his puppy walker. It's my job to give him lots of different experiences and prepare him the best that I can for when I have to give him back for more training in about a year."

"What? You're going to give him back? Ohhhh, Ike, I wouldn't give you back! No way—we'd run off and live happily ever after on a farm somewhere. Just you and me!" The two girls laughed while Jason shook his head.

"Well, that's not exactly the point of this." Jason sounded annoyed—like when I peed on the kitchen floor. "He's got an important life ahead of him. It's my job to give him a good start."

My massage stopped. The women looked at one another, clearly not appreciating Jason's serious stance on the matter.

"Whatever—bye, Ike, have a good life!" The two of them waved at me.

"That wasn't very nice of him," said the one friend quietly as they continued on.

Jason turned around and grabbed his bike with both hands. "Run away to a farm—what a stupid-ass thing to say. Did you hear what she said, Ike?"

I did—it sounded pretty good to me!

"Come on, bud—let's get to class."

After another few minutes, we pulled off the main walking path and arrived at an old yellow brick building. It was sort of like our home—pretty ordinary looking. And, it didn't look anywhere near as fancy as some of the other buildings that we had walked by in getting here.

Jason leaned his bike up against a sizeable looping steel contraption that had other bikes configured neatly within it. He then pulled out a long chain that he snaked in and out of his tires and the steel loops until he was satisfied. Finally, he locked the bike with the chain.

"Welcome to the University of British Columbia, Ike."

Jason reached into his backpack to gather me up. "See, that wasn't so bad. I told you you'd be safe in there." He put me down on the ground, grabbed my leash along with his panniers, and we made our way to a patch of grass close to the building.

"You know what, Ike? That's going to work just fine—we won't have to drive my car, which means I'm not payin' those ridiculous parking fees. Perfect!"

I sniffed around and took in all of the smells of who and what had been here in the last day or two.

"Come on, bud. Class starts soon and I still haven't spoken to the prof about you. Go busy—hurry up!"

He carried me into the main foyer and up two flights of stairs. "I think it's down here? Room 307—come on." Jason put me on the floor and I followed him down the hall until we stopped at an open door. He slowly stuck his head into the room and quietly knocked on the door frame.

An older male human wearing a neatly pressed white dress shirt was writing on the chalkboard. He turned around to face us. "Can I help you?" he bowed his head to get a better view of us over his reading glasses.

"Is this Canadian Physical Geography 200?"

"Yes. But class doesn't begin for another 10 minutes or so. You're a tad early."

"Ya, I wanted to catch you before class started. You see, I have this little puppy with me."

"I can see that," replied the professor, still standing by the chalkboard with his arm half-cocked, waiting to continue writing.

"I was hoping it would be okay if he joined me for this summer session."

"You want to bring a puppy to my class for the summer. Do I understand that correctly?"

"Ummm, yes, sir. I'm wondering if you'd be okay with that. He's a guide dog in training."

"Really? He looks a little young for that, no?"

The professor didn't seem too keen on the idea. He turned away from the large green board, slowly put his chalk down on his desk, adjusted his tie, and walked toward us.

"Well, he's living with me for about a year," answered Jason. "I'm his puppy walker. It's my job to get him used to things. Like..."

"Like attending a geography class for four weeks—two hours a day?"

"Well, kinda." I could feel that Jason was getting anxious.

"Kind of?" The professor was now standing right in front of Jason.

"You see, I have this special little jacket in here," said Jason as he pointed at his backpack. "It says he's with the Canadian Guide Dogs for the Blind." He reached in and pulled out my little beige and red jacket.

Have I told you how much I hate that thing?

"It's supposed to indicate to people that he's allowed to be inside... um, any building."

"Oh, so you are *telling* me that he will be attending my class, not asking?"

Jason was getting frustrated as he struggled to know exactly how to answer that question.

The professor paused for a moment and then knelt to look at me. He reached out his wrinkled hand and gently stroked the top of my head. "And, your name is?"

"Jason. My name's Jason."

"I was referring to the puppy."

"Oh, right. Ike—his name's Ike."

"Well, Ike, it appears as though you're going to learn a great deal about landforms, weather patterns, and the soil classification system of this great nation. Welcome to my class."

I could see the relief in Jason's face as the professor put out a hand to brace himself against a chair before slowly standing. Once steady, he turned to face Jason again.

"I really appreciate you letting Ike take your class—er, audit—I mean, attend. You know what I mean; thanks for letting him be here. I'll make sure he doesn't disturb you or anyone else—you won't even know he's here."

"Perhaps the two of you should sit at the back, to begin with—that might make it easier on everyone."

"You bet—good idea—whatever you think." He grabbed his things and, with my leash in hand, made his way toward the desk nearest the back of the class.

Over the next few minutes, the remaining students claimed their desks around Jason and me. Some curious individuals leaned over to say hello. Jason was getting faster at describing our situation.

When the professor had gathered the attention of his students, I curled up for a nap on the blanket Jason had laid out for me under his chair. Although physical geography was a required course for Jason, it certainly wasn't for me.

With the end of class came more pats and chin-scratches from the other students. I stood up and stretched while soaking up all of the attention. Jason stuffed his books and my blanket into his panniers.

After the last student had left, Jason stood up. "Come on, bud. We've got to get you outside before you pee all over the place."

We were the last ones leaving.

"Did you honestly think I would say no?" Jason turned to see the professor, arms crossed, leaning against his desk. "You know, I had a golden when I was first married. His name was Rusty. He was a beautiful dog, so intelligent and so well behaved. I swear he did a better job raising our children than we did at times. I haven't thought of him in years. Thank you, Jason, for providing me with a reason to remember him today."

"Ahh, no problem," Jason answered quietly. "Well, thanks again. We'll see you tomorrow."

"You will. Have a good afternoon. Goodbye, Ike!"

My first stab at post-secondary education flew by. Jason said I was a champ with our morning routine! Up early every weekday, fed and busied, zipped up into the backpack and onto his bike as we made our way to school with the precision of a Swiss watch. If Jason was anything, he was a taskmaster. He liked to get things done. And he seemed to take satisfaction in finding faster, more efficient ways of completing his long lists of things to do. Walk me, train me, get groceries, clean the house, tidy the backyard, do laundry, do homework, make meals with Pat and Trev—he rarely seemed to stop.

Me, I was okay with that. It got me out meeting new humans and doing what I was supposed to do—socialize. My favourite outing was our weekly Saturday adventure to Granville Island, located in the middle of the city. The Island had a huge food market with a bunch of restaurants scattered throughout. It was a smorgasbord for my senses. If it could be eaten, you'd likely find it there, or in my case, smell it! Also, artists would sell their paintings, sculptures, pottery—you name it. Very talented humans were all over the Island.

It was a festive place to be. Humans were almost always in a good mood there.

Most weekends, Pat and Trev would join us. We would all pile into Jason's car and make our way to the busy Island. There were hundreds of humans strolling the walkways as they relaxed and enjoyed the beautiful summer weather.

Although I would walk on a leash for most of the outing, I was assigned to Jason's backpack when we got to the market. There were so many humans inside that I could be a bit of a tripping hazard for shoppers. With his backpack facing front and me on Jason's chest, he would gather all of his groceries for the week while passers-by smiled and patted me on the head. Jason had stopped explaining about the guide-dog thing. I suppose it just took too long.

Once done, the boys would usually grab something to eat or drink and go looking for one of the many local musicians playing nearby. Jason loved music. He listened constantly. Any time we were in the car or doing chores at home, the stereo was playing. He liked all types of music—there really wasn't anything that he didn't enjoy.

Eventually, we'd pile back into the car with our bags of produce, fresh bread, and other goodies, and make our way home to our little house in Dunbar. The ride back was always filled with the usual antics of throwing digs at one another. As a trio, they were funny and, more importantly, terrific friends. It was always an entertaining way to start the weekend.

The active life I had anticipated in choosing Jason was coming to fruition. It was a rare moment when we sat idle. The only things I had yet to experience were the camping trips I had heard about in Roberta's description weeks earlier. But that was about to change.

On the last morning of summer session with no drapes on the windows and the sun streaming into our bedroom, I was up before

Jason. Standing beside his bed, I watched for signs of life. There were none. His eyes were locked shut and his mouth hung open with rhythmic audible breaths pushing into and out of the room. He was dead asleep.

No longer was I looking up at Jason's bed. Now I was eye-level. If I wanted to, I could've jumped up, found a soft piece of real estate by his feet, and stretched out without him even noticing. While I considered my strategy, Jason began to move.

"Don't even think about it, Ike. This bed is not yours. You've got your own—understood?"

Boy-oh-boy, how did you know I was standing here?

With one more long stretch, he sat up and reached over to scratch my ears.

"How'd you sleep? Clearly not that well if you woke up before me—you okay?"

His big strong hand moved down around my ears, along my neck and to my chest. Nobody knew how to scratch, rub, and pet me the way Jason did. Scratching his fingernails up and down my chest with just the right amount of pressure, he told me about the day ahead.

First of all, it was exam day—I could feel that Jason was nervous. The good news was that we were taking his car to school, which meant no backpack for me. But the really exciting news was that we were going camping right after his test. He said we would get on one of the big white ferry boats we saw with Colin and head over to Vancouver Island to some campsite "up north," as he put it.

Walking in from the parking lot, I discovered a new part of the campus. It was beautiful. There were giant trees everywhere—really tall ones and fat ones with big leaves that danced in the wind. Old stone buildings lined the sidewalks that weaved in and out of fancy gardens. Humans sat on benches drinking and eating while reading books or visiting with friends. What a neat place!

The smells were intoxicating. Fresh baked goods, as well as other breakfast stuff that Trev was always cooking, like bacon, sausage, and eggs. It was hard to focus.

"Come on, Ike. What's the problem? You seem distracted this morning."

Distracted? I'm in heaven.

As he carried me up the steps of the building, some of Jason's classmates spotted me and said, "Good morning, Ike."

Although Jason hadn't taken the time to get to know any of his fellow students, they were still pleasant to me every day. Don't get me wrong, Jason was polite to everyone—he just kept to himself. But, I was going to miss this group.

After waiting for a few minutes outside the classroom, the door finally opened. Our professor, wearing his usual perfectly pressed white shirt and classic paisley bowtie, greeted everyone with a warm and genuine smile. "Good morning, fellow scholars and geniuses." The group chuckled politely. "I trust your minds are brimming with the knowledge of orographic rainfall, plate tectonics, and our remarkable Canadian Shield." He nodded his head forward while tilting it to the left for effect. "As you walk into the classroom, please leave all of your backpacks at the back of the room. Please sit at the desks adorned with an exciting examination booklet filled with possibilities. Understood?"

The class acknowledged his instructions.

"Well done. Come in, and we will begin as soon as everyone is settled."

I stepped onto my blanket, made two turns to the left, and lay down, burying my nose in its usual spot. I had basically slept my way through the entire course. Given I was of no use to Jason, it was time to doze off.

I awoke to my name. "Ike—hey, wake up. Time to go." Jason tugged on my ear. "I'm done early. It was easy. Well, easier than I was expecting," he whispered.

He folded my blanket, grabbed my leash, and we made our way to the door. As we approached, the professor knelt down to greet me. "Lovely to have met you, Ike. I wish you a magnificent and meaningful life. I know you will have a tremendous impact on some very fortunate soul someday. Good for you." With that, he got himself back to his feet and turned to speak with Jason. "And, to you, Jason—thank you, again, for bringing this beautiful spirit into my classroom this summer. I have thoroughly enjoyed his presence. You take care."

Jason stuck out his hand to meet the professor's. "My pleasure. And, thanks for making physical geography so interesting." They both smiled. "My dad used to teach this class in high school—he would've approved."

"Thank you for saying so."

With that final goodbye, we were off for a weekend of camping.

By this time of day, the campus was packed with students sprawled on the neatly cut lawns eating their lunches. The mouthwatering smells were irresistible.

"That wasn't so bad, Ike—I think I might have actually done pretty well." We navigated between groups of students enjoying the warm sun as we hurried for the car. "Nice way to start our camping weekend, eh bud?"

"EXCUSE ME! Hello! Excuse me... I have a question about Ike." A woman from our class came running up behind us as we zigzagged along the main thoroughfare. "Hi," she said, trying to catch her breath. Jason turned. "Phew, you got away sooner than I had hoped. You must have done really well on the exam?"

"Maybe—I sure hope so. I was surprised that I finished so early," said Jason, clearly still unsure of his performance.

"Yes, I think I did well, also. That bonus question was fascinating. I could've written a book!"

Jason cocked his head back, becoming taller while doing so. Then, he frowned his eyebrows and turned his head slightly. "What bonus question? I didn't see a bonus question."

"Really? It was on the last page? The one about logging old growth forests in the Haida Gwaii—I thought that was a great question. My guess, he wanted us to reflect on the conversation we had as a class regarding protecting our rich natural resources juxtaposed with supporting local economies and working communities."

Jason couldn't look any more flustered. "My last page didn't have that question—at least if it did, I didn't see it!"

"Oh, well, I'm sure you did fine." The young woman smiled politely, trying to appear supportive. "Umm, the reason I ran after you was because I wanted to know a bit more about Ike. He's beautiful, by the way! I don't think I've ever seen a puppy as cute as him. I mean, the whole class talks about how adorable he is. And, I can't believe how well-behaved..."

"Yup—he's something else," interrupted Jason. "Look, I don't mean to be rude, but did you have a question for me, or did you just want to tell me that?"

The young woman stepped back.

"Ike and I are heading for the ferry and we're in a bit of a hurry."

"Can I walk with you?"

"Ya, sure." Jason shrugged his shoulders and began walking.

"Oh—my name's Susan. Sorry, I should've introduced myself."

"I'm Jason." He stuck out his hand to shake hers.

"Yes, I know. Our professor calls all of us by name. He's amazing like that. Not too many people take the time to learn names these days—don't you think?"

"You said you had a question about Ike?"

I couldn't figure out if Jason was shy, or just that impatient with other humans. He wasn't like this with Pat and Trev.

We began weaving in and out of the groups of students strewn on the grass. Each time we changed direction, I became overcome with a new smell. Once again, I was finding it tough to stay focused on where we were heading.

Mmmmm, chicken. Boy-oh-boy, cookies. Ahhhhhh, tuna and eggs.

This was torture. I was drooling, being this close to some of the best smells I had ever experienced, and I couldn't eat any of it.

"So, my parents recently retired," continued Susan, "and they have a lot of newfound time on their hands. I think volunteering to be puppy walkers would be great for them. We used to have dogs when I was younger. What do you think?"

"Sure. I mean, it sounds like they would be a good match. I will say, though, it's a lot of work. I find myself thinking about him 24 hours a day. I'm responsible for everything—feeding, house training, walking—and, you're supposed to only walk him a special way. It's not rocket science, but it requires a lot of attention to detail and effort."

"I think they'd be perfect." Susan appeared to get more excited the more she thought about it.

"Well, all they have to do is apply. They'll tell your folks straight-up if they're good to go."

"Terrific. Do you have a name and number of someone I could contact?"

Jason stopped and dropped his backpack down to the ground. "Here, can you hold this?" He went digging for his address book while Susan took hold of my leash.

"Hi Ike—come here, you little cutie." Susan knelt and put her hand out to welcome me. I would've gone in for the free scratches and attention on any other day. But not this one. All I could think about was the endless amount of food surrounding me. Goldens are well-behaved dogs, but food can make us crazy. I had to make a break for it. I slowly backed up until my leash was taut. Then, with one quick yank backwards, I was out of my collar and free!

"Ike? How'd you do that so quickly?" Susan stood up.

Jason stopped rummaging through his backpack. "What happened?"

"I don't know—he just got out!" Susan was now crouching forward, trying to grab me.

I continued to back up.

"Ike. Come here, bud. What are you doing?" Jason began walking towards me, unaware of what I was planning.

In an instant, the surrounding food cast its final spell upon me—I was overtaken. I spun around and bolted, running in every direction, in and out of students who sat in small and large circles. Some with food—others not. Transfixed, I kept running. My speed was impressive—my moves like a pro. I was possessed—in the zone—effortlessly finding gaps between humans and darting through them. Screams, cheers, and laughter followed me with each stride. Soon all of the students within earshot were watching me run as if my life depended on it. Knowing Jason was in hot pursuit, I had to plan my attack quickly. Then, I saw it. Straight ahead. A young woman slowly peeled back the paper that wrapped a mouth-watering chicken burger. I knew it was now or never. Getting caught was inevitable. What would make it okay would be getting that burger into my drooling chops!

With the precision of a hawk, I was tracking and timing the moment when I would have to pounce. As I got closer, I committed myself to making that burger mine. I leapt into the air, paws outstretched as I flew with great precision toward my target. My open mouth landed on that burger just as she lifted it to her mouth.

Our eyes met. Our jaws locked on the prize. Her look of horror was intense. Her scream, although muffled by our burger, was loud. She rolled back to the ground. I came with her, landing with my two front paws on either side of her head, pinning her. I stayed focused—I'd come too far to give in now. Finally, she relinquished. The burger was mine. I stood up and ran, burger in tow.

I had to eat and run which was, surprisingly, more challenging than I thought. I hit the brakes, skidding across the grass until I came to a standstill. My time was limited. I began to chew and swallow, chew and swallow, as fast as I could. Choking back that burger, it was only a matter of seconds before Jason would grab my neck with one massive hand and pry the burger out of my mouth with the other. I would get as much of that delicious chicken meat down my throat and into my stomach as I could.

"What that hell was that, Ike? Drop it! DROP IT!" Jason yelled at me while trying to retrieve my catch. I wasn't letting up. I had earned this. Frustrated, he eventually took his empty hand out of my mouth.

Jason turned and grabbed my collar from Susan and quickly pulled it over my head. Then, he attached the leash. He passed it back to Susan.

"Here—can you hold him again," said Jason, still breathing hard and trying to manage the anger that was brewing. "Umm, just be a little more careful this time—okay?" Jason marched off to find the woman whose burger I had devoured. Susan and I slowly followed behind.

"I'm sorry about my dog," said Jason to the young woman who was now wiping bits of leftover bun from her shirt. Her friends, meanwhile, were rolling on the grass in hysterics. And, soon, she was laughing too.

She stood up to meet Jason. "Don't worry about it. It was just some greasy chicken burger I got at the cafeteria."

"It doesn't matter what it was; he shouldn't have done that. But, sometimes, when food's involved, he loses his mind!"

"I'm okay," she insisted. "Don't worry, truly." She turned and looked at me. "He's certainly one adorable puppy."

"I suppose. But it doesn't excuse his behaviour. Here, let me pay for your burger." Jason got out his wallet and handed her some money.

"You don't have to, honestly."

"It's the least I can do." Jason was not impressed with my hunting adventure. I had never felt him this upset. His voice was low and powerful, his stance was wide and strong, and his brow was furrowed.

She reached out and took the money from his hand. "Thank you."

Susan handed my leash to Jason. "Sooooo, any chance I could still get that number?"

By the time we arrived at the car, Jason had mostly calmed down. Our weekend of camping likely hadn't begun the way he might have imagined; messing up his final exam, me creating a major scene at the university—those were probably not on his list.

He opened the passenger side door and tapped the floor mat with his hand—that was my sign to jump in. The car was hot. It had been baking in the sun for the entire morning. Jason got in on the other side, rolled down all the windows and cranked open the sunroof. Then, he started the engine, turned on the stereo, and plugged in a tape. Soon, we were in motion, and a breeze began to rustle my fur.

It had been a long morning. With Jason's music playing in the background, my full stomach, and the car gently swaying as we made our way to the ferry, it was time for some shut-eye.

getting there

Mid-afternoon, we finally drove onto the ferry. The car deck was loud and frightening. Being on the floor didn't help much—I couldn't see anything. Jason didn't seem too fussed, which helped me stay calm until the car was parked.

We made our way up several flights and out onto the main deck. With my guide dog jacket, we were allowed anywhere on the boat. We found a perfect spot to soak up some sun and take in the stunning view.

"Over there, Ike," said Jason as he pointed. "Those are the Coastal Mountains."

Once the boat began moving, the breeze made for a perfect temperature to enjoy the ride. We sat quietly side-by-side and watched the ferry terminal disappear as we moved out into the Strait of Georgia and on toward Nanaimo, our destination.

It didn't take long for some young children to find me. Soon, we were surrounded by little hands reaching to pat my soft fur and asking Jason a question or two. Children's questions were different—more to the point of wanting to understand what it was like to be a dog.

What does he eat? Where does he sleep? How do you know when he has to go poo or pee? And to Jason's credit, he took the time to answer all of them. Despite his tendency to get frustrated with himself and others, he could be patient with children.

Soon that same deafening whistle I'd heard with Colin and Trev blew out over the waters announcing our arrival in Departure Bay.

We headed north on the Trans Canada Highway. I could feel a difference in Jason. After spending more than an hour interacting with those curious children, he was lighter.

"Get comfortable, Ike. It's a beautiful ride—enjoy the view!"

Moments later, Jason pulled over. Realizing there was nothing for me to see from the footwell of the car, he quickly spread out a blanket on the back seat and slapped his hand on the top of it, signalling for me to join him. I climbed into the back seat.

"Not a word—got it?"

We were off—music blasting, sunroof open, windows down. The hot air flapped my ears and rustled my fur. I sat tall on my new perch and took it all in. Now I could easily see the entire view! Trees, mountains, streams—Jason was right, it was all so beautiful.

Jason snacked on carrots and apples that he had cut the night before. After a few moments of watching him eat, he caught my stare in his rearview mirror.

"Oh, so you think I'm going to share these with you? Ha—that's pretty bold! Especially after what you did earlier this morning." I looked back at him. He smiled.

"Okay, you know what, stealing food from someone picnicking with their friends is not cool—but, I have to tell you, Ike, that if I had been watching from a distance and you weren't my dog, I think I would've wet myself!" Jason let out an enormous laugh. It startled me. I'd never heard that from him. "Man, good thing Roberta didn't see that!"

Then, he tossed a carrot into the backseat. "Don't make a mess, bucko!"

I carefully grabbed the carrot and laid down. Holding it between my front paws, I took a nibble. It was actually good; crunchy and sweet. I took another. Next, a piece of apple landed beside me. That, too, got lodged between my paws as I tasted and then devoured it. It was no chicken burger, but I'd take it.

"I think this is it, Ike," said Jason as we pulled off the highway. "The map says that the road in can be bumpy—so, hold tight."

We slowed to a crawl. Huge ruts and potholes constantly forced Jason to adjust his course. Richly coloured green trees flanked the car, as well as massive stumps from what appeared to be trees that had been cut years earlier. Occasionally, the bottom of the car would scrape the road.

Eventually, we emerged into what appeared to be a parking lot. Jason got out to read the campsite rules posted on an old piece of plywood. I sat up and stuck my head out the window. The smells were intense—almost overwhelming for my young senses. A mishmash of odours from the thick forest surrounding the freshwater lake in front of us, all combined with the pungent aromas of the wildlife that lived nearby. It was like nothing that I had ever smelled before.

"Nothing too surprising, Ike. Honorary payment system. The usual stuff about fires and garbage. We're good to go, buddy."

A moment later, Jason gently eased the car up to the lake's edge. He turned off the engine and we both sat still and stared. "This is what makes that stupid road and every scrape worthwhile—isn't it beautiful, Ike? Just look at that mountain. Welcome to Schoen Lake, little fella."

After a few more moments of appreciating Mother Nature's precious work, Jason opened my door. I climbed out and had a big stretch. It felt good. I had been sitting for most of the day and longed to move my young bones.

"Okay, I've got lots to do. So please stay close and, whatever you do, don't try swimming yet," he said with a laugh. "Remember what happened last time?" He looked at me with a knowing smile. "If you want to help, we need firewood. We'll lose light in a few hours."

While Jason went to the trunk to find his gear, I walked up to the lake. It was enormous. There was a large log jam to the right and a pebble beach directly in front. The huge logs, gnarly and battered, looked as though they had been there for a while. Standing by the edge of the lake, I peered through the crystal clear water. I could see dozens of little fish darting this way and that in front of me. Jason had mentioned that this weekend was going to include swimming. Knowing I had webbed feet for a reason, I was keen.

I turned and walked back to our campsite. My stomach was complaining. I had enjoyed the carrots and apples, but they didn't satisfy my hunger the way a bowl of kibble could.

"You looking for something to eat? It's about that time, isn't it?"

Jason dug into a box of food he had packed and pulled out a container of kibble. He poured a heaping cup into my bowl and added some fresh water. I was already sitting and waiting for his command to begin—I had been a quick study in this pre-meal drill. "Here you go, Ike—enjoy!"

It didn't take long for Jason to set up our tent and get a fire going. After dinner, I curled up beside the dancing flames glowing bright orange with the black sky behind them. It had cooled off considerably, making the heat coming from the crackling fire feel soothing. Jason cleaned up and packed away all of our food into the trunk. He explained that was so any bears in the area wouldn't get at it. Wearing an extra sweater, he joined me, cramming his large frame into a tiny folding chair that barely fit him.

With my nose buried in my tail, his hand felt calming as he stroked my neck and rolled my ears between his fingers. We both enjoyed the silence of the day's end—aside from the odd crackle and pop that escaped from the burning logs. "Pretty nice, eh, Ike. It's so quiet—isn't this just perfect?"

I was too comfortable not to doze off, but I soon awoke to the hissing sound of Jason pouring water over the fire. "Bedtime, bud."

After a long stretch and a pee, I walked into the tent to join him. "Hmm, no crate, right? That's what you're thinking, isn't it!" He looked around the tent and smiled. "Well, I guess you can crash by my feet. Okay?" I curled up on his sleeping bag and closed my eyes. It wasn't his bed from home, but it was close. Besides, I could've slept anywhere after all of the fresh air that day.

Jason pulled out a book and began to read by the light of his flashlight. A few moments later he slapped the book down on his lap. "Can you believe I screwed up that exam today? What an ass." I lifted my head, tilting it slightly. "I know, right? That was so stupid—story of my life." His tone was harsh—like how he sometimes spoke to me when I made mistakes. He could be incredibly demanding, and if things weren't done just as he wanted them—look out!

"Screw it—we didn't come up here to get all pissed off about a geography exam. Did we?" He closed his book and turned off the flashlight. "Good night, bud." He rolled onto his side and I leaned into the backs of his legs. It was nice to feel the comfort and safety of his body as I drifted off to sleep.

schoen lake

The unzipping sound of Jason's sleeping bag woke me up.

"Hey, you—how was your first night in a tent?" Jason reached out and scratched my chin. "You ready to get this day going? Come on, let's make some breakfast!"

As we crawled out of our tent and met the morning air, I looked up to see a few scattered clouds. It was still warm, but a slight breeze was beginning to kick up.

"I think it's supposed to be clear. It's calling for mid-twenties just like yesterday. Either way, we're goin' swimmin', Ike!"

While Jason got breakfast organized, I returned to the lake. The mountain looked even more prominent in the morning sun. The tiny waves rhythmically lapped up against the shore. They sounded curious to me; perhaps louder than I expected. The little fish were back, too, but harder to see. For some reason, the water wasn't as clear as the night before.

"Okay, Ike—breakfast!"

I quickly trotted back to our campsite. Jason had made some porridge for himself and even added a spoonful to my kibble. "Here, this might make your breakfast a little more interesting."

After cleaning up, Jason put on some hiking boots and grabbed his water bottle and baseball cap. "Come on, Ike, let's check out some trails around the lake."

It was no longer an effort to keep pace with Jason's enormous strides. As he led the way, I followed comfortably behind, taking a moment here and there to stop and sniff all of the new smells surrounding me. Sometimes I would fall behind to check out a unique scent that required deeper, long-lasting sniffs. I could've spent the entire day just smelling the aromas of the rich forest.

After a long, long while on a winding trail, Jason stopped suddenly and turned to face me. Up until then, he'd been quiet—not a word spoken. Just lost in his thoughts, I supposed—he did that sometimes.

"Hey, Ike, answer me yes or no—did I miss the bonus question on the exam yesterday?" His eyes were piercing. I could feel his anger.

Goodness me, is he really waiting for me to reply?

"Sorry, bud—that's going to drive me crazy for a long while. Welcome to my world!" He spun around and continued plodding down the trail.

After a few more minutes, we were deeper into the forest, something bit me just above my left eye. I broke the silence with a loud and sharp yelp. It was intense and painful, like a hot burning ember had landed on my skin. Then, another bite. And, another! I whimpered and frantically scratched at my eyes and ears with both of my paws. I was under attack.

Jason sprinted back to see what was the matter. He removed his shirt and started swatting at the attackers that surrounded me.

"Come on, Ike—run! This way," he gestured for me to hurry up. "Those are mud wasps, and they're pissed!"

We took off as fast as we could. I could still hear the wasps buzzing beside me as I did my best to outrun them. Now Jason was cursing and swatting at the wasps that were biting him as well. Suddenly, he made a sharp turn at a clearing beside the lake and ran directly toward the water. I followed him. "Just keep running, Ike. Don't stop!"

Eventually, the water became too deep for him to run, and he fell forward with a dive into the lake. I stopped, not knowing what to do. I couldn't swim!

"Ike, just run until the water is at your chin. Get in—quick!"

Jason made his way back toward me. The wasps were still biting. I stood frozen, too frightened to know what to do. He quickly scooped me up, spun around, and headed back toward the deeper water.

"Hold on, Ike. We're goin' under...."

Then, like a familiar nightmare, I was once more underwater. I could feel Jason running his hands along my ribs and legs, looking for any hangers-on. Again, I opened my mouth wide and tried to breathe. And, once more, my lungs filled with the cool liquid that engulfed us.

Breaking through the surface, Jason held me high. I coughed and choked until I could finally breathe again. I squirmed against his tight hold. I knew he was trying to help, but I wanted to get back to shore.

"Hang on—I'll walk you in," he waded back to the shallower water. As we got closer, Jason let me down. I landed with a splash; my front paws broke through the surface of the water and settled on the pebbles below. Once I realized that I could stand in the lake and still breathe, I calmed down.

"That's a little better, eh? You okay?" he checked my face and body. "Those greasy little bastards are nasty. And those bites are going to hurt for a while. Sorry, bud—that's a lousy way to start the day."

I had pretty much dried off by the time we got back to our campsite.

"You must be starving, Ike!"

I was. With a generous serving of kibble before me, I dove in as fast as I could.

"Easy does it, bud—you know what happens when you eat too fast!"

I didn't care if I threw up. I was too hungry and enjoying my lunch immensely.

Jason pulled out his book and tiny chair and found a spot in the shade beside the lake. Me, I walked over to the tent and gently pawed the zipper.

"Are you serious? You want me to come over there and let you in so you can nap?" Shaking his head, Jason pulled his large lean frame out of his chair, stood up and walked toward me. "I've seen everything, now." I wagged my tail in approval as he got closer. "Oh, sure, lay on the charm, buddy." He zipped open the tent. "There—enjoy the bed," he said with a laugh.

It had been quite a morning. I had never walked that far before. Forget about the wasps and dunking—I was beat. I stretched out on the sleeping bag, making sure to position my head on Jason's pillow.

The familiar feeling of having to pee woke me. I laid there a while longer until I couldn't avoid the message Mother Nature was sending. As I walked out of the tent, Jason looked over. "Okay, now that was your longest nap ever!"

I turned and made my way to the bushes.

Then I sat down by Jason's chair. "Quite a morning for you," he said as he rubbed his hands over my body. "Are you sore?"

I was. Those bites were still stinging. But his big hands felt soothing. I leaned into him and tried to direct his scratches as best I could.

"How about another swim?" I looked at him and tilted my head sideways. "This time, I promise you won't go under!"

We walked over to the main swimming area. A few humans were sitting in lawn chairs, reading under an umbrella, enjoying the cool breeze off the lake. A mother and father played cards with their two children at a picnic table while another couple threw a stick into the lake for what looked to be a young Doberman Pinscher who was eagerly retrieving it.

"See, it's not so hard. That guy's probably about your age and he's figured it out. Do you want to give it a try?"

We slowly waded into the lake. As the waves lapped up against my legs, the water felt cooler than it had earlier. When the Doberman saw me, he dropped his stick and came running over.

He must have misstepped on a sharp stone because he awkwardly tumbled, splashing me as he came to an abrupt stop at my feet.

Not showing any sign of embarrassment, he stood up and greeted me. *"Hi."*

"Hi," I answered. *"You okay? That was quite a spill."*

"Ya, I'm good, thanks. Still figuring out my growing legs."

"I'm Ike."

"I'm Dash. Nice to meet you."

"Ya, same. How long have you been swimming?"

Still dripping wet, he gave himself a good shake. *"Well, we just got here today—so..."*

"No, I mean, in total. When did you learn how to swim?" I asked.

"That's it. Today, I guess. I learned today."

"You learned that fast?"

"I guess so. It's not that hard," continued Dash. *"Come on! I'll show you!"*

He turned and started walking toward the deeper water. *"Come on, Ike—follow me. Just wait for the water to lift you, and then... sort of run. Try It."*

I followed Dash out until the water was at my shoulders. He was already swimming. *"Keep going,"* he yelled, looking back to see how I was doing. *"Come on—you can do it!"*

I took another few steps and, just like he said, it felt as though the lake lifted me off my feet. I outstretched my front legs and began to, well, run. Sure enough, I moved forward—I was swimming!

"That's it—you're doing it! Keep going, Ike!"

Next, I tried curling my hind legs up under my belly and kicked them straight back one at a time. The sensation was incredible. I loved it.

"Look at you, Ike," yelled Jason, clapping as he watched from the shore. "You're a pro, buddy!"

I swam in large circles for a few moments while I figured out the breathing. Going through the waves still needed some fine-tuning. There were a few times when some water splashed up my nose. It was a little scary at first, but I soon learned to relax and not get too panicked.

Dash swam by me on his way back to the shore. *"Come on, Ike. Let's get something to chase."*

Before I got to shore, Dash had returned with his stick and dropped it at his human's feet. Jason had gone to find a stick for me.

While I waited for Jason, Dash took off, splashing into the lake for another chase.

"You ready?" Jason wound up to toss the stick. As it spun in the air far over my head, I turned and ran back to the lake, launching myself at the water. I landed with a splash and began running immediately like Dash had told me. I was away—this was easy.

For the next while, Dash and I retrieved countless tosses. Soon, I had mastered this swimming thing.

"Great, Ike!" Jason yelled. "With your webbed toes, you're built for this!"

Standing over my stick, soaking wet, I turned to see Dash charging toward me. I braced myself for another tumble. He hit the brakes just in time, with his paws outstretched in a play-bow in front of me.

With a mischievous look, he dared me, *"Bet you can't catch me! "*

"Bet I can...."

I answered his play-bow. He didn't move. I remained crouched and motionless, waiting for him to signal the start. He pounced left. I did the same. Then, he pounced right. As I moved to match him, he took off. The chase was on.

Pebbles flew through the air; we dug in and pushed as hard as possible to get up to speed. Dash was fast. His lean, long body could move on the straightaways. But I made up ground on the corners. Everyone at the beach watched and laughed as we did what young pups do so well—play!

Our chase involved large circles at first. Then, they became tighter until we ran a perfect figure-eight pattern. Even looking back, I'm not sure what it is about that shape, but it appears hardwired into us from birth. It's not mysterious or mystical or anything overly profound; it just feels good to turn in opposing directions over and over, again, because we can—feeling our speed and our agility. I loved those early days of discovering my legs and the possibilities they offered. It was a beautiful time of life.

Eventually, Dash's long legs got the better of him, and he spun out on a corner. I ran over and pinned him.

"See, told ya!"

I got up and bolted. Dash flipped over, stood up, and came after me. I had just learned that sharp corners were my best strategy to keep him at bay. As I heard him closing in, I leaned into my front right shoulder and spun around with such an abrupt change in direction that he ran far beyond where I had turned.

"Hey, that's not fair!" he yelled as he tried to answer my hairpin turn.

Our chase game continued for a while longer until neither of us could run anymore. I walked over to the lake, laid down in the cool refreshing water, and began drinking. Dash joined me.

"That was fun," he said between slurps.

"Sure was!"

Eventually, Jason waded into the water and made his way out to a half-floating dock anchored a ways offshore.

"Come on, Ike—come join me!"

"I'm out. I've had enough," said Dash. *"It was nice to meet you, Ike. Thanks for the playtime."*

"You bet, Dash. Thanks for the swimming lessons!"

Dash got up and returned to his humans while I swam out to be with mine.

"Swim over here, bud. There's a thick wooden ladder. You should be able to climb up onto the dock with my help."

When I got to the ladder, Jason grabbed the scruff of my neck from behind and pulled me. I braced against him and climbed up—it worked. The dock was barely afloat, with Jason sitting on the edge, his legs dangling in the water. I sat beside him.

I was surprised by how thin he was. He looked like Dash. In the sunlight, I could see his ribs and bony shoulders exposed. I had never really noticed.

"What do you think? Pretty nice, eh?"

It was nice. Beautiful, in fact. Even perfect. I had learned to swim, spent time with Jason, and made a new friend. Not bad for my first camping trip.

We made our way back to the campsite and a very satisfying meal. Nothing like a little hunger spice to make ordinary kibble taste amazing. As nightfall arrived, we settled beside the warm and noisy fire.

With Jason sunk into his tiny chair and me curled up beside him, I fought the sleep that was calling. It had been a long and exhausting day. But, thinking this would be our only summer together, I was keen to enjoy as many of these moments as I could. A year from now,

I was scheduled to be immersed in my final training for life with a blind human.

The next morning we enjoyed a short hike on a different trail heading around the lake in the other direction. Thankfully, there were no wasps to be found. Once back at our campsite, we jumped into the lake for a quick swim to cool off. Then we packed up the car and said goodbye to our perfect spot.

Arriving home, we found Trev and Pat sitting at the picnic table, enjoying their dinner and a cold beer. Jason had barely opened my door when I launched myself from the back seat. If you've ever seen an excited golden retriever try to run while managing their energy, it's quite a sight. You see, goldens don't just wag their tails; we wag our entire bodies. And, sometimes, we trip ourselves up.

"Ikester, buddy—how was the camping?" Trev knelt to meet me. Once close enough, I dropped to my back and enjoyed some belly scratches while the wagging continued upside down. It was good to be home. As much as I had enjoyed my time with Jason, I had missed our roommates too.

"How'd it go, Jase?" asked Pat.

"It was great. The campsite was right on the lake. It was clean, quiet, and Ike even made a friend."

"You made a friend, Ike? You social butterfly, you—just like your dad!" Trev winked at Jason and continued to rub my belly while I rolled from side to side.

"How about getting there—any problems?"

"Nope—all good. Ike was a hit on the ferry—both ways. With that guide dog jacket, we went everywhere. Let's just say he was popular."

"Ike—you rockstar, you," said Trev. "I'm going to have to find you some doggie sunglasses!"

"Hey, I forgot to ask—how did things go with your exam?"

"Don't bother—I'm trying to forget about it."

meeting allyson

With Jason's summer class over, our new morning routine began early every day with a long hike amidst the fresh-smelling trails of the UBC Endowment Lands near our house. Every time we entered the huge park, it reminded me that I had won the lottery. It was doggie-heaven. Trees galore and smells that could keep a canine nose busy for a lifetime. I loved our hikes in there. Jason would walk while I explored. Perfection.

A week into our new routine, Jason told me that I'd be meeting my new vet. I had met one before when my siblings and I were really young. An older man came to Roberta and Hugh's house to "check us over," as he put it.

Allyson was her name. A young doctor who, among others in the city, would take care of my siblings and me for the year we were with our PWs. The clinic was only a few minutes away. Getting there required walking along a busy street in a part of the neighbourhood that I hadn't seen before.

"You see these idiots speeding by, Ike? These are the asshats you want to avoid. Got it? Please, if you ever get out of the backyard, don't come anywhere near this street! Okay?"

As we walked into the office, the smell hit me like one of the speeding cars out on the street; cats and dogs, birds and hamsters, and everything in between. Those combined smells mixed with the pet food and cleaning products had me wishing for an open window.

After checking in with the human talking on a phone, Jason took a seat in the waiting room. He read a sports magazine while I curled up under his chair like I was supposed to. Soon, Jason was asked to bring me through the door furthest to the left and wait for the doctor. While we both stood, a younger human wiped down the examination table, changed the water in a bowl on the floor, and put cookies on the counter.

"The doctor will be in momentarily." She smiled and disappeared through another door at the back of the room.

"Pretty official, eh, Ike! I should've phoned ahead and told them to have more cookies ready for you. Two seems a little skimpy."

In walked my new Doctor. "Hello, Jason?"

"Yes, hello, and this is Ike."

I looked at her bright smile. She knelt on the floor in front of me and patted herself on the tops of her legs, gesturing for me to come over. "Would you mind if I have a closer look at you? I can give you scratches while I do."

I moved in, dropped to my back, and welcomed her warm and comforting touch. She was good. She knew all the right places—under my chin, behind my ears, and the top of my belly.

"There you go, Ike—you're such a good boy. Does that feel good?"

It does!

After a few more minutes of Allyson scratching and rubbing my belly while she spoke puppy-talk to me, she looked up. "Sorry, I don't mean to ignore you, Jason. I'm Allyson. I'll be Ike's vet until he moves on with his training in the spring."

Without getting up, she grabbed the strange thing with tubes and a round shiny part that was hanging around her neck. "Ike, this is my stethoscope. I'm going to put it on your belly and listen to your insides. Okay?" Then she breathed on it and rubbed it up against her own belly. Jason watched closely.

"Strong sounding heart. Lungs are clear. He's off to a good start." With her hands cupped on either side of my head, she moved toward me until her nose was very close to mine. *Hmm, no human has ever done this to me.* "Well, lover—look at you handsome boy—you're a healthy little guy. Next, we have to take your temperature and give you some medicine through a sharp needle. Both can feel strange. Jason, can you please grab those cookies on the counter?"

Jason passed them to her.

As I opened my mouth to enjoy the first cookie, I felt something cold slide into my backside. *Hey—careful with that thing!*

"Easy does it, Ike—just a few more moments." Allyson smiled at me. Her eyes were warm and friendly. I could trust her. The instrument in my backside beeped. "Perfect temperature. Ike, you're passing with flying colours." I rolled onto my front and stood up. "Two cookies is never enough, especially when my patients are as well-behaved as you. Let's say we go find some more—what do you think, Ike?"

I could tell she knew that asking a golden retriever if they wanted another cookie was actually a question you never needed to ask. I wagged my tail in approval.

"Jason, I'm just going to take Ike to the back so that one of our technicians can draw some blood. It's not standard procedure to check his levels at this age, but because of what he's destined to become, they want us to make sure there's nothing out of the ordinary going on with him. He'll also receive his scheduled shots. We'll just be a moment." Allyson turned to face me. "Okay, Ike, let's go find those cookies!"

We left Jason on his own.

The big cookies were in the back. However, so were the needles that reminded me of the wasps we had met up with at Schoen Lake. I yanked my leg back as the big needle bit through my skin. "Hold on, little guy. It'll just be a second." She pulled out the needle and pushed her thumb and a piece of white stuff over the bite. "There—almost done, Ike." Then two smaller needles, both at the back of my neck—they were easy.

I followed Allyson and her handful of cookies back to the other room to find Jason facing the wall admiring the prints.

"That's quite a pup you've got here, Jason,"

He smiled with pursed lips while he took hold of my leash. Allyson continued to feed me cookies and stroke my ears and neck.

"Ike and his sister, Iona, are the first guide dogs that I've volunteered to work with—she's a beautiful pup, as well," continued Allyson. "I'm pretty sure they live quite close to the clinic too." I perked up when I heard Iona's name. "Have you seen them in Memorial Park?"

"No, we haven't. I had no idea Ike had a sibling nearby. I'll keep my eyes open when we're out walking around."

"It's my understanding that most of the puppy walkers are either families or retirees looking for something to keep them busy. It says on Ike's file that you're a student?"

"Well, I'm hoping to be. I should get a letter from Emily Carr this week. It's a four year design program, but Ike will be with me for the first year." Jason didn't wait for Allyson to ask her the next question. He knew where she was going with this. "Look, I know what you're wondering. Why would a young single guy still in school volunteer to take care of a golden retriever puppy—forget about the guide-dog-in-training part, right?"

"Well, truthfully, that question had crossed my mind," admitted Allyson as she smiled.

"The short answer is, I've always wanted to have a golden. This program allows me that chance at someone else's expense. Yes, he's a lot to take care of while still in school, but I'll find the time. And, with his guide dog jacket, I can take him anywhere. We'll figure it out."

"I'm sure you will." Allyson knelt down and looked at me. "You take care, Ike—I'll see you again soon," she said as she gently rubbed my chest. I leaned forward and licked her face. "Awww, for that, you get another cookie for the road." She reached into her jacket pocket and pulled out her last one. "Can you sit? Ike, can you sit?

To which I wasted little time in plopping my backside on the floor. "Well, look at you, smarty-pants. How about shake-a-paw?" she asked as she held out her hand. I quickly raised my right paw and placed it in her hand. "Wow, he's good!"

Yup—not just a handsome face!

"You've done a good job so far, Jason. He's really quick," said Allyson as she got up off of the floor. "Good luck with that letter. I'm sure Ike will love going to art school."

"Thanks—ya, fingers crossed." Jason led me into the waiting room and over to the counter, where the human was busy with someone on the phone.

"Can you just hang on a moment?" She covered the receiver. "There's no payment, Jason. Ike's visits are billed directly to the Canadian Guide Dogs. We'll see you and Ike again in a few weeks. I'll call you when he's due." She smiled politely as we turned and made our way back out onto the busy street.

"How about that, Ike—you have a sister living nearby. Maybe I should phone Roberta and find out where?"

If I could've made that call myself, I would have. I missed Iona most of all of my siblings. Knowing she lived close and that there was a chance we'd run into her made me happy.

"Ike, let's go home a different way. We'll check out that park Allyson mentioned. It's not too far!"

The new park was different from the forest trails that we hiked every morning. There were fancy shrubs, planted flowers, and freshly cut grass. There were other dogs there, too; some playing fetch, others wrestling. It seemed to be a popular place.

"What do you think, Ike? Pretty nice, eh! Don't you love those enormous trees? Wait until autumn when the colours change. It's beautiful in here."

The grass smelled sweet. I wanted to roll and scratch my back on it, but Jason still had me on leash, which meant I was "working," as Roberta called it. "Okay, bud, we have to go. Don't worry, we'll come back, and I'll let you run around and play."

At home, Pat and Trev were in the kitchen making dinner. The stereo was playing loudly. Trev was singing along as he chopped vegetables.

"Hey, Jase—how'd it go?" yelled Trev.

Pat made his way to the stereo and turned it down. "Ahhh—there, I can hear myself think, again," whispered Pat.

"You got a problem with Sting?" asked Trev.

"Yes, I do—when the windows are rattling, I have a problem with Sting!"

"Don't mind him, Ike," said Trev. "He's just mad 'cause I didn't let him pick the music!"

I walked over to my bowl to get a drink of water while Jason dug into my bag of kibble and served up my dinner.

"Ike's in perfect health," Jason said as he hung up my leash and grabbed a paring knife to help out.

"What about the Vet—guy or girl?" asked Pat.

"Girl. Her name is Allyson. Ike sure seemed to like her," Jason began dicing a carrot.

"Pretty?"

"What do you mean, pretty?" asked Jason with a strange look on his face.

Trev turned and looked at Jason. "Which part of pretty are you having trouble with? Was she good-looking?"

Jason cocked his head sideways. "I suppose so. She kinda looks like that figure skater from a few Olympics back. You know, the one with that fancy haircut."

"Haircut?" Confused, Pat and Trev looked at one another. Then, after a moment spent pondering the riddle, Trev replied, "Get outta here. I know who you mean!"

"The American who won the Gold—that one?" asked Pat.

"Ya, that one—she looks like her," answered Jason.

"And you're not sure if she's good-looking?" laughed Trev. "Are you joking?"

"What—so she's pretty—who cares?" replied Jason.

"How old is she?" pressed Trev.

"I don't know—a little older than me?"

"Is she married?" was Pat's next question.

"How the hell am I supposed to know if she's married?" With an unflattering look directed at both of them, Jason continued, "What, I'm going to ask Ike's vet if she's married during an appointment?"

"It's called a ring finger," said Trev, as he grabbed his.

"Geezuz Murphy, I can't believe your obsession with this woman. She's Ike's vet—I didn't go there lookin' for a wife!"

"Ya, true—but maybe you could ask her out on a date?" said Trev. "She likes Ike. You like Ike. You've already got something in common." Trev elbowed Pat in the ribs. They both laughed. "Come on, Jase—we're just playin' with ya. But, seriously, when was the last time you went out on a date?"

"Trev, she has a job—a really good job. I don't—I don't even know what I'm doing come September. She probably has a nice home—a nice car. I live in a dining room with two... two...."

"Two what?" Trev smiled. "And careful how you answer that—I'm making your dinner!"

Jason took a deep breath. "Look, futon aside, I can put all of my worldly possessions into three suitcases. You think a woman like Allyson would seriously consider dating a guy like me?" Jason turned around and grabbed another carrot.

Pat and Trev looked at each other, surprised by Jason's comment. Trev quietly responded, "You might want to think about how you talk about yourself—your self is always listening."

"Hmph," Jason grunted. "Enough with your self-help garbage."

"Speaking of September, this came in the mail." Pat held up an envelope. And then slowly lowered it in front of Jason's face.

Jason dropped the carrot and knife. He looked at Pat, who had tilted his head and smiled. Jason slowly took hold of the envelope, walked to our room, and sat down on the bed. I followed him. Shoulders slouched, he stared at the envelope, then turned toward me and said, "Well, Ike, I guess this is it—cross your toes, buddy."

Slowly, Jason tore open the envelope and removed the letter. He unfolded it, turned it right-side-up, and began to read quietly to himself. After another read-through—just to make sure—he carefully refolded the letter and placed it on his desk. Then he got up and walked back into the kitchen. Pat and Trev continued to make dinner without a word. I followed Jason to the kitchen door to hear the news.

"I guess I know what I'm doing in September." Pat and Trev turned to face him. "Looks as though Ike and I will be going to Emily Carr."

"Yesss!" yelled Trev. "Awesome news!"

"Well done, Jase," added Pat, as he and Trev high-fived Jason and then caught him in the middle of a group hug.

"This calls for a celebration! Let's just leave all this stuff and head out for a bite. What do you say?" asked Trev.

"I'm in," said Pat. "And the fireworks competition is on at English Bay again tonight. I think it's Italy's turn? What do you say, Jase?"

"Sounds great, but I haven't left Ike alone yet. I'm not sure if he's ready for that."

"Well, only one way to find out," replied Pat. They all looked at me.

"True enough," agreed Jason. "What do you think, Ike—can you handle a few hours on your own?"

Piece o' cake.

"How about the Varsity Grill on 10th?" suggested Trev.

After a brief scramble of changing shirts, grabbing keys, and finding wallets, Jason came into our bedroom to say his version of goodbye.

"Okay, you—don't mess this up! We'll be a few hours. See you soon, bud." As he bent down to pat me on the head, he added, "Just make sure you stay off my bed—got it?"

"See ya, Ikester—be good!" yelled Trev, running down the outside stairs.

"Ya, don't burn the place down, Ike—see ya, buddy," Pat said as he locked the door behind him.

Silence—ahhh, no stereo. No bantering. I could handle this for a few hours. I walked into the kitchen and sniffed around, looking for any fallen carrot bits or other carnage from the stew. No luck. Then, over to my water bowl for a drink.

Hmmm. Jason didn't get me out for a pee...

***

Standing in our bedroom, panting, I heard the car pull up. Moments later, the sound and impact of Jason running up the stairs shook the house. Then the door swung open and he hurried in.

He flicked on the lights. "Holy crap—what smells?" He looked around and saw me standing by my crate. I bolted through his legs and ran down the stairs. I had to go busy—badly. "Ike, what's wrong? Where are you going?" Jason called after me.

I ran past Trev and then Pat, and hurried to my spot near the compost and squatted. "Ah, poor guy—looks like he really had to go," said Pat. Next, I took a long pee. Then I made my way back up to see Jason.

"Whoa—who died?" called out Trev as he walked in through the kitchen door and saw the mess. "Ike, buddy!"

As I came to the top of the stairs, I could see Jason on his hands and knees, cleaning up my accidents. I walked in slowly. "Ike, man, what the hell? We weren't gone that long—you should've been fine." Jason grabbed some more paper towels and continued to clean up the carnage.

Trev returned with a new roll. "Holy crap, Ike—that is some stinky!" Before he passed the roll to Jason, he tore off a few sections and got down on his knees to help. "Trev, I appreciate the offer, but he's my dog—I'll clean up when he craps all over the place."

"It's okay. Remember, I grew up on a farm in Saskatchewan—I'm used to this stuff."

"I grew up in Toronto—I'll supervise," added Pat with a laugh.

"Bastard," Trev smiled. "At least open some more windows, Mr. Supervisor, sir."

After Jason had finished mopping the floor, he came in to see me. I had been lying in my crate watching. I was still panting as he came closer to check me over. "Ike, what was that about? You okay? And, why is your belly so huge?" He reached his hand under my stomach. "Hey Pat, come have a look at this."

Pat came in to join us. "Yikes, his stomach is quite distended."

"I can't figure out why he's panting so much?"

Pat crouched down to inspect me a little closer.

Jason looked around the room until he spotted the scene of the crime. "What the... Ike, did you get up on my bed?" Jason stood up and moved to the end of his bed, where my big bag of kibble was leaning against the wall. "Look here, Pat. The bag is open. And, there's a tonne of food missing," he peered inside. "Holy smokes, Ike, did you climb into this bag from my bed?"

I got up and went over to my water bowl, which was empty. I stood there looking back at Jason. *Can a dog get a drink around here?*

"Oh my goodness, he must have eaten two days' worth of food in one go. No wonder his belly is so huge. And that would explain his panting as well. Yikes, poor guy—no wonder he crapped all over the place!"

"Can I give him some more water?" asked Trev.

"He drank that entire bowl? That would explain him peeing everywhere too."

"Man, rough night, Ike. Hopefully, he's learned his lesson," said Pat.

"Don't count on it. We had dogs on the farm that sometimes got into the bins that stored their food. They would eat so much, they'd puke. You might want to find a better way to store that big bag of food if you plan on leaving him alone again."

It was a long night. Aside from the continuous panting, I had to get Jason up three more times to go outside. Come morning, he was exhausted. And so was I.

waiting to begin

The following month was about getting ready for school. Despite all of the things that Jason needed to take care of, he always made time for our morning hike in the Endowment Lands. We would spend hours in there. The Clinton Trail, Sasamat, Sword Fern, Iron Knee—we explored all of them. My favourite was Sword Fern, I loved running fast along the winding parts. But it really didn't matter; I was just happy to be lost in there with Jason.

Most days, he hardly ever spoke. We just walked. Some mornings he would throw large sticks for me deep into the woods off the trails. Jason was a large human and had quite an arm. I was always amazed at how far he could launch those huge ones. And, after a moment or two, I would decipher his scent on the stick that he had just thrown and return it to him. It was easy. "How the hell do you do that, Ike? How do you find the right stick every time? Well done, buddy!" It was our morning rhythm.

I was nearly four months old. I was bigger, stronger, faster, and becoming more confident amongst the other dogs we'd meet each day. Regardless of which trail we chose, we would run into other goldens, labs, huskies, and everything in-between, pretty much every morning. We got to know the regulars. For the most part, they were all friendly. We would start with a greeting, a few sniffs, and then a play bow. If it felt right, we'd be off tearing in and out of trees and up and down trails. I loved the speed that I was developing. The sensation of running at full tilt in the woods, having to make last-second decisions to navigate safely through all of the obstacles—I never tired of it.

A few weeks after seeing Allyson, I got the scent of someone—something—that was oddly familiar on one of our morning walks. I wasn't sure who or what it was; I just knew the scent. I dropped my stick and began to trot along the trail with my nose high in the air.

"Ike, what's up? What are you doing?" asked Jason. With each inhale, the scent got stronger.

Why do I know this smell?

Then, suddenly, up ahead, I saw a dog that looked like me dart across the trail. I stopped. *I know that pup!* I looked a moment longer. *That's Iona!*

I was off and running full speed up the trail. *"Iona. IONA. It's me, Ike!"*

She came out of the woods and looked my way. *"Ike, is that you?"* For a moment longer, she stared closely and then broke into a sprint directly toward me.

We met mid-stride. I tumbled left and she right. Then we both got up laughing and came back toward one another.

"I can't believe it's you, Ike!"

"I know—it's so good to see you. I've missed you!"

"Me too. Do you live nearby?" asked Iona.

"Yes, we live just a few blocks from the entrance. What about you?"

Iona turned to look at her human, who was now calling her name and walking up the trail to find out what all of the commotion was about.

"We're close, too," answered Iona. *"But we live on the other side of that busy street. So just a little further than you."*

"Right, the street with the asshats!" I replied.

"What? Ass-who?"

"Never mind," I said. *"It's just what Jason calls the drivers who speed up and down there."* Iona tilted her head with a look of confusion on her face. *"Don't worry about it. How have you been?"*

Her human arrived. "Iona, you've found a friend!"

"It certainly appears that way," answered Jason.

"They look as though they're the same age."

"Wait, did you say Iona?" asked Jason.

Surprised, the woman answered, "Yes, why?"

"Well, my dog's name is Ike—I think they're littermates."

"That's fantastic! So nice to meet you—I'm Linda. We live a few blocks on the other side of Dunbar."

"I'm Jason. We're just a few blocks from here too."

"Oh, the student! I heard about you from Roberta way back when we decided on which dog we wanted. We looked at Ike, but we decided on a girl."

"You didn't answer my question, Ike... How have you been?" asked Iona.

"Right... Ahh, good. I've been good. How about you?"

"Same. I like my humans," answered Iona. *"Although, they have two young daughters who can make a lot of noise at times. But they have a lovely home, and I feel spoiled most days. Lots of chewy toys, a warm cozy place to sleep and cuddle with the girls, the house is always clean with a fenced backyard, and we walk here most days. Life is pretty good! How about you? How is the student working out?"*

"He's okay," I said. *"Although, instead of two children, he has two roommates—Pat and Trev. None of them like to cuddle, though. We're constantly going places, doing things—I never get bored; Jason takes me everywhere. We've been camping; I even went to school with him for a few*

weeks. It was quite fun. Nice humans. Lots of pats on my head, a few chin scratches, and some great food!"

Iona smiled. *"Sounds as if it's worked out perfectly for you. I mean, you said you were looking for someone who liked to be active, remember?"*

"Well, we're definitely active. That's for sure!"

"Really nice to meet you, Jason," Linda turned to head back the other way. "I guess we'll see you next week at the picnic?"

"Right, right, the picnic—we'll see you there! Stanley Park, correct?"

"Yes. I think we're meeting by the tennis courts around eleven and then finding a spot for a picnic where the pups can play."

"Bye, Iona," I said. *"Sounds like we'll see you again next week!"*

"Great—so glad I ran into you, Ike." Iona laughed. *"You know what I mean!*

the school

The following day, arriving home from our morning walk, Jason grabbed the hose from the side of the house and stretched it out to reach the middle of the backyard. "Ike, you stay here. I'll be back in a second." He then dashed up the stairs and returned with a bucket and some shampoo.

Then he turned the hose to face away from me while he adjusted the pressure. "Okay, Ike—hate to do this, but I'm afraid it's bath time, buddy."

Jason took hold of my collar and slowly moved the hissing nozzle closer to my back. Then the shock of frigid water hit me. I jerked as the steady-moving liquid slid down my sides and around to my chest and belly. "Easy, buddy," encouraged Jason. This seemed colder than Schoen Lake.

Jason rubbed the water into my fur and moved it around my entire body until I was dripping wet. Then he laid down the hose, grabbed the shampoo, and squeezed blobs along my spine. Next was the good part—Jason started rubbing, scratching, and massaging soapy suds into my fur over every inch of my body—heaven! Yes, the cool morning air was chilly, but the body rub was so worth it!

Unlike the cuddles that Iona had described with her family, my time with Jason had been mainly void of any physical affection. Sure, I got chin scratches, and belly and ear rubs, but they were few and far between and never felt this soul-satisfying—I longed for this.

Within moments, I leaned into the pressure coming from Jason's hands and groaned with audible approval.

Jason let out a roar of laughter. "Would you listen to yourself, Ike—you sound like an old man! It can't feel that good."

Oh, but it does.

"Okay, look out—here comes the rinse cycle. Almost done, buddy."

I braced myself as the cold water streamed down my body while Jason did his best to help the rinsing process. Covered in suds, it took quite a while to get my fur squeaky clean.

"Hey, Trev—I've got some old towels beside Ike's crate. Can you throw them down?" yelled Jason as he held my collar tight.

Within moments, I was under those towels with Jason's big strong hands rubbing and patting me dry. The moaning soon returned. Jason laughed again.

"Okay, Ike—that's it—we're done. You're as good as new!"

He released my collar and, almost instinctively, I was off. Standing in the middle of our backyard, Jason watched with pleasure as I launched into a crazed sprint around the perimeter of the fence, barely managing my balance with each sharp corner. After a few warm-up laps, I broke into a repeating figure-eight pattern as usual.

"Hey boys, check out this nutbar tearing up the lawn," Jason called to our roommates upstairs. They quickly appeared on the deck and cheered me on with encouraging whoops.

Having released my pent-up energy, I slowed to a trot and eventually stopped. I felt fantastic. I turned and followed Jason up the stairs to join Pat and Trev on the deck.

"That was impressive, Ikester—wish I could tap into just an ounce of that sort of speed during my runs," said Trev.

"Not sure why, but he always runs in that figure-eight pattern. I wish I knew what that was about?"

"I think they call it... fun," joked Pat. "You should try learning a thing or two from Ike for a change. Like having some fun once in a while, Mr. Serious!"

"What's up today, Jase—why the bath?" asked Trev.

"Big day—we're meeting with the dean of design at Emily Carr. So I figured a sweet-smelling dog wouldn't hurt!"

"Do they know about him?" asked Pat.

"Nope—but they will soon," answered Jason. "As long as Ike doesn't crap in his office, we should be good! Right bud?" He looked at me and smiled.

By now I was used to the drive to Granville Island. We had done it almost every weekend since I arrived in the spring. That late summer day, Granville Island was in its glory. The sun was high. The temperature was warm but not too hot, with the coolness of the ocean breeze balancing the heat. Finding a parking spot was easier than it usually was on weekends. Within minutes we were walking toward the school.

Jason paused outside the main entrance, pulled out my jacket from his backpack, and tied it around my chest. "I know, I know—you hate this thing. But it's what's going to allow you to come here with me for the year, buddy. So, grin and bear it—okay?"

With my jacket in place, Jason grabbed my leash and stood up. He took one final look at me, bent forward to straighten my ear, then gave me an approving pat on my head. "No pressure, Ike—but if you screw this up, we're toast."

We entered the building. It smelled like the harsh stuff my roommates used to clean up the house. Once we got further inside, I could smell food as well—cafeteria food. It reminded me of our summer class at UBC.

I wonder if they sell chicken burgers?

There were humans, mostly young humans, going this way and that, hurriedly carrying paintings and drawings in different directions. I wasn't exactly sure what everyone was busy doing, but there was certainly a buzz about the place.

Just inside the front door, a human sat at a desk. I wasn't sure why, but it seemed like every building had a human like that. She, too, was busy. I watched her quickly jot down notes while simultaneously speaking on the phone she held between her shoulder and ear. She smiled and waved at what I assumed were students as they walked by her desk. Which, by the way, was tall and fancy and red—it was huge. Surely too big for just one human.

"What's his name?" she asked. "He's beautiful!"

"His name's Ike." Jason moved us closer.

"What's the jacket for? Is he going to be a guide dog or something?" She got up from her chair and came around to see us.

"Yes, that's exactly it; he's in training to be a guide dog."

She bent down to greet me. "Hello, Ike. You're a good lookin' boy. I'll bet you attract a lot of women for your dad." She turned and looked at Jason and smiled. He blushed. I couldn't believe that my stern and stoic human was embarrassed by this woman's playful question.

"I guess."

"Of course he does. I know what you're up to, Ike. Tell your dad I'm hip to his plan." She laughed with a snort and walked back to her chair.

I had never seen Jason so flushed.

"How can I help you, Ike's dad?" Her smile had faded slightly, but she was still friendly.

"I'm here to see the dean of design? I have an appointment for 10:30."

"Really? You're here to meet with the big guy, Frederick? Hmmm, are you a student or something?" She leaned forward across her desk, looking at Jason over the tops of her glasses.

"Well, I—I'm going to be. I mean—I am. I just haven't started yet."

"Haven't started what?"

"School—I haven't started school here yet."

The woman laughed and leaned back in her chair. "I know what ya mean—I'm just messin' with ya, Ike's dad." She took off her glasses and peered down at me. "Hey, Ike, does your dad come with a name?"

I looked up at him. "Yes, sorry, my name is Jason."

"I love that name. My nephew is Jason. I call him, 'Jase-the-Ace!' Does anyone ever call you that?"

"Ahh, no."

Jase the Ace—I'll have to remember that one!

"Do you come with a name?" asked Jason.

"Ha, that's the spirit! See, Ike, now your dad's beginning to lighten' up. Yes, as a matter of fact, it's Rebecca—but people around here call me Becks."

"Nice to meet you, Becks," Jason stuck out his hand to shake hers.

"Oh my, look at this fancy gentleman—hand shakin' and all!" She stood up and took Jason's hand. "Your dad's quite a serious guy sometimes, eh, Ike?" She looked at me and smiled, then put her glasses back on to review her notes. "Let's see here. Ah yes, you're right on time." Becks looked up with a softer smile this time. "So you see those blue doors behind me?" She pointed over her shoulder. "Through there—down the hall—second office on your right. Freddie's got big brown hair and glasses to match. His shirts are pressed. His pants are pleated. He's all business just like you, Jase-the-Ace."

We made our way through the blue doors.

Jason tapped lightly on the door frame. "Excuse me, are you the dean?"

"Maybe." A man with very shiny shoes slowly turned around in his chair. "You must be Jason. Thanks for being on time. Have a seat," he said, gesturing to a small wooden chair in the corner of his office. "And, this little dog is here because...?"

"He's why I asked for the meeting." Jason looked tense; his posture was ramrod straight. I guess he wasn't kidding—this meeting was a big deal.

Frederick sat back in his chair, crossed his legs, and placed his hands on top of his head with his fingers interlocked. "I'm all ears."

"This is Ike. He's in training to be a guide dog. Hence the jacket."

"I can read."

Jason looked at me. "Well, you see, this jacket allows him to go into any public building while he's in training. Ahh, like this building, for example. So I was wondering if you would be okay with Ike coming to classes with me?"

Jason rolled my left ear in his fingers, waiting for Frederick to reply.

"Are you asking me or telling me?"

After a moment. "Asking?"

"It doesn't appear as though I have a choice."

Jason looked at me while he adjusted himself in his chair.

"Is it house trained?"

"Yes, he's house trained. And, he has this amazing effect on people, they just seem to light up when they meet him," Jason offered enthusiastically.

"Really," said Frederick, sounding less than impressed.

"He came to school with me this summer at UBC," Jason continued. "I took a geography course. He was a hit with all of my classmates, including the professor."

Frederick paused. "You're aware that he has bright red lipstick in the middle of his forehead?"

"We met Becks before we came in here."

Frederick nodded his head and turned around. Then he reached for a piece of paper on his desk. "It says here that you transferred from UVic. We don't get many students from there. At least not the kind who enrol in design."

"My painting instructor there asked me why I was in his class. He was trying to politely point out the difference in the work that I was producing compared to the other students. My work was based on realism and was graphic—he called it 'eye candy.'"

"Of course he did."

"He suggested I might be better suited here. So I put together a portfolio, had my interview a few months ago, and here we are."

"I see. Why design? Why not illustration, if realism is your thing?"

"I originally went to Syracuse back in the mid-'80s. I studied advertising design—and loved it. My instructors were incredible. But I transferred out here after two years to pursue something else, and now I want to get back at it."

"Really? Syracuse? They're an impressive university with an equally impressive design school. If you were good enough to get in there, you'll be just fine here." Frederick's tone seemed to soften as he brought his hands down from atop his head and uncrossed his legs. "What was the other pursuit, if you don't mind me asking—what brought you out here?"

Jason looked at the floor. "Hmm, just some crazy dream. It was nothing."

"Well then, Jason—and Ike, I suppose—welcome to Emily Carr. As a mature student, you'll enjoy it here. We have other students your age who, for whatever reason, find design later in life. The important thing to remember is that the difference between you and 'the painters,'" he said, air-quoting the word, "is that when you graduate, you'll get paid for your work." A dismissive smile slowly grew across his face.

"Thank you. And thanks for letting Ike come to school with me."

"Good luck." Frederick returned to his work.

Jason looked at me, scrunched up his face, and gave me the thumbs-up. We quickly made our way back to the main foyer. Becks was holding a coffee. "How'd it go?"

"Looks as though Ike's all set for September!"

"Ike, your dad looks a little less stressed than when you two arrived. Congratulations! I didn't realize it was in question. I thought you could go anywhere with that jacket?"

"We can, but I wanted to give him the heads-up."

"Hey, before you leave, you should check out the student show," suggested Becks. "There's some good work."

Jason nodded and began to walk toward the gallery. I didn't move. Instead, I braced myself for when the leash became taught. Then I pulled back and resisted.

Jason turned around. "Ike, what are you doing? Come on; it won't take long." He pulled me a little harder, but I continued to resist and tried to make my way to the door. I had to go busy, badly. "What's up? Come on—this way!" Jason gave my leash a sharp tug, and I followed. "Good boy, Ike—that's better."

Exposed steel girders framed large sections of the walls and combined to create a vast open space where the students had hung, placed, or leaned various art forms. Jason slowly walked from one display to the next without saying a word. His pace was slow and unchanging—his expression flat.

Meanwhile, my desire to find a patch of grass was growing urgent. The pressure, unstoppable. Once more, I tried to pull Jason towards the front entrance. And, once more, he told me to wait.

"This is what I've been worried about, Ike. Going to school with people who think this crap is art. This isn't art. Look at this—some jackass dragged a stop sign in here, cement and grass still attached, leaned it up against the wall, put a title on it—Dead Stop Sign—and deemed it art?"

"Excuse me, buddy, your dog just took a dump on the floor."

Jason spun around to see me standing beside a pile of what I couldn't hold anymore. "Ike!" said Jason with a loud whispering voice. "What are you doing? You just took a crap in the main art gallery of the school!" Unnerved, Jason turned toward the guy who busted me, "Here—hold his leash. I'll be back in a sec."

"What? I can't look after your dog—I'm supposed to be...." But Jason had disappeared into a crowd of humans spilling into the room. The student looked down at me sheepishly while I returned his gaze with the same sentiment. I was genuinely embarrassed. Aside from my night of mishaps all over the kitchen floor, I had never done anything like this.

As the students entering the gallery surrounded us, his embarrassed look slowly morphed into something more resembling awkward bravado. He stepped away from the pile and kept repeating, "It's not my dog. It's not my dog."

Finally, Jason reappeared through the growing crowd. He had a small plastic bag and some wet paper towels. He crouched down beside me and began cleaning up my mess. "Ike, buddy—Geezuz Murphy—that's disgusting." He continued frantically trying to wipe up my accident. "And, if that Frederick guy finds out about this, we're done. Why didn't you let me know?"

Tried to, twice.

"Hey man, is that part of the show?" joked a young student from the crowd.

His friends laughed. Jason, unamused, answered him under his breath, "Yah, it is—it was inspired by the rest of the shit hanging on the walls." Then he looked at me. "Okay, let's get outta here."

Jason stood up and grabbed my leash from the now-traumatized student. "Hey, thanks for helping."

We didn't wait for his reply.

"Jason! Jason, over here!" It was Becks. Jason veered us over to her desk. "I heard what happened, don't worry about it. If Freddie gets wind of this—no pun intended," she said with a wink—"I'll make up a good story. I got your back." She leaned over her desk and looked at me. "And you—you, ya big pooper! Go home and tell your dad it's going to be okay!"

***

Sitting around the picnic table later that evening, it was everything Pat and Trev could do to not choke on their meal as Jason colourfully relived the events of the day. Jason shared the comment from the young student who suggested it was a "performance piece." Trev had to get up from the picnic table and walk around, he was laughing so hard.

"Maybe he was expressing his views on the stop sign piece. I mean, it sounds as if Ike agreed with you, Jase," said Pat.

I was lying under the table, listening in on the conversation. I was still embarrassed having gone busy in front of what became a large group of humans at our new school. These three may have found it hilarious; I didn't. Given we'd be heading back there soon, the last thing that I wanted was to be known as "that dog."

"I wouldn't worry about it, Jase. Any guy who submits a stop sign as his final project for a course deserves to have a young pup take a crap right in front of it," added Trev. "Way to go, Ike. I'm with ya, brother."

Jason shook his head. "It's what I've been most concerned about all along. The possibility of having to endure four years with art students who think art is open to their interpretation." He paused. "Look, I know I can be harsh with my assessment of people and places and...well, pretty much everything. And, yes, I'm not the most open-minded at times. But having to sit through in-class self-assessments where students stand beside their work and bullshit their way to a passing grade is not what I've signed on for. That's why I barely made it through one year at UVic!"

"Maybe designers are a different breed? You said yourself that your classmates at Syracuse didn't do any of that. So my guess is Emily Carr will be more of the same?" suggested Trev.

"I'm going to hope so."

"If not, I'm sure you can teach Ike to crap on command," concluded Pat.

They all laughed in agreement.

Trev got up and began clearing the table. "So what do you and Ike have left to get done before school starts?" Pat and Jason grabbed the remaining dishes and followed Trev up the stairs to the kitchen. I followed as well.

"It's going to be a busy few days, that's for sure. We have a reunion with Ike's littermates at Stanley Park on Tuesday. His second appointment with the vet is on Wednesday. I've still got some supplies to pick up for school. And I'm hoping to head over to the Island one more time for the long weekend and our last camping trip of the summer. How about you guys?"

"Wait, you have another appointment with Ike's vet?" asked Trev. "The figure skater?"

Jason shook his head while he carefully put the dishes into the sink. "You mean the one who *looks* like the figure skater?"

Trev smiled in acknowledgment. "Ya, that one."

"Do you need some help?" asked Pat. "You know, someone to walk Ike up to the clinic? Or maybe take notes during the appointment?"

"'Cause Pat and I are more than happy to help. It's just who we are. You know, team players and all." Trev had an eager look on his face.

"I think I can manage. But thanks for being willing to take one for the team," replied Jason. Then, with half a smile, he turned and looked at both of them. "You two need help. Seriously, like there's something-wrong-with-both-of-you kind of help."

"Ouch—that hurts!" Pat looked at Trev and continued, "We're just trying to be good roommates. Right, Trev?"

"You know it, Pat. There's no ulterior motive here, Jase—if that's what you're inferring."

"Oh no, I'm not implying that you've got a separate agenda here at all." Jason rolled his eyes.

"Good. 'Cause if you think we just want to meet Ike's vet..."

"You mean Allyson," said Jason, annoyed.

"Oh, is that her name?" replied Trev with a smile directed at Pat.

Jason laughed. "You two are pathetic."

Pat and Trev high-fived each other. Trev began filling the sink with hot water and dish soap. "Grab a towel, Pat—be a team player and make yourself useful."

I was already settled into my crate for the evening. The sound of their playful banter was my soothing lullaby. I enjoyed their conversations and how they laughed at one another and themselves. My time with the three of them continued to be a reminder that family didn't have to come with four legs.

“So what about you two? What’s on before classes start for each of you?” asked Jason.

Pat and Trev were a few years older. Trev was finishing his master’s in marine biology while Pat was in medical school—both at UBC.

“I’m picking up a few extra shifts this week at the restaurant,” answered Trev. “Other than that—absolutely nothing.”

“There are some parties I want to go to,” Pat added, “but, otherwise, I’m just trying to get a head start on some of the assigned readings.”

“What about your birthday, Jase?” asked Trev.

“Hadn’t really thought about it. Maybe we can make dinner here or something like that. I prefer to keep it low-key, if that’s okay?”

“It’s your birthday,” said Trev. “We can do whatever you want.”

With the kitchen cleaned up and everything put away, each of my roommates retired to their rooms. Jason sat on his bed with his headphones on, listening to music while sketching in one of his many art books. Occasionally, he would break into air-drumming using his pencils as drumsticks. His limbs flung wildly in the air and his feet tapped in complete unison with the beat that escaped from the tiny speakers pushed up against his ears.

I had run out of steam. It had been a strange and exhausting day—it was time for sleep.

reunion

I loved driving throughout the city. It was spectacular. Tall modern buildings stretched to the sky surrounded by oceanfront beaches and seawater, bathed in the salty ocean air. I hadn't been to Stanley Park before. Jason assured me there would be lots to do. Trails and open fields for running, forests for exploring, a lake for swimming, and something Jason called "the seawall." But I remember being most excited to see my brothers and sisters again. Well, most of them.

Jason drove slowly, stopping sporadically as flip-flop-clad city dwellers crossed in front of us, making their way to the sand and water. Pedestrians appeared to own the streets. Whenever they looked as if they wanted to cross, drivers stopped to let them.

"Here we are, Ike. English Bay!" We parked and Jason gathered our picnic stuff. I looked out my window at all of the humans on the beach. There had to be hundreds of them—maybe thousands. Dogs too—everywhere; all splashing and swimming and enjoying the cool ocean water. Their playful shrieks, howls, and barks combined with the brightly coloured balls and frisbees hurling through the air made it harder and harder to contain my excitement. I began to whine and bark, objecting to how much time Jason was taking.

"Hold your horses, Ike."

I couldn't help myself; after my time swimming with Dash up at Schoen Lake, the sight of dogs playing at a beach proved irresistible. I howled again.

"Okay, okay, I'm coming." Jason got my leash ready. "I've never seen you so excited. It's just a beach, Ike."

As soon as the door opened, I took off.

"Ike. IKE. IKE—come here! STOP!"

I made the tight corner at the rear of our car and recalibrated for the straightaway sprint that would lead me to the beach. Three strides into my acceleration, there came a high-pitched squeal.

Then, with the force of one hundred full-grown golden retrievers, I was struck and lifted into the air. I floated sideways in what seemed like slow motion. As I dropped to my shaky paws a few feet away, I stumbled to a standstill. Sights and sounds diminished around me—Jason, the passing cars, the pedestrians, even the beach and the dogs on it. My focus was singular. Now on one thing—the big shiny metal car that had just sent me flying. I turned to face the vehicle. I crouched down slightly and slowly, purposefully moved towards it like a cat stalking its prey. Standing inches in front of the bumper, I summoned up the most intimidating growl that my four-month-old-self could muster.

"What the hell's your dog doing, man?"

As my next growl came oozing from deep inside my throat, Jason's hands gently wrapped around my chest from both sides. In the softest and most caring voice I'd ever heard him use, he asked, "Hey, Ike—you okay, bud?"

He began to run his hands slowly and strategically over my entire body, starting with my ribs. "Are you hurt? Is there a part of you that's sore when I touch it?" I looked away from the car and stared at Jason. I had never heard him sound so concerned.

"There's something wrong with that dog of yours, buddy."

Jason gently grabbed my collar and attached my leash. "Come on, Ike." He turned to walk toward our car. Jason opened the passenger side back door and patted the top of my seat. I jumped up.

"Holy shit, Ike! That was close!" Jason collapsed backwards onto the headrest. He closed his eyes and began moving his hand up and down my back, kneading his thumb and index finger into the muscles along my spine. He would pause momentarily every few passes to rub my neck. It felt soothing.

With his eyes still closed, Jason spoke slowly. "That was not okay." I laid down and put my head across his lap. "Oh, sure, now you're sorry." He moved his hand to my ears. "You big goof. Growling at a car? What kind of dog growls at the car that just hit him?" He took a deep breath. "Okay, not a word of this to anyone at the picnic, got it? If Roberta ever found out about this, you and I would be done."

Jason grabbed the backpack and blanket and we made our way down the busy beachfront street towards the entrance to Stanley Park.

The grass was soft, cool, and relieving under my paws as we stepped off the hot sidewalk. In the distance, we could see the tennis courts, and just to the left of the courts was a gathering of humans with their dogs—my siblings! By now I was excited to see all of them—even Indie.

As we got closer, Iona yelled, *"Ike, you made it!"*

Jason reached down and unhooked my leash. "Go say hello, Ike."

I was off, sprinting across the field to meet with Iona, who was running to meet me. *"Iona, great to see you again; how have you been?"*

"I'm great now. I'm so glad you came. Linda thought Jason wasn't going to bother."

"Jason? He's a little quiet sometimes. But he had planned on coming," I answered. *"Is everyone else here?"*

"Ian's humans aren't coming, but everyone else made it."

"Hey, Ike—how's life with the student? Are you getting enough to eat?"

"More food than I could want," I confirmed. *"Looks as though you're getting lots, too!"*

Indie didn't appreciate my comment. *"You little bugger, come here,"* he yelled as he charged me. I sidestepped his lunge and took off. The chase was on. Indie had always been the largest of the family. It looked like he was still growing at a rate much quicker than the rest of us. Not only was he taller than everyone, but he had also gotten a little chunky. After a moment of sprinting out into the open field, I looked back to see where he was. He wasn't making any headway in catching me, so I let up. I circled back and ran directly at him. It was time to have some fun!

He stopped and crouched down, preparing himself to pounce. Running at top speed, I got closer and closer, waiting for the last possible moment to deke left and leave my much slower-moving brother behind.

"Hey, get back here!" yelled Indie as I darted beyond his reach. Soon, my siblings chimed in with howls and barks, cheering me on as I taunted Indie. With each pass, he was becoming angrier and angrier. My speed and agility were easily out-performing his size and lethargy. Eventually, Indie conceded and went back to where our humans had gathered, at which point the rest of my siblings came charging for me—Iona, Ivy, Ishtar, Ivan, and Ivor. We all combined for one large pack of young pups running wildly in circles and figure eights, much to the amusement of our humans.

It was a fun-filled afternoon. Even Indie rejoined the group for some playful chase and a pile-on wrestling match just like we used to. By the time our humans were packing up their belongings, we were all exhausted. Stretched out beneath a large evergreen, enjoying its cool shade and the breeze coming in off English Bay, it was time to say our goodbyes.

"Ike, I'm glad that things have worked with your human," said Ivor. *"He seems like a nice guy, and you certainly appear to be happy with the arrangement."*

"Thanks, Ivor, I'm glad to hear how things have worked out with your humans. Their farm sounds like a great place to live."

"Come on, Ike—let's get going!" called Jason.

Iona came over to say goodbye. *"Hopefully, it won't be too long before we see each other again in the Endowment Lands."*

Sitting tall in the backseat, windows down, sunroof open, we made our way along Pacific Drive and over the Burrard Street Bridge. The sun was gradually lowering itself. It was late summer and the days were getting shorter and the evenings a little cooler. With the ocean air blowing through the car and my ears gently flapping, I reminded myself of how lucky I was to be living in such a beautiful city with Jason.

The reunion had been better than I imagined. Aside from my run-in with the car, I appreciated seeing Stanley Park and meeting up with my siblings for the first time. I was happy to know that we had all found good homes.

Despite landing the family with the biggest house, Indie seemed even grumpier than I remembered him. His behaviour was puzzling to me. A fancy house was what he had wanted right from the first day we started talking about our temporary humans. He had multiple beds throughout the house to nap on. There was a pool in the backyard that he could swim in. Instead of the regular kibble that we were eating, his humans made Indie special meals. There was lots to keep him amused; rawhide chewies, as well as balls and squeaky toys everywhere. It sounded like a dream to me.

But he never did much with his humans. They weren't very active and sometimes even went out and left him at home alone for long periods.

Sure, Jason could be a little cool at times, and perhaps reluctant to offer himself up fully. And my old foam bed with the stinky blankets wasn't anything close to what Indie had. But, for me, what I had with Jason, Trev, and Pat had outweighed what I didn't.

lover

"Just have a seat. The doctor won't be a minute."

Before Jason could get settled into one of the chairs, the examination room door opened and the assistant invited us to come in. Once inside, as he had before, Jason turned to face the walls and inspected the prints hanging there as decoration. Not surprisingly, they were drawings of animals—the ones that lend themselves to being pets.

"This is pretty good work, Ike. Gotta love that photorealism!" Jason continued to inspect each of the drawings. "Man, not sure who this person is, but they've got some chops when it comes to controlling their pencil."

Moments later, Allyson came in. As soon as she entered the room, she got down on her knees to meet me. I tried to move closer. Finally, Jason dropped the leash, allowing me the freedom to roll onto my back and receive Allyson's welcome.

"Ikc, you've grown! Look at you. You're becoming a big boy!" Allyson rubbed my chest and belly and put her face closer to mine. "How are you doing, Ike? How's my lover?" I continued to bathe in her affection for a few more moments. *Eat your heart out, Pat and Trev!*

Finally, she looked up at Jason, who, at this point, had a strange expression on his face.

"I don't think I've ever seen him like this. I mean, he's crying, for goodness' sake!"

"So, how's he doing? Anything to report?" asked Allyson.

Still looking surprised, Jason answered, "I think he's doing fine."

"Great to hear."

"Well, actually, there was one night he got into his big bag of food and ate about two days' worth of kibble in one go. He peed and pooped all over the place. But he seemed back to his old self within a day or two."

"What? A golden ate two days' worth of food in one sitting? I can't imagine!" Allyson crossed her arms and looked at me while she cocked her head sideways. "Ike—is this true? You silly boy!" Still on the floor with me, she grabbed my ears and kissed me on my forehead.

"My roommate said he'd probably do it again, given the chance—true?" asked Jason.

"Absolutely! Your roommate is correct. Did he throw up as well?"

"No. Just pooed everywhere."

"Of course, you didn't, Ike. You worked hard for that kibble. You weren't going to throw it up on the floor—were you?" Allyson laughed as she got to her feet. "Golden's—they're all the same—a stomach for their brain. Anything else been going on with this handsome pup?"

"Umm, actually," Jason answered slowly, "he kinda got hit by a car yesterday."

Allyson looked at me. "What? How do you kind of get hit, Ike?" She bent down and pressed her fingers along my ribs. "Well, he certainly doesn't seem lame anywhere. How did it happen?"

"We were heading to a family reunion in Stanley Park. He ran between my car and the one behind us and, when he got out onto the street, a car coming along Pacific knocked him into the air. It wasn't very hard. I mean, it could've been so much worse."

"What did Ike do after he got hit?"

"Well, here's the strange part—he slowly walked up to the car and growled at it."

Allyson roared with laughter. "Oh, Ike, you're such a man!" She bent forward again and patted my back. "What are we going to do with you?"

"I can't imagine having to make that phone call to Roberta. I was so lucky."

Allyson looked at Jason as she grabbed my leash and made her way to the door that would lead us into the back area. "We'll just be a second, Jason. He has some more shots due today and then we're done. I'm sure Roberta will be in touch with you regarding Ike's next appointment. It's for his..." Allyson looked at me and then back at Jason. Before continuing her sentence, she raised her hand to her mouth to block my view and then whispered, "... neutering."

Once back at the house, we joined Trev and Pat at the picnic table.

"How'd it go, Jase?" asked Pat.

Trev looked up and added, "Ya, how's our favourite figure skater—oh, I mean, veterinarian?"

Jason shook his head as he sat down to join them. "Pretty good. Ike's health seems fine. It was really just a checkup with some more shots."

"And Allyson?" Trev asked with an eager grin.

Jason paused for a moment. "First of all, you were right, Trev. Allyson said Ike would stuff his face with as much food as possible, if given the chance again. He didn't learn a damn thing that night he basically ate his body-weight in food!"

"Trev, did you hear that? Allyson thinks you're a genius! That might be your in..."

Jason interrupted. "She's amazing with Ike."

"How do you mean?" asked Pat.

"She greets Ike like nobody else—gets down on the floor with him and rubs his chest and his belly. She sticks her face right up against his. He rolls onto his back and starts crying because he's so excited to see her."

"Ikester, you got a crush on Allyson? Take a number, brother!"

"Ike sounds like a smart dog," added Pat. "Trev, maybe we just need to get ourselves some collars and leashes."

"There, now you're thinking like me, Pat!" Trev howled.

"Very funny, you sick bastards." Jason continued. "It was quite something to watch. I wasn't going to tell you guys this because I knew you'd freak out. But she calls him '*lover*.'"

"Ike's vet calls him her lover?" continued Trev. "Are you kidding me?" Trev slowly turned and looked at Pat. "We're going to the pet store right now—go get your wallet!"

"See, I knew I shouldn't have told you guys."

"Jason, she calls Ike her lover, and you don't think that's strange?" asked Trev.

"No! No, I don't," snapped Jason abruptly. "You had to be there. You have to hear how she says it—how she means it."

"So what does she mean by it?" asked Pat with a troublesome smile.

Jason paused and rubbed my ears under the table. "I'm not entirely sure—but obviously not what you two derelicts are thinking!" Trev looked at Pat and rolled his eyes. "I don't know; it's like she's saying, 'Ike—I will always look out for you. And, no matter what, you can trust me.'"

Pat and Trev's eyes grew wider. "And, now that I think about it, obviously, the word doesn't even matter. It's who Allyson is when she greets Ike—he's responding to that."

Pat leaned forward and slowly asked, "So what's so different about how you greet Ike versus Allyson?"

"That's a good question." I looked up at Jason. His eyes searched the giant evergreens that grew at the back of their house. "You know what? Maybe this 'treating Ike like a job' thing isn't the best strategy to make him into a great guide dog. What if I'm screwing this up by not getting attached to him? Or letting him get attached to me?"

"You're not attached to Ike?" asked Trev.

"Well, I like him. I mean, he makes me laugh sometimes. And I enjoy doing stuff with him," answered Jason. "But I don't get on the floor and do what Allyson does. Maybe I need to be more affectionate."

Trev quickly wiped his mouth with his napkin and started talking with his cheeks still stuffed with food. "Jase, do you hear yourself?" Jason recoiled as Trev continued. "It's not that Allyson gets on the floor to greet Ike; it's what Ike feels when she does that. I can assure you there isn't a chapter on 'How to show your dog affection' in your Canadian Guide Dog Instruction Manual. And Allyson likely didn't learn how to greet dogs in veterinary school. Affection is not a 'strategy,' as you keep calling it. It starts with a feeling. An emotion —called love."

Pat nudged Trev under the table with his knee, but Trev wasn't finished. "And it comes from your heart. Not your head!" Pat nudged Trev a little harder this time and he paused.

Jason sat quietly, considering what Trev had shared.

Pat continued, "Do you love Ike?"

"I don't know. I mean, if he left today, I would miss him. But I don't think I'd be heartbroken or anything like that."

"How long has he been with us?"

"Well, the middle of May to now. So what's that? Two-and-half months?"

"So Ike cries on his second visit with Allyson and he's been with you for over two months—correct? I'd say you've got some catchin' up to do."

Jason looked down at me. He looked embarrassed. I wanted him to know that I already loved him. I tilted my head and stared at him.

The three of them sat quietly for a moment. Then Trev continued, "Look, Jase, we don't mean to gang up on you. But Ike's a remarkable pup. My dad always said that a dog's eyes tell you everything you need to know about them." Trev leaned back and looked at me. "His eyes are soulful. The lights are on and everyone's home. Look at him. You should take some time to notice the gift you've been entrusted with. He's not just an eating, shitting, sleeping machine. He's a beautiful living-breathing creature with a loving spirit that will touch you if you let him. But that's the catch; you have to let him."

After a moment, Jason got up from the table and made his way to the outdoor steps. "I'm going to make a sandwich."

With the sound of clanging dishes leaking through the kitchen window, Pat quietly said to Trev, "I think Jason sees Ike as a rowing race—he's trying to win this guide dog training thing just like when we rowed together." Pat looked at me under the table. "Your dad was a competitive SOB, Ike—I don't think he's learned how to turn it off."

"Clearly, and Ike's no race. Are ya, buddy?" Trev's hands blindly searched for my ears. Once found, he rubbed them gently.

As I think back on the role that Pat and Trev played in Jason's life, I am filled with gratitude. I don't know that Jason ever appreciated the good fortune of landing those two as roommates. They were older and wiser, and in Trev's case in particular, more willing to reveal the emotional awareness that Jason so clearly resisted. Although their tactics could appear harsh at times, they were always fuelled by love. What those three humans shared was a beautiful friendship to bear witness to.

baby steps

After a hectic day of errands involving what seemed like a hundred different places, I was exhausted, tired of my jacket, and ready for a nap. But Jason still had a birthday to celebrate. And even though he had said he didn't want a fuss, the boys were able to talk him into going out for dinner.

As planned, during the long weekend we had gone up to the north end of Vancouver Island to another beautiful camping spot, this time on Atluck Lake. Unlike our previous trip, there was absolutely no one to be seen at our site. We had an excellent spot across from an enormous mountain that appeared to grow from the lake, which was clear and cold—but we still managed a lot of swimming.

The trails nearby weren't easily accessible so we mainly stayed on the dirt road that circled the lake. We enjoyed some beautiful long walks and, thankfully, there were no mud wasps this time!

Mind you, there were cougars! At least, that's what Jason led me to believe. "Have you ever seen a cougar, Ike?"

I stopped walking, looked back at him, and cocked my head sideways.

"I mean, if I haven't seen one, how could you, right?" He paused for a moment before continuing. "I heard that just because I haven't seen one doesn't mean that one hasn't seen me. That kinda gives me the heebie-jeebies."

I won't lie, I began checking the rock faces we passed more thoroughly. The last thing I wanted was a surprise visit from an overgrown pussy cat.

"Apparently, you likely wouldn't know a cougar is stalking you until it's on your back—they're that stealthy!"

Why are we talking about this now?

"D'you know what you need to survive a cougar or bear attack?" He paused for a moment. "You need to run faster than whoever you're with. I guess that means I'm screwed, eh buddy?"

Jason was undoubtedly more engaged this trip. Chatty, even. He had plenty of questions, thoughts, observations—sometimes it seemed as though he was expecting me to reply. I didn't mind. I was gaining insight into what I was beginning to realize was a very complex human being.

I was struck by how angry Jason could get. At what, I wasn't always sure. But there were plenty of things that "pissed him off," as he would say: line-ups at the grocery store, being put on hold while on the telephone, humans who were late, —patience was not a virtue with Jason. Oh, and "shit-awful drivers," as he called them.

At night in the tent, I'd curl up against his lower legs, and he'd continue talking about how much fun we'd had that day before finally saying good-night and pulling out a book to read. It was our best weekend together yet. I couldn't wait to tell Iona.

The following week when school began, finding a new rhythm was relatively easy. We woke up at the same time, got dressed and fed, but instead of heading out for a walk, we jumped in the car and made our way to Granville Island and the Emily Carr campus.

The weeks were long, with two 3-hour studio classes most days. Thankfully, lunch breaks were long too. We would head out for walks at noon almost every day. I was still young with lots of energy then, and as most dog owners know, a tired dog is a well-behaved dog. Jason would bring a ball, and we'd find a spot that was big enough for me to burn off some energy before heading back for his afternoon session.

Jason's classmates were friendly—and much younger. It didn't bother him. He told Pat and Trev that he didn't go there looking for new friends. Rarely did he socialize with anyone. Well, except Becks—the funny receptionist who smooched her bright red lipstick between my eyes on our first day. She made it impossible not to say hello. Every day when we walked through those large glass doors, she would call out my name and ask how I was doing. We spent breaks outside or going to the market to buy lunch. There wasn't much time for anything else.

It's not like Jason wasn't friendly. He was. On the first day of classes, he managed the usual barrage of questions without getting too frustrated. Even he could appreciate it was a novelty to have a young dog in the classroom. It wasn't something other students came to school expecting. But it didn't take long before I became part of the furniture.

To help pass the time, I would get up in between naps and visit everyone at their workstations. There were some incredibly talented artists in his classes. And Jason was pretty good too. I didn't realize he could draw so well until I saw his work up on the wall during class critiques.

Emily Carr was an excellent school. I heard Jason tell Pat and Trev how impressed he was with the facilities and his instructors—even though some of them were his age or just a bit older, he seemed at ease when they would chat during class.

There was no shortage of talented humans. Even though he used to tell me how much he couldn't understand the blue and purple hair, the tattoos, or the body piercings, Jason did his best to look past these forms of personal expression and see the inspiring artists inside. I didn't understand the big deal—it was no different than some dog getting a fancy haircut.

No longer was I his sole focus. Instead, Jason now had a whole host of responsibilities to juggle, including taking care of me. By now managing my needs was pretty easy as far as I was concerned. I was thoroughly house trained—I answered the "go busy" call every time, especially when it mattered most between classes. I slept through the night. I no longer threw up in the car. I'd stopped barking at anything I didn't recognize. And, most impressively, I was a pro on the leash. The only thing that Jason took extra time for was my exercise. We never missed our long weekend walks.

One particular Sunday morning started early like they always did. Jason was unusually quiet. No questions, no random thoughts. Not a peep from the moment we left the house until well into the trails.

I was off into the woods looking for the stick he'd just thrown, busy sniffing and searching the ground, when I heard a loud *whack* sound. It was strange and seemed out of place, but not worth interrupting my search. Then it came again—*whack*. Only this time, the noise was louder and was accompanied by Jason yelling. Then another *whack*. And some more yelling. This time, I stopped and looked up. Jason was smashing a large stick up against a tree over and over again.

Whack. Whack. Whack. Interspersed with curse after curse, the likes of which I won't repeat. Jason was in a rage. I'd never seen him like this. I began to back up as the strikes against the tree became more frequent and Jason's words became even louder and less discernible.

Finally, the thick branch snapped, and the far end came whirling at me. It missed me by less than a foot.

I slowly looked up at Jason. I was frightened. I didn't know what to think, or what to do. He stood still with his head down and one hand braced against the tree, taking deep breaths. He looked over at me. He seemed shocked at first and then embarrassed.

"Sorry, Ike," he said in between breaths. "That was stupid."

I slowly walked over to him. He knelt down and grabbed me on either side of my head. "I'm not having a great day, bud—you okay?"

I'm fine, but what was that? Did I do something?

After a few moments of rubbing my chest and stroking my back, Jason got up. "Come on, Ike, let's go home."

Back at the house Jason began making porridge. Pat came out of his room to join us.

"How was the walk?"

"Good. It was quiet. Ike is still a crazy-man chasing sticks like his life depends on it."

Pat reached down to scratch the top of my head. He paused for a moment before continuing. "How are you doing?"

Jason turned towards Pat. "Who, me or Ike?"

Pat tilted his head slightly sideways. "You."

"What do you mean? I'm fine." Jason returned to carefully cutting up his apple. "Why?"

Pat waited a moment before answering. "I saw the calendar hanging above your desk." Jason put down his knife and turned around with an intrigued look on his face. "You have today circled in red with the words, 'Seoul—5 years. Fuck!'"

Jason slowly turned back to the cutting board. His banana was next. "I still don't know what to think about that day. That race. That summer. How we lost so badly. Why we lost. All of it—I just don't know."

"I forgot it was today," added Pat. "Can't believe it's been five years."

"Ya, who would've thought that one of the guys calling that infamous race live on television would be my roommate five years later?"

They both smiled. "And we'd be together in this old kitchen talking about the unbelievable shit-show that unravelled at the Olympics that day in Korea!"

Jason slowly poured his vanilla soy milk into the mixing bowl of porridge with all of the nuts and seeds and fruit he'd prepared, then sat down to eat. I walked over to my water bowl to get another drink. Pat continued to nudge the conversation gently.

"Well, you can't do much about it now. I mean, I know it's shitty, but sometimes, races go sideways—even the ones that matter most. You can't beat yourself up about it five years later, Jase." Jason just kept shovelling large spoonfuls into his mouth while he looked out the kitchen window. "You've got other things—more important things—to focus on now." Pat was doing his best to support Jason around what I would come to appreciate was an enormous disappointment for him.

"Easier said than done," Jason replied quickly as he wiped away the soy milk that was running down his chin. "Believe me, Pat, I'd love to be done with this and just let it go. But the memory of that day keeps hanging around...like one of Trev's farts!"

"Hey—I heard that," yelled Trev from his room.

"Truth hurts," added Pat, as Trev walked out to join us.

"Sorry, Jason—I don't mean to eavesdrop, but this house is so tiny it's kind of hard not to hear everything." Trev looked at Pat. "For what it's worth, I remember when Pat's crew won in '84. We were roommates not far from here at the time. It was amazing to watch this guy I knew win an Olympic Gold Medal for Canada. We cheered and screamed—it was fantastic! But, when he got home and life returned to normal, he was still Pat. Pat with a beautiful shiny gold Olympic medal, but he was still Pat." Trev walked over and messed-up Jason's hair as they all laughed.

"I know winning that medal was the focus for you—I understand that. But, at the end of the day, Pat's my friend because of who Pat is. Not because of some medal he won. I don't care about that medal."

"Hey—I worked hard for that thing!" Pat smirked.

"I appreciate you guys listening and sharing your thoughts—I do. It's a strange one for me. On the one hand, I can rationally make sense of losing a race—it happens. But, emotionally, Seoul just keeps hanging on in ways that cloud everything. I find myself getting so mad about things. Small things—things that didn't use to bother me." Jason shrugged his shoulders and waited a moment before continuing. He clearly had something more to say. "Even," Jason stopped abruptly and looked at me. "Even this morning. I almost took Ike's head off when I bashed a big branch from the side of the trail against a tree. I just missed him. What the fuck is that about?"

Trev put on the kettle for tea and Pat made some toast. I got up and went to my crate.

"How about some music?" asked Trev brightly. "I think this Sunday morning needs a little rock 'n' roll to get it started!"

"If you're taking requests, how about some Rush?"

"Patrick—I like how you think," Trev called from the living room.

"Agreed—a little Geddy, Alex, Neil on the drum kit—Red Barchetta would get my vote," added Jason.

Rush was a band that I recognized because Jason talked about them all of the time and played them in the car constantly. I gathered he was a fan.

Moments later, Trev leapt into the kitchen. As the song began to build, he played air guitar until it was time to change instruments. Next, he grabbed some wooden spoons and played the drums and then bass guitar while singing along. Pat and Jason laughed at his antics.

I learned that Jason had gone to the Olympics in 1988 as a member of the Canadian men's eight in rowing. And, as Trev had mentioned, Pat had been a member of that same crew four years earlier. The only difference was that Pat's team had won. Five years later, Jason was still processing his race not going quite as he and his crew, and the media, had planned.

lost and found

After almost taking my head off several weekends earlier, Jason opted for another Sunday walk through the Endowment Lands. It had been raining all night and much of the day. Now with a pause in the rain, Jason took off his headphones, put away his sketchbook and grabbed my leash. "Come on, Ike." He leaned down and kissed me on the top of my head. "I think we're getting a reprieve. Let's get goin'!"

The park was empty. And quiet. The air smelled like nothing I had ever experienced before. It was as if every rain-soaked leaf preparing to fall, or that already had, was contributing their part to a sensory occurrence that could only be described as extraordinary.

The seasons were changing; my first autumn had arrived. I noticed the days getting shorter, the temperature cooler, and our walks in the crisp air amidst brightly coloured leaves that rattled as I dashed through them became a favourite pastime. And, afterwards, napping by a roaring fire tucked under Jason's legs as he listened to music and read a book or drew in his sketchbook.

There had been a shift in Jason since our last camping trip. He was often down on the floor with me, showing affection more than he ever had. And, as you just read, kissing me was now a regular occurrence—I loved it. But it wasn't just the belly scratches, ear rubs, and kisses. He felt more present—genuine, even. As if the job of creating the best guide dog possible had taken a back seat to simply having fun during the time we had left together. Don't get me wrong; it's not like he abandoned the training. Believe me, we still went through those drills every day. But it seemed there was more to the arrangement. I wasn't just an obligation he had signed up for. I could feel him opening up to me being a part of his life. Jason was learning to be my friend and not just my trainer.

That Sunday, as we walked amongst the trees and the resident creatures, Jason took the usual pleasure in tossing the biggest sticks that he could find at the side of the trail well into the woods. "Even with the rain and it getting dark, you have no trouble finding these things, Ike. You're amazing, buddy!"

Always happy to amaze. But I'm a golden retriever—it's what we do!

Jason never tired of this game and never ceased to be impressed with my ability to sniff out and return each large branch. It was a symbiotic connection that I was more than happy to be a part of.

We walked for close to an hour before it began to rain again. A little at first, but soon it was coming down quite hard. Then, amongst the white noise of the raindrops hitting the trees tops above us and the ground below, I heard a clattering racket off in the distance. I turned with my head perked up to see where the sound was coming from. I dropped the stick from my mouth. I stood frozen at the side of the trail. I'd never heard anything quite like it in this park.

Is that some kind of bird? An owl, maybe?

Although it was hard to hear at times over the noise of the rain, I could tell that, whatever it was, it was getting closer.

"It's okay, Ike. It's probably just some old bike. Nothing to worry about, bud," said Jason, trying to reassure me.

Some distance up the trail, coming over the crest of a short hill, a bright light appeared suspended in midair. As the light began eerily coming down the hill with increasing speed, the accompanying clatter grew louder and more alarming.

The flying object reached peak speed and sound at the bottom of the hill. But it didn't stop there. As it continued to advance directly towards us, I had heard and seen quite enough. As far as I could tell, we were under attack. I panicked, and bolted down the trail. Even as I reached my top speed, it wasn't enough to evade this imminent threat. I knew that my best strategy was to break from the trail and head into the woods where I could outmanoeuvre this loud and dangerous aggressor.

"IKE. IKE. It's okay. It's just a bike. Come on back!" I heard what Jason had yelled. But I was beyond reasoning. Instead, I was terrified and believed the only way to find safety was to run for my life. And that's what I did.

I ran deeper into the woods and further away from Jason. I continued at top speed until I crossed another path before proceeding into a different section of the park with the same thick wooded growth.

Eventually, my young legs had had enough, and I turned around to see if I was still being pursued.

Boy-oh-boy, what on earth was that? And, where's Jason?

My chest heaving, I assessed the situation. Now it was raining even harder as well as getting dark. I could hardly see. I didn't recognize the trees that surrounded me. A few moments later, I felt safe enough to make a move. My plan was to retrace my tracks as best I could. I couldn't see much—but I had my nose!

Soon, I was back to the first trail I crossed. There was no sign of Jason. And, if he was calling me, I couldn't hear him. The rain was too loud.

Eventually, I made my way back to where we had been when I bolted. There was no sign of Jason or my attacker. Now I was worried that something might have happened to Jason.

Had he tried to protect me? Did he end up getting hurt? Or worse?

I looked everywhere, but there was no sign or scent. Luckily, I was back on a familiar trail that would lead me to the entrance of the park. I gave myself a good shake and turned toward home.

Before leaving the park, I turned to look and listen for Jason one last time. There was nothing—just trails and trees that were now hard to make out in the dark. And, of course, pelting rain that made it almost impossible to hear anything else.

Having crossed countless streets with Jason beside me paying close attention to my every move, navigating through the neighbourhood was reasonably straightforward. I knew when to cross, and more importantly, when not to. It wasn't long before I was safely home. The house was dark. I pushed open the side gate and made my way around to the back and up the stairs to the kitchen door. I scratched at the door and waited.

I scratched once more, a little harder, and barked—still nothing. Worried about Jason, I gave myself another thorough shake and then curled up beside the door. The mat was itchy against my wet fur. I wiggled and tried to get more comfortable.

It was getting cold, and what little fat I had wasn't keeping me warm. I shivered. I considered returning to the woods, but knew that as hard as it was to wait, it was best to stay put.

After what seemed an eternity, I heard the side gate swing open. I raised my head and peered down the stairs.

Please be Jason!

A dark figure came into view and looked up at me. "Ike? You up there?"

I stood.

"IKE! You little bugger...." I flew down the stairs to meet him. "Where the hell did you get to? Come here, you!" He reached down and scooped me up off the bottom step and held me close against his body. "You're shivering!" He opened his jacket. "Here, let's see if I can warm you up a bit." His body heat felt soothing as he held me against his chest inside his jacket.

"Holy crap, Ike—man, you had me worried."

You were worried—I was terrified!

"I looked up and down those trails a million times. Didn't you hear me calling?"

"Everything okay, Jase?" Trev came around from the side gate.

"It is now."

"Why? What happened?"

"I lost Ike for about an hour in the Endowment Lands."

"He's soaked, did he make his way home all by himself?"

"Yup—he's a guide dog alright! He's cold, but aside from that, he seems okay."

Trev leaned closer to Jason. "Are *you* okay?"

"What do you mean? Of course, I'm okay," answered Jason. "I was worried as hell, but I'm all good now!"

"Are those tears I see shimmering down your cheeks?"

"What? No, it's raining, ya big nut-bar!"

"It was raining," said Trev with a gentle smile. "But it's not now!"

"I'm not cryin.'"

"Whatever you say, Mr. Tough-Guy." Trev moved his hand to scratch my chin. "Let's get Ike inside and warm him up."

Jason waited for a moment longer before joining Trev. "I was so worried about you, buddy." Jason stared at me closely. "Don't you ever take off on me, again, got it? I'm not sure what… ."

Yup, definitely tears.

Without finishing his sentence, he pulled my head under his chin and squeezed me tighter before heading up the stairs and into our warm house.

old habits

Life was busy. Generally, our days were filled with coming and going: Granville Island, classes, the market, the park, and everywhere in between. And that was just the weekdays.

I was growing too. Roberta dropped off a bigger collar with my new bag of food. And a new guide dog jacket—and, yes, I hated that one just as much!

Weekends were equally jam-packed. Jason took some time for schoolwork, but mainly we spent Saturdays hiking trails in the many parks in the Lower Mainland. Then, a quick bite out and a movie with the boys at night. Sundays were more of the same. We'd walk along the beach at English Bay after a feast of Jason's pancakes, followed by a house dinner where everyone contributed to a group meal. The evenings were quiet. I snoozed at Jason's feet, while he read or drew in his sketchbook and listened to music with his headset.

My training was still a priority for Jason. When we weren't hiking, we walked downtown on busy streets like Robson or 4th Avenue in Kitsilano. I had become quite adept at managing crosswalks, stores, restaurants, and those weekend movies. In fact, movies were my favourite—a floor covered in popcorn, nuts, and other snacks. Believe me, I scared more than a few moviegoers as I navigated my way under their chairs in search of treats.

Well into the second half of the first semester, we had established a good rhythm. Up early every morning and off to school for most of the day. Short walks around Granville Island during breaks and lunch. And then home for a longer walk on the trails before an evening of homework or visiting with the boys in our tiny living room.

I enjoyed going to class, except maybe photography. I wasn't allowed in the darkroom and, therefore, had to stay in the lecture studio by myself. The instructor called me a "tripping hazard." I was fine with that—the darkroom smelled anyway.

The school had a competitive environment. I could see why it was such a big deal to be admitted. The students were all extremely talented. Everyone worked hard during class time, and then most of them again at night. Jason, not so much—I got the sense that he did just enough. Rarely did he go beyond what was required of him.

I overheard that many of Jason's classmates were back in the computer labs or studios working on their projects into the wee hours most nights. Jason, however, had yet to return to the campus after dinner to work on anything.

He got along with all of his instructors, some more than others. Conversation was easy if they liked watching hockey or listening to Rush.

One of his instructors, Andrew, ticked both of those boxes. They were close in age and had a similar perspective on art and design. One Tuesday morning, when Andrew's introductory design class had just ended, Andrew asked Jason if he wouldn't mind stopping by his office after class later that day.

It was almost 4:00 pm when Jason tapped quietly on the door frame. "You wanted to see me?"

Andrew looked up from his computer. "Yes, yes—Jason, come on in." He stood and walked over to the only other chair in his office, and cleared away the pile of papers that occupied it. "Here, let's pull this up a little closer, so we're not having to yell at one another. And, Ike—you're going to have to lay on the floor, my friend."

"Don't worry about him. There are no couches in his world, so he doesn't know what he's missing." I laid down beside Jason and positioned my chin across his shoe.

"He adores you, doesn't he? I notice in class that he watches you like a hawk." Andrew closed his office door and returned to his chair.

"Well, we spend a lot of time together, so I think he's just used to me. And I would imagine it has a lot to do with the meals that I provide him multiple times a day."

Andrew chuckled politely. "Maybe." He grabbed a paperclip from his desk and began playing with it.

"Nice poster," said Jason, pointing to the wall behind Andrew that showed a large photo of Rush's drummer, Neil Peart, with his arms a blur of movement. "I saw them last time they came through town—the drum solo was his best yet. They don't call him 'The Professor' for nothing!"

"Hey, I was at that concert, too!" Andrew turned in his chair to admire the poster. "I think I could see them live every weekend. There's truly no band like them."

Jason nodded his head in agreement.

Andrew turned around and continued fidgeting with the paperclip. "I grew up on a farm in Alberta. My grandad had a yellow lab. Ike looks at you the way that old lab looked at my grandad. They were inseparable. In fact, I've never said this before, but I think my grandpa loved that dog more than anyone else in the family. Ha—maybe even more than my grandma!" Andrew leaned back in his chair and crossed his legs. Jason sat quietly. "Trust. 'It's all about trust,' is what my grandpa would say. Isn't that the basis of any good relationship?"

"Alberta—really? I wouldn't have guessed that. You strike me as someone from one of the Gulf Islands. I mean, you're so easygoing like most folks who live over there."

"Ah—yes," laughed Andrew. "My family lineage at work. My dad was a pastor. He taught me that nothing in life is worth getting upset about. 'Absolutely nothing,' as he would constantly remind us. He believed that when we choose to see every challenge as an exciting opportunity, even the worst predicaments can present scenarios that may have us coming out ahead. If we're willing to see life that way."

"I wish I had met your dad a few years ago."

Andrew smiled and nodded as he refocused his attention on the paperclip. Jason looked at me as the room turned silent.

"Listen, I don't mean to be rude, but traffic's not getting any lighter, and I've got some homework that's due for tomorrow. So if there was something that you wanted to talk about...?"

"Of course." Andrew put the paperclip down and leaned forward in his chair. "The reason I wanted to speak with you is that I'm trying to figure how a guy who has a highly competitive background—I looked through your files and saw the bit about the Olympics—is, is...I don't know...I just can't figure out why some of what got you to the Olympic Games doesn't appear to show up in class—ever?"

Jason took a deep breath and slowly exhaled, puffing out his cheeks while an audible stream of air escaped his lungs. "Busted."

Andrew smiled awkwardly. "That wasn't my intent. I'm not trying to *bust* you, Jason. I genuinely want to know why—"

"There's only one way I know how to compete, and it's ugly," interrupted Jason. "I'm not proud of who I was as an athlete. I'm not proud of what I did as an athlete. And I'm certainly not proud of how I treated people in getting to the Olympics. So I simply choose not to go there anymore." Jason reached down, put his hand on my head, and gently began rolling my ear between his fingers.

"Look, I'm not trying to be your parent or your coach. You're a grown man with lots of life experience. But, watching you from the sidelines, to use a sporting analogy, it's like you're just coasting. Like you're afraid to try. Or be even the least bit competitive with your classmates. You're a talented artist, Jason. It's easy to see that in your work. But talent will only take you so far." Andrew stopped talking and waited for Jason to reply. He didn't. Instead, he looked directly at me. He appeared lost. "You're not going to say anything?" asked Andrew.

"What do you want me to say?" snapped Jason. "Okay, you're right—I don't try. I don't compete with my classmates. Congratulations, you've figured out my operating system—way to go!" Jason leaned forward in his chair and continued, "Yes, I'm playing this safe. And, therefore, I'm not realizing my potential here. I know, brutal, right? But I've seen who I become when I want something badly—when I *compete* for something." Jason paused for a moment, leaned back in his chair, took a deep breath, and looked anxiously around the room. "That guy scares me. And I don't want to bring him to the party anymore. He's an asshole, plain and simple. Look, I like all of my classmates, even the ones with blue and purple hair. And if that guy shows up, all of this ends—all of it."

Boy-oh-boy, that explains a few things!

They both sat quietly for a moment. I leaned my head against Jason's leg until he reached down and began rubbing my ears again. It was painful to hear the frustration in his voice.

"I know you're just trying to help, Andrew. I do. And I'm not pissed that you went looking through my files—that's your prerogative. I just need to figure this out on my own. But, until I do, this is how I manage that part of me. For now, I'm not willing to compromise." Jason looked directly at Andrew. "I spent the younger part of my twenties chasing something that never materialized. I was obsessed with achieving that one goal. I gave it everything I had—everything. And I have fuck-all to show for it. If you think I'm going to do that again—chase something like my life depends upon it? It's just not going to happen."

"Okay." Andrew nodded. "I understand. I'm glad we talked; at the very least, I have some clarity as to what's going on for you. If you ever want to talk again, or consider a different strategy, I'd be honoured to help."

"You bet. I appreciate the offer." Jason stood up and reached forward to shake Andrew's hand. I got up and stretched.

change of plans

The following Sunday, after pancakes and a brief snooze, we decided to change things up and head to the nearby park to chase sticks through the piles of leaves accumulating under the trees that towered high above.

It was energizing to burst through the fragrant leaves. They crackled and crunched beneath my paws. Some flew into the air only to flutter once again to the ground. The crisp pungent air intoxicated me. Jason tossed stick after stick and I eagerly returned each one to his feet.

I could feel my coat thickening in the cooling air. That week, Trev had commented that there were fewer bundles of dog fur on the floor, hiding behind our living room chairs.

On the next toss, I heard the leaves rustle beside me.

"Bet I can beat you to it!"

"Iona!" She and her human had come to the park, too! *"Bet you can't!"* I dug my claws deeper into the damp grass as we both sped toward the stick. Seconds later, a tug o' war ensued.

Eventually, we both started laughing so hard we lost our strength and collapsed to the ground.

"What a great surprise to see you here, Iona!"

"We usually come here on Sundays. I'm so happy to see you! How have you been?"

I looked back at Jason. Iona's human, Linda, had joined him, and they were busy visiting.

"I'm good. I'm excited to tell you that there's been a shift in Jason. He's not so businesslike anymore. I mean, we still do all of our training, but he's so much more relaxed—affectionate, even. It's been great!"

"I'm happy to hear that. But, if you're still doing all of the training, what happened last weekend?" asked Iona.

"What do you mean? Oh, the mall test?"

"Yes, the mall test! I tested shortly after you left. I heard Roberta telling Linda that things didn't go so well for you!"

"Really, Roberta said that?"

"Yes, and she said that if you don't do better the next time, she's going to have to start taking you on weekends for extra training to make sure you don't fall behind." Iona looked concerned. *"She said you were pulling her to the side so that you could rub your body against the walls. And, at one point, you dropped to your back and tried to wiggle out of your jacket. What was that about?"*

"I hate that stupid thing!"

"So do I. So do all of us. But, we don't behave like that in public—especially when Roberta's there!"

I looked away. I was embarrassed for Jason. *"What else did she say? Did Jason get into trouble?"*

"I don't know. But I don't imagine he was thrilled." I looked down at the stick. *"Extra time on weekends? Maybe that wasn't such a good idea."*

"Maybe what wasn't a good idea?" asked Iona.

I turned and looked at Jason. I wondered if they were talking about my test as well.

"Ike, did you do all that on purpose?"

"Well, kind of—I mean, I guess I did."

Iona took a step backwards. *"What are you talking about? Why would you purposely mess up your test?"*

I looked directly at Iona. *"Okay, you have to promise you won't tell any of our siblings—especially Indie! Promise?"*

"Okay, I promise."

"That would explain why Jason was so quiet on the ride home from the mall. Roberta must have given him an earful." I shook my head as I imagined the scene.

"Ike—your test. Tell me about the test!"

"I thought that if I failed out of the program, maybe I could stay with Jason and not move on to live with another family?"

"Are you kidding me? Ike, that's the stupidest thing I've ever heard! Not become a guide dog?" Iona moved closer. She was furious. *"That's why we're here. That's why you're living with Jason. It's an honour to be a guide dog and wear the harness that says you're in service of someone else."*

I understood the part about it being a big deal; I did. But I still wanted to be with Jason. Deep down I knew that I was meant to be with him—I wasn't meant to be a guide dog.

"You're right. It was a stupid idea. I'm sorry."

"Ike, I understand what you're thinking. I like my family too. But, it's not my choice." Iona walked over to the stick. *"Just do better next time."* She pawed the stick with a mischievous look in her eye. *"Come on, let's get back to some fun!"*

christmas

With the end of Jason's first semester, project due dates came fast and furious. Jason continued with his predetermined effort and subsequent pace—he did enough to get the work in, and that was about it.

With a three-week break for the Christmas holidays, the plan was for us to fly back to his parents' home in southern Ontario. The night before we left, Pat, Trev, and Jason had planned a house dinner together. They had all of the fixings—barbecued salmon, roasted potatoes with vegetables, homemade bread, and an apple crumble to finish off. The smells were beyond tempting and my mouth was watering uncontrollably. I was hoping there might be some leftovers.

The three of them sat around the living room, each with their TV dinner trays. With the stereo playing Christmas music and the warm fire crackling, it could not have felt cozier.

"So, Jase, would you consider Ike's first semester a success?" asked Trev as he took another bite of his salmon.

Jason put down his fork, leaned back in his chair, and considered his answer. "I'd say so. I mean, there were no more doggie-dumps in the front gallery!" He looked at me lying in front of the fireplace. "Right, Ike?"

Trev got up from his chair and made his way to the kitchen for seconds. "That was a memorable start to the year for you, buddy!"

"Ike did really well. I was struck by how well-behaved he was during our long studios, especially. His sense of time is amazing. Towards the end of November, with about ten minutes to go in each class, he would get up, stretch, and start walking around to visit with other classmates. Eventually, he became like a class alarm clock, letting everyone know when it was time to pack up."

"Atta boy, Ike! Keeping all those artists on time—you're a star pupil," said Pat. "And how about you, Jase?"

Jason took another sip of his water and looked at me. "You know what, it's been a good lesson. Ike doesn't see all of the surface stuff we see. When those patchouli-smelling types come up to Ike with their piercings, tattoos, and dreadlocks, he's excited to meet them as he is anyone else. And, because I was left standing there holding his leash, I had no other option but to talk. They'd ask questions about the whole guide dog thing. And I soon realized—behind all of the *stuff*—they're normal people, not much different from me. I mean, you wouldn't find me dead wearing patchouli, but I've actually become friends with a few of them."

"Normal people?" Pat repeated as he and Trev laughed. "You make it sound like they're another species."

Jason shook his head. "You know what I mean," he said, and then began laughing as well as he realized how that must have sounded. "Seriously, Ike's been quite a good influence. And not just on me. I see it with other people everywhere we go. They smile when they see him; they relax, laugh, and are more playful. People talk to him like he's a little kid and just seem to become better, happier people. I think we should—well, I know I should—try to be more like Ike when I'm around others."

"You're not getting soft on us, are you, Jase?" asked Pat with a smile. "Are you going to get a tattoo and start growing dreads in the new year?"

Trev roared at the suggestion. "Can you imagine Jason with a nose piercing and a tattoo of a dragon on his arm!" Trev and Pat laughed harder. "I'd pay good money just to see your button-down-wearing-ass looking like that, just once!"

As the meal ended and the conversation and laughter continued, I realized that this was what I treasured about my time with Jason, and with Pat and Trev as well. Their friendship—the trust they shared was palpable. This was where I was meant to be; this was home.

The next day, with help from the boys, we made it to the airport on time. It was a huge building packed with humans rushing this way and going that way. I couldn't believe the noise. I could see stress on the faces of most of the travellers. Even I couldn't garner many smiles.

Once we found our gate, we sat down and waited to board. No surprise, I was a hit. With so many families travelling, it didn't take long before young children surrounded me. Jason managed question after question with more patience than I had ever seen in him. He was laughing and joking with all of them, and he even struck up a few conversations with the parents as well.

Then, Jason's name was called over the loudspeaker, directing him to go to the desk to speak with an agent.

"Sorry, everyone—Ike's going to have to go."

The children leaned in and gave me hugs and pats while Jason gathered his things.

"Hi, you called my name?"

Without looking up from her screen, the woman answered, "It says here that you're visually impaired?"

"No, I'm not blind. I have a dog that's training to be a guide dog. I phoned ahead and told someone that."

"Oh. Okay. Just stand over there—" she pointed to the entrance to the boarding ramp— "and one of the flight attendants will be up to assist you."

Moments later, a young woman wearing a dark blue dress and matching jacket walked up to Jason and offered her arm. "When you're ready, my arm is just to your right. If you want to take hold, we can make our way to your seat."

Jason smiled and looked at her. "I appreciate your help, but I can see. He's in training. I'm not blind."

The flight attendant looked at Jason and began to laugh. "Oh my goodness, that's so embarrassing. I'm very sorry!"

"Don't worry about it. This is Ike. He's a guide dog in training. This is his first flight, so it's kind of a big deal! Ike, say hello."

"First flight!" The woman knelt to greet me. "Well, look at you, Ike—so brave. Flying is easy. And I'll take extra good care of you —promise!"

She stood up and said, "I'll walk with you, anyway. Just to make sure Ike finds his seat."

We were the first on the plane. It was smaller than I thought it was going to be. The attendant put us in the front row in a window seat. Jason laid out a small blanket on the floor and patted his hand on it. "Right here, bud. This is your spot for the next few hours—just a little longer than a studio class. Lay down and get comfortable."

As the rest of the travellers came on board, some children noticed me, smiled, and called my name. "Hey, mom, look—there's Ike! He's learning to be a guide dog!"

"You're amazing—you know that. No matter where we go, you bring out the best in people." Jason leaned forward and stroked my back.

"Can't wait for my family to meet you. There's a lot of them, though—so be prepared to be the centre of attention."

It wasn't long before things got incredibly loud and we began to move. I remember feeling myself being shoved up against Jason's feet. A strange sliding sensation got stronger as the plane started to lift. Jason bent forward to brace me while he scratched my ears. "It's okay, Ike. It'll level out soon."

Within minutes the noise subsided and I stopped sliding. I got up and readjusted my position while Jason reached into his backpack for his headphones and sketchbook.

"Everything okay?" I looked up to see our flight attendant smiling and leaning forward to check in with Jason.

"All good. That was a piece of cake. Apparently, this little guy's a world traveller."

"Good to hear! Just hit the notification bell on your armrest if you need anything."

Jason nodded and got back to his drawing. I closed my eyes and buried my nose in my tail. Sleep was my go-to for passing the time.

Landing was pretty much the opposite of taking off—after the big thud, I slid away from Jason this time. He reached forward and grabbed me while the plane slowed down. Then the flight attendant came over. "That wasn't too bad, eh, Ike—you're a pro at this flying thing!" After a goodbye pat on my head, she ensured that we were the first to get off the plane.

Jason gathered his luggage before we made our way through a set of oversized sliding doors into a mass of waiting humans.

"Welcome to Toronto, Ike—this place is massive! Stay close. Paul's going to meet us out front."

As we walked out into the darkness, a blast of cold air whipped around us. The hard frozen concrete bit at my feet. It was cold—unlike anything I had experienced. At first, it was even difficult to breathe. The air burned as it came in through my nostrils. It made me sneeze. My coat had thickened up to match our West Coast winter, but this weather was a whole different game. This was going to take some getting used to.

"There he is, Ike—there's Paul!"

While Jason put his luggage into the trunk, his brother got out of the car and came around to say hello.

"So you must be Ike!" I could see his breath as he spoke. It looked strange. "Good to finally meet. I've heard so much about you!"

After Jason covered the back seat with my blanket, I jumped in and got settled. The two siblings quickly hugged in the cold night air before climbing into their seats. Within moments, we were away. Driving on the highway, I had never seen so many cars. We were surrounded. As far as my eyes could see, there were lanes upon lanes of cars, all driving at speeds faster than I had ever travelled before. Watching out the window, I saw an endless stream of concrete and steel buildings, most of them lit with brightly coloured lights. If there were mountains or an ocean nearby, I couldn't see them.

As we pulled off the highway, Jason announced, "Won't be long now, Ike. Five minutes, tops!"

Jason told me that St. Catharines was where he had been born and raised. His family home was in an old neighbourhood in the downtown core, where the houses were made of rusty-coloured brick and surrounded by enormous trees with bare branches. It was quaint and cozy as we meandered the old streets until we eventually pulled into a long driveway.

"We're here, Ike. Time to meet more of the family!"

I had never held a pee this long before. I wouldn't need a go-busy cue—I was ready to burst. As soon as Jason opened the door, I dashed out and onto the lawn. The grass, frozen beneath my feet, felt cold and scratchy as I squatted. *Whew, what a relief!*

"Looks like he really had to go," said Paul as he opened the trunk.

"Yup, that was a long haul for him," answered Jason. "Good busy, Ike!"

I caught up to them as they made their way to the side of the house. Before we got to the door, it opened. Standing there waiting to greet us were Jason's mom and dad.

"Come on in," said Jason's dad as he held open the door. "Gosh, hurry up!"

"Get in there, Ike—quick," said Jason. "Man, it's cold out here!"

I walked into the kitchen and began exploring while the humans hugged and said hello. The kitchen led me to the main hall and into the living room, where I found a roaring fire. *Ahhh—now we're talking!* I walked closer to feel the heat emanating from the popping flames. It was soothing to feel such warmth after the bitter cold outside.

"Ike?" I turned around to see Jason come into the room with his parents and Paul behind him. "Mom and Dad, this is Ike."

I made my way over to meet his mom, Eleanor, and his dad, Carl.

"Goodness me, he's such a handsome dog," said Eleanor. "He looks like one of those movie dogs."

Jason, as he bent down to pet me, said, "Agreed, he's a looker, alright, but there's so much more to him." Jason stroked my chest. "Why don't you sit down, and then he'll come up to you and you can pet him?"

I moved closer to Jason's parents, who were now sitting on the couch. They looked much older. When they smiled, wrinkles appeared on either side of their eyes. And, when Carl sat down, I heard his knees pop. *That can't be good!*

"Can you sit, Ike?" I sat. "Well, would you look at that," said Carl with a tone of surprise. "He's smart, too!"

"How much training does this little guy do?" asked Paul.

"Every day. Whether we're walking to school from the car or in the backyard at home, there are a bunch of drills we go through and rules we have to follow that will help him get ready for what's coming in the spring. Yikes—four months away, Ike. Our time's running out."

I made my way out to the kitchen for a drink of water, some more exploring, and then back to the living room and the fire. The house smelled like the outdoors. There were plants everywhere. That, combined with the fire—good smells.

With the heat now caressing my back, it wasn't long before sleep was calling. I drifted in and out, listening to Jason and his family catch up on school, life on the coast, and the family plans for the time we were home. Later, Jason woke me up to tell me that it was time to go back out into the cold for a pee before bed.

"It's supposed to snow tonight," announced Paul as Jason put on his coat. "We're supposed to get a foot and a half by tomorrow."

"Ike, we timed this perfectly. It looks like you'll get your first snowfall!"

The next morning, we did indeed wake up to a winter wonderland.

"Hold on, bud. Let me get my coat." Jason sat on the bench by the kitchen door and put on his boots. Next, he grabbed some mittens and a hat. "Mom and Dad, do you want to see this?" he called out. "I'm going to let Ike out into the snow for the first time! Paul, come on out here and watch!"

I stood by the door and eagerly waited. "Okay, Ike, here we go." Jason's parents and Paul stood by the kitchen window.

The door opened. It was white—everywhere. *So, this is snow.*

"What are you waiting for, Ike? Get out there!"

I slowly stepped into the snow. Immediately, I sunk to my chest. It felt cold but soothing in a strange way. I walked a bit. Slowly at first, then into a trot until I was springing like a rabbit through the deep white stuff surrounding me. I burst into a full sprint, bounding from one landing to another. With snow flying everywhere, I dashed around the perimeter of the yard. Soon, my hardwiring kicked in, and a figure-eight pattern emerged.

"Look at him go," I could hear Carl say from the step of the kitchen door.

"Don't ask me why, but he always does that," said Jason.

Later that day, more family arrived. Wendy, Jason's sister, and Erik, her husband, and their children, Jenny, Laura, and Mark, from Edmonton. And Scott, Jason's oldest brother, and his wife Rose, along with their children, Ryan and Kaylyn, arrived as well. The house was packed. I had never been in a house with so many humans. The smells were like nothing I had experienced living with the boys. Sweet aromas seemed to follow the female humans throughout the house, while the younger humans had food scents sticking to their hands and clothes as they devoured the snacks Eleanor had laid out. My nose was in overdrive and I was loving it!

While the older humans stayed indoors, I played with the cousins in the backyard. I was a hit. Their playful energy was infectious. It reminded me of being with my siblings. They were amazed at my ability to find a tennis ball even when they threw it into the deep snow. When the sun came out, the snow became a little thicker and heavier. The ball chasing ended when the young humans began rolling the snow into big balls and piling them up to make a snowman.

Before dinner, Jason and his brothers came out and began throwing snowballs at one another. This part was especially fun as I chased the snowballs that didn't land on their desired targets. I could sense from their banter and the speed at which these snowballs were travelling, there was more than a bit of competitiveness among them. Eventually, their hands became too cold, and we all went inside for the evening.

There were two dinner tables set—one for the young humans and one for older humans. As I soon discovered, Carl had a knack for dropping food. I found my spot at his feet. Accidentally or on purpose, I didn't care—I was too busy enjoying every morsel that fell from above.

Soon, Jason was onto the gig. "Dad, you're not supposed to feed him from the table—it could screw up his training."

Eleanor playfully scolded him. Carl, smiling mischievously, would utter, "What? It was an accident!" Carl was my new best friend!

Later, with the sleeping arrangements for everyone complete, Jason came in to find me outstretched between his parents on their enormous bed. Eleanor with her book on one side of the bed, and Carl with his newspapers on the other side. Me, half-covered in those newspapers, lay somewhere in between.

"Dad—he's never slept on a bed before!"

"What?" Carl collapsed the newspaper he was busy reading and did his best to look surprised. "Oh, Ike, when did you climb up here?"

"Sorry, dear," said Eleanor. "I told him Ike should probably stay on the floor."

Jason sat on the end of the bed and cleared some of the papers. "Thought I wouldn't see you, eh, bud?" Then, he gently whacked my hind leg. "You little goofball—you know you're not supposed to be up here."

"Come on now, son—just for the holidays. It won't hurt him." Carl smiled with his reading glasses perched on the end of his nose while he stroked my ears.

"Okay, he can sleep here, but just because it's Christmas," conceded Jason as he shook his head. "I swear, we're going to get home and he will have forgotten everything!"

Jason's mom closed her book. "How's his training going, anyway—do you think he'll pass?"

"Well, a few months ago, I would've said, 'no.' At his first assessment in the fall, he absolutely bombed."

"Has he had another test since?" asked Eleanor.

"Yup—a few weeks ago."

Carl sat up and put down his newspaper. "How did he do?"

"A-plus! Roberta said it was like she was working with a mature dog who had gone through months of training. She also said that she had never seen a pup so well trained."

"Gosh, son—well done," said Carl. "That's got to feel pretty good."

"Well, he's a smart dog. I don't think I've done anything extraordinary. We've just followed the guidelines."

"So, there's no way he'll likely fail out?" asked Eleanor.

"Probably not—not if he keeps behaving the way he can when he's focused."

"That's a shame," said Carl. "I'll be honest; I was hoping you might get to keep him."

"Dad—there's no way I can keep him. It's best if he moves on and becomes someone's eyes—believe me, it's better that way."

"I don't know how you're going to say goodbye to this boy. He's something special, son. And you two have a bond. I can feel it. He follows you around and is always watching you."

Eleanor smiled warmly. "And, well, don't take this the wrong way, Jason, but you seem better with Ike. Not as angry as you were when you were rowing. Especially after Seoul. That was unbearable for me to watch."

"Your mother's right, son. You do seem lighter. Ike's been good for you. It would be a shame to lose him."

"I suppose. But I can always get another dog someday. And it's not like he's leaving tomorrow. I mean, we still have a few months together. I'll continue to enjoy his company, do the training, and when he heads to Ottawa—well, I knew that was part of the deal."

Jason's parents were dog humans; they had that energy. Carl, especially. They didn't get too fussed about things. They could laugh at each other, and they didn't try to manage my behaviour too much. They knew I was a dog—not a piece of furniture. I had a personality. And, like humans, sometimes that personality could mess up. They were easy to be around and I was enjoying that ease. I loved Jason. But his intensity could be exhausting at times. It was interesting to hear that he hadn't always been this way. That somehow his time spent rowing had magnified this trait. He sure hadn't learned it from Carl or Eleanor.

Jason was clearly still in progress. Even as a puppy, I knew he had come a long way, but there was still much work to be done. Sure, he deserved credit for how well he had trained me. I knew the drills. I knew that booklet inside and out. But the nuance of feeling who I was—my soul—and what I could offer him had yet to sink in. He was still too caught up in keeping my behaviour within the lines—controlling me.

I knew that, given a lifetime with Jason, he'd get there. But we didn't have that time. We had months. And I was a puppy; I wanted to enjoy what time I had with him.

The next morning, I got up early with Carl and Eleanor. We made our way downstairs to avoid the chaos that was certain to descend upon the kitchen very soon. It was quiet when Eleanor flicked on the coffee machine. She got out their cereal bowls, two spoons, and some orange juice. The napkins were already on the table. I imagined this had been their routine for decades. It happened without a word spoken. Carl, still busy reading, waited for his wife to sit down and join him before he neatly folded his morning newspaper and laid it on the floor.

"Not sure what to feed you, Ike. We'll just have to wait for Jason." Eleanor gently patted me on the head.

"Why don't we give him a bowl of cereal? That should be okay—don't you think?"

"Honey, you don't feed dogs bran flakes! For heaven's sake, all we need is for Ike to have diarrhea while he's staying with us." Eleanor poured some milk over Carl's cereal. "And please don't you feed him from the table!"

While Carl and Eleanor ate their breakfast, I waited patiently for mine. I was hungry and feeling a bit restless. Normally, by now, I would be out for a walk with Jason. Instead, I was lying on the floor, having to contain the energy that was building inside of me, including the urge to pee. I noticed that Carl had some bright and cheery red Christmas socks on. I gave them a sniff. They smelled clean. Then I gave them a playful nibble.

"Gosh, honey, what in the Dickens is he up to?"

"What are you talking about, dear?"

"The dog—he's nibbling on my socks."

Carl pulled his foot away. "You leave those socks alone, Ike."

This was getting boring. I needed something to do. I looked around for something to occupy my time but returned to those red socks. I wiggled myself closer and took another sniff. Then I grabbed hold and pulled.

"What on earth! Honey, he's got my sock!"

I stood up with Carl's red Christmas sock locked in my mouth and his foot still in it. I began to back up, attempting to pull that sock off his foot. Next, Carl braced himself with one hand on the table and the other against the counter. He was sliding closer and closer to the edge of his chair. Carl began to giggle as he reached for his sock while trying not to fall. I shook my head back and forth, trying to dislodge his foot. His giggle turned to laughter—uncontrollable laughter. Soon, he was in a fit of hysterics so loud that Eleanor couldn't help herself, and she, too, began to laugh.

Finally, the sock released, and I shot backward. Feeling quite proud, with my prized possession hanging from either side of my mouth, I walked towards Carl with a confident young swagger. I figured announcing my accomplishment to the entire house was in order. I began baying loudly. My bark was muffled by the sock, but it was loud enough to cause Carl and Eleanor to laugh even harder as they tried to shush me.

The cousins came running into the kitchen to see what the commotion was all about. Arriving to find their grandparents both in hysterics only invited them to join in, and the infectious laughter spread.

Soon after, Jason and his siblings joined us. I got let outside, and then fed, as did the children. Within an hour, we were on our way to a nearby park for a hike.

It was the day before Christmas and more snow had fallen in the night. The park was beautiful. The snow emphasized the barren branches. Each tree looked like its own modern sculpture—stunning. It didn't take long for me to find a stick. With some instructions from Uncle Jason, the children took on the role of keeping me occupied with retrieving every stick they could find.

Upon our return home, exhausted from chasing countless sticks, I went in search of the warm crackling fire. With his red Christmas sock back on his foot, Carl was sitting in his chair reading another newspaper and snacking on nuts, cheese, crackers, and other delicious-looking treats. With good posture, I promptly sat by Carl's side and flashed him a cute sideways head-tilt that garnered me a reward.

"Don't tell anyone, Ike."

Are you kidding—not a peep!

While I dozed and snacked the afternoon away, the kitchen was abuzz with activity. The house smelled festive, with all of the inviting aromas floating into the living room and eventually my nose. With stockings hung, the tree decorated, and everyone looking their holiday best, the stage was set for another evening to visit and catch up on life's events.

I assumed my place at Carl's feet, grace was said, and soon after, my prayers were answered—food began to drop from the heavens.

The conversation was lively. The competitiveness I witnessed with the snowball antics the evening before continued at the table. The subject of rowing came up often. I learned about the history of the sport within the family. Jason's dad, grandfather, and his two older brothers had all rowed.

Eventually, the conversation landed on Jason's race at the Olympics. And then the Canadian rowing team's new direction after those Games were over. It wasn't just Jason's crew that had performed poorly; it was the entire national team. Following the '88 Games in Seoul, coaches and administrative staff were fired. As is often the case, it was time for new leadership and a different focus.

"You should've hung on, Jase," said Paul. "You should have never retired. Look what would've happened—you'd be an Olympic Champion. You would have chased your dream and won! Man, that would've been so cool."

The room went quiet. Paul was talking about the Canadian men's eight crew returning to the following Olympics in Barcelona four years later under a new coach and winning. Some of Jason's teammates from the 1988 crew were in that 1992 boat. Knowing the frustration that I had witnessed from Jason, I don't imagine he appreciated being reminded.

"As I've said many times before, Paul, given how I was doing after Seoul, there's no way I could've hung on for four more years. This is not the time or place to get into the details, but there's just no way."

Silence, again. I got up from below Carl and made my way down the table to put my chin on Jason's lap. I could feel the shame still alive in him.

Jason had indeed struggled with the outcome of those 1988 Games in Seoul, as had many of his teammates. And, as I was beginning to understand from our many long walks and camping trips, he had taken the anger that he had felt from the loss of that race and redirected it inward. The result of which was a very unhappy and bitter young man. Now, five years later, he was finding ways to let go of some of that anger, and I was beginning to figure out that maybe I was just as important to his healing as he was to my training.

"And if you were still rowing you might not have met Ike," added Wendy.

"I would agree," said Eleanor. "Ike is a wonderful addition to the family."

"It's too bad Ike'll be with his new family when we go to the cottage!" yelled one of the cousins from their table in the living room.

"He would love that place," said Carl, slipping me a delicious piece of turkey skin.

"Don't think I haven't thought about that," said Jason. "The lake. The runs. The lake. The dinners. The lake." Everyone laughed. "The bonfires."

"The lake!" yelled the cousins in unison.

This was the first time that I had heard about the cottage. It sounded like a dream—swimming all day, playing with the cousins, catching food falling from Carl at the table—I could've gotten used to that.

***

Christmas morning came with the excitement of a herd of elephants. The grandkids waited at the top of the stairs while their grandad made sure Santa had arrived in the night. On his word, they came flying down the stairs and into the living room to find their stockings loaded with goodies.

Santa had even made me a stocking! It was red with white trim and had cut-out snowflakes glued to the side. I supposed it was one of the perks of having an artist for your human. The best part being, of course, was what was inside. Cookies. Chewies. Two squeaky toys and a couple of orange street-hockey balls. *Jackpot!* I was thrilled! This whole Christmas thing was a very good tradition.

I wasted little time grabbing one of the chewies and parking myself directly in front of the roaring fire. I could enjoy watching the others open their gifts from that vantage point while munching on my salmon-flavoured treat.

We spent the remainder of the day at home, heading out to the backyard with Jason and the cousins to chase one of my new orange balls, which was easy to find in the snow. Otherwise, the day was filled with a steady flow of company, which included more extended family and friends. I had never met so many humans. I certainly was popular. I received more head pats than I could count. Not surprisingly for me, every visit ended with a, "I don't know how you're going to give him up!"

And, by then, I was wondering more than ever, what about me? How am I going to give up Jason?

When the last guest had left and everything was cleaned up and put away, Jason grabbed his jacket, mittens, and boots, and we went out into the winter night for a quiet walk through the city before bed. The snow began to fall lightly, then much harder.

"They call these Charlie Brown snowflakes, bud. Just like in the cartoon. They're so big, you can see the intricate design of each flake." Jason caught one on his mitten and lowered it to show me. "Pretty cool, eh?" They were quite something, and easy to see so perfectly lit up by the street lights. "Do you remember that time in class when Andrew said that Mother Nature was the world's best designer? I think you could argue a good case."

It was quiet and peaceful as we walked block after block. The snow dampened the city sounds. All we could hear were Jason's boots crunching through the snow. I could've walked all night—just me and him.

Back at the house, everyone had gone to bed. We moved into the living room where the fire was still burning just enough to see.

"One song, Ike. I just want to hear one song." Jason went over to the stereo and placed a CD into the tray, hit play, and turned the volume right down. "This is my favourite Christmas hymn, bud. 'Once In Royal David's City.' It always reminds me of being a young boy and singing in the choir. I used to love when we sang this one."

He sat on the floor beside me in front of the fire, and we listened to his carol and watched the flames slowly flicker out.

***

"Wonderful to meet you, Ike," said Jason's dad as he bent to scratch me under my chin. "Thanks for bringing him home, son. He's quite a dog."

"I'm glad you and Mom got to meet him."

Carl stepped forward and gave Jason a handshake, not a hug. He was old school, a veteran of the Second World War who wasn't much for emotions.

"We thoroughly enjoyed having Ike as our guest," added Eleanor as she smiled at me. "And, you, too, of course," she said as she got up on her toes to hug Jason goodbye.

"I'll see you two at the cottage!" Jason grabbed my leash and climbed into the car after me.

Getting to the airport and boarding our flight was as smooth as it had been getting there. The flight attendants were friendly, and when they saw my vest we found ourselves with front-row seats again. This time, we had company.

"He's a beaut!"

"Yup—he hears that a lot!"

"What's his name?"

"His name's Ike. I'm Jason."

"Nice to meet both of you. My name's Bob. My wife and I retired to the West Coast a few years ago. We live up in Whistler. How about you?"

"Dunbar, with a few roommates. I'm studying graphic design at Emily Carr."

"How about this little guy? I see he's going to be a pair of eyes someday. Good for him."

"That's the plan—I have him for about another four months."

This was where I checked out. I had heard about my future so many times, some days, I thought I was already living it. I curled up at Jason's feet and proceeded to do what I did so well—sleep.

"Ike. Ike—wake up." I opened my eyes and looked at Jason. He seemed concerned. "I think you peed in your sleep, Ike. You had an accident," he whispered. *I did what?* I sat up and immediately felt that my lower belly was wet. He was right. I began licking my fur. I couldn't understand; what had gone wrong?

While Jason frantically tried to pat dry the carpet, the flight attendant came by and asked, "Is everything okay with your pup?"

Jason looked up and tried to smile. "All good, thanks. We're fine. I think I spilled my apple juice, and I'm just trying to clean it up. Sorry about that."

"This plane has an overnight in Vancouver to get a thorough cleaning. So the carpet will get steam-cleaned. Please don't fuss."

I don't think Jason was too worried about the carpet. It was me he was concerned about. I wondered too. Why had I peed in my sleep?

We made our way to the front of the airport where Pat and Trev were waiting. I was so happy to see them that I jumped into the car and tried climbing into the front seats to lick their faces.

"Ike—easy, buddy! Yes, we missed you, too, little fella!" Trev tried to contain my wagging body and not let me get to Pat, who was busy driving.

"Good flight?" asked Pat. "How'd Ike make out?"

"Seasoned pro," answered Jason. "He was great going there. He charmed the entire boarding area at our gate. Every child waiting to fly to Toronto came over to see him!"

"Ike—rockstar status!" Trev reached back to pat me on my head.

"But coming home, it was weird—he peed in his sleep."

Trev turned right around this time. "He had an accident on the flight?"

"Yup—and not just a little, but a lot. The carpet underneath him was soaked."

"Yikes, that's not good," said Trev.

"Are you going to call Allyson?" asked Pat. "I would let her know sooner than later."

***

When Jason returned from brushing his teeth, he knelt down to say goodnight. "Are you happy to be home, Ike?" He rubbed my neck as he looked at me. "I bet you're going to miss my parents' bed." He laughed. "Well, we'll keep that between us—got it?" He leaned down and kissed me on my forehead. "Good night, bud."

He turned out the light and climbed into bed. I got up and circled a few times to see if I could make this combination of old foam and blankets feel a little more comfortable. After a few more tries, it just wasn't working. I got up and walked over to Jason's bed, laid my chin on his blanket beside his face, and sighed.

"Ha—are you kidding me? What, so now you've been spoiled so badly you can't sleep in your smelly old crate? I knew it! I should never have let you sleep with Mom and Dad."

Jason reached out his hand to pat my head. "Listen, bud; you have to sleep in that crate. We have to get back into your training."

I didn't budge.

Jason continued to stroke my ears.

"So, that's it? It's my bed or nothing?"

He's caving—I can feel it! Come on, Jase. What's the big deal?

"Okay, up you get."

Yes—knew it! I leapt up and curled into the back of his legs. It wasn't his parents' bed. But it would do.

"I can't believe it. You are such a spoiled little boy now." Jason reached down and playfully whacked me on my hind leg. "Okay, you, have a good sleep. And not a word to anyone!"

I was awakened a few hours later by Jason's worried voice. "Oh my goodness, Ike. What the hell? Wake up, bud—you've soaked the bed. Come on, let's get you outside."

I sat up immediately and noticed that my lower belly and legs were wet. I had peed in my sleep, again. I'd had my bedtime pee; I hadn't drunk much since dinner—nothing had changed. Yet the bed was soaked.

"Come on, Ike, go busy; it's freezing out here." Jason stood in the middle of our backyard in his boxers and t-shirt with just his Birks on his feet. I emptied what little I had left in my bladder. Jason knelt down and called me over. "Hey, you okay?" He asked, putting his arm around my chest. "We'll call Allyson first thing in the morning. Don't worry, Ike, we'll figure this out."

After Jason had finished changing the sheets, he laid several towels down where I had been sleeping and patted his hand on the bed for me to come back up. "Here, bud, just curl up here. Get some sleep."

The following morning, Jason called the vet clinic as soon as it opened. This was strange—other than my two accidents, I felt fine. Why couldn't I hold my pee when I slept like I had been doing for months?

"Hello, I'm wondering if we can get in to see Allyson this morning? It's kind of important." I could hear the concern in his voice.

Jason looked at me with a pensive smile.

"Well, it's the weirdest thing. He peed in his sleep last night and the day before during a nap." He paused again. "Great, thanks. We'll see you then."

"Okay, bud, they're going to squeeze us in this morning. We have to head up there soon. Don't worry, Allyson will figure this out."

***

The last time I was at the clinic, she had cut off my you-know-whats. And it hurt a lot for at least two weeks. I was a little apprehensive about what might happen on this visit, if I'm honest.

While we waited, we both stood quietly, staring intently at the door. Finally, it opened.

"Hi, Jason." Allyson smiled as she came through the door. "I don't have a lot of time, but I wanted to get Ike in to check him over."

"Thanks for making the time. I figured you'd want to see him right away." Jason looked at me. "He soaked the bed last night, and he peed on the flight coming home. Other than that, he seems just fine."

"Well, let's have a look. But first, our hellos?" Allyson put down her clipboard and took off her stethoscope while she knelt on the floor. "Come here, Ike. Come say hello, handsome boy." She patted the tops of her thighs and Jason dropped my leash. I skidded on the floor, trying to get to her quickly.

"Oh, look at you—you look beautiful, Ike." I dropped to my back to encourage some tummy rubs. "And look, your sutures healed up perfectly. Have you forgiven me for that yet? I know—I know. That was a dirty trick, wasn't it? I told you that you were just going to have an afternoon nap." Allyson laughed. "Sorry, Ike. You're still a manly man to me!"

Jason snickered while Allyson continued to fuss over me on the examination room floor. If this was her idea of an apology, she was forgiven.

"Okay, Ike, let's go to the back and draw some blood—shall we? And, you know what's back there, don't you—the gigantic cookies. Come on!" Allyson grabbed my leash and stood up. "We'll just be a moment."

When we got to the back, Allyson gave me two of those enormous cookies while those little bee bites drew some blood. *Easy-peasy!*

"I'll give you a call with the results of his bloodwork, Jason. And I'm going to call Roberta and recommend that we do some x-rays to see if we can find out exactly what's going on in there. He's way too young to be experiencing this type of incontinence."

Jason took hold of my leash. "Thanks again for seeing him so quickly."

"You were smart to call right away. Canadian Guide Dogs will want to know what's going on with Ike. Try not to worry. We'll figure this out."

While Pat, Trev, and Jason were all in the kitchen preparing dinner, Allyson called. The blood work had been inconclusive, so we had to go back in for more tests. In fact, this was so serious that Roberta had asked for a specialist to have a look at me.

Two days later, we went back to the clinic for x-rays and met with the specialists. And, after another two days, we sat in the examination room about to meet with Allyson and hear the results.

"As it turns out, Ike's incontinence is a bit more serious than we had originally thought. The x-rays revealed that only one of his kidneys has developed." Allyson paused while she put up my x-ray and flicked on the light-box. "As you can see, the other kidney has remained underdeveloped. It's about the size of a peanut and is likely not functioning at all."

"So what does that mean?" asked Jason as he looked more closely at the x-ray. "How do we fix that?"

"Well, we don't. Perhaps, more specifically, we can't. At this stage, if Ike's kidney hasn't developed, it never will."

"What does that mean for Ike?"

"Well, it means he may not live a full life," answered Allyson. "Or he may. We just never know in these cases. He could live a year. He could live five years. And he could quite possibly live longer; we just don't know with these things. It all depends on the strength and health of that one kidney."

I remember being confused; that was a lot of information for a young dog to understand. But when I saw the look of terror on Jason's face, I realized I was in big trouble.

Jason pointed at the peanut-sized kidney. "There's no doubt about it, that thing's smaller." Then he turned and looked at Allyson. "So this is what's making him pee the bed?"

"No. That's another issue we're looking at. You see, there's a sphincter between his bladder and his urethra, and it's malfunctioning. When he sleeps, it's supposed to remain closed like a draw-string and prevent his bladder from draining. But, instead, it's relaxing and letting his urine drain freely, which is essentially causing him to wet the bed. We have some meds and strategies that can help manage this, but he's likely going to have this condition for life."

Jason looked down at me. He looked even more worried. *This isn't happening.*

"So what about being a guide dog? How does his future owner deal with this?"

"I guess that's the silver lining here."

"Silver lining?"

"Jason, I spoke with Roberta this morning. She said she would call you later, but she asked me to tell you that if you were interested, you could keep Ike as a pet."

"Keep Ike? Forever? Are you sure?"

Jason looked at me again. Now he looked as confused and scared as I was.

Allyson smiled and came over to stand in front of Jason. "Isn't that terrific news? Ike would be yours forever, Jason." Allyson began to tear up. Clearly, she was more excited about this turn of events than he was. "I can help you manage the incontinence. And we'll just keep checking his blood work every year and see how that one kidney is doing. But there's no reason why he can't live a normal, long, and healthy life."

"Forever?" Jason's face went blank.

"Yes, Jason, forever. I'm so excited for you two!" Allyson put her arms around Jason and hugged him. Not the most affectionate human at the best of times, but this was the stiffest hug I'd ever seen, even for Jason.

Then Allyson got down on the floor with me. She placed her hands on either side of my head and kissed me on my forehead. "Ike, did you hear that news? You are going to live with Jason from now on. And you won't have to wear that annoying jacket anymore—you can be a regular old golden retriever. Isn't that fantastic?"

I, too, was trying to understand what had just happened. *Live a year? Did I hear that right?* That news from Allyson was going off like a siren in my head. I wanted to live longer than that. Sure, living with Jason forever was what I wanted, but I also wanted it to last longer than just a few more months. This was going to take some time to process.

We walked home in silence.

Trev met us at the door. "Jase, what happened? You look like you've seen a ghost?"

Pat came out of his room to join us. "Ya, how's Ike doing?"

Jason undid my leash and sat down on the couch. Pat and Trev were both quiet as they sat in separate chairs, waiting to hear Jason's answer.

"Ike's been removed from the guide dog program. He's mine to keep if I want him."

"What?" Pat and Trev said simultaneously. They looked at one another and smiled.

That's not how Jason reacted!

"He's got some medical issues that compromise his ability to do his job. So he's out. He's mine to keep. If I want."

"If you want? Why wouldn't you want to keep him?" asked Trev.

"I can't afford to have a dog right now. Are you kidding me? As it is, my student loan barely gets me through the month. Now I'll have to take care of his food. Not to mention the vet bills—especially now with all of the medication and special treatments that he'll need." Jason looked over at me. "And his jacket—I won't have his jacket. Which means I can't take him to school. Which means he has to stay here all day long by himself. I can't do that to him. That was the whole point of this—so that I could take a dog to school with me."

I remember thinking at the time, *Wow, so that's it—we're done because of my future vet bills and a jacket?* I knew Jason was as practical as they came, but his reaction surprised me. I thought even he was more emotionally invested than that.

By bedtime, Jason had calmed down. And so had I, for the most part. I simply decided that a few more months or, if I was lucky enough, a few more years with Jason was better than none at all.

Jason, on the other hand, wasn't convinced. Pat and Trev had done their very best to persuade him that I was worth keeping—regardless of the extra costs. They told him that he would find a way and that if he gave me up for financial reasons, he'd live to regret it someday. Jason seemed to hear that but was still quietly going over the pros and cons. I heard him tell Roberta over the phone that he would think about it. And, knowing Jason, he was going to think—long and hard.

Having taken some new medication to help me make it through the night, I lay curled up at his feet. With the streetlight spilling into our room, I could see that Jason's eyes were still open.

"What do you think, Ike—can we make this work? You and me?" He reached down and stroked my back. "I just don't want you to become one of those dogs that has to spend all day at home. I would never do that to you, bud."

The next morning, before Pat and Trev were up, we left for the trails. Deep in the woods, Jason did his best thinking. Although, that day, it was more like he was lost in the woods, deep in thought!

While he pondered the possibility of our future together, I explored the forest floor and revelled in the mid-winter damp, musty smells of the rotting leaves.

After spending the first half of our hike in complete silence, Jason finally knelt down and called me over. He grabbed hold of my collar and looked straight into my eyes. *He seems lighter.*

"I think we can do this, Ike—or, perhaps, I think we should do this! But, just so you know, I can't promise you fancy digs for a while. It's going to be what you've had so far for a few more years, at least. You know, until I can start earning some money. But, if you're okay with that, I say we give this our best shot—you and me. What do you think?"

Instantly, I ran off the trail to find a big stick, then I bounded back towards Jason with it locked in my mouth. My excitement was spilling out of me—my entire body wagged. It was hard to stay upright with a large, heavy stick in my mouth and my back-half swinging side to side. As I got closer, I barked excitedly in celebration. As the stick muffled the sound. Jason roared one of his loud laughs.

"Well, I guess that's a yes, eh buddy? Good boy!" Jason reached for the stick and took hold of one end. Then he pulled it closer to his face with me attached. "One thing's for sure, Ike; if you've only got a year or so, I'm going to make it the best one ever. I promise." He stood up and cocked his right arm, preparing to toss the stick. "Are you ready for this?" Then he wound up and sent the stick spinning like a helicopter far into the woods. "Go get it, Ike. Go get it, bud!"

We arrived home to the sweet smell of pancakes and Trev standing by the stove in his boxers with a spatula in his hand.

"I thought I'd make them for a change." Trev turned to greet us. "Hope you're hungry!"

"I am for sure—thanks, Trev! And I know Ike can always make room."

"Quit your yappin' and keep flippin'!" yelled Pat from his room.

"Get out here and make yourself useful, you lazy dawg," Trev turned and winked at me.

Pat came out to join us in the kitchen. He grabbed some plates and began to clear space at the counter overlooking the backyard. "Any more thoughts on Ike? What's your gut telling you to do?"

Jason looked down at me and smiled. "Well, I think we'll give it a shot."

Trev spun around. “Really—that’s great news, Jase!” He turned and looked at Pat. “Get in here, Pat. Time for a family hug.” Trev put down his spatula and hugged Jason with some help from Pat.

“You won’t regret that decision, ever,” Pat said. “What about school? Are you going to tell anyone?”

“Nope. I’m just going to keep taking him until someone asks. Then I’ll figure out what to do from there.”

“Ikester—just keep showing up like you own the place, buddy. They won’t mess with you,” added Trev.

“There’s probably a lot of truth in that,” said Jason.

one year old

My first birthday was April 27th. I had made it to one year with no sign of, well, leaving. I'd take it.

Everything seemed to be falling into place. Health-wise, Allyson suggested a special diet to support my kidney. Lots of fruits and vegetables, if you can believe it. Anything with high water content was now on our shopping list. I grew accustomed to apples, pears, berries, carrots, broccoli, and celery sticks! I actually enjoyed it when Jason gave me a big carrot to wedge between my paws and gnaw away on. It was no soup bone, but it would do.

Jason, whose diet was already mainly plant-based, simply made extras for me on certain nights. That, combined with some special kibble, and I had never felt better. As for me wetting the bed, Jason simply pulled my water dish up after dinner. And he made sure that I had a late-night pee. Along with some meds prescribed by Allyson, that made the night mistakes rare. I was living a pretty healthy lifestyle and enjoying every day of it.

As for school, Trev had called it perfectly. For the entire second semester, Jason showed up for classes every day with me in tow, and not one question about my missing jacket was raised. Explaining why I was still around in September—now that would require a little more thought.

Yup, life was good being a regular old golden retriever. And it was about to get better. Pat and Trev enjoyed running on the trails in the Endowment Lands, through Stanley Park, and along the Baden Powell trail, which meandered through the North Shore Mountains of Vancouver. Jason had taken some time away from running for his year with me and was keen to get back into better shape. Allyson had told him that I could start running with him on my first birthday! Something about my hips setting and being ready for that sort of activity.

Furthermore, in the name of making this the best year of my possibly short life, she also okayed his idea for how to celebrate my birthday from a culinary standpoint. You see, Jason thought it would be fun to serve me a meal I wouldn't normally have. In this case, a homemade burger with fries, complete with a dealcoholized beer to wash it down, and carrot cake and ice cream for dessert, with a candle on top! Allyson said it wouldn't be her first choice from a health standpoint, but she understood the sentiment of wanting to spoil me. Gotta love Allyson!

Before I dove into that chef's special, we were going to head out for my first run! The boys were all in their running garb, stretching in the backyard. Me, I was just eager to get going.

The pink cherry blossoms had just finished blooming, but the air still smelled sweet as we came out of our back alley and onto the sidewalks that would lead us to the trails.

"Nice to have you along, Ike," said Pat.

"Ya, what a nice treat, Ike," added Trev. "Remember to take it easy on your dad. He's not exactly built for speed."

"Hey, you bastard—appreciate the vote of confidence."

Running through those trails was a different experience of the woods than before when we just walked. There was no stopping to sniff the new smells or find a perfect stick to retrieve. Instead, we kept plodding without ever stopping.

When running, we covered far more distance than we ever did merely walking, and I discovered new trails. I couldn't get over the size of the park. It was enormous. One trail led to another, and another—we just kept going. It wasn't even tiring. To match the pace the boys kept required a simple trot from me. I loved the sensation of the breeze in my face—it sometimes lifted my ears when we ran a little faster. Eventually, without even knowing we were heading back, we arrived at the main trail we had started on. I had been so swept up in the beauty of the place, I'd lost track of time and location. Soon after hitting the neighbourhood streets, we came through the alley and into our backyard.

"How was that, Jase?" asked Pat.

"Considering it's been a year off, it felt pretty good. I'll likely be sore as hell tomorrow, though."

"Thanks for the run, boys," said Trev. "I hear we've got a birthday to celebrate this evening?"

"We sure do!" said Jason.

"The big one-year mark for the Ike-monster!" added Pat.

"Hey Trev, do you mind if we use your barbecue for the burgers? I picked up some beef for Ike's burger."

"What was that like, veggie-boy?" asked Pat.

"It was for a good cause."

It was a fantastic celebration. The burger and fries were outstanding—the cake and ice cream, perfect. I liked my kibble and carrots, but this was a whole new world of flavours! Like the goodies that Carl snuck me under the table at Christmas. I wondered if this was how Indie ate every day? However, the beer—not so much. The fizzy bubbles were hard to manage. I tried a little bit, but it wasn't for me. Although, I sure appreciated how much effort Jason put into that special meal. He not only baked the cake, he also bought me a card and wrote some things I had never heard him say before. Such as being glad that he had chosen to keep me. And that he was excited to make every year we had together the best possible. He even signed it "Dad." I hadn't thought about our relationship like that. But I was good with it!

A few weeks later, Jason finished his first year at Emily Carr. There was no big fanfare. He was just glad for a small break before he'd begin, again, his summer academic coursework at UBC. In order to graduate with a degree from Emily Carr, he needed several academic courses that he relied on UBC to provide.

Jason's sister, Wendy, called from her home in Edmonton to congratulate him on making it through his first year. She suggested that he come for a visit and bring me as well.

"You up for a road trip, Ike?"

I was. And, a few days later, we were up early and heading for Wendy's place. Although the scenery was beautiful the entire way, 14 hours is a long time for anyone to sit still. So Jason had planned a trail-run midway, starting from the side of the highway.

We pulled into a designated rest stop. After exploring the trail map posted by the washrooms, we chose a route and began our run. Before long, we were deep into the surrounding forests. The trees were taller than anything I had seen before. Everywhere I looked, enormous evergreens were reaching for the sky and their fair share of sunlight.

Soon we ran out of trail. "That wasn't long enough, Ike!" he proclaimed. "What do you say we do some bushwhacking?" While Jason looked around at our options, I explored the smells. "How about we just head straight up and see where it takes us? We should be fine.

It sort of looks like an old logging road up there. Let's see if we can find something to follow."

We were off again, heading straight up. As we came out onto a plateau, there did appear to have been a road there. "This should do—come on, bud."

We were off, again, running amidst what seemed like never-ending trees and stumps. Some of the stumps appeared large enough to be small cabins. I had no idea that trees could grow to that size. We soon found a nice pace as we made our way in the cool shade of the silent giants.

Then, the silence was shattered by a strange noise. "Geezuz Murphy, what the hell was that?" We both turned in the direction of the cracking sound. "Holy crap, look at the size of that guy!" We stood frozen, not wanting to draw attention. Before us was the largest dog I'd ever seen. And it had branches growing out of its head. "That, my friend, would be a moose," whispered Jason.

It stopped, turned, and looked at us from a close distance.

"So we're just going to stay still, Ike," whispered Jason. "Don't move, bud."

The moose continued to look in our direction. It appeared to look beyond and around us but never really focused on either one of us standing there, frozen.

Soon, the creature lifted its head as if to take one more big sniff. Then, it was off—trotting along our new trail, heading away from us.

"That was frickin' close, Ike. I've only ever seen a moose from a car. Amazing!"

***

Our week at Wendy and Erik's was just what Jason needed. He was tired. He could sleep in, go for some long trail runs, and just hangout and visit while I played with *my* cousins. Well, that's what they called themselves, anyhow. I was quite enjoying these human terms of endearment.

The cousins were all young like me, and the idea of having a dog in the house was a novelty. Not surprisingly, I was the centre of attention. There were lots of walks, pets, and scratches to be had, and even a backyard bath before we made our way home again.

Jason's time with Wendy and Erik had been good for him. I could tell he admired his older sister. She and Erik had a good life together with their three children. They lived in a small home in a nice neighbourhood. They were both teachers and active coaches.

It was a life that Jason knew all too well growing up in his family home. Wendy had obviously appreciated something about their dad's example. For his entire professional life, he had worked hard as a teacher, a coach, and a housemaster at a boarding school. During the summer months, he enjoyed spending time with Jason and his siblings. Late one night, I heard them talking. Jason said that lifestyle, although not on his radar for the moment, was something he could imagine building for himself one day.

Once home in Vancouver, Jason resumed his classes at UBC. We'd get up early, head out for a run, and then he'd bike up to the campus without me. I had outgrown Jason's backpack by that stage, and he knew there was no way he'd be allowed to bring me to class. So I'd stay home with Pat or Trev, or sometimes by myself. It was easy by now. And, with the early run, I looked forward to napping away the rest of the morning after Jason left for school.

Camping season was back as well. We wasted little time heading off to some new sites over on the Island. Jason loved exploring over there. The campsites were smaller and generally less busy than on the mainland. He wasn't much for having neighbours. I think he also liked knowing that we had little to no chance of ever running into a grizzly if we stuck to the Island. I was okay with that too.

Mid-July brought a trip Jason had planned when he thought I would've been gone to Ottawa to complete my training. He had applied for and was chosen to be a counsellor on a tall ship sailing from San Francisco to Hawaii. Confined to a boat for ten days with nowhere to run didn't sound like much fun to me. And, with no sailing experience either, seemed strange too. But Jason seemed keen, nonetheless. He was going to be in charge of running the physical fitness program for the teenage campers aboard. Rough seas and exercise? No thanks. But, for Jason, the tougher, the better. It seemed at every turn he was constantly looking for ways to challenge himself, or prove himself.

When the day came to leave for the airport, with a small suitcase in tow, he kissed me on the ear, scratched my chin, and was off. On the way out the door he reminded me to listen to Pat and Trev and mind my manners. Whatever that meant.

they called it a miracle

The first few days were okay; Pat and Trev did their best to keep me occupied and distracted. But each day without Jason became more of a challenge. I was even finding it hard to sleep! After spending every moment of every day together for more than a year, it was really strange to be suddenly apart. The day he left, he had told me that he wouldn't be gone too long. But I was beginning to wonder what "too long" even meant.

One beautiful Saturday afternoon in July, the birds were active and loud outside our wide-open bedroom window. The breeze coming through the house was warm but relieving. While Pat studied in his room, I passed the time in our bedroom on the cool wooden floor, trying to nap.

"Ike! You up there? I've got someone here you might want to see," yelled Trev from the backyard.

What now? I raised my head, got up, and stretched before slowly walking out onto the deck. Trev encouraged me to join him in the backyard. "Come on down, Ike. I've got someone here who wants to see you!"

Jason stepped into view from behind the house.

"Ike—it's me...."

I flew down the stairs. Jason knelt on the grass and braced himself for my impact. I launched myself at him. I twisted and contorted with joy like an oversized water balloon before collapsing to the ground beside him. Not nearly finished with my welcome, I rebounded onto his chest with my front legs braced against him while I reached forward to lick his face. With his mouth firmly closed, he turned his cheek to provide a target for my lapping tongue. When his face was sufficiently covered in licks, I dropped to my back and welcomed Jason's belly rubs. My coos and cries showed my obvious pleasure in reuniting with him.

"Hey, you—so good to be home, Ike. I missed you all day, every day!"

The following morning we got up early and took off for a short run. It was so good to have Jason beside me again. Despite enjoying my outings with Pat and Trev, especially when Pat felt like racing, I missed listening to Jason talk as we wound our way along our favourite trails. He was forever conversing—with me, the trees, the birds—whoever was there to listen. I had missed that.

But on our first run, he was quiet. There was the odd, "Good to be running with you, again, Ike. I sure missed this!" But, otherwise, silence. Something was on his mind.

After a quick breakfast, Jason showered and shaved, put on some dress pants, a shirt, a tie, and a blue blazer. An outfit I had never seen before. He looked so different. No t-shirt. No khaki shorts. No Birkenstocks. And no baseball cap.

"Whoa—look at you, fancy boy," said an equally surprised Trev as Jason walked into the kitchen. "Where the hell are you goin' looking so formal?"

Pat came out of his room to see what the fuss was about. "Man, I'm surprised you remembered how to tie that thing," he joked. "Lookin' mighty fine, Jase!"

"Yup—still got it. When you start wearing ties for school at twelve, it stays with you." Finally, Jason grabbed some very shiny burgundy shoes. "I'm off to church."

"What? Something happen on the sailboat you want to tell us about?" asked Trev jokingly. "Did you meet God up in the crow's nest?"

"Funny you should say that," answered Jason as he gently slid his heel into his shoe. "It's kind of a long story—I'll tell you when I get back."

"You okay?" asked Trev, stepping a little closer to Jason.

"I don't know. Something did happen on that boat, and I can't stop thinking about it. I haven't been to chapel in years, but I thought about going on our run this morning."

"What about Ike?" asked Pat.

"You know that old chapel in Kerrisdale?" Pat and Trev nodded. "I drove by there a while ago and noticed a sign out front that said, 'All of God's creatures welcome.' So either they're desperate to grow their congregation, or they've got a cool Padre. Either way, I'm going to take him." Jason grabbed his car keys. "We can chat when I get back."

"Here, give me a hug," insisted Trev, as he stepped in to grab hold of Jason. "You say a prayer for both Pat and me while you're there—got it?"

Pat cringed. "Yikes, don't do that, Jase—the roof will fall in!"

As we approached the chapel, the "Padre," a grey-haired gentleman with a warm smile, welcomed Jason with an exuberant handshake and me with a gentle pat on my head.

"Lovely of you two to join us," he said. "My name is Phil."

"I'm Jason and this is Ike."

"Nice to meet you, both," he said, beaming with genuine excitement. "And you'll notice there are some other dogs here today, Ike," he added, bending down to address me directly before gesturing with his hand to enter the chapel.

We stepped into the back pew. "Just like high school, Ike—my favourite spot." Jason whispered.

The organist played softly while the latecomers filed in. The old wooden floors were worn and dusty. I could see some other tails sticking out from under the pews ahead of us as I looked around to get a better sense of the place. The windows were detailed in brightly-coloured glass. And there were white sculptures of various humans adorning the walls at the front. The breeze coming in from the large main doors behind us was cool and soothing. I was tired from the run and soon found myself nodding off.

Periodically, I'd stir as Jason stood to join in the singing. But, for the most part, as soon as Phil began to speak, I was out cold again.

I felt Jason put his hand on my hind leg. I lifted my head to see what was up. "I think we're almost done, bud."

"Before we end this beautiful Sunday morning, I want to try something different," announced Phil. "I want to open the space up to you, the congregation. I've been speaking long enough today. Now I'm curious if any of you have something you'd like to share? Is there anything on your mind? Anything at all?" He peered out at the group. "And it doesn't even have to do with my sermon." He paused before asking again, "Anyone? Anything?"

Jason squirmed. I looked up at him. He looked as if he was considering the invitation. For a guy that found simply speaking in class challenging, I would've thought he'd be slinking down in his seat to avoid Phil's gaze. Instead, he slowly raised his hand.

"Jason, is that correct?" asked Phil as he moved closer.

"Yes, it's Jason."

"Did you have something that you wanted to share with us?"

"I'm not sure. Actually, if I'm honest, I'm not even sure why I came here today. Until, perhaps, you asked that question." One by one, the congregation began turning around in their pews. "I've had something on my mind for the last week, and I don't know what to make of it."

Phil gestured for Jason to stand. "We're all here for you. When you're ready, if you'd like to share what's concerning you."

Jason slowly got up and moved to the centre of the aisle. I sat up.

"I'm not exactly clear on where to start, so I'll just share the whole story, if that's okay?"

Phil smiled and nodded.

Jason took a deep breath, looked over at me and then began to speak. "I just got back from this sailing trip. I was a counsellor on a tall ship that sailed from San Fransisco to Hawaii and back to Victoria. About 20 teenagers onboard—the average age was probably 17 or 18. I think most of the kids were from Quebec."

"Despite a lot of sea-sickness, myself included, we eventually made it to Hawaii. You know, it's funny, there's this saying with sea-sickness that only those who have experienced it can appreciate. It goes, 'At first you're afraid that you're going to die, and then you're afraid you're not going to.' I understand that now!" There was some soft laughter from the group. It seemed to relax Jason. "After a few days in Hawaii, we began our return trip. It took a little more than a week to get there and we were expecting the same coming home. We were about three days out from Victoria—I think a few hundred miles off the coast of Oregon, give or take. It was a normal afternoon. The kids were doing different activities. I was in charge of running the fitness program onboard—easier said than done on a sailboat, believe me!" The laughter was louder this time. Jason was slowly finding his voice. "I had been on watch with my roommate from midnight to three in the morning the night before. We were having a mid-afternoon nap down below deck in our bunks."

"About 30 minutes into our sleep, we were both awakened by a loud thud. A noise neither one of us had ever heard before. As we looked at one another, wondering what the heck had just happened, a young camper came barging into our cabin. He yelled that Sara, one of the campers, had fallen from the crow's nest." The congregation turned further around in their seats as their engagement heightened.

"We ran up the stairs and out onto the deck. One of the young girls had fallen roughly 80 feet and landed on the ship's steel deck. I won't go into the details, but she was in rough shape. Broken bones and bruises in numerous places—but she was conscious. She was aware of what had just happened, and more strangely, it seemed, aware of the question on everyone's minds—'How on earth are you still alive?'"

Jason paused for a moment while he gathered his thoughts. He looked at me once again before adjusting his glasses. "Like I said, we were days from shore and any sort of hospital or proper care. The only thing to do was put out a Mayday call, which our captain did immediately. Within minutes, several ocean liners had answered the call and were steaming toward us. We were relieved and partially hopeful. In the meantime, our nurse did everything she could to keep Sara comfortable.

"But then, about ten minutes later, we got a call from the USS Abraham Lincoln. It's an American aircraft carrier. It was somewhere off the Pacific West Coast involved in military manoeuvres and training. We were told they would answer the Mayday and instructed all other ships to stand down. The tone immediately changed on our ship. Now there was real hope. I mean, say what you will about the US military, but on this day, their Navy was coming to rescue a young Canadian girl." Jason paused as he began to choke up. He took a moment to gather himself.

"About 15 minutes passed before we heard this roar getting louder from a distance. It was foggy, so it was hard to see what was coming. Then, a huge jet fighter flew overhead—maybe a few hundred feet above us. It was deafening. Everyone on deck was abuzz with excitement. Sara was still conscious and doing her best to remain calm, but even she seemed more hopeful. The jet circles back overhead and disappears from the direction in which it came. Then, another 15 minutes goes by, and we can hear a helicopter approaching. Sure enough, out of the fog emerges this Navy helicopter. It hovers off the port side for a moment. Then this Navy Seal jumps out of the side door and into the sea. I can't believe what I'm seeing—it's right out of a movie. Then, without taking a look, this guy comes to the surface, already swimming, and arrives at our portside ladder as calm as if he's back from a dip in the pool."

"He steps onto the deck, smiles at everyone, and introduces himself to another counsellor and me. With the introductions complete, he calmly asks to see Sara. While he's attending to her, the helicopter gets into place over the stern of the ship so that it can hoist her aboard. Within moments, Sara is being reeled up to safety. Then the Navy Seal shakes our hands, wishes us good luck, and leaps back into the water. Seconds later, he's dangling in the air, being pulled aboard the helicopter. With all of us now leaning against the portside railing watching in complete awe, the helicopter tilts forward as our Navy Seal sticks his head out of the side door and gives a salute. Everyone erupts in cheers as the helicopter speeds out of sight. The campers are going crazy. People are crying. It's nuts. And it wasn't just what he did that everyone cheered for. It was who he was—how he showed up. I swear the guy should've been wearing a cape. He was so confident, and calm… So caring."

The congregation was spellbound. Phil appeared to be in shock. No one moved. "Later that night, during my watch, I came through the classroom and saw something written on the chalkboard. A student was there, reading a comic book. I asked him if he knew what it meant. He told me it was Hebrew—'Today we witnessed a miracle.'"

Jason looked at me and then back at the congregation. "So I guess that's why I've come here today. I'm trying to make sense of why this young girl is still alive. We got word that she was flown from the Abraham Lincoln to the Portland Trauma Center, where she received life-saving care. She's going to need some rehab, obviously, but she'll be okay. She's going to walk again and lead a relatively normal life."

The congregation began looking at one another in absolute disbelief. There was a low murmur until the entire group began to applaud and cheer. Jason adjusted his glasses one more time before finishing his story.

"I know it sounds like a James Bond movie, but it happened just as I described it. And now I'm left trying to make sense of it. What's in store for that young girl? Why was she saved? And who...who saved her? Was it... Was it God? Was it sheer luck? Even the US Navy—did they just happen to be there?"

Phil joined us walking to the car. "Jason, I want to thank you for coming here today and sharing your story. I can't tell you how profound that was for everyone in our congregation, including me." At the car, Jason turned and faced Phil.

"I like to believe it's not just about God," Phil said. "It doesn't matter who it is. It could be Buddha, Allah, or some guy named Steve." Jason laughed and then reached down to scratch my head. "For me, it's simply about faith—faith in a higher order of things. That's what gives me comfort and allows me, as you said, the ability to make sense of things that seem nonsensical. People don't normally fall 80 feet and live to tell about it, correct?" Jason nodded. "I take comfort in knowing that sometimes events happen that don't become clear as to their purpose for years to come. When we can trust there is a purpose—a higher purpose—we don't get as rattled as we might otherwise." He paused and smiled at me. "You take good care of yourself and that beautiful dog of yours, Jason. And come back anytime—you tell a good story."

Arriving home, we could see Pat and Trev sitting at the picnic table. Before we got out of the car, Jason reached back and rolled my left ear through his fingers. "You were going to be a guide dog. That was your purpose. Now you're not. Now you're just my dog."

Jason stared into my eyes. I had never seen him so serious. "Life was so much easier when I was rowing, Ike. My days were planned. My goal was clear. Now I feel lost." He took a deep breath. "Come on, bud—let's go get some lunch."

robyn

For the next few days, I was glued to Jason's side. Whether he was doing laundry, making a meal with the boys, or having an afternoon nap trying to catch up on his sleep, I was with him. It was comforting to have him home again. I had genuinely missed him.

Laying at his feet on the cool grass under the old wooden picnic table and listening to the three of them banter back and forth during dinner was music to my ears. I loved this time of day.

"Jase, did you hear the message on the answering machine from Fiona?" asked Pat. "Something about you meeting a woman for a date over in Victoria?"

"Who's Fiona?" asked Trev. "And why is she setting you up with women in Victoria?"

Jason wiped his mouth with his napkin. "She's a massage therapist that Pat and I know. She travelled with the Canadian team in Europe. We've stayed in touch and become good friends. When I was living in Victoria, she was forever setting me up with every eligible woman in the city."

"How do I find a friend like Fiona?" Trev elbowed Jason in the side.

"Help yourself. So far, none of them have amounted to much—all dead ends."

"Are you going to call her back?" asked Trev.

"There's someone she wants me to come over and meet tomorrow. I said I'd think about it."

"Think about it? Think about what? Jase, when was the last time you went on a date?"

"It's been a while."

"How about more than a year," said Trev. "Maybe two!"

"I've been busy. School. Ike. And other stuff. I'm too busy," said Jason, dismissing the idea.

"You're too picky," insisted Trev. "You're looking for the perfect woman—someone to marry right out of the gate."

"What's wrong with that?" Jason shrugged as the kitchen phone began to ring. "I'm tired of dating; it just ends up being a waste of time. Besides, I'm beginning to think what I'm looking for isn't out there."

Pat ran up the stairs to answer the phone.

"Jason—it's Karyn," yelled Pat through the kitchen window. Jason had met Karyn a few years before. They had discovered a mutual love of running and began training for marathons. Running together mile after mile, they became good friends.

Jason looked up at Pat. "What does she want?"

"She wants to know if you're interested in going to Victoria with her tomorrow?"

I wasn't sure where Victoria was, but apparently we were heading there soon!

Early the next day, Jason and I picked Karyn up at her apartment and headed straight for the ferry. As we waited in the terminal, Karyn turned in her seat and smiled at Jason. "So Pat tells me you have a date in Victoria today?"

Jason tilted his head forward. "Bastard. Really? He told you?"

"Why didn't you tell me? Did you really think you could go on a date and keep it from me?" She laughed out loud.

"I don't know. I'm so tired of this game."

"You haven't even been in the *game* for, what… two years?

"I've been too busy!"

"You're not too busy! You're too scared."

"Geezuz Murphy! Trev says I'm too picky. You say I'm too scared." Jason shook his head and looked out the window.

"It doesn't have to be work, bucko. You could just have some fun. You know, with another person?" Karyn sat quietly.

"If you're waiting for me to say something, I've got nothin' to offer."

Jason continued staring out the window. I had heard this tone many times before. It meant he was up in his head, *thinking*!

"What are you afraid of, Jase?"

Jason turned to face Karyn. "Honestly—you want to hear?"

"I wouldn't have asked otherwise."

Jason took a deep breath and slowly exhaled. "I'm looking for a person that doesn't exist. And I want things just so. I mean, ask Ike—man, he'll tell ya! And I get so pissed off when things don't go the way I expect or want. Since retiring from rowing, I get so angry at...stupid things. I am afraid. I'm afraid of finding out that the person I'm looking for isn't to be found—anywhere!"

"Let's play a game." Karyn reached into her backpack and pulled out a pen and notebook. "Best-case—worst-case. Tell me, what would make this person a best-case scenario date?"

"That's a stupid game."

"Don't be such a loser. Answer the question, lover boy!" Karyn raised her notebook and readied her pen.

"I'm not playing."

"Here. I'll start for you, grumpy pants. One—she'd be hot. Two—she'd be an athlete. Three—she'd like running."

Jason turned and looked at her. Then, reluctantly, added to the list, "She'd like running with dogs. Golden retrievers, obviously."

"Okay, that's four—she'd like dogs. What's five?"

"Five—she'd be funny. Have a good sense of humour."

"See—it's easy! Keep going..."

"Six—she'd be smart. But not too smart."

Karyn scrunched up her face. "Umm, what was it that Trev said about being too picky?"

"What? I don't want to date some nerd."

Karyn shook her head as she added it to the list.

"Seven—would want to have children. Maybe lots of children. Eight—comes from a small town and a big family. Nine—confident. She'd be strong and not put up with my bullshit."

"Yikes, she'd have to be more than strong—crazy comes to mind! Okay, any more?"

"Ahhh, ten—she'd be ambitious. Have big goals that she's trying to achieve."

"Nice—I like that one," added Karyn as she looked over the list. "Is that it?"

Jason looked at her sheepishly. "Maybe one more."

"Okay—shoot. What is it?"

"Umm, sex—she has to like sex," said Jason.

"What?"

"Sex—I'm looking for someone..."

"I heard what you said, you donkey. I was asking *what* because I can't believe you said that! You're such a guy!"

"You asked!"

"I'm not adding such piggery to the list! Besides, you're not going to find that one out on the first date, anyway!"

"How do you know?" Jason's mischievous smirk grew across his face.

Karyn shoved him. "That's it—I'm going to join you on the date and tell her what you said!"

"Okay, okay—take it easy! You can scratch that one off."

Karyn shook her head again. "I can't believe how pathetic men can be." Then she flipped to a new page. "Okay, worst-case scenario?"

"What?"

"Tell me, what would make this a worst-case scenario date?"

"Easy—the exact opposite of every one of those ten points. Which is a combination of every other woman that Fiona has set me up with!"

After a beautiful ferry ride to the Island and a relatively short drive, we arrived at the university. Karyn got out of the car, turned around, and leaned in through the passenger window.

"I thought of one more item for the list," Jason said.

"Oh—okay, what?" asked Karyn.

"Her mom would be a librarian," replied Jason.

"What is wrong with you?" Karyn shook her head and looked at me in the back seat. "Ike, do we even dare ask why that would be important?

"My mom was a librarian—and she's an awesome mom! So maybe that would make her an awesome mom as well."

"Sometimes you say the strangest, loveliest things. I don't know any guy like you!"

Jason turned and looked at me, not knowing what to do with that sideways compliment from Karyn.

"Okay. I'll be done my meeting around 4:30—maybe 5:00. I'll meet you back here," added Karyn.

"Sounds good. Have a good meeting, Karyn. And wish me luck!"

"You don't need luck. She'll either knock it out of the park, or she won't—no big deal. Be open to her being exactly what you're looking for, Jason. What's her name, anyway?"

"Robyn."

"Nice. Take care of him, Ike. Make sure he behaves!"

The beach where we were meeting this woman—Robyn—was down a long hill a few minutes from the campus. It was called Cadboro Bay. And—no surprise—it was beautiful! It was a long gentle u-shaped beach lined with spectacular homes. The soft sand was intermixed with small pebbles and massive logs that had washed ashore during winter storms. And there were plenty of humans leaning against the logs. Lots of family picnics with sun worshippers, swimmers, and castle builders, as well as sailors and windsurfers. All enjoying another perfect summer day on the coast.

Jason's date wasn't due to show up for another 30 minutes or so. Instead of waiting in the car, he grabbed my leash and we began to explore the park. First thing's first—I went looking for a throwing stick.

I caught up to Jason as he was getting close to the water. I ran by him, ensuring that I whacked him in the back of his leg with my new stick.

"Hey, Mr. Subtle."

I dropped the stick on the hot sand.

"If you're going to get wet, you have to promise me you won't jump up on Robyn."

I dashed for the edge of the water, spun around, and waited for Jason while the waves lapped at my feet. He launched the stick far offshore. I was off, dashing through the waves with powerful leaping bounds until I had to swim. I was full-grown at this point. I remember my strength being so impressive. I loved feeling all that youthful energy pulsing through my body—I felt so alive.

I wasn't overly excited to meet this Robyn human. I figured Jason and I got along just fine without a significant female human in his life. Why did we need one now? It would likely mean more time away from me. I was hoping this was another one of Fiona's dead ends.

"Come on, bud—we're supposed to meet her over by the swings."

Reluctantly, I came out of the water and caught up to Jason as he made his way through the maze of families picnicking on the beach. The smell of food everywhere—it was hard to ignore.

"Don't get any ideas, Ike!"

Jason looked around. "She's late." He glanced at his watch again. "Maybe she'll be a no-show and we just enjoy the beach on our own."

Just then, I saw a female human with bouncy red hair coming toward us. She was slender, not too tall, and had legs that looked like they belonged to a greyhound. I had never seen legs like that on a human.

"You must be Jason," she said as she came up behind him. "Fiona said you'd have a beautiful golden retriever with you."

Score: one point for the human lady!

Jason spun around. "Yes, hi, I'm Jason—you must be Robyn?"

Jason reached out to meet her tiny hand. As he closed his around hers and began to squeeze, an audible popping sound appeared to come from her wrist.

And, another point—she didn't grimace or draw attention to Jason's overzealous introduction.

"So do you live in Victoria?"

"Well, this is where I train. So it's home for now."

"Train? What are you training for?"

"Oh, sorry, I thought Fiona might have said something. I'm a middle-distance runner."

"As in, national team runner?"

"Yes."

"Get outta here, really? Fiona didn't say a thing about that. How long have you been running?"

"I came out to UVic about nine years ago and began training with the group. I've been here ever since."

"Wait, you were at UVic in 1985? I was here in '85!"

"Yes, I moved out from Nova Scotia. I grew up in a small town across from Cape Breton."

Jason was spellbound. I could smell the excitement coming from his pores. He was intrigued by this human. Question after question, Robyn ticked all the boxes that he and Karyn had determined earlier would make this a best-case scenario date. She was even born number seven of nine littermates—one more than me! I don't know if that meant she wanted children of her own, but it was highly possible. Even the librarian box got ticked—it was uncanny.

Robyn seemed intelligent and funny and she was clearly a runner. As for ambition, she was training for the 1996 Olympics in Atlanta—it would be her second time going.

Jason was about discover her strength of character. After three hours of walking back and forth multiple times along the beach, Jason finally began to ask some questions about Robyn's running career. He discovered that she'd be competing in the upcoming 1994 Commonwealth Games that Victoria was hosting over the next couple of weeks. Robyn was entered in the women's 3000 metre and 1500 metre events.

"I'm not sure how to ask this," began Jason. "You seem ridiculously humble, so I'll just ask you straight up...are you a good runner? I mean, are you going to win your event next week?"

"I don't know; do I have to win to be considered a good runner?"

Oh boy—take cover, Robyn!

I don't think Jason knew exactly what to say to that. But if he was being honest he would've yelled, "YES, of course, you do!"

Robyn talked about how she had struggled with a compromised immune system throughout her winter and spring training, which had restricted her ability to garner her usual peak level of performance so far that season. She told Jason she wasn't feeling very fit and not all that prepared. However, she was still keen on getting out on the track and doing her best.

"Why even bother if you don't think you can win?" Jason was taken aback by Robyn's approach.

"How will I know where I am with my training if I don't get out on the track and test it?"

"Can't you do that in practice? I mean, if things go sideways, it could be embarrassing."

"I don't see it that way. Whether I win or lose, I want to enjoy the feeling of running fast on the track. I want to see what I can do with my competitors there to challenge me."

Jason didn't know what to make of this young runner who clearly didn't see competition the way he did. Sitting in the car or running beside him on the trails, I had heard his rants. I knew how critical—how harsh—he could be. I could only imagine the inner dialogue racing through his mind while he listened to Robyn confront his life-long narrative.

"Robyn, no offence, but in all my years of rowing, I've been around a few track athletes. And, I can guarantee you, none of them—none—would agree to race if they weren't ready."

"What's the worst thing that can happen? I lose? I come last? I don't finish the race?"

"Umm, okay, ya—all of those would qualify as worst things in my book. Wouldn't that be humiliating? I mean, in front of all of those people? And your parents!"

"If any of those things happen, I'll learn from it and move on. After the race, I'll likely go out for dinner with my mom and dad. They'll still love me." She laughed. "Jason, you sound more worried than I am!"

Robyn might have ticked all the boxes, and she might have even been a fast runner, but she couldn't throw a stick to save her life. Twice, it barely made it to the water's edge. And her aim needed some work too. She almost took off Jason's head with one toss that went astray.

I couldn't believe Jason and Robyn had been talking the entire time. Their easy conversation about all kinds of issues reminded me of how Jason would talk with Pat and Trev sometimes—minus the swearing, of course.

We stood beside Jason's car to say goodbye.

"Well, that was a nice way to spend a few hours, Robyn. Thanks for the walk and the chat."

"I enjoyed meeting you both." Robyn looked over at me. "Thanks for letting me throw the stick, Ike. I promise to be better next time."

"Can I give you a ride somewhere?"

"No, it's okay. I'm just staying up at the university in the dorms. It's not far."

"We're actually heading that way. I'm meeting a friend there in about ten minutes."

"Great—thanks. I'm just going to use the washroom. I won't be a second."

"Perfect. I'll just get Ike settled into the car."

Get Ike settled into the car?

Jason was nervous—and smitten. He opened the door and patted the seat. "Come on, bud—up here." I jumped up and spun around before plopping myself down on the seat. "I don't want to get too far ahead of myself, but I think you just met your mom?"

No, not too far ahead at all! Seriously, did you just say that? Besides, I didn't need a mom—I already had one. I couldn't believe Jason had said that. How could he know so fast? *A three-and-a-half-hour walk and you've just met your future wife? Come on, Jason, grab hold of yourself.*

We pulled up to the residences and Robyn got out of the car. Just before she closed the door, Jason asked, "Is it too late to get a ticket?"

Robyn looked at him sideways, unclear what he was asking. "For your race?"

"Just call UVic, I guess? The race is here at the new Commonwealth Stadium."

"Okay. I will. I mean, if you're okay with that? I don't want to be a distraction."

"Why would you be a distraction? If you want to come to the race, that's fine with me."

"Great. Thanks. See you, Robyn—and good luck."

As we pulled away, Jason looked for me in the rearview mirror. I knew exactly what was coming next. "A distraction—what a stupid-ass thing to say!"

Knew it.

Karyn was sitting out front as we pulled up to the building. Jason reached over and opened the door. "So was she hot?"

"Nope."

Karyn looked at Jason strangely. He smiled. "She was better than hot; she was beautiful."

"Aww, Jason, you've just redeemed yourself."

Jason smiled at Karyn as he put the car in gear and drove off. They found some takeout and another beach closer to downtown. Sitting on a bench facing the water, they laughed and joked about the list while I ate my kibble.

It had been a fun day. Jason had enjoyed spending the afternoon with Robyn—that much was clear. However, given her throwing arm, she had a long way to go before she'd get my stamp of approval. But, for now, if Jason was happy, then so was I.

the race

Jason was different after the date. I had never seen him so relaxed—playful, even. It was strange to see him laughing and joking with Trev and Pat far more than usual. I wouldn't have guessed that meeting a female human could change a male human's demeanour so dramatically.

Jason called and purchased a ticket to Robyn's race. That surprised me. I figured he'd have no interest in watching someone run around a track with no intention of winning.

That told me that there was something about this "beautiful redhead," as he'd described her to Pat and Trev, that intrigued him beyond just her good looks and muscular legs. There were plenty of attractive women at Emily Carr. And we passed lots of women running on the trails. Perhaps it was her confident demeanour? Or her aspirations of going to the Olympics for a second time? I wasn't sure. Maybe he was simply curious to see for himself how her supposed race strategy would play out?

"She's going to get killed. It's the Commonwealth Games, for goodness' sake. We're talkin' some of the best runners on the planet—from

Great Britain, Australia, New Zealand, Kenya—not to mention some of her teammates. I mean, who would line up against those runners knowing they weren't prepared?" Jason shook his head as he described what he found so confusing about Robyn's decision to enter the race. "Pat, you know there's no way in hell we'd agree to race against crews of that calibre if we weren't ready. No way!"

Pat, nodding his head, replied, "True. But maybe she just wants to see where she stands with her training at this point. Maybe she knows the season's likely a write-off. So she's got nothing to lose?"

Trev put down his fork and chimed in. "Did you ever consider that she doesn't buy into the same competitive beliefs you do? Maybe, just maybe," he added for emphasis, "she's racing this weekend because she loves running?"

"We're not talking about some high school track meet here, buddy—this is the world stage!" Jason wasn't buying what Pat and Trev were selling. "I sure as hell wouldn't risk the embarrassment. Not to mention what her sponsors might think!"

"I guess you'll find out tomorrow," said Trev, as he cracked open another can of beer. Then he looked down at me on the grass below the picnic table. "Cheers Ike—here's to Robyn kickin' some ass tomorrow!"

Jason dropped me off with Fiona. From the moment he left until he got back from the race, we were busy. We went to the beach and, unlike Robyn, Fiona had an arm! We spent a few hours with me charging in and out of the waves. It was my idea of a perfect date!

Then she took me to a dog bakery—yup, a place that actually made dog treats. The best dog cookies I'd ever tasted. And, finally, we went back to her home where she massaged some fancy dog lotion into my paws—couldn't believe it!

When Jason finally got back from Robyn's race, I was crashed in the backyard.

"Yikes, what'd you do to him, Fiona?"

"A little of this and a little of that—we had a great time! He's such a wonderful dog, Jason. You're so lucky to have him. I would love to have a dog like Ike." Fiona rubbed my belly.

"Well, he's sure whacked, whatever you did."

"Now tell me about Robyn's race—how'd she do?"

Jason grabbed a lawn chair and placed it down in front of Fiona. Then he sat down and stared at her with a funny smile, obviously searching for the best way to answer the question.

"What? What's so funny? What happened at the race?"

"Well, that's a great question. In fact, I'm still trying to understand what exactly *did* happen at that race!"

"What do you mean? Is Robyn okay? She didn't win, did she?"

"No, she didn't win—but she came close."

"Really? Robyn won a silver medal?"

"Well, I wouldn't consider it winning a silver medal—she had to lose to come second, right?"

"Oh, for goodness' sake, Jason—you and your rowing talk." Fiona waved her hands back and forth in front of her as if trying to swat his words out of the air. "Did she really come second?"

Jason paused to rearrange his long limbs in the lawn chair. "I still can't believe what I witnessed; she was tied for last for the opening laps."

"Oh, my."

"To be honest, I was hoping she'd just step off the track and DQ. But she just kept running."

"So how did she go from last to second?" asked Fiona.

"That's the part I'm really having trouble understanding." Jason paused and smiled again. "It was like nothing I've ever seen. Five laps into the race, about halfway, she was way back from the lead group in the second pack. She was so far out of contention—not even close to the front runners, I was embarrassed for her. But then, after another lap or so, she passed someone. I thought, okay—a bit late, but at least she appeared to be trying to race."

"So then what happened?"

"That's when she took off. Fiona, if I hadn't seen it, I swear, I wouldn't have believed it. She just started passing runners like they were standing still. Eventually, she made up the ground between the two groups and was right there with the lead runners. With two laps to go, she was fourth. Angela, her teammate, was leading. The crowd was going nuts! Robyn moved again and now she's third. Bronze and gold for Canada if she can just hang on. But she doesn't stop there." Fiona was spellbound. She raised her hands to her mouth as Jason continued.

"Finally, with less than a lap to go, Robyn passes the second-place runner and takes off down the home stretch to finish behind Angela. It was crazy! The people in the stands were screaming and cheering—it was mayhem!"

Wow—so that explains her legs!

"Oh, my goodness—yay, for Robyn—that's so exciting!"

"I got choked up! And it wasn't just me. Others around me were caught up in the moment as well. There was just so much excitement in the stadium."

"Well, I'm so happy that you were there to see it. Did Robyn see you?"

"I don't think so. But her victory lap with Angela was something else—every sports writer's dream, I'm sure! People were on their feet, cheering while Canadian flags waved back and forth everywhere—right out of a movie. I'm not sure where her parents were sitting, but they had to be proud. Fiona, it was the most incredible race I've ever seen. Honestly!"

"Wow, that's saying something coming from you—I've never heard you talk about any rowing races like this!"

Jason shrugged his shoulders. "Sure, gold would've been better—obviously. But it's remarkable she pulled that off."

"Did you make plans to see her this evening?"

"No, I figured she'd be with her folks."

"Would you like to go down to the inner harbour tonight? There's a free concert—the Crash Test Dummies."

"Sounds great—but, first, I need to close my eyes. Watching that race was exhausting!"

Fiona laughed before disappearing inside to make dinner while Jason crawled into the hammock. I got up and moved closer to him. He hung his arm over the side and rolled my ear through his fingers.

"Ike, this woman can run. You should've seen it—she's crazy fast. Maybe even faster than you, buddy!" He poked his head over the side of the hammock and smiled at me.

After dinner, I returned to the coolness of the backyard while Jason and Fiona left for the concert. I was fine with an evening on my own. Jason was right—I was whacked.

The next morning, I lay under the kitchen table and got caught up on the evening's activities while the two of them ate their breakfast. By the sounds of it, I missed quite a night!

Fiona took a bite of her toast, which was dripping with peanut butter and strawberry jam. It looked delicious. My mouth began watering.

"That was quite a moment when Robyn and Angela walked out onto the stage during the concert and were introduced by the band—it was a sign!" Fiona laughed. "You two are meant to be! Did you get to see Robyn after I left?"

"Well, I decided that one way or another, I was going to meet her backstage. But there was a security guy at the gate. He stopped me and asked what I was doing. I tried to play it cool—'I'm here to see

Robyn,' I told him." Fiona was smiling in anticipation as she waited for more details. "He got on his walkie-talkie and told someone backstage that there's a guy named Jason looking for some woman named Robyn. He told them I'm waiting for her."

Jason stopped there and took another sip of his tea. "Can I make some more toast?"

"No, you can't make more toast—not until you tell me what happened! Did Robyn come out to see you?"

"Ahhhh—sort of. But it took more than an hour. At which point, me and my new friend, the security guard, weren't sure if she was coming out to see me or just leaving."

Fiona scrunched up her face. "Well, at least she knows you're patient."

"Or a stalker! She came over to the gate. I said hello, she said hello. We were both standing on opposite sides of the fence and I couldn't help myself."

"What do you mean, 'you couldn't help yourself'—what on earth did you do, Jason?"

Jason shook his head and looked out the window. "She looked so beautiful. The street lights were sparkling in her eyes. Her hair was all shiny. Jason looked down at me. "Ugh, what was I thinking!"

"JASON—WHAT DID YOU DO?"

I couldn't believe what I was hearing. I had never seen him so flustered, especially over a female human. Finally, he looked up at Fiona and sheepishly answered. "I reached out and grabbed her hand."

"So why was that so bad? What did Robyn do?"

"Umm, she pulled her hand away—immediately."

Fiona scrunched her face again. "Ooooooo—not good!"

The security guard put his hand up to his mouth and spun around quickly, trying not to laugh out loud. Then he just walked away and left me there feeling like a big dumbass."

Fiona nodded, chewing her toast.

"I just kind of lost my mind there for a second. She's something else, Fiona, and, I don't know—I can't stop thinking about her. I've never met anyone like her. You finally did it with your blind dates—Robyn's a home run. No, she's a grand slam! I just don't know if she thinks I'm the Gordie Howe hat trick I think she is?"

Fiona put her tea down and reached forward with both hands to take hold of Jason's. "Well, first of all, I can assure you that Robyn wouldn't use sporting analogies to describe you!" Fiona shook her head and leaned in closer. "Jason, you have to appreciate that Robyn's different. She's not like other athletes. Or like other women, for that matter. And she's definitely not like the rowers you hang out with. She doesn't hate her competitors—goodness, she doesn't hate anyone! She doesn't think about killing the other runners when she's beside them in a race. There's no ego with Robyn—it's all soul. She runs because she loves running. In fact, I don't even think she cares if she wins. The medals mean nothing to her. She doesn't buy into all that macho garbage that I heard you and your teammates talk about when I travelled with your team in Europe."

Jason looked away.

"If you're going to date this woman, you have to learn to understand her world."

"You know what she did before the start of the race—she hugged some of her competitors. What is that about?"

"Jason, you didn't hear a word I said!"

"What? What didn't I hear?"

Fiona shook her head in frustration. "Listen to me—I've never worked on an athlete like Robyn. If I'm being honest, she's the most talented runner I've ever met—and she doesn't fit the traditional stereotype of an athlete. She's so much more than just her running. Yes, she loves it, but it's not who she is. She's a complex person, Jason. She doesn't date just anyone. You're going to have to be incredibly patient with her if you plan on being in her life."

I got up and walked over to Jason. He reached down and stroked my ears. He was rattled, I could tell. And for good reason—he could barely spell patience.

"And, one last thing. Are you listening?" Jason rolled his eyes. "Take it slowly. I understand you lost it for a moment, and you just wanted to hold Robyn's hand. It's quite sweet, actually. But that's not Robyn's style, and it's definitely not taking it slowly."

After breakfast, Fiona and Jason took me for another walk. They talked some more and laughed a lot. I had to hand it to him; at least Jason could find humour in his obvious blunder. And, if this Robyn human was going to be in our lives, he would require some serious coaching from Fiona. That much was clear to me. He was a capable guy with many talents, but dating wasn't one of them. I imagined some rough patches ahead.

Arriving home later that same day meant lying on the grass, listening to the replay of the date, for the boys. Only this time, it was a little more colourful, and, of course, although Jason mentioned that he reached out to hold Robyn's hand, he somehow forgot to mention that she had pulled hers away.

"I'm just happy you're back in the dating game," Trev said. "Robyn sounds like quite a catch."

"And an impressive runner! I would've loved to have seen that race for myself," added Pat.

"I thought I would invite her to the party on Friday. It's a long shot, but you never know?" Jason said.

Trev gave Jason an encouraging pat on the shoulder. "March up there right now, grab one of your invitations, call her, and read it to her. If you don't ask, you don't get—we'll wait here."

"You want me to call her right now?"

"Jason, the party's on Friday. It's Wednesday evening. At least give her two days' notice."

"Okay, okay." Jason slowly got up from the table and made his way to the kitchen, where the phone sat by the window.

"Trev, take it easy on him," smiled Pat. "He's a little gun-shy."

"That's what roommates are for," said Trev with a smile. "If someone doesn't give him a kick in the ass, he's gonna end up a monk!"

Moments later, we could hear the murmur of Jason speaking on the phone. Then, nothing.

Jason came down the stairs, walked over to the table and sat down.

"Well? What'd she say?" asked Trev.

"Nope. Can't make it."

"How come?" asked Trev.

"She's off to Europe to race."

"Wow," said Pat, surprised. "That was quick."

"Yup—given her results the other day, her agent wants her to run some races overseas and see how things shake down."

"Good for her," said Pat. "Sounds like she's turned her season around."

"Apparently so," confirmed Jason. "Then she's off to India for some fancy track meet. And I think she said something about the New York City Mile?"

"You sound disappointed," said Trev.

"No, I'm happy for her. I am," answered Jason. "It's just a reminder of what it was like when we rowed. There was something big to shoot for—a purpose. I miss that." Jason leaned back and reached under the table until he found one of my ears to rub. "Travelling overseas for big races is fun."

"Well, if nothing else, at least she knows you're interested," confirmed Trev as he landed a loud smack on Jason's back.

I could feel and smell how disappointed Jason was. The excitement I had sensed in him that week was gone.

The invitation Trev was referring to was something that Jason had made up a couple of weeks earlier and sent out to family and friends. It was a nod to the fact that he was turning 30 years old and his life wasn't anywhere close to what he had imagined it to be as a teenager. It referenced three goals that he had made for himself when he was 18.

Be married.

Have six children.

And be a millionaire.

The invitation finished off with a final self-deprecating comment: "Clearly, I have some work to do!"

From what I had gathered in my short time with Jason, his Olympic defeat had completely knocked him off-course, and then some. I still wasn't clear on the details, but it was obvious that he had no trouble reminding himself and others of his shortcomings. Sure, as a 30-year-old, he may well have been behind the standard life pace of his peers. But I didn't care about his list. When I was with him, we had fun together; that was enough. Besides, Jason with six little humans? I couldn't even imagine.

The party was a huge success. It was hard to believe our little home and equally tiny backyard could hold that many humans. Using the occasion to celebrate the end of summer and the beginning of another school year, Pat and Trev had also handed out invitations to their friends and classmates. Good thing, because Jason hadn't invited that many humans at all—not even one classmate. Based on my time with him, he had a small handful of humans he was close with, and he seemed content with that. His brother Paul had flown in from Toronto to represent the family. It was a pleasant surprise for everyone.

The bonus for me was the many half-eaten burgers left on tables and countertops. If I was quick, and I was, I could make off with someone's burger before they noticed. By the end of the night, I was stuffed and content.

Pat and Trev gave Jason a fancy new sleeping bag. The old one he had been using for our camping trips was far too short for him. But, given how expensive new sleeping bags were, he had just made do. When he opened the gift, the look on Jason's face was both shock and genuine appreciation. For all of the teasing and bravado that these three dished out to one another, it was clear there was a real bond and friendship between them.

We left for one of our usual spots on the Island two days later. It would be our last camping trip of the summer and the perfect opportunity to try out Jason's new sleeping bag.

slow learner

After the first week of school, Jason called Fiona to see if she had heard anything about Robyn's racing overseas. She hadn't. All Fiona knew was that Robyn had just stopped in Nova Scotia to visit her mom and dad.

It was Sunday morning. Jason was cutting kiwis, bananas, apples, and oranges for the fruit salad he was preparing for brunch.

"Why don't you call her up?" Trev suggested.

"What am I going to say?"

"Wow," Pat said. "It has been a long time since you dated anyone!"

Trev walked over to Jason and put a hand on his shoulder. "You could start with, 'Hello, Robyn, how was your trip? Did you see some sights? How did your race go? How's the weather in Nova Scotia?' Holy crap, do you want me to make the call, myself?"

"Of course not. I know all that. What, do you two think I can't do this?"

Pat and Trev looked at each other and then back at Jason blankly.

"Here, give me the phone—I'll show ya!"

"Now that's more like it!" Trev gave Jason a high-five.

Jason used directory assistance to find Robyn's parents' number.

"Well, that was easy. Now the hard part."

"Just be confident. You two held hands, for goodness' sake. A phone call is nothin'!" Trev winked.

Jason paused before finally dialling the number. "Hello, is Robyn there?"

Trev and Pat leaned toward the phone.

"Yes, it's Jason. I'm a friend from the West Coast."

More silence as they waited to hear the reply.

"Yes, she had mentioned something about that race. Oh, and any chance I could get that number?" Jason looked at the boys. "Great. Great. Thank you very much." He quickly scribbled across a scrap piece of paper.

"Who was that?" asked Trev.

"Her mom. Robyn's at her sister's for dinner."

"So call her there."

"Hold onto your frickin' horses, Trev. I just want to get my head straight here."

"What was the part about the race?" asked Pat.

"She's on her way to New York this week for the New York City Mile."

"Wow, good for her—that's a great race," said Pat. "She must have done okay with her races overseas."

"Ask her if you can come down and watch her!" Trev said with a big smile.

"I'm not flying down there to watch her race. Don't be stupid."

"It's not stupid—it's brilliant, actually," said Trev defiantly. "Get a cheap flight. Stay with Pat's brother. Go watch the race. Cheer your head off for Robyn as she runs by. Go out for dinner and celebrate her victory. Boom! You're in, brother! This could go down in history as the most romantic second date ever." Trev turned and winked at Pat. "Oh, and you're welcome!" He smiled at Jason.

"It's actually not a bad idea," said Pat cautiously. "Although, it sort of reminds me of something you'd see in a movie, which probably means it won't end well." Pat shook his head before continuing. "If it works, it's something you'll tell your kids. If it doesn't, you may never see her again."

"See! Go big or go home, Jase. Make the call, buddy."

"Ugh—all I can hear is Fiona reminding me to 'be patient and take it slow.' This is neither of those."

Trev grimaced. "Just pick up the phone and call her. Imagine if she's blown away by this—you'll go down there and have an amazing time."

Jason looked over at me lying on the floor. "Ike, what do you think, bud? Should I call her?"

I don't think Jason wanted to hear my answer—I was in Fiona's camp.

After another moment of pondering his decision, Jason picked up the phone.

"That's the spirit, Jase—get in there and take control!" Trev was worked up at this point. Pat was quietly standing by to see how this played out.

"Put it on speaker, Jase—that way, we can coach you," suggested Trev with a whispering voice.

Once the phone started dialling, Jason hit the speakerphone button.

"Ooohh, it's ringing," said Trev enthusiastically. "Confidence, Jase. Just be confident."

"Hello?"

"Robyn?" asked Jason tentatively.

"No. This is Heather."

Jason scrunched up his face.

"May I speak with Robyn?"

"May I ask who's calling?"

Trev encouraged Jason to breathe with big flapping arm motions.

Jason nodded his head in agreement. "Um, it's Jason. I'm a friend of Robyn's from the West Coast."

Trev flashed the thumbs-up signal to Jason.

"Hello?"

"Robyn, hi—it's Jason."

There was a pause. The boys looked at each other, wondering if the line had gone dead.

"Jason who?"

Pat and Trev immediately flinched, as if a firecracker had gone off at their feet. Jason turned to both of them with a desperate look spreading across his face. Trev made a "keep-it-movin'" gesture with his hands. Pat stood quietly with his forehead resting on his thumb and index finger, waiting for this train to crash.

"Uhhh, it's Jason. Fiona's friend. We met for a walk with my dog Ike a couple of weeks ago?"

"Oh, that Jason—hello! I'm sorry. I just wasn't expecting a call from you while I was home."

Trev lunged and fanned his arms apart imitating a baseball umpire making a safe call.

Jason began to laugh and had to turn away from Trev. "Don't worry about it. Umm, is this an okay time?"

"Yes, yes it is. Is everything okay?"

"Everything's great. I just thought I'd give you a call and see how things went overseas."

Relieved that Jason had found his legs, Pat and Trev left him to finish the call. I, on the other hand, wasn't going anywhere. I wanted to know if Jason would be leaving me in a few days. As much as the boys were excited for him, I wasn't. Robyn continued to represent a distraction from me. It's not like I didn't want Jason to be happy—

I did. I just didn't look forward to having to share him with another human.

"Well, it sounds as if you really turned things around. Congratulations!"

"Thanks, I appreciate the call," answered Robyn graciously. "Now it's off to New York and the road mile race. I'm keen to see what I can offer on that course."

"About that race..." continued Jason. "Umm, I was thinking...how would you feel if I flew down there...to watch you race?"

Pat and Trev slowly crept into the kitchen to hear her answer. They waited. And waited. "Robyn, are you there?" Jason spun around and looked at the boys. They both shrugged their shoulders.

"I'm not sure that would be a good idea, Jason. I don't want to feel that I have to entertain you or somehow be responsible for you if you fly down. It's a distraction that I would prefer not to have. Does that make sense?"

"No, no, don't apologize. That makes perfect sense. I just thought I'd ask. And the last thing I would want is to be a distraction. I get that, Robyn," Jason sounded more confident. "If I were racing, I wouldn't want to have to entertain someone either. I should've thought of that."

"Listen, my sister is telling me that dinner's ready. So I have to go. But why don't you give me a call in a couple of weeks?"

"Sounds good. Safe travels and I hope everything goes well for you in New York."

Jason turned and looked at Pat and Trev. His face was expressionless. "You know what, I totally understand." Jason moved closer to the boys.

"At least she knows you're more than a little interested and it didn't scare her away," said Trev.

I was relieved. Jason wasn't going anywhere. Instead, he refocused on school and ensuring our weekends were packed with outdoor activities. Hikes in the local mountains, swims at Kits beach, and our favourite go-to trails in the Endowment Lands—always a win for me.

Following Robyn's lead, Jason called her up a few weeks later. Fiona had suggested that Jason come over for the weekend and make dinner for Robyn on Saturday night. Fiona would spend the evening with some girlfriends.

After some meal planning and a quick grocery shop, Jason was busy in the kitchen preparing some fancy meal intended to impress Robyn. Actually, he was a pretty good cook. I could smell fish with hints of orange and dill. And there was basmati rice cooking too. Always a favourite with the boys—I couldn't wait for the leftover scraps!

While Jason prepared dinner and Robyn set the table, the two of them caught up. It was fascinating to hear about Robyn's trip to these faraway places. Her description of Pune, India was incredibly detailed. The food sounded amazing. Sure, as a golden, I had a reputation for eating anything—including horse poop—but, given the choice, I'd be all over this Indian food.

When she described her World Cup race in London, England, I couldn't understand why so many humans sat side-by-side crammed into a stadium watching other humans run around in circles. Jason sure seemed intrigued. Mind you, Robyn could've been talking about the weather and he would've been hanging on her every word.

When Robyn asked how school was going for Jason, he quickly dismissed it. "Okay," he said. And that was it. No talk of his interesting instructors and no mention of the colourful characters he spent his days with—nothing. He seemed more focused on dinner and trying to figure out Robyn. There was no questioning Fiona's assessment—Robyn was intelligent, soft-spoken, and had world views that didn't align with Jason's. When she described a friend of hers who had dreadlocks, I thought Jason was going to drop the steaming pot of rice he was carrying to the kitchen table.

“I grew up eating a lot of fish, but this is fantastic! Not sure what you did, Jason, but it’s delicious!”

I’m hoping you save me some!

“Glad you like it.”

“I’ve heard the workload at Emily Carr can be heavy. How do you manage that?”

Jason quickly wiped his mouth with his napkin and took a drink of water. “I don’t. Well, I mean, I do just enough—that’s how I manage. Basically, I see my classmates busting their asses to get work in, and they have no lives, and they look like shit most of the time. I just refuse to do that.”

Robyn looked at Jason inquisitively, not fully understanding his response.

He continued. “Look, it’s not like I blow off my classes. But I also know how I get when I decide to go after something. And I don’t want to do that anymore. So I decided last year to keep my time with Ike a priority and not get too fussed about school. My marks were okay last year. Not the best. But I’m good with my decision.”

Robyn paused from eating her dinner.

“That’s interesting. When I told you, the first time we met, that I was going to simply go out and do my best in my Commonwealth Games final, you seemed surprised. Like you were disappointed that I wasn’t trying to win? And yet, with your school, you’re taking the same approach?”

Oops!

Jason kept eating. I couldn’t imagine the frantic rebuttal he was preparing inside his head. Robyn was the first human I knew of to ever challenge him.

“Are you comparing a world-class running race to my art school homework?”

Here it comes...

Robyn thought for a moment, and then just as she was about to answer, Jason continued.

"Cause if you are, they're not the same—at least not in my world." Jason sat up; his tone had changed. I knew this voice from driving in heavy traffic—it was never a good sign. "*Your* race was about trying to win a gold medal against the best in the world. My homework is about satisfying some graphic designer who can't find enough work and ends up teaching at an art school. I couldn't care less what my instructors think of my work."

Robyn got up from the table and went to get some more water. Jason looked down at me and reached for my left ear. He looked lost amidst the growing and awkward silence. I was hoping he would just stop—leave this topic alone and move on. But, like I had seen so many times before, he just couldn't help himself.

"Robyn, have you ever been boxed in during a race?"

" A few times."

"What have you done about it in the moment?"

"I've tried to manoeuvre myself as best I could to get out and move up on the outside."

"Has it always worked?

"No; sometimes, the pack is so dense, you literally can't move for long stretches of the race."

"Have you ever lost a race because of that?"

"There have been a few times where it's negatively impacted my performance—so, yes."

Jason took a drink of water before continuing. "If it were me, I would do whatever it took to get out of that box and make sure that it never happened again. A shove, a kick, a clothesline—anything to get free."

"Well, there are rules against that. You'd be disqualified," said Robyn calmly.

"Maybe—but it would be the last time I'd get boxed in."

"Can't say as I've ever considered that strategy," added Robyn with a gentle smile.

"Do you understand my point? You train all year long to prepare for a race, and then someone decides to impede your ability to show up and win. Not okay. If someone did that to me, I'd make damn sure they understood that."

Robyn smiled again. "I'll keep that in mind for next time, Jason."

That was Robyn's signal to shut it down. To move on and talk about something less threatening. Something that could salvage a night that actually started out okay. Jason missed her cue entirely. It went from bad, to worse, to unbelievable. He just wouldn't let up. Part of me was quite content to let the train wreck unfold uninterrupted. Jason was sealing the deal on never seeing Robyn again. And, at this early stage in the relationship, I was okay with that. But another part of me was confused and, quite honestly, sad. I wasn't sure where his aggressive tendencies were coming from. Why was he so mad—at everything?

It was as if he were steering the conversation to intentionally confront her ideas. He was looking for a fight, plain and simple—something to win—even if only in his own mind. I could see that he was also announcing his insecurities to Robyn. Trouble was, Jason never let up long enough to notice.

It was horrible. I remember being embarrassed for him. It was still relatively early on in our relationship, and I didn't yet fully appreciate his complexities. Life was comfortable for Jason when he stayed in his narrow lane. When others pushed him out, it was like he was drowning emotionally—thrashing and clawing, trying to get back to safety.

Jason tried to convince Robyn that she'd likely win more races if she hated her competitors and used that as a strategy. He told her that hugging competitors before a race was weak and disabled any sort of killer instinct she could call upon when she needed to "finish them off." He explained that if rowing were a contact sport, he'd waste little time using his oar as a weapon if that would help him win—a comment that was met with more awkward silence. However, to Robyn's credit, she continued to gently invite Jason to look at competition with a "more holistic outlook," as she put it. To which Jason laughed dismissively. "Sounds like something you'd read in a new-age self-help book," he said. "That stuff's too flakey for me."

Thankfully, Jason was saved by the front door opening. "Hello, I'm home!" called Fiona from downstairs. "How are you two doing? How was dinner?"

"Dinner was delicious," answered Robyn graciously as she stood up to say goodbye. "But it's time to be getting on home. I have a training session at the lake tomorrow morning."

While Jason did the dishes, Fiona sipped her tea. "So tell me how the evening went. Robyn sure left in a hurry. Did you two make plans earlier to see each other again? Because she didn't say anything about getting together before she left. What did I miss?"

First, Jason described how he had made dinner. My mouth started watering again. And then he went on to explain how he had challenged Robyn's "weak" approach to competition. He was smug as he reiterated the advice he had "generously" shared with Robyn. He seemed quite proud of himself.

"Are you hoping to see her again?" asked Fiona.

"Of course." Jason seemed surprised by her question.

"Which part of this evening do you think Robyn enjoyed?"

"Well, you heard her—she said dinner was delicious!"

Fiona shrugged. "Anything else?"

"I don't know—we talked for a long time about sports and stuff. You'd have to ask her?" Jason rinsed the dishcloth and began wiping the countertop.

"I don't have to. I can tell you right now, with great confidence, that there wouldn't have been much." Jason stopped wiping and turned around. "I've heard it too many times from you, Jason. I know exactly what kind of macho crap you puked all over poor Robyn."

Jason crossed his arms and heaved a heavy sigh while he looked at me and leaned back against the sink.

"Jason, aside from the next time Robyn's hankerin' for a yummy plate-o-fish, I can't imagine why she'd ever want to see you again. Why do you feel so compelled to share that garbage? Until you're willing to let go of that destructive narrative, you're going to be a very lonely young man."

Jason turned, walked into the living room, and sat down.

"And, just to be clear, I'm done setting up dates for you. I arranged for the most remarkable, beautiful, amazing, talented, you-name-it kind of woman for you to meet—and you have the nerve to play your tough guy games with her?"

The ferry ride home the following day was quiet. Fiona had hit the bullseye with her comments. We didn't even bother getting out of the car once we got onboard. Jason just sat slouched at the wheel and stared at the back of the car in front of us.

As we prepared to dock, he finally spoke up. "What the hell was that last night—where does that guy come from?" Jason shook his head and looked at me in the rearview mirror. "Fiona's right—about all of it. I'm not sure why I find it so amusing to crawl up someone's nose and piss them off. I've got to figure this out, Ike. Or, like she said, it's going to be a lonely ride."

never too late to ask

Despite Jason's concerns regarding the start of the school year without a guide-dog training-jacket, we began classes without a hitch. The welcome I received from everyone, including Frederick the dean, was positive. Everywhere I went on campus, it was, "Great to have you back, Ike!"

Becks was her usual self. Bubbly. Loud. And hilarious. From the first day back, our morning greeting went off like clockwork as we entered the main building through the heavy glass doors.

"Hey, who's that good lookin' guy?" She would yell across the foyer from her perch. Jason would smile awkwardly and wave. "Good morning, Becks."

"I'm talkin' about Ike!" Then she'd laugh and slap the top of her desk. "Oh, hi, Jason—I didn't see you there." She never missed a day.

It was a reminder that Jason attended an art school. One filled with some eccentric artists, but Jason seemed to be finding a home in the cold modern architecture, as well as with its interesting and friendly occupants. Although he wasn't remotely close with any of his classmates, they all seemed to like him, and he appeared to genuinely like them too. But there was a line. As a tall guy, he was intimidating enough. Combine that with his intense personality and you had a boundary that was tough to cross. I couldn't figure it out; they all seemed like nice humans to me.

Our daily rhythm at school still included lunchtime runs along the False Creek seawall. It was a great way to drain my tank, and for Jason to let off steam too. Unlike our weekend runs in the Endowment Lands where he would talk to me, the trees, himself, and anyone else who cared to listen, he rarely spoke during these shorter outings. The politeness and professionalism that he manufactured for class-time crumbled into brooding energy that spilled from him with every stride. I could feel his intensity.

Our weekends were still all about grabbing a break from the demands of school and getting outside to enjoy time with mother nature. Meals with the boys were always a favourite for me. I loved the banter and the leftovers! The more we did that didn't include schoolwork, the better Jason's mood. Even with a heavier workload, he maintained the same outlook as the previous year. He was going to do just enough—no more, no less.

Despite the debacle a few weeks earlier, Jason was still interested in a future with Robyn. He'd talk about her on our runs. Yes, he was that stubborn and that smitten. Not surprisingly, he was still mad at himself for "screwing things up." But he was also embarrassed. So much so, he hadn't even called her since their dinner date. Instead, he would check in with Fiona regularly to see if there had been any progress—had Robyn mentioned him during one of her massage therapy appointments? Fiona was honest but gentle. She encouraged him to reach out to Robyn on his own. "That's the only way you're going to find out," she suggested. "But, go slow—be patient." Patience was always the order of the day. Still not a trait Jason appeared to want to hone.

One Friday night, Pat came into our room and tapped Jason on his foot. Sitting on his bed, listening to music with me curled up against him, he was busy drawing in his sketchbook. "What's up?" Jason pulled one of his headphones aside.

"Trev's mom just called."

"Okay?"

"Trev's dad had a heart attack."

"Fuck—really?"

"He died a few hours ago."

Jason looked down at his sketchbook.

"She wants us to go find him at work and let him know."

Within minutes, they were heading out the door. "We won't be too long, Ike. Hang tight, buddy."

I hadn't met Trev's dad, but judging from the stories of life back on the farm in Saskatchewan, it sounded like Trev had inherited his dad's best traits. Friendly. Hard working. Always willing to lend a hand. And a great sense of humour!

I curled up on the bed and waited. I thought about my family. My mom, especially. I knew I'd never see her again, but in that moment, I remember being grateful for everything she had done for me—she was selfless. I wanted to be more like her.

The next day, Trev flew home to the prairies. The house was quiet without him. Not just in his absence, but, in reflection, Jason and Pat were quieter as well.

On Sunday, after our morning run, Jason called his parents while eating his mixing bowl of porridge. The tone of their conversations always struck me. I wasn't exactly sure what speaking to parents was supposed to sound like, but I figured it wasn't supposed to sound like this. He seemed somehow too relaxed—too comfortable when he spoke. It usually sounded like he was talking with a couple of friends.

This time was a little different, however. I could hear concern in Jason's dad's voice even through the cheap phone speaker. He knew something was up.

"Everything okay, son?"

"Kind of—I mean, I'm okay, but Trev... well, Trev's dad had a heart attack—and died."

"Oh, I'm sorry to hear that. How's Trev doing?" Eleanor was on the line too.

"Quiet. But what else would you expect?"

"True. And how are you and Pat doing?" asked Carl.

Jason's voice sounded funny. I looked up at him from the kitchen floor and noticed his eyes were turning red and beginning to glisten. He stopped speaking.

After a moment of silence, Jason's mom asked again, "How are you doing, Jason? Are you okay?"

Jason dropped his spoon and pushed away the bowl of porridge. "I heard you!" He seemed mad that his emotions had choked him up.

There was more silence. Jason's dad eventually spoke up. "And you're concerned about me? Wondering if I'm next—if I'm going to have a heart attack?"

"Yup." Jason took a deep breath.

"Ohh, Jason, I wish I could be there to give you a hug," said Eleanor.

Jason, still unable to speak, just waited.

His dad's voice sounded far away through the little speaker. "I guess I'm just not worried. I trust that the good Lord will take me when it's my time. Until then, I have faith in that belief. When my purpose here on earth is complete, I'll be done—I'm okay with that, son. When it's time, it's time. And I'm not going to worry about it. Until that moment, I'll welcome every day the same—each one as a blessing."

"What if... What if I don't have that faith?" Another deep breath. Jason was beginning to settle and find his words more easily.

"Son, you don't have to go to church to have faith—to have that trust. You just have to know your purpose. To believe in it," answered Carl.

"What if I don't know my purpose?" asked Jason quietly. "I mean, I used to have a purpose—winning an Olympic gold medal. That got me out of bed every day."

"Dear, that was a dream—an exciting dream, yes—but it's not your life purpose. You have so much more to give than just a rowing race," said Eleanor.

"It was a big deal to me, Mom!"

"I know it was—we both do. But maybe it's time to move on?" suggested Eleanor. "Find something that stirs you the way rowing did."

"That's the problem—move on to what? Life mattered more when I was rowing. Trying to win that medal was something worthy—special. Now I'm just a guy going to art school—who gives a crap?"

"Son, if you recall, that Olympic dream was more than ten years in the making," said Carl. "It took years for you to realize that dream—you call it your purpose. It can happen again. For the time being, school is simply a stage of your life that will enable you to find your next purpose. And there will very likely be many more after that. But, they don't always appear the morning after one comes to an end. Be patient; it'll happen for you—you have to trust that."

"Easy for you to say."

"True. But, if you remain open, it will reveal itself to you—I believe that much." It looked as though Carl's voice was reassuring Jason. He exhaled. His shoulders lowered.

Jason seemed better after the phone call. And it wasn't temporary. In the days, weeks, and months that followed, he felt lighter.

Jason eventually forgave himself enough to reach out to Robyn. He didn't even mention their last conversation together, let alone apologize. I heard him tell Fiona, "Why even bring it up—maybe she's forgotten?" I could hear her laughing through the phone.

We went over and stayed with Fiona. Sunday morning, when Robyn wasn't training, we met for another walk. However, there was no talk of running or rowing or any sport, for that matter. Not even a "how's your training going?" Instead, they discussed school, religion, health, politics, and even their life aspirations.

And amidst their topics of conversation were plenty of laughs. Jason's sense of humour had been revealed to me during his exchanges with Pat and Trev, but this was different. Jason wasn't laughing at someone else's expense the way he would with the boys. Don't get me wrong, they were never mean to each other—it's the way male humans can sometimes be. With Robyn, they laughed at simple life observations—it seemed kinder and more genuine. And Jason lit up when he laughed with Robyn. I had never seen that before.

We walked at different spots each time we came over to the Island to visit. Ocean beaches, lakes, and mountain trails, each of them stunning in its own way. I was beginning to understand Jason's intrigue with Robyn. Like Fiona had said, she was different. Sure, she was thoughtful, kind, and generous, but she was more than that. Her ability to listen—to be truly present when Jason spoke—I could feel her sincere interest in what he had to say. And Jason was different too. When he was with Robyn, he was softer—more relaxed and less intense. Better, even. We had more fun when he was with Robyn.

Believe me, he still had his moments with plenty of missteps and blunders. But, most times, he caught himself and knew enough to either change the topic or stop talking. Robyn, always gracious in those moments, never drew attention to his flaws but instead allowed them to fade.

Despite her many attempts, and even some coaching from Jason, Robyn rarely threw a stick far or even straight. After too many close

Grabbing a nap on the boat after my first adventure at sea with Colin, Trev, and Jason. *Photo Credit: Colin Savage*

Rescued from my first accidental swim—Jason thought it was pretty funny! *Photo Credit: Colin Savage*

My first official swim at Schoen Lake with Jason and Dash on the sinking dock. *Photo Credit: Hannah*

Our first family reunion at Stanley Park. That's Indie beside me, and then Ivor, Iona, and Ivan. *Photo Credit: Roberta*

My first winter hike in the snow with my cousins at Burgoyne Woods Park in St. Catharines. *Photo Credit: Jason*

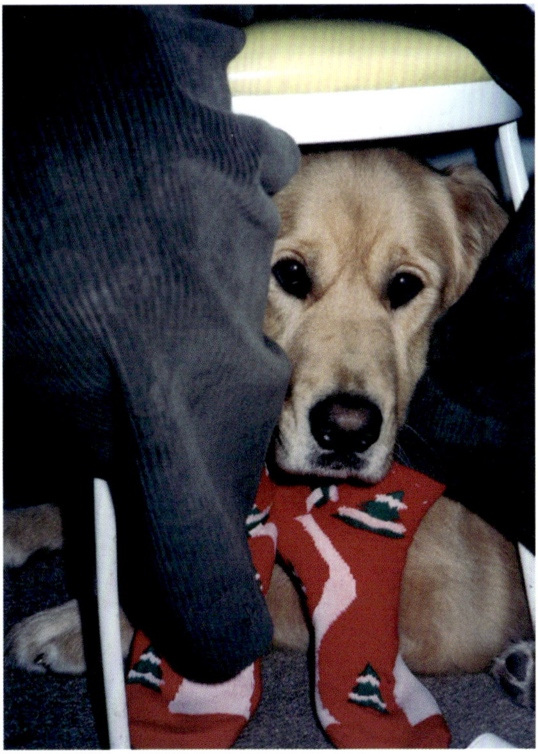

Me with Grandpa's red Christmas socks after I had finished wrestling with them.
Photo Credit: Jason

Canoeing with Jason after dinner at the cottage in Bobcaygeon.
Photo Credit: Wendy VanDrunen

Rabbiting for Robyn on a training run along the Fraser River in Abbotsford. *Photo Credit: Erin Hayashi*

While Jason was busy accepting our Emily Carr diplomas, I took a moment to say hello to the audience. *Photo Credit: Unknown*

Ian and Jason selling Skeet & Ike's Not Just Nuts Spread at Granville Island Market. *Photo Credit: Peggy Walker*

Hanging out with Jason on his old futon and his new sleeping bag.
Photo Credit: Robyn

Robyn phoning family with the news of their engagement.
Photo Credit: Jason

Robyn and Jason share an impromptu dance at an "East Coast" kitchen party in Edmonton. *Photo Credit: Wendy VanDrunen*

Left: Robyn and Jason recite their vows. Right: Robyn shares a smile after their wedding ceremony. *Photo Credit: Lawrence McLagan*

Benson and I pause between classes for a photo with Jason in the staffroom at Shawnigan Lake School.
Photo Credit: Unkown

The year after I left, Jason presented this drawing to Robyn. It was from a photo taken atop Black Mountain moments after they were engaged. I love this drawing. It reminds me of happy times!

calls, Jason had learned to subtly move out of the way each time it was her turn.

On our last visit before we left for Christmas with his family in Ontario, we arrived at Fiona's house to a surprise—a new puppy! A black lab named Brodie.

"Isn't he beautiful?" Fiona beamed with excitement and pride.

"He's a handsome boy, that's for sure," agreed Jason. "And, he's big—holy crap! How old?"

"He just turned ten weeks. Do you think I'm feeding him too much?"

"He'll likely lean out as he grows. But our vet Allyson always told me that one of the best gifts you can give your dog is a lean body. Too much chub and they'll struggle later in life."

"That sounds like good advice. Did you hear that, Brodie? We can't let you get too chubby!"

"Great—now she's goin' to starve me." Brody sniffed Jason's legs, then my nose.

"Oh, well, I'm sure you'll survive. My name's Ike. Nice to meet you, Brodie."

"Nice to meet you, too, Ike."

"You sure landed a keen mom. Fiona's a very kind and generous human—you're in for a good life!"

"I think you're right," agreed Brodie. *"The first two weeks have been amazing!"*

"I'm picking up Robyn around 1:00 pm for a walk at the lakes. Would you mind if we take Brodie?" asked Jason. "I'm sure Robyn would love to meet this little guy, too!"

"Of course! That would be great," she answered. "But it's supposed to snow—will Brodie be okay?"

"Fiona, he's a lab puppy—not a china doll! He'll be fine. Besides, he's got plenty of insulation," Jason said as he elbowed her in the ribs.

That walk with Brodie marked the first of many we took together. Brodie and I would become fast friends. Although I was a little older than him, it wasn't long before he was taller and definitely broader than me. The chub never went away. But it never bothered either one of us. Brodie loved to run and chase and swim as much as I did. I appreciated his easy-going approach to life. Nothing ever got to Brodie—nothing.

On that particular hike, the snow did come, and like most snowstorms on the West Coast, it accumulated quickly. By the end of the walk, Brodie was leaping from one of my footprints to another as he followed behind me. This was my first snowfall on Vancouver Island. It was nothing like the snow I had first experienced at Jason's parents' place in St. Catharines. This snow was wet, and the snowflakes were bigger.

Robyn and Jason were caught unprepared for the weather as well. By the end of our walk, they were both cold, wet, and eager to climb into a warm car. With the engine running and the heat blasting, Brodie and I dried off in the back seat.

Before we drove back to Robyn's place to drop her off, Jason asked her a big question. I knew the question was coming. He had talked with Pat and Trev about it before we came over.

There was no, "Umm, Robyn, I was thinking..." Instead, he was straight to the point. "I enjoy our time together on these walks, Robyn, but I'm wondering about becoming more than friends. What do you think?"

Robyn paused before turning to face Jason. That one gesture was her answer. I knew what was coming, and so did he.

"Jason, I've really enjoyed getting to know you better over the last number of months—I have. I've truly looked forward to our time together. However, with the Atlanta Olympics being less than two years away, I'm trying to limit my commitments. Having a serious relationship right now is just not what I'm looking for. I would like to stay friends, though?"

Jason laughed. "Ha—just ask Fiona—I've got enough female *friends* to rock the Queen Mary. I guess our timing's off. Speaking of which, have you ever heard a song on the radio, and thought that it was written specifically for you and what was going on in your life?" Robyn nodded. "Well, there's this new song from Larry Gowen—it's called, 'When There's Time for Love.' Have you heard it?"

Robyn nodded again. "I think so. It has a pretty melody if I'm thinking of the correct one."

"It's the lyrics that struck me. Here, have a listen," he said as he put the CD into the stereo player. "It says everything I'm feeling."

The two of them sat quietly in the car while the CD began to play. As the guitar intro broke the silence, Robyn looked at Jason and smiled.

As the lyrics unfolded and revealed Jason's honest intent, he took a deep breath and turned to look out the window. Appearing quite focused, Robyn looked straight ahead and listened closely to every word.

Jason wasn't kidding. The lyrics spoke perfectly to their individual circumstances, and what was preventing their relationship from moving beyond just friends. Call it bad luck, but their timing seemed to be the obvious culprit.

When the song ended, Robyn put her hand on Jason's wrist. "Aww, Jason, that was truly lovely. And, believe me, I completely understand you wanting more than a friendship, and I also appreciate you understanding where I am with this."

"Of course. I get it—I remember what I was like when I was training for Seoul." Jason smiled at Robyn. "But we don't need to talk about that—do we?"

Robyn smiled, too, before turning around to look at me and pat my head. "And you too, Ike. Sorry if I've not improved much with my throwing arm!"

With that, Jason had his answer. Robyn disappeared from our lives.

moving on

With my official guide dog status gone, there was no flying first class anymore. Instead, I was relegated to a cold plastic crate in the plane's underbelly.

I remember our first flight with me travelling in the crate. I caused quite a scene at the airport, refusing to succumb willingly to my new flying accommodations. Finally, Trev stabilized one end of the crate while Jason held the top with both hands and used his midsection to force my rigid body into the tiny space. When Jason slammed the door shut, sealing my fate, he was frustrated with my behaviour.

"Well, that was a bit of Christmas cheer for all of the stressed-out holiday travellers, I'm sure," said Trev, still laughing at what had just transpired.

"Holy shit—I know you're not happy, Ike. But it's this or leave you at a kennel. And there's no way I'm doing that." He pushed some cookies through the wire door for me. I ignored his peace offering. "Hang in there, Ike. It'll all be worth it once you cozy up on Grandma and Grandpa's bed."

Later that evening, with the fire roaring and his parents there to welcome me, I had to agree.

With Carl and Eleanor on either side of the bed and me stretched out between them, Jason came in to say goodnight.

"It sure looks as though someone has made himself right at home. Eh, buddy? See, I told you," he said before sitting down on the end of the bed and leaning forward to rest his head on my chest.

"I didn't think I'd ever get to see this boy again." Carl lowered the top half of his newspaper. "I'm so glad things worked out the way they did. You must be thrilled."

"It feels like this was always the way it was meant to be. It's hard even to imagine not having Ike in my life. I can't explain it, but I trust that this is how it was always going to work out." Jason rolled my left ear in his fingers. "He's an amazing dog."

Jason's mom lowered her book and rested her hand on my neck, "And how are you doing, Jason?"

"Still spending my days at school—still doesn't stir me the way rowing did. But I'm trying to stay open to what's going to show up next."

"And how are you doing otherwise?

"Well, I met this woman."

Carl looked at me from behind his paper and winked as a smile grew from the side of his face.

"We're not dating or anything. But you'd like her."

Carl looked at me again and puffed out his lower lip to make a pouty face.

Jason spoke very slowly; I could tell he was cautious talking about this with his parents. "Let's just say we got off to a rough start. Sometimes I'm not very nice, and it kinda freaks me out...I don't remember always being like that. I don't like how I behave sometimes. So I've been thinking about...who I want to be instead—and I've noticed a difference. I've been trying to...let things go. It's not easy."

"I was telling your father that I thought you seemed lighter during dinner—not so angry." Eleanor looked at Carl, who had now completely lowered his newspaper and was listening intently.

"It's quite obvious to us, son—you seem so much better."

"I always felt that, as your mother, I failed you when you got home from the Olympics. Dad and I agreed that we'd just leave you alone to figure out what you were going through on your own. But now I see that we should have never done that. We should have talked with you and tried to support you more. I'm sorry for that, Jason."

Jason lifted his head and sat up. "Mom, don't be crazy. You couldn't have made me talk. I needed to work through my disappointment on my own, anyway. I certainly don't blame you guys for what I went through and how long it took—so please don't blame yourselves."

They talked for quite a while longer—school, life after school, Pat and Trev, the loss of Trev's dad, and of course, Carl wanted to know more about Robyn. Eventually, it was time for sleep, but before I dozed off, Jason got me out for my late-night pee. There was no way we wanted to risk an accident on their big comfy bed.

Jason kissed me on the ear and left. Carl lowered his paper then quietly turned and whispered to Eleanor, "Robyn sounds like quite a gal—wouldn't that be nice! Ike, you need to work some magic!" Carl stroked my forehead gently before I drifted off to sleep.

The following two weeks in St. Catharines were busy. Long runs with Jason in the crisp white snow along the creek that ran through the centre of town; walks with his siblings, nephews, and nieces in the wooded park near the golf course; and, my new favourite activity, tobogganing on the escarpment. It had been a year since I had last romped through the snow. Now, I could easily bound up the hill we were sliding down. The difference in my strength and speed was noticeable as my young cousins tried unsuccessfully to catch me.

Every evening, after plenty of outdoor adventures in the snow, Jason's family would gather for long meals around the dining room table with a glowing fire crackling in the background. Me, I always found my spot on the floor next to Carl. I hadn't forgotten the source of those goodies from my first Christmas.

Carl had to be strategic when deciding on the ideal moment to sneak a treat to me. A piece of chicken or turkey, a carrot end, a nibble of stuffing—even a tiny bit of crust from his apple pie. All of it was delicious, and I appreciated every single morsel.

The time flew by. After our last meal together, and a final photo gathered beside my cousins in front of the tree to mark the end of another Christmas vacation, it was time to go home.

At the airport, I wasn't too happy about being crammed into my crate again. We waited for the baggage attendant. A woman came over to speak with Jason. I watched through the bars of my crate.

"Sir, what are you waiting for?"

"I'm waiting for the baggage guy to come and grab my dog."

"Sir, your flight leaves in 20 minutes. If you don't head to the gate soon, you're going to miss it."

"I'm not leaving him here unattended."

"But, sir, you're going to miss..."

"Sorry, I'm not leaving him."

"But..."

"Do you have children?"

She paused and then frowned.

"Would you leave your child in a plastic crate in the middle of this airport, alone?"

She scowled at him for a moment longer and then turned and pulled out her walkie-talkie.

Jason knelt. "How's it goin', bud?" I avoided eye contact. "Really, you're giving me the cold shoulder? Look, I told you—if I could take you with me in the cabin, I would!"

"Excuse me, sir, someone will be here momentarily. And they're going to hold the gate, but you're going to have to run."

"Thanks. I appreciate that."

She nodded. "What's its name? The dog, I mean—what's their name?"

"His name is Ike. He's my firstborn." Jason looked at the attendant and smiled, but he still didn't head for the gate.

"Hello, Ike. Someone will be here for you any moment now."

Soon, a large man dressed in a full-body orange suit covered in bright yellow plastic stripes arrived.

Jason looked directly at him. "Hi, this is my dog, Ike. He's not a huge fan of this crate. If you could be gentle, he would appreciate it!"

"You bet, man—let's roll, Ike," he grabbed the dolly with me on it and sped off.

"See you in Vancouver, buddy!"

***

My late-night pee ritual, along with the meds from Allyson, had kept me pretty much accident-free for over a year. What began as a significant health scare had fizzled to a slight inconvenience—mainly for Jason. Although troublesome enough to keep me from guiding a blind human, it didn't stop me from living a vibrant and full life with Jason. We ran together, hiked, swam, camped, pretty much anything a dog like me would want—life couldn't have been any better. And Allyson was happy too. My one kidney continued to do the work of two. It was, "carry on" from her!

With the beginning of 1995, more challenges arrived. In March, with the cherry blossoms coming into full bloom, school was still the foundation of our weekly rhythm, and weekends were spent training for a 50 km trail race that Jason had entered called the Knee Knacker.

One Friday afternoon the landlord called and told us that the house was for sale. We had to be out by the end of the month.

For Jason, losing our home was one thing. Losing the support of Pat and Trev was something altogether different—more significant. Not only had they been generous in their willingness to help with my care, but they had also been kind with their support of him. They had proven to be an ideally-sized pair of kid gloves that helped keep Jason out of the weeds. Pat and Trev had balanced encouragement with caution. They respected Jason's perspectives on life, albeit hard to stomach at times, and had been there to offer feedback and guidance when called upon. From something as simple as challenging his narrow view of how humans should look and dress, to his tough-guy approach to competition, I saw that their combined efforts had helped Jason grow tremendously.

Pat had found a room in a house full of medical students and Trev was going to move to the Island. Which left Jason to fend for himself. He was about to discover how hard it was to find a room to rent in Vancouver with a full-grown dog.

Ever the strategist, he covered all of the bases. He scoured the newspapers looking for rentals, and made dozens of phone calls. He posted signs with his name and number on housing notice boards at the Granville Island Market. He got a few calls, but when he mentioned me, the calls ended. He was stressed.

With less than a week to find a new home, Jason received a call from a long-time school friend named Wendy. They had known each other since their early teens. They swam club together and had even rowed on the same team in high school.

Wendy and her husband, Mike, had purchased a home in the suburbs just east of the city, in a quiet neighbourhood with massive evergreens. Wendy offered us a spacious room on the second floor with a huge bed—a place to call home until we could find another suitable spot. What made this move so interesting for me was that it came with a young black-lab-mix named Maddie. Wendy and Mike were excited to have a live-in playmate for their young pup. In a word, Maddie was hyper, like no dog I'd ever met. But she was fun! And always up for a wrestle, or a run with Jason and me.

With the move came a long commute every day. Combine the drive with studio time, and we were both ready for some quiet trails come the end of the day. We'd head to Mundy Park, with chip trials that looped and meandered through a mishmash of beautiful trees. It wasn't our beloved Endowment Lands, but it would certainly do.

Moving our run to the end of the day so that Maddie could join us meant we had a new chunk of time to fill during lunch. So we walked. Everywhere. On the Island, off the Island; we explored every nook and cranny the surrounding neighbourhoods had to offer. Aside from those evening runs, lunchtime was my favourite part of the day. The darkness Jason had shown on our lunchtime runs even a few months earlier seemed to have passed. Now he would talk to me.

Even our commute was better. Jason and rush-hour hadn't always gone well together, but now he rarely lost his temper. Jason seemed to have shifted into a better place. As far as I could figure, the disastrous dinner conversation with Robyn had been the catalyst. It was his proverbial rock-bottom. Ever since that night, he had been slowly and steadily trying to show up as a better human. I could feel it.

Although Robyn still wasn't in the picture, and there was little indication that she would be anytime soon, with Fiona's gentle encouragement, Jason had gone on a few dates with other women. They were nice, but I was reminded after each one, "They're not Robyn." True enough, but Robyn wasn't calling.

There was even one who had a great arm—I couldn't believe how far she could throw sticks. She was pretty, intelligent, outgoing, and her laugh matched Jason's. Still, he had taken a pass.

Our runs had a new focus—distance. As in, 50 km of distance. The Knee Knacker would have Jason running 8000 feet up and 8000 feet down along the Baden Powell trail that traversed the North Shore Mountains from Horseshoe Bay to Deep Cove.

Starting that January, Jason turned up his mileage with three long runs during the week and one four-hour run along the racecourse every weekend. Allyson had given her blessing for me to join Jason in his preparation, despite the possibility of increased wear and tear on my joints. The main reason? Jason was, well, slow! Rarely did I ever break out of a trot, and all of the runs were on soft trails. And, as Jason reminded her, "It could be his last year—I think he'd enjoy this." That was his go-to with Allyson. Anytime he wanted her blessing, he pulled out the lifespan card!

Every weekend, Maddie and I would climb into the back seat of Jason's car and we'd make our way to the North Shore, for those beautiful training runs. My favourite was the first section of the race. We'd head straight up Black Mountain, sometimes through the clouds; at the top we would look back on the city and the Gulf Islands off in the distance. Even Maddie, who easily covered twice the distance we did as she maniacally ran off the trails in pursuit of added adventures, seemed to pause for a moment and take in the stunning vista.

Spring arrived. It was still cool atop the mountains, but the snow we had grown accustomed to navigating was beginning to melt. On one particular weekend in early March, the air was rich with the smells of plants and animals waking up from the long winters' nap. As we crossed over the top of the mountain and began our descent into the valley below, I caught the scent of something so strong and pungent it stopped me.

"Hey Maddie, do you smell that?"

She looked over at me with her nose already in the air and her hackles up. *"Yuck—what is that?"*

I looked ahead to where Jason was plodding along. A large black bear was rummaging in the bushes.

"Do you see that?" I asked Maddie. *"Jason's running directly at it."*

"Come on, let's go!" she yelled.

We were off—full speed down the trail. Thankfully, the bear hadn't noticed Jason yet. That gave us the advantage of surprise. I couldn't understand how Jason hadn't seen that bear, either.

Just as he came within a few feet of the bear, Maddie and I caught up to him. Maddie started barking before I did. The bear shot up and spun around.

As he caught sight of the bear Jason jumped off the trail. "HOLY FUCK! HAH—GET GOIN', BEAR. GET OUTTA HERE. SCAT! GO ON!"

Maddie and I, side by side, put on the most fearsome show we possibly could in the hopes that would be enough to dissuade the bear from engaging. Shocked by our sudden appearance, the bear stood up upon its hind legs and assessed the situation. With Jason yelling and waving his arms, and Maddie and I barking and periodically charging the bear, eventually, that giant smelly creature got down onto its four legs, turned, and ran. Maddie gave chase while I stayed with Jason.

"Holy crap, Ike—that was way too close!" Jason knelt down and hugged me. "Man, if you two hadn't been here, goodness knows what might have happened."

Maddie came running back to join us. Panting from her sprint, she gave Jason some licks while he grabbed hold of her and rubbed her back in appreciation. Maddie and I stayed on high alert for the remainder of the run while Jason yelled, "HEY, BEAR!" every few minutes. It was the first and last time we saw a bear.

Still in his third year at Emily Carr, Jason knew that part of the requirement for fourth year was giving a public presentation on his thesis project. Although he seemed to have no problem speaking to me and the trees when we ran or hiked, and publicly, as I had seen with his impromptu chapel story, the idea of doing so in front of strangers terrified him. In classic Jason style, he joined a local Toastmasters group in the hopes of learning some basic public speaking skills that could help him manage those fears head-on.

Part of the initiation was delivering an "Ice-Breaker Speech" within the first few months. The idea was to share something significant about your life—perhaps even something that you'd never told anyone else before.

Jason had been talking about it on our lunchtime walks. Sharing how the thought of getting up in front of his fellow Toastmasters and talking publicly about something meaningful scared him to death. But, I could tell, he was determined to conquer his paralyzing fear.

As the day approached, he still hadn't practiced speaking his words out loud. Instead, he methodically finger-punched at his keyboard for hours, trying to perfect his speech.

Mike's sister Karyn, Jason's "best-case, worst-case" friend, came into the house while he was busy downstairs finalizing his speech. She was a teacher at a high school nearby and often stopped in. "Anyone here?" she yelled.

Jason didn't respond. He was still typing away as Karyn came to the top of the stairs.

"Jason, are you down there?"

"Hi, Karyn. Yup—down here."

Maddie and I got up to welcome Karyn.

"Big night! Are you ready?" asked Karyn excitedly. "You're going to be great—I just know it!"

"I'm glad one of us thinks so!"

"You'll be fine, Jase. Just keep breathing—so you don't pass out!"

Jason chuckled. "I'll try to remember that."

As the printer nattered, the two of them sat quietly. Jason reached down and rolled my left ear between his fingers.

Karyn got up and walked over to the printer. She handed the papers to him and said, "Why don't you practice reading this to me? I've got time."

"Really?"

"Of course. I'll just sit beside you—that way, I don't have to look at you. Or, I mean, you know what I mean!" Karen laughed. "Jase, you do whatever you need to do."

Jason looked at me lying on the floor in front of him, smiled, took a deep breath, and began.

"Have you ever had a dream? I mean, a real-life dream? One that controlled every aspect of your daily life? Where nothing was more important than that dream? Where your health, your friends, your family—everything—took a back seat to your all-consuming dream? Not one where you say to yourself, 'Yah, that would be kind of nice.' But one where you say, 'I would do anything and give anything to have that come true.'

"I had a dream like that. It started as an innocent fantasy when I was eight years old. By the time I was eighteen, it had grown into what some might call an obsession. And for the next six years, it would influence where I went to university, my social life, and ultimately who I am today.

"In the early afternoon of the 25th of September 1988, in Seoul, Korea, I had my one shot at realizing my lifelong dream. It was the Olympic final of the men's eight in rowing and I was sitting three seats from the bow, in lane six, wearing a Canadian singlet. Canada had won the gold medal in Los Angeles in 1984 and that made us defending

Olympic champions. Although we had four members from that winning crew in our boat, we were not the same crew. We were bigger, stronger, and faster. During the two races leading up to the final, we had shown tremendous speed in certain sections of the race. This was our chance to put those two pieces together and row the race of our lives. Going into the final, the Australian coach had said, 'If the Canadians are anywhere in contention with 500 metres to go, the race will be over.'

"Less than six minutes after the starter's command, we crossed the line in sixth place. Far from what we had expected of ourselves, and perhaps farther from what others had expected of us. My emotions ranged from anger to disbelief to nothing. My senses were completely numb. Years of sacrifice—physically, financially, and emotionally—all for what? That was it; my one shot was gone. I would never have that chance again. Winning that Olympic gold medal had meant everything to me. As I saw it, it was the only reason for going to Seoul. *Getting* to the Olympics was not the dream; it was merely part of the process. To go to the Olympics and not come home with that medal meant failure. It meant that all those years of training were for naught. Going to the Olympics was not about representing my country or competing with the best in the world; it was about medals. And the one that mattered most was gold.

"When I returned home, I read the Globe and Mail from September 25th. On the cover of the sports page was a picture of our eight, slumped over our oars after the finish of the race. The headline read, 'Canadians Bomb Out in Seoul.'

"My family and I never talked about the race. They simply said they were proud of me regardless of the outcome, and we left it at that. I didn't phone anyone when I got home. I didn't want to see anyone. I didn't want to talk to anyone. I just wanted to hide. When I did run into people, it was always the same thing: 'What happened?' And that just brought it all back. So I figured the best thing to do was go somewhere where nobody knew me. I chose Australia. After five months in Melbourne and one month travelling the East Coast, I felt I was ready to come home. My plan was to return to Vancouver Island and resume my training for 1992. I wasn't ready to give up on my dream just yet.

"I began training in September of 1989. At first, it went well. I felt my strength and endurance returning with each workout. However, with those improvements came flashbacks of the race in Seoul, and those flashbacks were beginning to wear thin on my emotions. Initially, I used the loss in Seoul as a form of motivation. It was vindication I was after. I saw my next Olympic race purely as revenge. As I found out, revenge is a powerful force, but the effect is short-lived. With revenge comes an enormous amount of hatred and anger. Maintaining those emotions was making me an extremely miserable young man.

"My dream had become too much. I began questioning my reasons for wanting to go to the Olympics a second time. What if I lost again? Train four more years for 1996? Then 2000? When would it end? I was not about to find out. Six months into my training, I decided that I had had enough. If I continued at that rate, I wasn't going to make it to 1992, not physically and especially not emotionally. I phoned my coach and told him. He said he understood. We reminisced about old times for a few minutes. I hung up, had a good cry, and said to myself, 'That's it. It's over. Never again.'

"Was it over, though? Was the obsession with Olympic gold truly out of my life? Sure, I could say the actual physical hands-on side of rowing was gone, but what about the mental side? All those emotions leftover from Seoul—what about them?

"Since that day, there have been more talks and more tears, and along with them, a growing realization of what the Olympics now mean to me. The feelings from the race will always be there. The disappointment. The pain. The frustration. The 'what ifs?' What if things had been different? What if we had won? How would that have changed my life? Would that have affected the person I am today? Lots of questions, but no answers. There will never be answers. But what there will be is a stronger belief in, 'Yes, I went to the Olympics, and I didn't win a gold medal. But maybe I truly am a better person for it.'"

Jason stopped. He looked at me and forced a smile. His eyes filled with tears until they spilled down his cheeks. "Who knew, eh?"

He took a deep breath. Karyn reached out and grabbed his hand. "There's no rush, Jason. Take your time—breathe."

Jason wiped his cheeks with his sleeve, took a big breath and continued.

"Perhaps it was a test that I will continue to learn, strengthen, and grow from until one day I can return that knowledge and strength to someone else.

"Looking back, I don't regret having gone to the Olympics. It was a dream. It was my dream. And I gave to that dream everything I had.

"Sure, falling short hurt like hell. But that's life. Sometimes things work out the way we want. And sometimes they don't. But that doesn't mean we shouldn't all have dreams. I still have dreams. I dream of someday being a great husband and dad; I dream of being a teacher who makes a tremendous difference in a child's life. And I'll go after those dreams the same way I went after my Olympic dream. And if they come true...great. And if they don't, well, I'll have more dreams. Because when we stop dreaming, we stop living."

I got up, moved closer to Jason, and stared directly at him. He stared back. "What? Listen, buddy, that took some doing—so don't be giving me any grief!"

"Jason. That was beautiful," said Karyn. "How does it feel to share all of that?"

"Well, it's long overdue. I've been avoiding the truth for too long. It feels good to talk about it. And, having shared it with you, I feel better."

Karyn slowly got up off the couch and gestured for Jason to stand up too. She put her arms around him and hugged him, then stepped back and grabbed both of his hands.

She stood close and looked directly into his eyes. It was clear Jason's speech had touched her. "I know you don't write something like that for external validation. But I want you to know that, as a friend, I am so proud of you for giving this speech tonight." Karyn paused for a moment while she gathered her thoughts. "I hope you realize how much of a big deal this is."

Jason looked down at his feet. Karyn lifted his hands to recapture his attention before continuing. "Jason, I know you hate hearing this stuff, but those people are so lucky that they're going to get to hear this." Karyn let go of his hands and stepped back.

Jason shrugged his shoulders. "Right now I'm just focused on getting through it. And not throwing up on anyone!"

The two laughed as Karyn stepped forward to give Jason a high-five.

After a shower and a quick meal, Jason left a copy of his speech on the kitchen table for Mike and Wendy. "So how do I look? Is it too much—the blazer?" I didn't think so. "I haven't worn this Rowing Canada blazer in forever. I figure, 'go big or go home!'" Jason looked down at the maple leaf on his breast pocket, then knelt and called me over. "Ike, wish me luck, buddy—I'm gonna need it!" He kissed me on the forehead and disappeared out the door.

He was only gone a moment when Maddie came up behind me and intentionally bumped into my side. She dropped to the ground with her front legs splayed and her butt up in the air. Classic play-bow beckoning that she was ready to kick my backside. Or, at least, try.

We dashed around the living room, in and out of sofas and fancy chairs, trying to outmanoeuvre one another. Maddie was fast, agile, and relentless. Even when my age and experience aided me in pinning her for an obvious win, she was unwilling to let up. Unlike some of my siblings, her energy was endless. I loved her for it.

Wendy and Mike soon arrived home and let us out into the backyard, where our roughhousing continued. Later that evening, the headlights of Jason's car shone brightly across the kitchen wall. He was finally home. I moved to the door to greet him as he came in.

He smelled a bit strange—like he'd rolled in something! My guess was that the speech had been more taxing on him than he might have been willing to admit. I dropped to my back to invite some belly rubs. They always seemed to calm him down. Despite his odour, he was lighter than when he had left. His eyes were wide and his energy was fired-up—giddy, almost. I had never felt this from him before.

"Jason!" yelled Mike from the bedroom. "Get in here!"

He took another moment to say hello to Maddie before getting up and making his way to their bedroom. Mike and Wendy were already in bed reading. Mike waved the copy of Jason's speech. "Oh, look at you, Captain Canuck—looking pretty fancy, sunshine!"

"As you should, Jason." Wendy interrupted. "You look very nice. Don't listen to Mike."

"Okay, just so I'm clear, is this the speech you gave tonight?" Mike's mischievous smile widened across his face.

"Maybe."

"Maybe? You're full of shit—you gave this speech tonight, didn't you?"

"Mike!" Wendy tried to settle him. "Why don't you *politely* ask Jason how it went?"

Jason cleared some of the newspapers from the edge of the bed and sat down. I sat at his feet. He began to rub my neck and ears.

"Jason, that's a beautiful speech you wrote," offered Wendy. "I'm so proud of you."

"Thanks, Wen."

"It's more than a beautiful speech—it's amazing!" Mike said. "I can't believe you read this in front of complete strangers tonight. Did you cry? Because we cried. Both of us—blubber, blubber, blubber, the whole way through it."

It was true; when Mike read Jason's speech earlier his face looked like it had sprung a leak.

"That's kind of you to say, Mike." Jason looked at me, smiled, and raised one of his eyebrows. I could tell Jason appreciated his words.

"What did the people there have to say?" asked Wendy.

"Most of them came up to me afterwards and said some really kind things. Some of them even cried. Man, I had no idea sharing my story would touch people like that. But I'm glad I did it. I feel like I've finally kicked open a door that's been locked shut for way too long."

"What's with all of those pieces of paper in your hand?" Mike asked.

Jason looked down and saw the small pieces of paper spilling out of the folder that held his speech. "We share feedback at the meetings. We have this system where everyone writes..."

"Get outta here; people have to write down what they thought?" asked Mike.

"Yah—it's part of the whole Toastmasters thing, I guess."

"Have you read them?"

"Not yet."

"Well, pass 'em over, bucko, and let's have a look!" Mike clapped his hands together loudly and began rubbing his palms.

"Maybe Jason would like to read them first! And, *maybe* they're a bit personal," said Wendy.

"Personal? He doesn't care—pass 'em over, Jase! And speaking of personal, that soft-talker you've been pining over for way too long left a message on the machine."

"Really?" Jason sat up taller. He looked as though he had grown a foot!

"Go listen for yourself! And tell her to get a new phone—I couldn't understand a word she said!" Mike cackled and slapped the bed. "Or maybe it's her maritime accent—either way, good luck making sense of it!"

Before Mike could finish his sentence, Jason was on his way to the kitchen. I followed along. He bent down close to the answering machine and hit play. "Yikes—Mike wasn't kidding, I can barely hear her. Oh, well—who cares. She called. There's still hope, buddy!"

The next few months involved several trips to the Island to visit Robyn. We'd stay the night at Fiona's and Jason would make dinner without any of his previous commentary on how he felt Robyn should transform her running career.

Given that Robyn and Jason lived on limited budgets, their "dates" were simple and inexpensive; walks along the ocean beaches in Victoria, hikes in the mountains north of town, and picnics at local parks. The bonus for me was that I was included in all of it. And we almost always brought Brodie along too. He and I were becoming great friends. He was the most laid-back dog I had ever met. And he could still run and wrestle when he had to, or perhaps, more honestly, wanted to. He was stocky and strong and, sometimes, the effort it took to get him going was more than he felt like giving. For instance, on the days Jason and I did long runs, he'd walk with Fiona instead.

Robyn would also come over to Vancouver and stay at her sister's place. She'd come into town and we'd meet at Stanley Park, or Kits Beach, or even our favourite running spot, the Endowment Lands.

The pace was always what Jason could manage. He had explained to Robyn that he was no "speed demon," as he put it. Yes, he was competitive, but he wasn't stupid. He knew Robyn would win any run he decided to challenge her on. So he never bothered. Besides, Robyn didn't seem to mind. They would run for hours, talking the entire way. Me, I trotted along beside them and listened. I loved it. I was so fit by then, I could've run all day.

I wasn't sure what had changed for Robyn. Jason never asked. "Why upset the apple cart—she wants to spend time together, I'll take it!" And, there was something different about Robyn too. This time, she was more playful with Jason, and she was now calling to suggest getting together.

On one particular weekend, after twisting his ankle on a training run during the week, Jason decided it was best if he walked. So it was just Robyn and me.

"Go ahead, Ike. See if you can keep up with her. I hear she's pretty fast," Jason smiled at Robyn.

"Come on, Ike—it'll be fun!"

Jason bent down and kissed me and then whispered, "Take it easy on her, buddy!"

We were off. I had run with Pat and Trev by myself, but never alone with Robyn. At first, we eased our way along the trails. She was a quiet runner—light on her feet. I had grown accustomed to the sound of 200 lbs hitting the trails one slow-moving stride at a time. Not only was Robyn tiny, comparatively, she also had finesse when she moved. She reminded me of a whippet that I had met on the trails before. Quick moving and agile. There were no extra movements with Robyn. Everything flowed forward.

After a while, her watch beeped. "I'm going to speed up a bit, okay, Ike?"

Speed up? This was already so much faster than I ran with Jason.

Within three strides, she was off. I had never seen a human move so fast, let alone run with one. I sped up until I was beside her, moving at the same speed. Robyn was impressive. It felt thrilling to run at this pace, in and out of the trees and along the trails. For the entire run, we would speed up when her watch beeped and then slow down a bit when it beeped again. I wasn't sure why. I didn't care. I just knew this was the most fun I had ever had on these or any other trails.

After the run, Jason surprised me with a burger and some fries in my bowl beside the car in the parking lot. I gobbled it up. I wasn't sure why he had brought it. But I was more than happy to indulge.

Then he lit two candles that were stuck into the carrot cake he'd baked the night before while they sang Happy Birthday. Next, he opened a card and read aloud his note to me:

"Dear Ike, The best thing I ever did was decide to keep you.

Happy Birthday, buddy!

Here's to another fun-filled year!

Love, Dad"

Robyn smiled her approval. Sometimes he had a funny way of showing it, but I could feel how much Jason loved me.

"I don't know if I've sung Happy Birthday to a dog before." Robyn laughed.

"It's something I started last year. Given his health challenges, every year's a bonus with this handsome boy. I don't want to ever take him for granted. Celebrating Ike's birthday is a simple reminder for me that life is precious. We don't know how long we've got together."

"I love that, Jason. Thanks for including me," said Robyn. "Ike's a lucky boy to have a dad like you."

I agreed. There was so much Jason did for me that others didn't notice. My favourite was waking up from naps on the concrete floor at school and realizing that Jason had slid my blanket under my head while I was asleep. I was glad Robyn was getting to see that side of him.

We spent a lot of time with Robyn during those months, and I grew accustomed to having her as part of our routine. She still couldn't throw a stick or a ball if her life depended on it, but if that was her idea of trail running, I could get used to having her around.

Technically, they still weren't dating, but they had undoubtedly become very good *friends*. Jason finally heeded Fiona's advice and stopped *chasing* Robyn. She had become much more than a trophy girlfriend; she was Jason's trusted companion. Their long talks had resulted in a palpable connection; one that enabled Jason to feel safe enough to talk about almost anything. Usually, that was a good thing. However, his tendency to stumble over his old beliefs continued to haunt him.

I remember one time the conversation drifted towards Robyn's pre-race ritual of hugging her competitors. Once again, he suggested forgoing the hugs for one race just to see what happened. Robyn smiled and asked Jason to explain to her why geese fly in formation.

"So they can fly faster for longer," he answered.

"Exactly," continued Robyn. "I run *with* my competitors, not *against* them. If we all run faster and further, then we *all* run faster and further!"

Jason turned his head for a moment while he thought about Robyn's strategy. Then he looked at her and smiled. "You know, I've never thought of it that way."

"Together we fly—that's my racing mantra, Jason."

Until Robyn, if you didn't see the world as Jason did, he wasn't interested in spending time with you. But Jason became willing to absorb Robyn's enlightened approach to life that opposed his caveman views. Sure, he saw Robyn as beautiful, but he also found her way of being and her outlook on life equally attractive, and intriguing. It was a monumental shift for him. That said, it's not like he was buying up every self-help book he could find or watching Oprah every morning—far from it! But there was a lightness to him that had been missing when he first looked into my eyes.

I was beginning to wonder if, on that fateful day when they first met and Jason dared to suggest that he had met his future wife, maybe he wasn't kidding. I could see there was something special about these two when they were together. It wasn't always flawless—but when they clicked, it was pretty good. The respect that they showed for one another was obvious. And they looked out for each other. Jason seemed enamoured with how Robyn challenged him. Ever the glutton for punishment, he approached their relationship the same way he had with every other meaningful endeavour he'd embarked upon—head down, stubbornly moving forward.

The Knee Knacker race was a perfect example. The morning of, he rolled over, took his resting pulse, and proclaimed his strategy for the 50 km run.

"Thirty-six beats per minute, Ike. I'm not sure my body could be more prepared. But, you know what?" I looked up at him as he scratched under my chin. "I'm going to try something different today. And don't tell Robyn. In every race I've ever been in, I've hated anyone and everyone who came alongside me. Today, I'm going to run *with* everyone on the course—not against. No bad thoughts. No bad language. I'm just going to focus on doing my best." He looked almost embarrassed. "What do you think? Too soft? I mean, I'm not doing the 'together we fly' mantra thing, but it's a start, right?" I rolled onto my back and encouraged those scratches to move to my belly. Jason laughed, jumped out of bed, and got himself ready for the race.

There's no way on earth he would've arrived at that strategy without Robyn's influence. His relentless intrigue—examining her every move and thought, trying to understand what made her tick—had lured him into trying out bits of what he'd discovered about her.

Later that evening, when he was describing the race to Robyn over the phone, he shared how he had approached the day.

"I know—shocking, right?" said Jason with a laugh. "At first, it took some doing. I mean, it's an old habit, right?" He laughed harder. "But, after a few miles, I was able to reign in those 'kill or be killed' thoughts and just focus on my running." Jason looked at me with wide eyes, as if to say, I can't believe I just told her! He smiled as he listened to her response. I could tell he felt good about sharing his shift with her. "It was the most fun I've ever had racing. And my finishing time was so much better than I was expecting. I couldn't believe it!"

Jason patted the couch, signalling me to come closer. I sat down beside him and welcomed his strong hands, massaging my neck.

"It does feel pretty good—I have to admit."

While still not an actual thank-you, the conversation was an enormous step for Jason. As I said, there were glimmers of hope, with a long way to go.

The following week involved slow, gingerly walks. Jason's body would need some time to recover. Lugging his 200-pound frame up and down 8000 feet of elevation for seven hours would require some healing. Robyn had encouraged him to consider that the Knee Knacker might be his last long-distance running event. "You're a Clydesdale, not a mountain goat," she told him. He assured her he would take her advice into consideration.

That summer, having finished his third year of graphic design courses at Emily Carr, Jason was wrapping up his last academic courses at UBC. I wasn't sure where all of this schooling would take him—based on what he said on our runs, he wasn't either—but I, like Jason, was eager for a new adventure.

summer fun

In mid-July, Robyn came over for another visit with her sister and brother-in-law in Abbotsford. This time, we got invited for brunch. Yes, Jason and I would meet some of Robyn's family. Remembering she had eight other siblings, it was a start. And Jason saw it as progress.

No surprise, I had to suffer a bath before we could go. After brushing out my hind legs and tail feathers, Jason stepped back and admired his work.

"Sometimes I forget how handsome you are. Man, you're a good lookin' dog!" He smiled as he stroked my clean, soft fur. "Remember to charm their pants off, eh, buddy!"

On our way out to Robyn's sister's, we listened to the mixtape Jason had made for Robyn the night before. "Is this another great song, or what, Ike?" Jason turned up the volume. He was quite proud of his musical taste. I couldn't argue. Although we listened to a lot of Rush, he had a diverse appreciation of music. The tape included Sting, Annie Lennox, Bryan Ferry, The Cure, UB40 and many more artists.

"Notice the subliminal message, Ike?" Jason looked at me in the back seat. "Pretty clever, eh, buddy! Do you hear how each song is about love?" Then he paused, folded his eyebrows, and looked at me again. "Wait, do you think that's too cheesy?"

You said it, not me!

I could tell he was nervous. Jason dropped his keys as he got out of the car, and then the flowers, too, landed upside down on Robyn's sister's driveway, knocking some petals off.

He bent over to gather them up. "Way to go, Jase—you ass!"

"I wouldn't worry about that," came a voice in the front of the car. "I really appreciate the gesture." Jason spun around. Robyn's sister was waiting to greet him. She put out her hand to meet Jason's. "I'm Erin. Robyn's in the shower."

They shook hands. "Nice to finally meet you—I've heard a lot about you and Kuz. And sorry about the flowers."

"Don't be silly—I'll fix them up! And nice to meet you as well. Robyn's told us lots about you too."

"Really?" Jason tilted his head. "I mean, nice. Good. Uhh, am I early?"

"Nope—Robyn's late. She has a—let's call it a unique relationship with time." Erin bent forward and peeked into the back of the car where I was sitting. "And you must be the famous Ike! Have we heard *a lot* about you!"

Jason opened the car door and let me out onto the driveway. I wiggled and wagged as Erin rubbed my back and stroked my ears. "He's soooo soft. What a gorgeous dog you are, Ike."

Erin led Jason and me into their home. Her husband Kuz was at the stereo, choosing some music. He quickly made his way over to greet both of us. Kuz was short for Kuzumi. Smiling as he bent down to welcome me, I noticed his eyes. They were the warmest I'd ever seen.

While The Mavericks began rocking from the giant speakers strategically placed around the room, I got lost in the smells emanating from the kitchen.

"Hello Jason!" said Robyn as she walked into the kitchen. "Oh, and you, too, Ike—a big hello to you as well!" Robyn bent forward to rub my ears and back as she looked up at Jason. "How was the traffic coming out—did you have any trouble finding the address?"

"Nope—easy," answered Jason. "I just followed the delicious smells." Jason smiled.

"Two points for you, Jason!" said Erin with a wink. Everyone laughed as she pulled out ginger-pear pancakes from the oven.

On the table, there was a fruit salad, yogurt, maple syrup and, of course, peanut butter. Erin had heard about Jason's odd habit of eating pancakes covered with peanut butter.

"Can he have a small piece, Jason?" asked Erin.

"Sure, just make sure it's in a bowl and not from the table. It's the one thing I've managed to avoid—a dog that begs."

I followed Erin to the kitchen and gobbled up the pancake. *Delicious! Please don't screw this up, Jason—these are good humans!*

The humans stayed sitting around the table, drinking coffee and tea, and sharing stories. We were getting the lowdown on Robyn from one of her big sisters. And Erin wasn't holding back. However, to Robyn's credit, she laughed and joked along as Erin shared some particularly fun childhood memories.

Running full speed at the bed sheets hanging from the clothesline as they billowed in the wind pretending to be bulls, with their index fingers pointing forward for effect, and meeting headfirst the large boat they forgot was parked on the other side. Or, long past bedtime, listening in on their parents talking with friends at the kitchen table through the air vent in the bathroom upstairs. And holding their noses tight so as not to laugh when they heard things they likely shouldn't have.

As the stories continued, I began to appreciate why Jason had included "Comes from a large family" on his best-case date list. Robyn had lived experiences with all of her siblings. She was the byproduct of those; the bonds, the tears, and the laughter.

Lying at Jason's feet, enjoying the conversation, the time flew by. Soon it was mid-afternoon and we had a flight to get packed for. The next day, we were heading back to Ontario for two weeks—after cancelling last summer, we were finally going to visit Jason's family at their summer cottage I'd heard so much about.

***

Driving through the gate, the sign read, "Sunny Pines." Which made sense, considering there were tall pine trees everywhere and the day was, in fact, bright. I could make out an old wooden cottage and the lake behind it through those trees. I stood in the back of the car, eagerly awaiting my first swim. As soon as Jason opened the back door, I was off.

"Ike, what the heck?" yelled Jason.

I couldn't help myself. The day's travel had taken hours—most of them locked up in that tiny plastic crate. I immediately ran for the dock. Arriving at the edge, I took in the calm water below me. I shook anticipating my first plunge. *Two weeks of this? Pinch me!*

Just then, an orange hockey ball went sailing over my head and splashed down in the water a few feet in front of me. Then another. And another!

"Go on, Ike—go get 'em!"

I turned around to see Jason walking towards me with his entire family—parents, siblings, as well as nephews and nieces—in tow.

I leapt off the dock and chased after the first ball. Jason's family walked down and onto the dock, yelling encouragement and laughing.

I swam from one ball to another, trying to fit two at a time into my mouth. The crate was a distant memory.

The rhythm was simple. A morning run, followed by a swim, breakfast, then all day sunning and swimming from the dock. I remained wet from morning till bedtime. *So worth the wait!* Having the young nephews and nieces nearby meant I always had a willing arm to throw a ball or two into the lake.

Jason spent most of his days horizontal, reading in the hammock slung between two of the many large pine trees beside the lake. It was good to see him so relaxed. No classes. No homework. No chores. No training. Just quiet time with his family and me.

A few days after we arrived, Robyn called to see how we were doing and to let Jason know that she'd torn her left hamstring during training and wouldn't be heading over to Europe for the upcoming track meets. Her season was over.

Jason was disappointed for her. He knew that Robyn's world ranking played into her government funding, influenced her sponsors, and meant she wasn't earning the appearance money she'd be making at those top track meets. Unlike rowing, top international runners got paid to race. The summertime was when Robyn earned a good portion of the money she lived on throughout the year.

Robyn was one of the hot topics of conversation at most family dinners that capped off each day. With everyone crammed in around the dining room table and me at Carl's feet, they'd gather to share a delicious meal and discuss the day's events, and Robyn.

"When should we plan for the wedding?" was always the question that initiated the banter. Jason didn't mind. He played along. He wasn't shy about his "friendship" with Robyn, as he described it. He sounded comfortable and relaxed when he spoke of her. There was more respect. Less objectifying. She was no longer something he was trying to win over. They had become close friends and he seemed content with that for the time being.

"Well, 'friendship' or whatever you want to call it, you're different," announced Jason's sister, Wendy. "I haven't heard you laugh like this in a long, long time. I vote that you keep this woman in your life. And," she added with a smile. "I wouldn't be upset if I had a wedding to go to on the West Coast next summer!"

"Well, don't hold your breath. We both have a lot going on in our lives, and Robyn has many more years of competition ahead of her. So it will depend on her timing. And, besides, we're honestly just really good friends at this stage. Do I want more? Of course, but I'm trying to move at her pace."

By now I was so used to Jason talking about his long-term plans with Robyn, nothing surprised me anymore. And, truthfully, I had come a long way with Robyn too. True, she still couldn't throw a stick, but as a running partner she more than made up for it. The thought of having her as a life-long human mom was something I could easily get used to.

Eleanor, sitting to Jason's left, put her hand on his arm and smiled a motherly smile.

"But, don't worry, Mom—you'll be the first to know!"

With that, it was back to teasing Carl regarding his insistence that his portion of dessert was smaller than everyone else's. He complained every time. In his defence, it was. But, as Eleanor always reminded him, "You didn't go for a run this morning, dear."

It was nice to be a part of such a tight family.

By the end of the first week, Jason said I was *ripe*. "A wet golden is one thing, but a golden who's been wet for days is another."

Rose, Jason's sister-in-law, suggested the kids bathe me. I didn't mind; five pairs of tiny hands scrubbing and scratching me, then a quick rinse in the lake, and I was as good as new! Rose was happy, and I was back to chasing those orange hockey balls.

On our last night, we all sat around the fire pit. With an early departure scheduled for the following day, Jason's mom and dad wanted to hear about his plans for his final year at Emily Carr.

"I know, Dad, you keep reminding me—this is my ninth year of school. But I'll graduate with a degree and not just a diploma, which means if I decide to pursue another degree sometime in the future, I can."

"Gosh, more school?" responded Carl. "Son, I think it's time you found a job and started earning some money!"

"Honey!" Eleanor put her hand on Carl's arm.

"Believe me, I want to start earning some money, too, Dad. I've had quite enough of living like a student."

"What does your final year look like?" Jason's mom asked.

"We have different subjects that we have to take. But our main focus is what they call our thesis project. I think the school is just trying to make their program sound fancier than it is. Basically, we choose a topic that relates to design, and we work on it for the entire year. We show all of our steps and chronicle our creative process. Explain what we've learned, why we did what we did, and document it. Display it at the grad show and then present it to our instructors and professional designers who work locally in Vancouver. It's a pretty big deal. I'm told it's a ton of work. So it's going to be a busy year."

"What's your topic?" asked Carl.

"I'm not sure."

"*Christmas!* Don't you think it might be time to choose one?"

I loved the way Carl said, "Christmas"...it was as close to cursing as he ever got!

Jason shook his head. "Yes, Dad, it's time."

"Well, it all sounds fascinating to me, Jason," said Eleanor. "We're very excited to come out in the spring and attend your graduation."

"It's been a long time comin'," added Carl.

Eleanor slapped her hand across Carl's knee. "What?" responded Carl.

"Don't worry, Dad." Jason laughed. "I'll get you front row seats!"

Carl's frustration was warranted. Jason had been a distracted student during his first five years of university. And that distraction was rowing. Now, finally having moved on, he was finishing a degree that his dad and many others, including friends or family, thought should've been done years ago.

On our first day home, Robyn called to invite us out to Erin and Kuz's place for the upcoming weekend. Another sister, Shannon, and her husband and children were coming from Saskatchewan for a visit. Robyn wondered if we would like to join them for dinner Friday night.

Another bath for me and another chance for Jason to get to know more about Robyn and her family! With dirt being dished from both ends of the table, Robyn had little choice but to smile, laugh, and take it!

After dinner, plans were made for an afternoon at the beach the following day. Once again, Jason and I got invited—we were on a roll! As much as the smells and company of dinner had been enjoyable for me, a beach day was going to be more to my liking. No bath required—I was goin' swimming in the ocean!

We arrived to find blankets and food laid out on the sand with everyone gathered, enjoying a perfect afternoon. As much as the mouth-watering spread tempted me, the ocean won out! Robyn ran up from the beach to greet us. "Hello, you two—welcome! Ike, my nephews are keen to see you swim."

Happy to oblige! Freed from my leash, I took off for the water. I ran in until chest-deep, turned, and waited for those orange balls to rain down from above.

Except, today, Jason hadn't brought any. I stared at him in anticipation.

"Hang on, Ike—I'll find you something." He searched the shore for the perfect piece of driftwood. Within moments, a smooth, ideally-sized piece of doggie entertainment helicoptered over me. Before it could land, I was in pursuit. *Splash!* Through the waves, I made my way to the target and quickly returned it to Jason for another round—this was going to be a great day!

A few tosses later, I was surprised when my stomach began to gurgle. There was no delaying it—I had to go busy big time. As I made my way to the shore, stick in mouth, I found a spot that would do. No privacy meant no pride. I squatted and began the deed.

"Ike, what the heck? Right here? Come on!"

Hey, it's not like I planned it—you think I'm enjoying this?

"Robyn, can you grab me a poopy-bag from my backpack, please?"

I returned the stick to Jason for another toss and I was off again. The urge soon returned. Confused and annoyed, I ran for the shoreline again.

"Ike, what the hell's going on with you?"

This time it was loose—humans refer to it as diarrhea. Horrified, Jason did his best to remove my mess from the beach. Once more, I was off, only to feel the urge continue. *Again? How could that be? I'm empty!* But that undeniable lower belly tumbling persisted. Only, this time, I wasn't stopping.

With every stride a stream of ocean water shot from my backside. It was the strangest feeling. Clearly, I had consumed more saltwater than I had initially thought. With every toss, I ran through the waves in pursuit of my prized stick, with the same humiliating reaction.

"Ike, buddy," yelled Jason. "You've got water shooting from your ass!"

"Look at that lab," Robyn pointed from where she stood in the water beside Jason. "The same thing is happening to him!"

"I know one guy who's definitely not swimming today!" replied Jason.

"Jason, we have friends whose dog does the same thing every time they come to this beach," said Erin.

I didn't care much. I was having too much fun. And, for the next few hours, I chased my perfect beach stick while expelling ocean water with every stride, much to the amusement of the little humans and the disgust of everyone else.

Back at Erin and Kuz's home, I gobbled up my kibble. While the humans prepared their dinner in the kitchen, I joined the rest of Shannon's family in the backyard. There were orange balls everywhere. Shannon had gotten word of my favourite pastime and showed up with a bag of them. My playtime continued until everyone gathered, once more, around the dining room table. I found my spot at Jason's feet and passed out. Even the smells of Erin's cooking couldn't keep me from slumbering.

Hours later, I stretched and awoke from my long nap.

"Well, look who decided to join us," said Jason. "You tired, handsome boy?" He reached down and stroked and then patted my belly. "Thank you for managing to keep dinner inside of you!"

Robyn came over and knelt beside me. "How's our little Pooh Bear?" she said as she gently rubbed my ears.

"Pooh Bear?" asked Jason. "Where'd that come from?"

"I don't know—he just reminds me of Winnie-the-Pooh sometimes."

"You're right, Robyn," added Erin. "He does look a bit like Pooh."

"Are you sure you're not just referring to what happened earlier today at the beach?" The little humans responded to Uncle Kuz's comment with howls of laughter. "I think we should call him 'Ike the Poo Monster,' instead." He raised his hands like a bear and growled at the kids. Their laughter filled the room.

"You know what, I think you're right." Jason looked closely at me, as if for the first time. "He does look a bit like Winnie-the-Pooh."

Ikester, Pooh-Bear—it didn't matter; whatever humans wanted to call me was just fine. I was happy to be on the floor and on the receiving end of so much attention.

"Oh my gosh, it's late," announced Shannon. "Bedtime, for all of you," she looked around the table at her kids.

A chorus of disapproving "Awwwwwwws," answered their mom's decree.

"Yes, bedtime for us as well, Kuz," added Erin.

"What?" objected Kuz. "I was just about to put on some more music!"

Erin shot him a wide-eyed look. "It's late enough, Kuz."

"Oh, right, I guess it is kinda late." Kuz quickly got up from the table and joined in on the goodbyes to Jason and me.

Within a matter of moments, Jason and Robyn sat alone at opposite ends of the table.

"Well, that was kind of awkward," said Robyn, smiling.

"I think it was cute—just trying to give their younger sister some alone time with Ike and me."

"Jason, I don't think it's Ike they were trying to arrange alone time with," said Robyn with a laugh.

"Fair enough," Jason grinned. "You've got a nice family. I've had fun these past two days."

Robyn smiled, too, acknowledging the compliment. "Yes, my sisters and I get along really well. Even the ones you didn't get to meet. Lots of stories, growing up in our tiny home."

"You were a good sport."

Robyn nodded. "What are you up to tomorrow?"

"I have a house to look at. It's walking distance to school—well, a 40-minute walk, but that's not too bad. Ike will like that. And we're close to Queen Elizabeth Park. Which he'll love."

"Does the landlord know about Ike?"

"Nope. I've decided not to say anything. Screw it—I've been honest about him every time so far and no one's given him a chance. So I'm just not going to bring it up this time." Jason shrugged.

"What if he asks?"

"I'll decide in the moment—we need a place to live," answered Jason. "I have to change up my strategy."

I remember being surprised by this admission. This was not typical for Jason. He was honest and trustworthy to the core. However, I understood his frustration. We *did* need a place to live, and he was willing to bend the rules to make that happen.

"How about you? Are you heading back to the Island tomorrow? Do you need a ride?"

"I'm going to stay here one more night, and then Kuz will drop me off at the ferry on Monday on his way to work. But thanks for the offer."

Jason nodded as the room turned quiet. They appeared to have run out of things to talk about. Or was it just becoming so painfully obvious, to me anyhow, that now was time for Jason to retest the waters?

What are you waiting for, Jase? Reach out and take hold of her hand, buddy. She won't bite! I could hear Trev coaching him in my mind. *Now's your chance, big guy!*

I had to agree. Now was the time to move the dial. Even from under the table I could sense that Robyn was interested in their friendship becoming more than just walks, talks, and homemade dinners together.

Finally, in an attempt to nudge open the door, Robyn got up and moved to the chair beside Jason and put her hands on the table.

Come on, Jason, I like this human—a lot—it's time!

As if he heard me, Jason lifted his hands from under the table and slowly reached forward and placed both of them on Robyn's hand and forearm. She smiled. Jason smiled.

Yes—that's more like it!

From that night onward, their friendship deepened. Jason began to trust Robyn in a way I had never witnessed him opening up to another human before; his confidence was reborn; the heaviness that so often consumed him was relinquishing its hold; he seemed content, happier, and just more fun to be around. His intensity could still rear its ugly head, as I assumed it always would, but somehow, now, it was gentler.

Our last night at Wendy and Mike's house came a few days after Jason's birthday. They celebrated Jason with a huge feast. Even Maddie and I got a burger fresh off the barbecue.

It was hard to tell who was more excited about our leaving, Jason or Mike. Mike lifted his beer in a toast. "To the houseboy who came for a month and stayed for seven!" Jason and Wendy laughed. "In all seriousness, Jason, it's been a lot of fun having you and Ike as roommates! Maddie has loved every minute of it." Mike looked at Wendy. "We may have to come visit for doggie playdates!" Wendy smiled.

"Happy Birthday, Jason, and good luck in your last year at Emily Carr. We know you're going to do great things," Wendy clinked her glass with Jason's.

"I honestly don't know what we would have done without your generosity. You've been amazing, and we both—" Jason looked under the table— "have truly enjoyed our time here. I don't know how we can ever thank you."

Jason had secured the rental on Cambie and was getting settled into his room on the second floor. His decision to keep me a secret had paid off.

Our new home was perfect. Karyn was on the second floor across the hall from Jason, Pat moved into the front room on the main floor, and Carolyn, another UBC student that answered their "roommate wanted" posting, lived on the main floor as well. Most importantly, the backyard was big enough to chase balls and, as an added bonus, was completely fenced. Jason couldn't have asked for a better arrangement.

After our first day of classes, Jason spoke with Robyn on the phone. They talked about the day, got caught up, and made plans for her next visit.

"No, I'm sitting at the kitchen table, why?" Jason asked.

I got up and moved closer to him to enjoy a back rub...and to listen in.

"Hold on. I think I can probably see it from the deck." Jason got up and walked out the kitchen door. I followed him onto the deck, where he turned and looked up at the moon brightly shining in the dark sky.

"There, now I can see it." Jason smiled and continued talking with Robyn.

"What were you doing out there?" asked Pat as Jason and I returned to the kitchen.

"Umm, I was talking to Robyn," answered Jason.

"Ya, but you were looking at the moon?"

"What's the big deal?" said Jason defensively. "Robyn thought it would be nice if we both looked at the moon together."

"Awwwww." Karyn, who was also in the kitchen making some tea, elbowed Pat. "Jason, don't listen to this donkey. He's just jealous. I can't wait to meet this Robyn—she sounds like a sweetheart!"

Our morning walks to school weren't like our walks through the Endowment Lands at all. Instead, we meandered through numerous Vancouver neighbourhoods. To add to the scenery, the air was cool and crisp, and I could smell the changing leaves—I loved how we began our days together. Jason was in a good place; I could feel it, and hear it! Gone were the rants about lousy drivers and greedy landlords. Instead, he'd speak of all of the exciting things happening in our lives and his plans for a life with Robyn. He'd also landed a terrific spot to live, with wonderful roommates.

Incredibly, I was still a welcome guest at Emily Carr. In fact, Jason heard more complaints from his classmates and instructors on the days he didn't bring me. Becks still leaned on the same corny jokes to welcome us every day. Jason cringed less when she drew attention to him. Becks was my favourite. She kept cookies behind her desk, and after sitting and shaking-paw for her, I would get a treat. Jason's classes were more focused, less about theory and practice and more about execution. The big challenge remaining for him—what topic would he choose for his yearlong project?

One afternoon, Jason stopped in to meet with Andrew, his instructor from first year, and explore some possible ideas. "If I'm going to work on this for the whole year, it has to be worthwhile," said Jason. "I'll need more than a letter grade to motivate me enough to keep me engaged."

"Thousands of students before you have managed to find something to hold their attention for the year. I'm sure you will do the same."

Walking home, I knew Jason was trying to think of what that thing could possibly be. Given his sketching talents, I hoped that he would find something that involved illustration. He was running out of time. Final idea submissions had to be in by the end of September, with the project due date being the end of the school year in May.

With his birthday money, Jason had purchased a brand new Champion Juicer and had begun making fruit and vegetable juices after school each day. He would often mix some of the vegetable grinds in with my kibble. It was actually quite good. Reading through the juicer's recipe book, he discovered that his new gizmo could also make his favourite food—peanut butter. "Ike... I've got an idea." He looked at me. "Come on, let's go get some nuts!"

Back at the house, he pulled out several bags one by-one and placed them on the counter. He had peanuts, pecans, walnuts, almonds, and different seeds like pumpkin, sesame, and sunflower. He even had chocolate chips and butterscotch chips, as well as coffee beans.

Soon, the Champion was grinding out different combinations of savoury and sweet nut butter. Karyn, Pat, and Carolyn were Jason's taste testers. Some of the mixtures garnered a thumbs-up and others did not. Jason kept at it.

For an entire week, every evening after dinner, Jason continued to do what he did so well when he put his mind to something—work hard at it, with laser focus.

The next day, Robyn came to visit. We walked down to meet her at the bus stop.

After Robyn stepped off the bus, they kissed and gave each other a long hug—I was still getting used to their new human greeting ritual. For so long, the physical component—the romance of dating—had not been a part of their relationship. Now it was.

Robyn pointed to her suitcase—it was pretty big.

"How long do you plan on staying?" Jason laughed.

"What? I have my running things, something to wear if we decide to go out..."

"I'm just teasing you," said Jason. "Stay as long as you want!"

Back at the house, Robyn met the roommates. With Pat and Karyn, the conversation quickly progressed to Robyn's running. In particular, her hopes for the following summer's Olympics in Atlanta. While Jason made dinner in the background, Robyn became the centre of attention.

Eventually, conversation shifted to the concoctions Jason had been busy making.

"Have you tried Jason's nut spreads?" Karyn asked.

Pat spit up his beer while Jason started chuckling.

Karyn turned and looked at Pat. "You are so inappropriate!" Then, she looked back at Robyn. "Sorry, Robyn, I'm still getting used to living with these two *boys*—sometimes, I feel like I'm back in junior high!" Karyn smiled and rolled her eyes while she opened up one of the cupboards. She grabbed a jar of nut spread. "*This* nut spread!"

Robyn turned to Jason. "No. It's the first time I've heard of it."

"I was going to surprise you with it after dinner," said Jason. "But we can try some now."

Jason got out all of his different flavours along with some tasting spoons. Robyn tried each of them. And, like the other roommates, some she approved of, others she didn't.

After dinner, Robyn pulled out the chocolate nut spread from the cupboard with a sheepish look on her face. "Can I have a schnick more for dessert?"

"You like them that much?"

"You're really onto something here. They're delicious, Jason! I'd buy them if they were in a store!"

"She's right, Jason." Karyn had just come in to get some more tea. "I'd pay for these too. They're wicked!"

That was all the convincing Jason needed; he had just found his project for the year—designing the packaging system for a food item.

Later that night, I finally realized the downside of Jason and Robyn "dating." I was now relegated to the floor! "It's a soft-cushy blanket," he said. "You'll be fine, Ike."

If it's so soft and cushy, then why don't you sleep here?

The next morning, Pat, Karyn, Robyn, and Jason took off for Stanley Park and a run around the seawall with me in tow. The sun was shining. Humans were out and the city was waking up.

Once home, with pancakes on the griddle, Robyn pulled out a large paper bag and passed it to Jason.

"What's this?"

"Consider it a late birthday present."

"You didn't have to do that." He stuck his hand into the bag to find Robyn's gift. "*The Artist's Way,* by Julia Cameron."

"It's a book, but it's kind of more than just something you read. It's a workbook, as well," explained Robyn.

"A workbook? I thought you said it was a gift?" Jason laughed as he got up to clear the table.

"Well, you hand-write three pages of free thought every morning. You just get up, grab some tea, sit down, and write."

"Three pages? Geezuz Murphy—that'll take me forever," declared Jason. "And what do I write about?"

"You simply write about the topics she suggests you consider. But the key is to write, and not to stop writing until you've written three pages—every morning. Even if you have nothing to write about. In fact, she suggests actually writing that down, 'I have nothing to write about.' Or, 'I'm not sure why I'm even doing this?' Whatever—until something comes to you...and then you can write about that."

"What's the point of all of this writing?"

"Just read the book, Jason," said Robyn. "And see what happens."

Jason flipped the book over and read the back. "Have you just given me a self-help book?" He smiled and waited for her to answer.

"Why are you so opposed to experiences that might teach you something about yourself? Something that might bring you more self-awareness?"

"Simple—weak people do this kind of stuff. I don't need it!" declared Jason. I hadn't heard that harsh tone in his voice for months.

Robyn waited for a moment before turning her chair to face Jason. Then she reached out and took hold of both of his hands. "This is not about being weak or being strong—being right or being wrong. It's about being open—open to learning about yourself. Julia Cameron uses 'morning pages' to enhance her creative writing. It's called *The*

Artist's Way for a reason, Jason. I thought it might support you in your final year of *art* school."

Jason looked at me, which is what he often did when he didn't know what to say to the human right in front of him. "See what she did there, Ike?" He turned back to face Robyn. "Man, you're good at that." He let go of Robyn's hands and reached for the book. "Okay, I'll try it, but only because it's going to help me with my fancy peanut butter project! Not to turn me into some flake looking for spiritual growth!"

Robyn smiled and shook her head. "Okay, Mr. Tough Guy—whatever allows you to get up and write every morning."

"I'm no wuss trying to find himself! Right, Ike?"

He was doing it again. Totally out of his comfort zone. *Sorry, dad—you're pathetic!*

But Jason was laughing as he went to the kitchen cupboard full of nut spreads. Walking back to the table, he held up a jar and announced, "These little concoctions of fancy peanut butter are going to knock people's socks off! And I'm going to design a packaging system that my instructors have never seen before!"

Robyn stood up to meet Jason. "I love the idea, Jase. I can't wait to see them in stores!"

Jason scrunched up his face. "In stores?" He thought for a moment. "Now that is a frickin' idea worth celebrating!" He reached out and grabbed hold of Robyn. "Ike, we're going to start a peanut butter business!" I got up from under the table, happily wagging my body in agreement. "And, you can help! I'll find you a job, buddy—official taster!"

Jason wrote every morning for the next few weeks; three pages of whatever he could muster. Many times, he'd stop and look at me while he bounced his pencil like a drumstick on the dining room table. "Ugh—this is brutal, Ike. I never should've agreed to this." But, soon enough, he'd put his head back down and return to his writing.

I could see there were some benefits to being as stubborn as Jason—he was realizing one of them.

During his second week, the writing appeared to get easier. He swore less and rarely stopped. Soon, he was writing the three pages nonstop. The first morning he did, he had quite a sense of accomplishment about him. "Well, would ya look at that, Ike!" He couldn't wait to tell Robyn during their evening call.

Some mornings, he'd finish writing and appear to be still processing the thoughts he'd laid out on the paper. Whatever this practice was meant to uncover, it had a noticeable effect. Jason dug into whatever questions were presented in the book with the same tenacity I'd seen in him many times before.

Jason sat at the desk in his bedroom with the phone on speaker. "How's the training going? Are you back to full speed yet?"

"I'm not having any discomfort when I run, so that's a good sign," Robyn said. "I'm grateful to be back on the trails and enjoying my time in nature."

Jason rolled his eyes. "I'm glad to hear that, but it's also kind of a big year, no?"

"It's simply *another* year," said Robyn. "I'll train as best I can and hope it all comes together in Atlanta."

"Okay—I'll stop asking."

"You can ask. I'm just not looking at this year as any different than the others," replied Robyn. "How's the writing going? What have you noticed?"

"Lots! Mainly that my mind never shuts off. That the thoughts banging around inside of my head are not helping my cause."

"That's quite a discovery," said Robyn. "Meditation would help with that."

"Did you say meditation?" Jason flared his eyes. "If you think for one lonely moment that I'm going to sit my ass down on a purple pillow, cross my legs, and chant while some hippie incense stinks up the room—you're crazier than I thought. I'm willing to write every morning. But, the m-word, that's where I draw the line."

Robyn laughed. "The m-word? Come on, Jason—it's not that bad."

"Next topic. This discussion is over." Jason smiled at me.

"Okay—how about your peanut butter project? How's that progressing?"

"Ha—today the Dean reminded me that Emily Carr is not a business school, and that the purpose of the project is to explore design, not start some *peanut butter side-hustle,* as he put it. What a jackass!"

"Well, I can understand his point. It is an art school, after all," replied Robyn. "Maybe just keep the business part to yourself."

Jason still needed a brand name. And, with only a week before the deadline to submit a concept proposal to his panel of advisors, he was under the gun.

The next day while running through the trails in the Endowment Lands, one at a time, Jason shared his ideas with me. And, one at a time, he declared all of them unworthy—or "shit-awful," as he liked to say.

Then he suddenly stopped dead in his tracks and gazed up at the clouds with his hands clasped on top of his head. I turned and walked back toward him to make sure he was okay.

"Ike—I've got it!" Jason stared into my eyes. "I've been looking everywhere for inspiration, and all of this time, it's been right beside me! You! I'm going to name these nut spreads after you. They're playful. They're fun. They're delicious—well, I don't know how that part relates to you, but...who cares!" Jason knelt down and motioned for me to come closer. He grabbed hold of my collar and rubbed my chest. "I'm going to get you on this label. You are going to be forever immortalized on jars of fancy peanut butter—how cool is that, bud? Everyone will know about the golden retriever named Ike—I love it!"

Standing there in front of Jason, I remember being a bit overwhelmed. I was two years old, and it was too much for me to consider that I was that important to him. It was one of the best moments I can recall with Jason. I had never felt that loved before.

The remainder of the week was spent refining the name and creating some rough sketches to indicate his visual direction. On Thursday afternoon following classes, Jason had arranged a meeting with Andrew, who had agreed to be one of his panel members.

Jason knocked at his door while I wagged my tail at the passing students greeting me. "Come in," said Andrew. "Jason—perfect. Come in, come in. Ike, buddy—how's my favourite student?" Jason laughed. Andrew laughed as he cleared the paper mess. "Okay. I'm all yours. And, just so you know, Deborah and I spoke earlier about the direction you've chosen. She said you two met yesterday—correct?"

"First, I appreciate you taking the time to meet," said Jason.

"Of course—it's my job!" Andrew smiled. "Where are you with things?"

Jason took a slow deep breath and looked at me. "I'm guessing you heard that I'm going to name the nut spread after Ike? That I'm going to put him on the label?"

"Yes," replied Andrew. "That's what Deborah indicated."

"Well, she wasn't too jazzed about the idea when I told her. In fact, she said, 'I like my dog, too, Jason, but come on.'"

"That sounds like our Deborah. Have you met with any other panel members?"

"No, just her. Look, I can see how some people might think that the product is for dogs. I get that. So, I've decided to put my name on there with him. You know, like, a guy and his dog—his loyal companion. This brand represents values like trust, relationships, looking out for one another—stuff like that."

Andrew nodded his head while he continued listening. "Okay—I like what I'm hearing so far."

"So I'm going to call it Skeet & Ike's Not Just Nuts Spread. My nickname is Skeet—my rowing buddies from Ontario called me that. It was my dad's nickname growing up—I inherited it from him. Ike is self-explanatory. And, as for the spreads, they contain more than nuts—dark chocolate, butterscotch, M&Ms, coffee, seeds, and other stuff."

Andrew nodded his head more deeply. "I get that. And it's a bit of a play on words as well—right? Not just nuts—as in, you're not just nuts, this is a legitimate product."

"Exactly!" added Jason. "Glad to see I'm not crazy!" Jason's knees were bouncing fast; I could tell he was thrilled that Andrew understood his concept.

"What about an illustration style? Fonts? What's the look and feel you're heading for?"

"Cottage. I want it to look like grandma's kitchen. Not corporate. Not slick. Just a guy and his dog who've created this fun and feel-good product. I want the look to follow that lead."

Andrew waited for a moment before speaking. Jason sat anxiously. "Jason, I like it. I do. I like everything about it. It has a nice feel to it. I can picture the label and the marketing. I can even see them on store shelves. So, my answer is yes—go for it!"

Jason exhaled slowly. "Andrew, thank you. Thanks for being open to this."

"Hey, don't thank me. It's a good idea."

With Andrew's blessing, Jason jumped full-on into researching other products that seemed to fit the same branding direction he was considering. When he didn't have classes, he would arrange meetings with local entrepreneurs to hear their origin stories and ask questions. How had they begun? How were things going now? If they could start again, what would they have done differently?

To his amazement, the meetings were easy to schedule. One after another, prominent local business owners with jam-packed calendars gladly made time to share their advice with a keen and ambitious student. Almost without fail, they all shared that someone had taken the time to meet with them when they were starting out. The meetings were paying that generous entrepreneurial spirit forward.

Jason also visited local grocery stores to photograph products that captured the visual direction he was considering for his nut spreads. Again, store managers seemed more than willing to help a student pursue a school project. Where, typically, pulling out a camera and snapping pictures of products on the shelves of any major grocery chain would likely get you kicked out—Jason had a green light every time. Each night, I would listen in as Jason would share with Robyn about the meetings and stories of the humans he'd met. He was on fire!

To help figure out what his future customers might prefer, Jason created a questionnaire asking shoppers to answer a few simple questions. Aside from the usual purchasing habits, he was keen to determine from the get-go whether having a golden retriever associated with a food product would interfere with a potential sale. To his amazement and relief, only a handful of humans responded negatively to a dog—me—on the label.

Most shoppers found it cute and intriguing that a dog was on the label. When asked to describe what feelings a golden retriever evoked in them, the answers confirmed his original thinking. Friendly, fun, and trustworthy were the descriptors that were consistently mentioned.

In the evenings Jason would combine all of his research from the day and sketch out the ideas he was developing. With me curled up beside him on his bed, and music playing in his ears, Jason busily drew up label ideas. As if expecting feedback, he would constantly show his work to me and ask, "What do you think?"

I just remember feeling excited that he and I were going to be on a food label together, and every human who purchased a jar would learn of our story. That made my insides feel warm.

Regardless of what some of his panel members had expressed concerning me being a figurehead for the design project, Jason was determined to proceed. Bold defiance seemed to energize his resistance. Every time we left a meeting, he was more entrenched in the idea of "his handsome boy" being on the label. "Screw 'em, Ike—we're doin' this, buddy!"

I don't think those instructors knew what they were up against. The more they told Jason he shouldn't, the more he believed that he should. With Andrew and two others in his corner, Jason was eventually granted permission to proceed as he had originally intended. Then the real work began.

Between school, runs on the trails, time with his roommates, and connecting with Robyn every night, Jason was very busy. His Tuesday night Toastmasters meetings had resumed as well. He seemed less anxious about attending this year—almost excited.

Since Jason's agonizing ice-breaker, he had steadily progressed through the required speeches. His fifth Toastmasters speech was to explore the use of physical gestures and vocal variety. It was scheduled for the end of October.

Like the first four, Jason would practice aloud while we ran, and then try to capture his thoughts on paper when we got home. Although I had heard some snippets here and there, I still wasn't sure what he had chosen to speak about.

A few weeks later, he asked Pat to come along to his Toastmasters meeting and bring me. After everyone was gathered in the main meeting room of the local community centre, Jason excused himself to meet Pat and me just outside the door. We entered an adjacent room with sliding partitions that allowed Pat and I to sit quietly in the next room and wait for Jason's cue. I still wasn't clear what he had planned.

After a while, it was Jason's turn to give his speech. The meeting organizer reminded everyone of the purpose of the fifth speech—show the meaning of the speech, don't just tell it—then he introduced Jason. I stood up and moved closer to the gap between the hanging partitions that divided the rooms.

"Not too close, Ike," whispered Pat. "It's not time yet."

Not time yet? What are you talking about?

Finally, Jason stood at the podium, cleared his throat, looked around at the members in the room, and began.

"Do you remember the speech we heard a couple of weeks ago about 'the mystery of friendship?' How a true friend is described as someone you can reveal your genuine colours to with no hesitation? Where two people establish a relationship based on complete trust and honesty—sounds pretty special, doesn't it? How many of us can say we have a friendship like this? It wasn't until I heard that speech that I realized I had that kind of friendship.

"You see, I have a friend with whom I don't censor my actions, or thoughts, or moods, or anything. I am completely myself in his presence. I trust him with my most personal insights. There isn't anything I don't feel comfortable discussing with him. He makes it quite easy, though—he's a great guy!"

I wasn't sure whom Jason was talking about. Was it Pat? Is that why he had him come along?

"He has the most amazing outlook on life. He's always positive—but never obnoxious about it. No matter what the situation, he will always try to make the best of every predicament. On days when I've had a stressful time at school, or if someone is really getting under my skin, all I have to do is tell him about it, and things seem to improve immediately. He's a great listener. I can always tell he's truly immersed in our conversations, and I feel the connection when I speak with him.

"No matter what the topic, he always has a solution for my troubles. It's almost Zen-like. He would never suggest he's got life figured out—he's not that brash—but when you watch him, it certainly appears as though he does. It's hard not to notice his remarkable confidence.

"He rarely challenges, but when confronted, he shows no hesitation in defending his values and standing up for what he believes in. He doesn't have a temper, but he's so strong-willed that I feel sorry for people who try to outdo him. He's more determined than anyone I know. But, at the same time, he's relaxed and laid back. His loyalty is unquestioning. He has no time for insincerity. You're either in, or you're out. If you try to play little mind games, he'll call you on it. I've seen him do it, and it's not a pretty sight. When I've let him down in the past, he doesn't really get upset but instead seems confused by my actions. Deception is a concept he has no grasp of.

"He treats everyone equally. He knows no prejudice. The car you drive, where you live, what you do, or how much money you make does not impress him. If you really want to impress him, tell him what you did for fun last weekend. Self-important people who are caught up in their busy schedules don't do much for this guy. And, if your mood changes like the wind, he'll avoid you.

"He is fun-loving and always has a smile for everyone. In fact, I've watched him smile at complete strangers. In most cases, they return the gesture.

"Although he has no regard for his appearance, he gets complimented on his looks all of the time. When we go for runs together, he doesn't avoid muddy puddles; he seeks them out. If his hair gets a little messed up, he's not concerned. If someone can't accept him for who he is, he wants nothing to do with them.

"I've never seen him get really down about anything. He always tries to turn every situation into a fun-filled learning experience. His approach to life is that we have one shot—so it had better be a good one!

"I remember the first time I met him. It was a family gathering. I watched him wrestle with some of his siblings. After a few minutes, his siblings began to tire of the game, but not him. He wanted to keep going. I suppose he hadn't had enough fun yet. Talk about foreshadowing—I was to learn that fun was generally the underlying theme of his every endeavour.

"I met him again about two weeks later. That was the first time I held him in my arms. He was an eight-week-old golden retriever puppy. I remember looking into his eyes and thinking I was going to teach this little guy so much. I couldn't have been more wrong. It's he who has taught me—more than I could've ever imagined.

"Initially, it was my job to take care of this little pup. You see, he was going to be a guide dog for the blind. My job was to expose him to as many different social settings as I could for one year and then... give him back. Sure, we went to a few restaurants, he came to school with me, and I taught him some obedience. But, in the end, none of that comes close to what he has taught and given me. I have the utmost respect for my dog, Ike.

"I can't imagine the term 'unconditional love' having more relevance. I screw things up far more often than he does, and yet he's always there when I need him.

"Someday he'll leave me..."

Boy-oh-boy—at the time, I thought, *Leave him? That's not going to be for a long, long time!* And here I am...leaving him.

"...but he will have left me the memories of our time together. And his teachings will never get old. When I think of him, I'll smile as I imagine that look he'd give me when it was time to play."

"Get ready, Ike," whispered Pat. "You're going to run into the room and over to your dad, got it?"

"And, if I want him by my side again, I'll just whistle like I used to—and he'll be there."

"Now, go, Ike—go, buddy!" Pat directed me through the gap, and once through, I ran over to see Jason.

As the members noticed me enter the room and run for Jason, they cheered loudly. It was fun and not what I was used to. Generally reserved in his expression of how he felt about others, Jason's speech had caught me completely off guard. I knew he cared about me; I had known that from the start. I just didn't know how much.

Jason knelt to greet me as I ran toward him. "Hey, Pooh-Bear," said Jason quietly. "Imagine seeing you here!" He rubbed my chest with his strong hands before standing up to look for Pat.

The meeting was adjourned for a ten-minute break. Jason stuck his head between the dividers, "Thanks, Pat. Appreciate you helping out."

"No problem—that was neat. Everyone sure loved Ike!"

"They sure did; I'll keep him for the rest of the meeting."

"Okay, and, nice job on the speech—that was really clever."

Jason headed for the kitchen and the oatmeal cookies he enjoyed so much. While getting there, many of his peers congratulated him. Once he was alone, a man with a dark complexion approached him. He wasn't as tall as Jason—not many humans were. He was lean, wearing jeans, a thick sweater, and a brightly coloured scarf. His face was weathered and surrounded by dark curly unkempt hair that was beginning to grey. His eyes were piercing—steel-blue but warm and kind.

"Jason, I loved your speech, my friend," he said with an accent and a big smile.

"Oh, thanks," replied Jason, looking up to see who was speaking to him. "I'm sorry, I didn't see you at the beginning of the meeting. Did you come as someone's guest?"

He nodded. "Listen, Jason—I was wondering if I could ask you a question about the speech?"

"Sure, what do you want to know?" he replied as he bit into his cookie.

"I'm wondering, Jason, if you could please tell me what the speech was about?" His smile disappeared.

"I don't know." He looked at the man strangely. "You were in the room—you tell me."

"I was, indeed, my friend. You are correct," continued the gentleman. "But I was just wanting your clarification."

"Well, I would say the speech was about Ike. This handsome guy beside me." He smiled and pointed at me standing beside him.

"Ahh, yes, he is a handsome soul. I agree. But I don't believe your speech was about Ike—not at all."

Jason recoiled his head and scrunched up his face. "What do you mean, it wasn't about Ike? I wrote the speech—I should know!"

"Yes, true—you did write the speech. But that speech was about you, not Ike."

Jason's face went blank.

The gentleman moved closer. "I'm aware you've had some difficult years. I know it has not been easy for you. What you told us about Ike is what you want for yourself. You are learning, and Ike is a beautiful and important teacher for you. But you also have others who are watching over you."

"Who are you?" Jason asked sharply.

The man stepped back. "My name is Mercy. I came here tonight to help a friend."

"Okay, everyone, let's return to our seats!" instructed the meeting organizer.

"Oh, I must go," said Mercy. "It was a pleasure to meet..."

"Wait, you can't leave now—there's the second half of the meeting. And..."

With a bright smile, Mercy reached out and put his hand on Jason's shoulder. "Jason, after much turmoil, you are finally on your path. Be patient, my friend. Have faith that it will lead you to where you are most needed." Mercy squeezed Jason's shoulder, turned, and walked out of the kitchen toward the meeting room.

Jason grabbed his juice and a few more cookies. "Was that weird or what?" Jason said. "And, Mercy? What kind of a name is that? Who names their kid Mercy?"

Jason carefully placed his juice on his desk and neatly stacked his oatmeal-raisin cookies. After sitting down, he looked around the room. Then he leaned toward the woman sitting beside him and quietly asked, "Where'd that guy go who was here for the first half of the meeting? The guy with the bright scarf?"

"He just left," she answered.

Jason quickly pushed back his chair and got up. "Come on, Ike. Quick. Let's go!" We hurried through the door and out into an empty hall. Jason looked both ways.

"Mercy? MERCY!" he yelled. He listened for a moment and then ran down the hall. He stopped at the men's washroom, shoved open the door and called inside, "Mercy?"

Quickly, Jason and I ran to the front doors and out into the parking lot. It was dark, foggy, and silent—not a sound. "What the hell, Ike—he couldn't have disappeared that quickly." Jason looked in every direction. There was no sign of him. Mercy had vanished.

On the phone later that night, Robyn was spellbound. "Jason, that was quite a moment."

"I'm still not sure what to make of it," said Jason. "One thing I'm getting a bit tired of, though, is everyone's advice being about *faith*.

My dad said, 'Have faith," when I called him, and we talked about death. Allyson said it when I was unsure if I should keep Ike. The Padre said that about Sara falling from the crow's nest. And now this guy, Mercy. Faith. 'Have faith, Jason.' Faith in what? Would someone please tell me what I'm supposed to have faith in?"

The phone went silent for a moment. "What does faith mean to you?"

"Well, I know what it's not—it's not religion," answered Jason quickly. "I interpret faith to mean trust... That everything's going to be...? I don't know. That's the part I don't get—trust what?"

"What do you have to know to have faith?" continued Robyn. "To trust?"

Jason took a deep breath and exhaled loudly. "Well, nothing, I suppose. I mean, trusting allows me not to worry as much. When I'm able to do that—I can simply let go."

"Maybe that's enough." She paused. "Do you remember reading about synchronicity at the beginning of *The Artist's Way*?"

"Yup—why?"

"Well, Julia Cameron suggests that a byproduct of journalling can be a heightened awareness of moments of synchronicity. Your experience with Mercy—coincidence or something worth paying attention to?"

"I'm not sure."

"His words, 'you're finally on your path'—what would it feel like to trust that?"

"Umm, good, I guess," answered Jason. "How could it not?"

"I would agree. So why can't that be enough?"

He hung up the phone and patted the outside of his leg, inviting me to move closer so that he could rub my back while he pondered their conversation. Like during most of his phone calls with Robyn, Jason sat for a moment longer after they finished speaking. As much as Jason liked Robyn to think that he wasn't paying much attention to her wise counsel, he was. He would often think long and hard about her advice.

put your hands up

Every morning, Jason continued to sit at the dining room table with his morning tea, pencil, and paper, and write three pages.

A month before the Christmas break, Jason's commitment to his final school project had ramped up. Skeet & Ike's had become more than a final letter grade for him; the plan was now about starting a business venture. That shift was enough to ignite a drive in him that I had never seen before. For the first time in his four years at Emily Carr, Jason would occasionally return to the campus after dinner, like most of his other classmates had done for years.

I was happy to see him so engaged. But I missed our time together. I still went to class with him during the day, but he didn't take me at night. I would doze on the kitchen floor and wait for the sound of his car pulling in under the deck. Then I'd quickly run down the stairs to the basement and meet him at the door.

One evening, Jason had stayed particularly late. It was long past our bedtime when I heard his car.

"Hey, bud—how are you?" I leaned into Jason's legs and soaked up his pats and scratches. "I know, I'm late tonight, eh? You just have to hang on a little bit longer. We have our break coming soon."

Jason put down his books and gestured for me to come outside. "Come on, bud—get out here and go busy." Most nights when Jason got home late, instead of using the bathroom, he would join me outside for my before-bedtime pee. Our backyard was surrounded by trees and shrubs, and, therefore, had plenty of privacy.

As I stepped outside, I could smell something different. I could smell dogs. And not just BonBon, the neighbour's dog. I could smell a scent on our grass. With my nose to the ground, I quickly darted around the backyard to investigate. As I got closer to one of the shrubs, I smelled a human. I crouched and growled. Whoever was in there wasn't moving. So I lunged and let out a series of intimidating barks.

"Ike. Ike, what are you doing?" asked Jason in a whispering yell. "What is wrong with you? There's nothing in there. Come on back!"

Oh, yes there is; there's someone hiding in these bushes. I can smell them!

Jason came over, grabbed me by the collar, and pulled me back closer to the house. He then bent down and began rubbing my chest and scratching my ears.

"It's okay. Just relax, Ike."

I was still tense and facing the bushes. If someone was going to come out, I was going to be the first to meet them.

"Hey, easy does it, Ike." Jason continued to rub my chest. "So are you excited to see your mom this weekend?" I looked at Jason. I had forgotten that Robyn was coming over for a visit. "I got most of my work done this evening, so we can just do fun stuff this weekend. Hikes? Runs? Swims down at Kits beach?"

I hadn't seen Robyn in a long time. And, no offence to Jason, a visit from Robyn also meant some runs that allowed me to really stretch out and run fast.

“Come on, let’s get inside and go to bed.”

As we came up the stairs, Carolyn was coming out of the bathroom. She, too, had been up late doing her schoolwork.

“You’re late—everything okay?”

“Yup. All good. Just getting some extra stuff done at school before Robyn comes over tomorrow. How about you?”

“The usual—just writing up more research.” Carolyn bent down to greet me. “What was all of the noise about, Ike?”

“I don’t know what got into him,” Jason said. “It was weird. It was like there was something—”

Before Jason could finish his sentence, the phone rang. Jason and Carolyn looked at one another with raised eyebrows. Carolyn picked up the receiver and quietly answered. “Hello?”

We could hear a woman’s voice, but couldn’t make out what she was saying. “Yes, this is Carolyn. Who’s calling, please?” Carolyn’s eyes opened wide as she reached for a pen and paper.

“What’s up? Who is it?” asked Jason.

Carolyn continued to listen to the human on the line as she grabbed a pen and began to scribble something down.

“Why are you drawing a gun?” asked Jason.

Carolyn placed the phone up against her chest. “It’s the Vancouver Police Department. She’s telling me the house is surrounded by SWAT team members. And she wants to speak with you.”

Jason slowly took the phone. “Hello?” As he answered, Pat’s bedroom door opened and he came out into the hall to join us. “Yes, this is Jason.”

“Did I hear you say there’s a SWAT team surrounding our house?” asked Pat.

Carolyn nodded. “Yes. She said they’ve been there since 7:00 o’clock. She doesn’t sound like she’s kidding, either.”

Pat wasn’t buying it. “Jason, ask her to prove she’s with the police.”

Jason nodded to Pat as he continued to listen to the woman. "Umm, no offence, but this isn't exactly a call that we might get every night. So any chance you could prove that you are who you say you are?"

Jason listened intently, his eyes grew wider, and wider. Finally, Jason covered the receiver and lowered the phone. "Okay, it's definitely the police!"

"How do you know?" asked Pat.

"She knows that I just got home a few minutes ago. And that I was out back with Ike, taking a pee before I came in the house."

"Yuck, you peed in our backyard?" asked a rather disgusted Carolyn.

"She wants us to come out the front door one at a time. And they want you to start, Pat."

Pat stepped back and pointed to himself. "Why me? What did I do? "

"Here, take the phone; she wants to talk to you. I have to go wake up Karyn. She wants all of the lights on as well as the blinds open. Carolyn, can you open the curtains in all of the rooms on the main floor?"

Moments later, we all stood in the front hall with Carolyn taking directions from the officer on the phone. "She says to open the front door and wait for instructions from the lead SWAT team member."

Pat slowly opened our windowless old wooden door. Its loud creak didn't help with the tension. With no way for us to see what was on the other side, we had to quietly wait for the door to open and then cautiously lean forward to peer through the screen door. It was completely quiet. Just some distant late-night traffic coming from Cambie. The street light in front of the house was bright enough to see that no one, especially someone resembling a SWAT team member, was in sight.

"She's full of shit," announced Pat. "There's no one out here. This is a crank call." Now he was clearly perturbed.

Jason, still looking through the screen, answered, "Ya, but how did she know that I peed outside with Ike?"

"Eww, you peed in our backyard?" asked Karyn.

"Oh, for God's sake, can we forget about that for a second?" Jason said. "Besides, Ike pees out there every night! What's the big deal?"

"She wants you to go out onto our front step, Pat," instructed Carolyn.

"This is ridiculous—when I find out who's behind this stunt, I'm gonna be pissed." Pat shoved open the screen door and moved onto the front step. "There. Now what? *Put my right foot in and shake it all about?"*

Jason and Karyn sheepishly smiled as they looked at one another.

"She says to wait."

"Oh, sure—now she wants me to wait. Sorry, don't mean to hurry the big bad SWAT team," said Pat. "I mean, it's not like it's the middle of the frickin' night!" Pat turned to face the street. "Hello! Mr. Big-and-Bad-SWAT-Team-Man. I'm here. Come and get me," yelled Pat as he raised his arms in the air.

The roommates began to laugh. It was kind of funny. Whoever had pulled this off had done a perfect job.

Just as their laughter grew loud enough to spill onto the street, the house suddenly lit up as if someone had borrowed the sun. Enormous portable lights made a loud *clack* as they shattered the darkness, shining powerful beams of daylight from every direction.

"Holy shit! This is no prank," whispered Jason.

"PATRICK, THIS IS THE VANCOUVER POLICE DEPARTMENT. PUT YOUR ARMS IN THE AIR AND SLOWLY MAKE ONE COMPLETE TURN. THEN WALK IN A STRAIGHT LINE TO THE SIDEWALK. DO NOT VEER FROM THAT STRAIGHT LINE. AND DO NOT FOLLOW THE PATH AND GO BETWEEN THE TALL HEDGE TREES. UNDERSTAND?"

Pat began to carefully turn in place. His face had gone grey and his eyes were wide and bright. Karyn, Carolyn, and Jason had also stiffened. I could feel and smell their tension rising as they watched Pat walk away from the house. Clearly, this had just become a very serious matter.

As Pat arrived at the sidewalk, a SWAT team member appeared from behind a vehicle parked on the road. He slowly approached Pat with his large assault rifle pointed directly at Pat's chest. We could hear the man speaking, but couldn't make out what he was saying. Then, with the same caution he had shown while turning in place, Pat slowly and methodically got onto his knees and lay down flat on the ground, placing his hands behind his back.

"Geezuz Murphy, that's a huge frickin' gun! Do you see the size of that thing?" Jason sounded panicked.

"They're putting him in handcuffs. What the heck is going on here?" Karyn, too, was getting more upset.

"Okay, Jason, she said you're next."

Jason turned to me and put his hands on either side of my head. "Okay, Ike, this is going to be a little strange. You're going to stay here without me. But, don't worry, I'll be fine. And no barking or freakin' out—got it?"

Jason slowly opened the screen door, moved to the front steps, and immediately received the same instructions. Except, in his panicked state, he followed the footpath to the sidewalk, instead of going straight .

"Shit, Jason's going between the trees," said Karyn. "The SWAT guy said specifically not to. What the hell's wrong with him?

"JASON, DO NOT FOLLOW THE PATH. MOVE IN A STRAIGHT LINE," yelled the SWAT Team officer.

"Uh-oh, he hasn't changed. He's still on the path!" said Karyn.

"JASON DORLAND, DO NOT GO BETWEEN THE TREES."

"Oh my, please don't shoot him," pleaded Karyn. "Come on Jase, don't go between the trees."

This was not okay. I knew something was wrong the moment I smelled a human in our backyard. I lunged at the screen door and then frantically scratched and barked. I had to help Jason.

Thankfully, he arrived at the front sidewalk alive while the SWAT team leader appeared to just give up and stopped yelling at him.

Once Jason was handcuffed, Carolyn looked at Karyn and said, "Sounds like you're next."

This time, the instructions seemed to change. When Karyn arrived at the sidewalk and was met by the same SWAT team member, she wasn't handcuffed. Instead, she was simply escorted to join Pat and Jason who were sitting out front of our neighbour's home.

Next, it was Carolyn's turn. "Okay, Ike. She wants me to put you in the backyard before I go out there. Something about clearing the house with the sniffer dogs."

Carolyn opened the kitchen door and I walked out onto the deck. The dog smells from earlier had become more intense. I stretched my nose straight up into the night air, trying to decipher what direction they were coming from. As I sniffed intently, I heard someone talking from down beneath the deck. I ran to the edge. There were two stocky men dressed in black, each with a German shepherd on-leash. I launched myself at the railing that ran around the deck. I barked and growled as loudly as I could. They didn't move. Instead, one of the men told me to be quiet. I was having none of that. I turned quickly and ran for the stairs. Once on the grass, I sped towards the fence and leapt at them. Again, I barked and growled at the intruders with my hackles on full alert.

"Hey, take it easy, pup," yelled one of the men. "Goldens are supposed to be nice and playful—what's up with you?"

This was my home and my humans lived here. There was no way I was backing down. Finally, realizing that I wasn't going to let up, they walked away, and I returned to the deck.

After what seemed like an eternity, the lights out front dimmed and darkness returned to our backyard. I stood on the deck waiting for Jason. Then I heard laughter coming from the front yard. *What's going on?*

Finally, Jason opened the kitchen door and let me into the house. The dog smell was now equally as intense inside. I took off immediately to see who was in our house. "Ike, it's okay, buddy. The sniffer dogs were having a look around. We're just fine."

I darted in and out of every room and, when I came back downstairs, there were two large police officers sitting in our living room with my roommates, having tea and laughing.

"That's the golden retriever our canine squad was talking about?" asked one of the officers. "He looks harmless!"

"What are you talking about?" asked Jason.

"I heard one of our canine guys come over the radio and say that they couldn't get close to the back of the house because of some dog in your backyard—that's saying something!"

"Really?" Jason looked at me strangely.

"So you guys waited out there for how long?" Karyn asked.

The older of the two officers answered, "Five, maybe six hours."

"Why so long?" asked Jason.

"Because if we started the process of clearing your house and then you showed up, that could get tricky."

"So you just sat and waited?"

"We did. In fact, we had three snipers staked out on your neighbours' rooftops the entire time."

In perfect unison, the roommates answered together, "What*?* You had snipers out there?"

"It's standard protocol," answered the same police officer.

"So why us? What did you think we had done?" asked Pat.

"A squad car just happened to drive by your house earlier and spotted Carolyn's car parked out front. It matched a suspect's licence plate number that we had received from a witness. Sometimes that info is wrong. Anyhow, the suspect was known to be armed and dangerous. Anytime there's an 'A and D' the SWAT team takes the lead."

"My partner and I stick around afterwards to make sure everyone is okay and understands what went on and why. And, if things had gone south, there were a number of ambulances parked around the corner while we were clearing your home."

"Oh, you mean, like if I had been shot for walking between the trees?"

Karyn laughed nervously. "Ya, what the heck was that about, Jason?"

"I heard the guy's instructions—I did—but I froze and my feet wouldn't listen!"

With that, the police officers stood up. "Well, it's late, and if you're all okay, we'll be heading off."

I made my way upstairs to our bedroom. This had been a long and stressful night. And I'd had quite enough.

The next morning came as it always did—with pangs of hunger. When you're a golden, food wins out over sleep every time. As much as I was tired, breakfast called! There would be plenty of time for sleep during the day.

Rising with a long stretch, I made my way over to Jason, who was still sleeping. Yes, I was no longer sleeping with Jason on his bed. The sleepovers with Robyn had started it and, unfortunately, I still had the odd accident when I slept. I understood. Besides, I now had a nice new soft bed of my own.

I leaned against his bed and wagged my tail. The gentle thumping sound soon registered and he stretched himself awake.

"A few more minutes, buddy. Come on..."

I continued to wag my tail and move my muzzle closer to his face. After a few sniffs, Jason left me no other options. I licked his face.

"Really? That's how you're playing today?" Jason recoiled and rolled over. "You realize we've only had about four hours of sleep."

If I could make my own breakfast, believe me, I would.

I moved to the other side of the bed and employed the same strategy—a wagging tail and doggie morning-breath. A few licks later and Jason was sitting up. *Success!*

One-by-one, our very tired-looking roommates joined us in the kitchen. There were intermittent moments of giggles and laughter. "Okay, was I dreaming, or did we have a SWAT team outside our house, and snipers on the neighbour's roof last night?" asked Karyn.

"I've been asking myself the very same question," said Pat. "Was that crazy or what?"

"Remind me never to answer the phone if it rings after midnight," added Carolyn.

Jason chimed in. "I'm thinking I've got a great speech for Toastmasters,"

Eventually, everyone made their way to their respective schools. Jason shared the story during his morning studio class. His fellow students, including his instructor, were completely caught up in the details. Later, when Robyn arrived, I got to hear it all over again. At least that time he told her while we were driving to the beach for a late afternoon run.

"What do you think happened when you just kept walking along the path?" asked Robyn. "Were you scared?"

"When I met the officer in charge of the raid—the guy who was yelling at me—he apologized. He told me that he knew immediately they had the wrong guys, he said seasoned criminals wouldn't have got that flustered," laughed Jason.

"What was it like to have a high-powered rifle pointed at you?"

"Not fun—at all," said Jason. "It was surreal. Standing, with my arms straight up in the air, in front of this short guy—built like a brick shithouse—dressed all in black. He had black face paint, holding this big-ass gun, and pointing it directly at my chest." Jason shook his head while we sat waiting for the light to turn green. "I could literally feel my heart pounding in my chest. I mean, I wasn't really worried about being shot, but still—looking at that gun—it was hard not to freak out."

"That must have been terrifying!"

"When I climbed into bed last night, I was thinking, 'What if I actually *had* been shot?'"

"And—what did you discover?"

We pulled into the Kits Beach parking lot. Jason turned off the car and looked at me in the rearview mirror. "When I found out that Ike may only have a year to live, it changed how I experienced our time together. It became more precious—like the cliché? But last night was different—I could've been killed. Very unlikely, but it could've happened. So I was thinking as we walked to school this morning, "What if I knew I only had a year to live?' What would that change?"

Robyn reached over and put her hand on Jason's. "It's a big question. And the majority of us never consider our own mortality."

"Guilty as charged," said Jason. "I mean, it's kind of a downer, right? Thinking about dying—bit of a buzz-kill."

"It doesn't have to be," Robyn looked directly into Jason's eyes. "What happened to your relationship with Ike when you considered life without him?"

"Hmm, good point." Jason nodded, looking at me with a gentle smile. "I made an effort to do more with him and to cherish those moments. I guess I actually started living more, too, once I was aware of our limited time together."

"Was that a 'buzz-kill,' as you called it?"

He smiled. "Not at all." Then he reached out and scratched me under my chin.

For me, there was no question—life had been wonderful these last few years. Despite the news from Allyson, I felt extremely grateful for how things had turned out.

Jason flared his eyes. "Do you want to get out there and show your mom how it's done?"

I jumped up and barked at the passenger side window.

"I think that's a definite, yes," said Robyn.

christmas on the coast

For our first Christmas together, Robyn and Jason decided to avoid holiday travel and stay put. No flights. No airports. And no crates! I certainly wasn't going to miss getting stuffed into that plastic jail cell, but I would miss my time with his family. Especially his mom and dad—and their big cozy bed!

Instead, we were going to spend a few days with Erin and Kuz, and their cats. Yes, cats—two of them, Snow and Spook. I hadn't met them yet even though I had smelled them every time we had gone out for a visit. The cats had always disappeared under the couch or into another room to avoid me. This time, with a sleepover in the mix, at some point it was likely we would meet.

Arriving at Erin and Kuz's home always filled me with a special feeling. They welcomed me into their cozy home with excitement and generosity. Erin always had special treats waiting for me. There wasn't much I enjoyed more than dozing off under their dining room table with my head on Jason's foot, as the sound of laughter and the Gypsy Kings filled the room.

This time, arriving at a house decked out in Christmas decorations and mouth-watering smells was exactly what I was expecting—perfect! *This was going to be a fun few days!*

The next morning, on Christmas Eve, Jason and I met Snow coming out of her litter box—she was pure white. But there was nothing soft and fluffy about her. Instead, she was like late-winter snow—hard and crusty. I stopped in my tracks. Snow didn't. She just kept walking toward me.

"Are you blind or just this bold?" I asked. The hall definitely wasn't wide enough for both of us.

"Move, dog!"

Not wanting to cause a scene, I leaned up against the wall. As Snow walked by she raised her right paw, spit at me and said, *"Don't get too comfortable."*

"Yikes—that's one bad-ass cat." said Jason. "Thanks for accommodating. You're a good house guest, Ike!"

Returning from outside, we met Spook. He froze, took one quick look at me, then screeched before darting into the living room to hide under the couch.

After breakfast, we were off to the banks of the Fraser River for a long run. With the Coastal Mountains on both sides of us, and the river winding through farmland, there was plenty to appreciate.

In the evening, we gathered in the living room. Andy Williams played in the background and I curled up in front of the warm and crackling fire. Their tree reminded me of being at Jason's parents for Christmas. Bright coloured lights, shiny ornaments, and long strands of tinsel magically transformed the tree into a festive centrepiece for the room.

Jason had purchased a hand-blown glass bulb from an artisan on Granville Island, painted a tiny scene of the three of us walking along Kits Beach, and written *"Merry Christmas 1995"* on the other side. He had put a lot of thought and effort into his gift for Robyn. Now he just had to wait for her to open it.

"Jason, Robyn shared your speech about Ike with us," said Erin. "I have to tell you, I was quite moved."

Jason looked at Robyn.

"You said I could!" Robyn tilted her head as she waited for Jason's response.

"I'm not upset. I just didn't think it would impact people that way it has."

"Well, when was the last time you spoke about anyone the way you did about Ike?" asked Erin.

"Never. I've never said those things about another person—even my parents." Jason paused for a moment. "I don't think I'm alone, though. I mean, dogs are safe, right? We can tell them stuff like what I said in that speech and not have to worry about it being reciprocated. And, let's face it, Ike's pretty expressive when it comes to how he feels about Robyn and me. But I guess it wouldn't hurt to tell others what they mean to me once in a while."

Robyn looked at Jason and smiled.

"You shouldn't feel bad about it. I think we all struggle with sharing our emotions sometimes." Jason nodded. "Your speech got Kuz and I thinking about getting a dog. No offence to Snow and Spook, but we don't connect with them the way you and Robyn do with Ike. Even the way Ike greets *us*. He's so generous with his...well, his love. He shares his love everywhere he goes. And with pretty much everyone he meets. I want that in our lives. So we're going to keep an eye out for a puppy."

"Did you hear that, Ike? You're going to have a new puppy to play with when we come out here!" Jason reached down and scratched me under my chin.

You may want to let the white cat know—she might have something to say about it!

"Okay—who wants to open a present?" asked Kuz excitedly. "Cause I sure as hell do!"

"Oh, Kuz," Erin grinned. "Be patient. Maybe it's not a tradition for Jason."

"Opening a present on Christmas Eve?" asked Jason.

"When we were kids," Robyn explained, "our parents and older siblings would wake us up after midnight Mass and we'd each get to open a present, and then we'd eat rabbit pie!"

Jason looked shocked.

Erin joined her sister. "Dad made the best rabbit pie in all of Mulgrave."

"Did you have any Christmas traditions, Jason?" asked Erin.

"Well, the four of us would sit at the top of the stairs Christmas morning while Dad went downstairs and into the living room to see if Santa visited. Then he'd say that same thing every year, 'Well, it appears as though Santa did find his way to our home last night. Come on down and have a look.'" Jason smiled. "It was magic. Those were special moments for sure." Then he turned and looked at Robyn. "I can't even imagine what that must have been like with nine children!"

"So that means Jason understands the whole Christmas tradition thing," said Kuz excitedly. "Let's all open a present!"

"Oh, for goodness' sake, Kuz," laughed Erin as she shook her head. "Jason, would you mind if we all opened a gift?"

"I'm good with that—Kuz, you go first!"

After Kuz opened his gift, Jason walked over to the tree and grabbed his gift for Robyn. "Here, you go next, Robyn."

Robyn smiled as she slowly and methodically undid the wrapping.

"Geezuz Murphy, you open presents like my grandmas—just rip the thing open!"

Robyn stopped and looked at Jason with a patient smile, then continued carefully removing the wrapping paper. Robyn opened the lid to the small white box and gasped. She slowly removed the ornament from the soft white tissue, revealing the painting that covered it.

"Oh, Jason," Erin whispered. "It's beautiful!"

Robyn sat quietly looking at her present, meticulously turning the ornament in her hands, inspecting every detail.

Jason, growing ever more impatient, finally asked, "Um, is it okay? Do you like it?"

She got up and walked over to Jason grabbing both of his hands and gesturing for him to stand up. Then she hugged him. "It's beautiful, Jason. Yes, it's more than *okay*—I love it," she said. "Thank you!"

"Phew," he said.

"Now *that's* a gift!" confirmed Kuz.

"You should've seen the guy blowing the glass. I got to watch through a window. Crazy talent, those guys!"

Robyn was spellbound. She continued to admire her gift.

"I'm thinkin', if things don't work out with us, it would make a really cool sound when you throw it against a wall!"

Everyone laughed, as Robyn playfully dropped her head and slowly shook it side to side.

"Well, for what it's worth," Erin said, "I hope that never happens."

Robyn smiled and looked at Jason. "Me, too," she added softly.

I could feel Jason getting uncomfortable with all of the gushy comments.

"How about you, Ike?" Kuz to the rescue. "Do you want to open your gift from Erin and me?"

"Close your eyes, Ike." Jason got up and came over to gently cover my eyes. After the sound of shuffling beside me, he removed his hands to reveal a beautifully decorated gift bag.

"Merry Christmas, Ike—perhaps, your dad can get you started?"

Jason peered into the bag and pulled out my favourite—an orange road-hockey ball.

"Looky-here, Ike—Allyson would approve, buddy," said Jason as he handed it to me. I took it in my mouth and wagged my tail. "Wait, there's more!" I dropped the ball while I anxiously waited to see what else was there. "Look at this, bud—a bunch of flavoured chewies. And a Christmas card." Jason passed it to Robyn to read aloud.

"'Dearest Ike, we want to wish you the merriest of Christmases, and thank you for bringing so much heartfelt happiness and playful joy into our home every time you visit. You are a lesson to us all. A reminder to find the best in each and every one of us, every day. We hope 1996 is your best doggie year yet! Much love, Erin and Kuz.' Awww, that's so nice, you two."

"Yes, thanks—both of you," added Jason,

"I told you, your speech inspired me," said Erin.

Kuz stood and walked toward the tree. "What else did you get me, Erin?"

"It's that big lump of coal burning in the fireplace—Santa heard you've been a naughty boy this year!"

We all laughed hysterically. I loved my time with these humans.

New Year's Eve was quiet. Robyn, Jason, and me in our empty house. The roommates had all travelled home to be with family. After a late dinner, Jason grabbed my leash hanging by the kitchen door. With my favourite humans bundled up, the three of us made off for our favourite neighbourhood walk in Vancouver. We didn't get snow often, but when we did it was a treat.

The old mansions of Shaughnessy were even more beautiful with the falling snow and brightly coloured lights perfectly placed to accentuate their stunning architecture. Jason was quiet as we slowly made our way along the uneven sidewalks that were steadily being shoved out of alignment by the powerful tree roots below. I could tell he was tired. The end of school term had come with many deadlines and late nights.

"These decorations—" he pointed at the house across the street—"I'll bet they cost what our entire house pays for one month's rent. Who spends this much on Christmas decorations? They're beautiful, but come on, who has this much money?"

"People who aren't in school," answered Robyn as she chuckled. "For some people, it's not that significant." She put her arm around Jason and squeezed him as we continued to walk amongst the falling snow. "You're certainly putting in far more hours and effort with your schoolwork than you ever have. You seem to be trying harder."

"My reason has changed—now it's about Ike. It's more real life."

"What do you mean?"

"The first three years were about projects and letter grades. That's it. Now it's about trying to build something bigger—I care more."

"I'm talking about our conversation around you not wanting to become *that guy*, again. When you told me you didn't want to try too hard at school because you didn't like who you became when things mattered. When you competed."

"When I first started at Emily Carr, true, my strategy was to not fully try. I see now that was just an attempt to save me the shame of not *winning* again—you know, not being the top student. Believe me, I've considered this many times. It makes me feel shitty when I think about it. Am I so gun-shy that I won't ever get back in the ring again?"

"You sure like your sporting analogies," said Robyn as she looked up at Jason.

"Ha—they just make sense to me."

"And, regarding your question...*about getting back in the ring*." Robyn smiled. "I'm not sure you have to answer it right now. I think just being aware of your thoughts is enough. Just knowing that there's a part of you that might think being competitive with others is a risky proposition. Maybe it's true. Maybe it's not. But, when you find yourself averting your best effort for fear of not being the best, that might be something valuable to explore."

"Hmm, you're not just a pretty face, eh?" Jason laughed and clapped his hands together, shattering the quiet of the old neighbourhood. That laugh was his go-to during uncomfortable situations.

"Fear doesn't appear to be holding you back with your Skeet & Ike's project. And I would imagine there's a lot more on the line than just a letter grade..."

"But this *is* different. This is about something so much bigger. This is about Ike. I want every Canadian to know his name when I'm done. I want his face on every kitchen table across this country. This isn't about trying to impress my instructors or my classmates, or even trying to sell a ton of peanut butter; this is about a promise I made to Ike."

Robyn stopped and hugged Jason. "Ike's a lucky boy—to have a dad like you."

Ditto.

Jason stepped back from Robyn. "I know I'm spending a lot of time on this. But it's important to me. I owe it to this little guy. He's given me so much. I want to share his story with anyone who will hear it."

I didn't see it as just my story. This was our story. Jason wasn't giving himself enough credit again. Sure, I understood the uniqueness of our relationship and how it was solidified by my jelly bean of a kidney. But, the way I saw it, it took an equally unique human to commit to sharing our story the way Jason did. True, dogs have lots to offer, but humans have to be open to receiving it. However painful to witness at times, Jason was "in the game," as he would say, and trying more and more to "play harder."

"Clearly, I can get a little obsessed with things that are important to me. I'll have to make sure I'm not neglecting Ike while I'm trying to get his name out there."

“I’m sure Ike will let you know when he needs some lovin’!”

Jason turned around and looked at me. “You’ll tell me when I’m *losing the plot,* won’t you, Ike?”

the final push

With his last term of classes underway, Jason seemed to find yet another gear. His commitment to his Skeet & Ike's project only intensified. He finally decided on an illustration style and font, and his logo was almost complete. He also took many more trips to the bulk food store as he refined the recipes for each flavour.

All of the spreads were built around a peanut base accentuated with different ingredients to achieve unique and delicious flavours. There was yogurt and almond, butterscotch and pecan, dark chocolate and coffee, M&M's, and—my favourite—a savoury combination of seeds and other nuts. In a word, it was perfect!

Despite his pace, Robyn made sure we still found time for play as she continued to visit us in Vancouver and insisted we visit her every couple of weekends as well.

Unfortunately, Robyn lived in an apartment that didn't allow pets, so I would stay with Fiona and Brodie. With the cookie jar always well-stocked, I could handle a night or two on my own. Each morning Jason and Robyn would come by to pick us up and head to Elk Lake for a run. While Robyn did her workout, me and my two Clydesdale running mates brought up the rear. Usually, I would take off with the speedy redhead. But I enjoyed hanging back with Brodie as well.

Almost every time, we'd find a large stick and parade it around the lake together, me on one end, Brodie on the other. The looks we'd get from the other runners added to our amusement. And, sometimes, when we were lucky, we'd scare up the resident otters. They'd make a horrible screeching sound as we chased them out the shrubs that surrounded the lake and back into the water. We loved it. Although not the fastest guy around, Brodie had a nose like no other. He could smell those slippery creatures a mile away.

After our adventures at the lake, we'd come back to Fiona's for a nap by the fire while Jason worked on his project, and Robyn read or visited with Fiona. These short trips seemed to re-energize Jason.

With his presentation deadline approaching, Jason focused on finding a business partner. Having help from a business mind to get this venture off the ground was a no-brainer for Jason. If rowing had taught him anything, it was if you're going to assemble a good team, you go find the best players. Ian, the younger brother of a high school friend, had just graduated from university with a degree in business and entrepreneurial studies; Jason figured he'd fit the bill just fine.

The three of us hiked up Black Mountain, discussing what starting Skeet & Ike's could look like. By the time we reached the top, the partnership and the plan were settled with a handshake. As Ian put it, "I don't know much about running a peanut butter business, but I'm willing to try."

That was good enough for Jason.

As the deadline approached, Jason hit his first snag. Part of the requirement for graduation was assembling a display in one of the main buildings to showcase each student's work for the graduation show. There was a draw to see who would get which spot in the building. Jason drew perhaps the best location, right by the entrance, for everyone to see. He was thrilled.

However, after a few days of work, one of his panel members complained about some of his sketches protruding past the top of the divider. She told him he'd have to redo the display. After a year of her petty comments, Jason had had enough. He took down all of his work and exchanged his prime spot with one of his classmates. At the back of one of the studios, he simply glued a jar of nuts spread to the wall and called it a day. Jason had a line. His classmates were surprised that he would give up his prime real estate for the show. But, as Jason told me on our way home, "Fail me—I don't care. We've got bigger fish to fry, Ike!"

Maybe so, but this was a prime example of the mule that could inhabit Jason. One step forward, a thousand steps backward. Even Robyn couldn't convince him to reconsider his knee-jerk reaction. He was decided—however irrational. She knew his heels were dug in and they weren't moving.

Now, without the visual setup to worry about, Jason simply focused on his impending presentation and making sure he was prepared for the barrage of questions he was convinced he would hear about having me on the label.

"Are you all set?" asked Robyn.

"Yup; nut spreads are made, jars are labelled, my slides are all in order—I've tripled-checked. I even bathed Ike!"

"Is he going to be there?"

"Are you kidding me? He'll be front and centre! Ian's coming as well."

"I'll be sending you and Ike lots of positive vibes and love."

After Jason proceeded through his slides with me lying at his feet, the time had come to answer questions. One after the next was about me on that label. "Why a dog? How will consumers react? Do you think having a dog on the label might make people think the product's dirty?" That one, I took exception to!

As it was a public presentation, anyone could ask questions. Ian came to the rescue. "Did you do any research regarding the receptivity of consumers around having a golden retriever on the label?"

"I did—in the form of surveying shoppers in front of approximately half a dozen of the busiest high-end grocery stores in town. Undeniably, people were intrigued by the idea," answered Jason. "Shoppers saw the image of a golden retriever as contributing to a brand that is friendly, playful, and trustworthy."

"Interesting." Ian winked.

Jason smiled. "Any more questions?"

A gentleman from the back of the room piped up. "Will I be able to buy these in stores?"

"Funny you should ask! We've rented a booth at Granville Market for next weekend. Come on by and sample any of the nut spreads."

The man nodded his head and smiled. "Congratulations! What tremendous publicity for the school!"

Andrew began to clap. One other panel member joined in; the others closed up their notebooks and left without a word. Jason smiled at Andrew.

Later, on the phone with Robyn, he shared the events of the evening.

"I'm so happy for you, Jason. But it seems now the actual real work begins. How does Ian feel about it all?"

"There's still lots of stuff to do. With Ian's regular job during the day and then making the nut spreads in the evening at a local kitchen we've rented, he'll be whacked."

Jason's juicer worked overtime as he and Ian prepared the five flavours they'd be debuting; Savoury Seed, Coffee and Dark Chocolate, M&M, Butterscotch Pecan, and Almond Yogurt.

Jason printed, cut, and glued the labels onto each Mason jar. He also created signage for the table and picked up a new white tablecloth and a cash box. They had a long to-do list, but by Thursday night they were ready.

Ian's day job was his priority, so Jason's roommate Karyn helped him transport everything—including the beautiful wooden display shelves her dad had made—to Granville Island.

"Well, Ike—wish me luck, buddy!" Jason scratched his hand up and down my back. "Love you, Pooh Bear." Then, he kissed me on the forehead. "Time to spread the news; Ike makes the best damn peanut butter in town!"

Finally, after a run with Pat and a long afternoon of napping on the deck, I heard Jason's car pulling into our back alley with Ian's truck close behind. Jason called out my name as he got out of his car.

I ran down to meet him at the gate. "Ike, I've got some good news and some not-so-good news." He squatted down to greet me. "Good news first—you were a hit! We sold over 80 jars! Everyone, and I mean everyone who stopped by, wanted to know where you were! Question after question about you and your story. 'Is Ike even a real dog or just something you made up for the label?' It was crazy, buddy! The place was packed!"

"What's the not-so-good news?" asked Pat.

Jason looked up to see Pat on the deck.

"Well, just like Jason described," Ian answered, "it was insane! Even in my wildest dreams, I would never have predicted this response."

"So what's the bad news?"

"If the same thing happens tomorrow, we've got nothing to sell on Sunday!"

"And guess what—two of my panel members came by right in the middle of the busiest time of the day. Andrew was so excited for us.

He couldn't stop smiling. He even bought a jar! The other instructor—not so much...."

"Oh well," said Pat. "Just enjoy the good stuff and leave the non-believers behind."

After a long phone call with Robyn, Jason labelled the rest of the jars. Clearly, they had underestimated the response. Although Jason was tired from the day, he was energized and excited too. He and I sat on the deck and looked out over the city. The sky was orange and red with wisps of clouds disappearing into the distance. The trees were lush as a result of the spring rain, and the city traffic softly hummed in the background. Feeling Jason so content was soothing for me.

"Well, Ike—that was quite a day!" He rubbed his hand up and down my back. "Can you imagine if this thing takes off?" He smiled at me. "Hang on, bud—I think we're just getting started."

Ian pulled in under the carport the next morning, right on time. The two of them quickly loaded the cases of newly labelled jars into the back of Ian's truck before heading off for their second day at the market. I curled up on my bed.

Well, it turned out they did have another crazy day selling every remaining jar of their nut spreads. They had to notify the market managers that they couldn't come back on Sunday because they had nothing more to sell.

The debut was an overwhelming success. Better than either one of them could have envisioned. Especially Jason. Never in his "best-case scenario" did he imagine the response to not just the nut spreads, but his choice to include me on the label. Humans were genuinely touched by his story of wanting to immortalize me on his fancy spreads.

When our other roommates came out to join us, he shared some highlights from the day. "Ian and I were busy getting samples ready behind our display shelves when this older gentleman slammed an empty jar down on the table. When we looked up, he said, 'I want to make a complaint!'"

"Oh my," said Karyn. "What was the problem?"

"He said it was 'too damn good,' and that he couldn't stop eating it. He finished the whole jar with a spoon in one sitting!"

"No way!" said Carolyn.

"Yup—then he laughed and bought another jar!"

graduation

After eight years of university education, there was no way Jason's parents were going to miss his graduation. Two weeks after Skeet & Ike's successful debut at the market, Carl and Eleanor arrived in Vancouver for the occasion.

The place, an old vintage theatre in the heart of the city, was packed—standing room only. Proud parents and friends crammed into their seats to applaud as members of the Graduating Class of 1996 from the Emily Carr Institute of Art and Design collected their diplomas and paused for a moment of recognition.

When Jason's name was called, he and I made our way across the large wooden stage. Several sharply dressed dignitaries were waiting for us as we walked toward the podium.

Jason, wearing the same fancy clothes he had worn to chapel that day long ago, collected our diplomas and shook hands with the line of esteemed guests—and, I say "our" diplomas because one of the department heads had made a diploma for me recognizing my graduation as well. He labelled it "Dog-torate" and went on to explain that, given I had attended four years of classes, "he must have learned something in that time!"

While Jason shook hands and accepted their congratulations, I walked to the front of the stage. As I peered out at the hundreds of faces looking back from the audience, I began to slowly wag my tail at the sight of so many smiling faces. Their response was to giggle. I wagged my entire body as enthusiastically as possible when I heard that, soaking up the crowd's appreciation. The giggles quickly turned to laughter and applause. If you're wondering whether or not dogs can smile...we can. I had one plastered across my face. I was thrilled for Jason. It hadn't been easy at times, but he had made it—he was a graduate!

Back at the house, Jason and Robyn put on a delicious spread for all of the guests. Barbecued salmon—my favourite—along with all sorts of salads, different breads, and yummy desserts. There had to be at least thirty humans in our home. Along with our roommates, there were Jason's parents, Erin and Kuz, Fiona, Trev, Wendy and Mike, Ian, local cousins, and to top it off, some old high school friends flew out to join in the celebration. It was a terrific gathering.

Jason even gave a short speech, which of course included some self-deprecating remarks. "Mom and dad, I know it's been fifteen years since high school, and you probably imagined this day arriving sooner, but I sure appreciate you hanging in there!" Carl played along, chiming in that he thought he'd never live to see the day. Jason thanked all of those who had patiently supported him in getting to this moment, including many of the friends in attendance.

"And, finally, I want to acknowledge Robyn and Ike—yes, you bud," he said as he smiled at me laying beside the couch by Carl's feet. "I'm not saying I wouldn't have made it to this day without them—it just wouldn't have meant so much. Yes, I learned a lot from my instructors at Emily Carr and UBC, and I'm excited to utilize that knowledge as we grow Skeet & Ike's. But what I've learned from these two has been so much more important. I want to thank you both for your patience and care. It's been bigger than you know!"

Oh, I know—it's why they gave me a Dog-torate!

Robyn smiled graciously. Having her in Jason's life had been profound. I was glad that he was able to articulate how much.

This wasn't just about the end of school for Jason, but also the beginning of something very exciting. Carl and Eleanor were thrilled by the news of Skeet & Ike's first weekend at Granville Island and were undoubtedly intrigued whether this school project would grow into a viable business.

The day after the out-of-town guests left, we met Ian in the parking lot at Lynn Canyon on the North Shore, for a West Coast-style business meeting—otherwise known as a sunny summer hike along the Baden Powell Trail. And while Ian and Jason talked about their next steps, I explored the sights and smells of the forest that grew tall above the city.

They planned to continue selling their nut spreads at the market twice a month. "Pay-day weekends," as Ian would say. When humans had more disposable cash in hand, they were more likely to buy. And so, every other weekend throughout the summer, they rented a table and sold as many jars of Skeet & Ike's nut spreads as they could. They would use the money they earned to pay for the ingredients and supplies for the next round. It seemed like a reasonable plan.

Ian and Jason recognized the importance of having direct access to paying customers so they could ask detailed questions about household purchasing and eating habits. They were trying to determine if this product had legs. Would shoppers make regular purchases or was it a once-in-a-while treat? Having a cottage-industry-type product that was a nice-to-have and not a have-to-have would be harder to make a go of.

With the two of them engrossed in the day-to-day tasks of keeping their business moving forward—ordering supplies, making nut spreads, printing labels, and selling at the Granville Island Market—Robyn prepared for her second Olympic Games in Atlanta. Coming off a strong spring training regimen, she seemed ready for her upcoming competitive season. She had a timed run along Spanish Banks that we would do together when she would come over on weekends. It was clear that her fitness was improving as she continuously posted faster times with every run.

Jason called me her "rabbit." It was a track term used to describe the human in charge of setting the race pace. Except in this case, it was me! According to Jason, I must have done a good job. In early summer, Robyn won the Canadian Olympic trials in Montreal, and arrived in Atlanta, Georgia for the Olympics weeks later as Canada's top-hope in the women's 5000-metre event.

Jason decided to fly back to the cottage to be with his family while the Olympics were on. Two weeks of chasing orange hockey balls into the lake all day long wasn't a hard sell. Every morning after making his tea, Jason would grab his journal and wander out to the end of the dock and sink into a lawn chair. I'd patiently lay at his feet with a ball between my paws. He'd write and write. Three pages, just like he was supposed to. I had no idea what he chose to fill those pages with, but gone were the days of him tapping his pencil on the dining room table, searching for topics to delve into.

Then he'd close up his journal, grab the ball, and launch it far into the air while I waited for splashdown. I'd look at him; he'd turn and look at me and say the same thing every time. "What are you waiting for, Ike—go get it, buddy!"

Permission granted, I'd take three quick strides and blast off the edge of the dock. Jason would head up to the cottage for breakfast before we'd leave on a run. Then it was back to the lake for the entire day. I'd swim after balls for as long as I had a keen tosser.

One of my favourite after-dinner activities was to climb into the canoe and explore the lake with Jason. The water was calm, and it was incredibly quiet. Nothing to hear but Jason's paddle disturbing the water and the loons' last calls of the day.

Bobcaygeon, like its name, was a quirky little cottage community northeast of Toronto. The lakes were shallow and warm. If I could've slept while floating around the dock, I would have. Honestly, if there was a better place on earth—I couldn't imagine it!

Race day finally arrived for Robyn. On our run that morning, Jason had told me what Robyn was likely doing as she prepared for her first race. A limited amount of just the right foods. A morning jog with some stretching. Followed by a day of keeping her thoughts positive and not thinking too much about the race. Then he shared what he would've done. *Boy-oh-boy, I'll spare you the antics—too much swearing!* But then he laughed. Never before had I heard Jason laugh with regard to his rowing career. I took it as a good sign.

Despite his dark humour, he was genuinely nervous for Robyn. I could feel it. He knew this was a big day. Her first chance to test her speed and suss out her competition. "I think being a spectator is worse than racing, Ike. I wish I could be there to help."

With the family closely gathered around the old cottage television to watch her heat, we yelled and cheered at the tiny screen. However, to no avail. The race wasn't what any of us expected. Nor Robyn, I'm sure. She finished last and didn't advance into the final. Speaking with her later that night, she told Jason she'd come down with a bug and spent the night before her race with chills, cramps, and rushing to the toilet. *Like my time at the beach—I could relate!*

We walked down to the dock after the race. Jason sat and dangled his feet in the water. I lay beside him. "That's shitty, Ike. Man, I feel for your mom right now. Blowing up on the world stage is no fun, trust me." He took a deep breath, looked out across the lake, and continued rubbing my back. "Hopefully some asshole doesn't put her on the front page of Globe and Mail with some disparaging headline."

Years earlier, Jason had shown me the front page of the sports section from the day after their Olympic final. I remember thinking humans were strange animals. I never understood how they could be so mean to one another.

Robyn's summer races in Europe were also impacted because of her poor showing in Atlanta. She wasn't invited to any of the top track meets on the circuit. That meant she'd be staying home and continuing her training—for next season. Although Robyn wouldn't get a chance to race overseas, I was happy to have her home with Jason and me. As she said, "The silver lining is more time with you and dad. There'll be other races—don't you worry, Ike. I'm not done yet!"

With a summer of successful weekends at the market under their belts, local store owners were now taking notice. Ian had convinced several high-end grocery stores to feature Skeet & Ike's on their shelves. With each new store came a day of demos for Jason. He would set up samples in high traffic areas and do what he did well: tell our story and feed humans!

Soon, Skeet & Ike's arrived at a crossroads. Jason and Ian decided to "Go big or go home," as Jason would say. It was time to fully commit. Ian quit his job. They found investors and soon the partners were drawing a salary and selling fancy peanut butter with my face on it, full-time.

Ian and Jason were looking for office space while the roommate situation was evolving. When Karyn moved out, Jason moved across the hall and into the bigger room with Robyn while he and Ian rented his old bedroom as their new "office." Yup, Robyn was movin' in! Jason saw it as the logical next step—no more ferry trips, and no more paying two rents. Robyn didn't disagree, but for her, moving in with us in Vancouver was about more than just saving money. She saw it as a commitment to their future together. When Robyn tried to explain the significance of this move, Jason answered, "...Okay?"

Clearly, I had more work to do!

I was thrilled. Robyn was going to be living with us and Jason would be working a few feet from our bedroom. No more long days waiting for him to come home, and more time spent running with Robyn on the trails—jackpot!

It didn't take long for television and radio stations to get wind of my story. Soon, Jason and Ian were doing interviews on local radio and television stations. One day, Jason and I had to get up extremely early and make our way into the centre of town for a morning television show. It was still dark outside when we arrived. I had no idea that so many humans got up this early. The place was bustling with activity. Serious-looking humans wearing headsets and holding clipboards walking this way and that way, barking out instructions to any humans who would listen. I was exhausted just watching them.

We were eventually led into a waiting room. Jason was given a name tag and told to sit tight until another important human came to get him. We sat quietly with some of the other sleepy but pleasant human guests. I made the rounds, greeting everyone with my wagging tail and smiling face.

Eventually, the human who had told us to wait came rushing in to gather us. "Jason," she chirped. "This way!"

She needs a walk in the Endowment Lands, badly!

Jason walked out onto the set with me following close behind. The morning hosts got up from their chairs and greeted both of us warmly. Each of them took a moment to reach down, scratch my ears, and say hello.

"Quiet on the set!" yelled one of the clipboard-toting humans.

"Welcome back, everyone. This morning, we're glad to be joined by this handsome boy, Ike," said one of the hosts. "And his owner, Jason—who both live in our beautiful city and have created a new and unusual nut spread."

And off they went. A few questions about Emily Carr, a few questions about me, and then a few more questions about the nut spreads. I don't think Jason could've asked for the interview to go any better. Then, just as they were wrapping up, the other interviewer asked Jason if I liked the nut spreads. To which Jason answered, "Well, he's a golden, right? And, if you know golden's, you know there's not too much they won't eat. So I don't know if Ike's necessarily a good reference."

"Well, let's find out!" The host grabbed half a bagel from the display that was covered in the Savoury Seed spread and tossed it to me.

I hadn't had breakfast, I was starving, and there was no way I was going to miss the opportunity to snag the spinning snack heading toward me. I opened my mouth wide and let the whole bagel land at the back of my throat. I began chewing and swallowing—mainly swallowing. However, the bagel wasn't going down as easily as I first thought. Jason could sense I was in trouble. He immediately pried open my mouth to retrieve the nut spread covered bagel, but it was already halfway down my throat. He stuck his hand in trying to grab hold. I was getting panicked. This thing was stuck. I kept swallowing, trying to encourage the gooey bagel down my throat.

The host who had thrown the bagel crouched down beside us. "Is he okay?"

Soon, the bagel made its way to my stomach and I could breathe again. It was delicious, but that scared both Jason and me.

"I'm sorry," said the host. "I was just trying to have some fun."

Jason turned to him and said, "He's okay now. But you can't throw a doughy bagel covered in peanut butter at a dog and not expect there's going to be some trouble. I'm sure he's already forgiven you, though!"

The upshot of the interview, and my brush with asphyxiation, was that Skeet & Ike's was getting attention. Ian was having more and more success placing the nut spreads in stores. More stores meant more jars, more labels, more ingredients, and more grinding! They had reached a point where their hand-grinding Champion juicers could no longer manage the volume.

Eventually, they hired a local manufacturer to co-pack the product, which allowed for more volume with greater consistency. They also reached a point where printing and hand labelling each jar no longer made sense, either. Soon, they had thousands of beautifully printed labels for each flavour. Jason and Ian's little company was booming!

With the business on an upswing, Robyn and Jason took advantage of weekends to run together, make some meals, and sometimes visit with Erin and Kuz.

Every day, Jason continued to make time for writing his "morning pages" while I lay at his feet. Whatever process Robyn had set in motion had stuck. Something had grabbed hold and offered him a platform to clear his mind, and soul, and sort out whatever challenges arose. As much as he hated to acknowledge it, a year in, this thirty-minute daily writing and reflection ritual was making a profound difference in all aspects of his life.

During one of our evening walks to the park, Robyn and Jason sat on their usual bench under my favourite tree. Robyn leaned close and asked, "What has surprised you most about journalling every morning?"

"I'm not sure I know what you mean?"

"Has anything emerged that you didn't see coming? Have you written about things that have caught you off guard?"

Jason watched some of the other dogs and humans who had joined us that evening and thought for a moment. "How heavy do you want to get?"

"Try me."

"Okay...admitting that my eating—or lack of eating—got out of control after I retired." Robyn looked directly at Jason and waited for him to return her gaze. Once he had, he added, "Wow—did I just say that out loud?"

"You did. And I'm still sitting here with you. I didn't get up and walk away." Robyn smiled softly and reached for his hand.

"Maybe 1990 to '91 I was at my worst—before I moved in with Pat and Trev and met Ike, I was only eating a bit of fruit for breakfast, a V-8 and a few rice-cakes for lunch, and then some rice and tofu with salad for dinner. Couple that with an obsessive workout regimen, and I was down to about 170 lbs. My body was desperately trying to tell me this was unhealthy—night sweats, dizzy spells, blood in my urine. Rationally, I knew this was messed up, but when people would comment on how thin I was looking, it was fuel to keep going. Any attention was good attention back then, even if it was the wrong kind."

"What changed?" asked Robyn. "How did you get back to healthy eating?"

"Living with Pat and Trev—simple. Things were still a little funky at first, but when we ate together, which was almost everyday, I really didn't have a choice. They never commented on my weight. They accepted me." Jason paused and looked down at me. Then he smiled. "Hmm, and the laughing. We laughed a lot. Eventually, I gained some weight and started feeling better. Then when Ike showed up, that was it—I was so focused on him I lost interest in getting attention for myself."

"That's pretty big, Jason."

"Feels good to tell someone. Thanks for asking."

"You're welcome." Robyn smiled. She looked beautiful in the early evening light. I could feel how present she was with Jason. If a herd of elephants had run by, I'm not sure she would've noticed. She took a deep breath. "Anything else you want to tell me?"

Jason let out a big laugh and reached down to grab my right ear and begin twirling it. "Are you kidding me? That's not big enough?"

"I'm simply asking if there's anything else you want to share with me?" Jason looked away. "Now that you know I'm not going to leave."

Jason continued rolling my ear. "Ike, man, she's making my hands sweat!" I got up and lowered my chin onto his lap. I could feel the tension rising in him. "See, even Ike's starting to wonder what the hell's going on!"

"You don't have to say anything, but if..."

"I blamed myself for our loss in Seoul."

Robyn reached over and put her hand on Jason's back.

"I can't believe I just said that—holy fuck!"

"We've talked about your race, but not this. Do you want to tell me more?"

"What's more to tell? I created a reason to go again and train harder by blaming myself. I win in Barcelona, I'm off the hook—I clear my name, right? Simple as that. So I tried a comeback. Six months in, I was done. I hated rowing. I hated myself—Geezuz Murphy, I hated everyone."

"Do you still believe that?"

"Hell, no—there was so much that went wrong that summer. Our training was off. Our crew was off—in fact, we weren't even a crew. It was bullshit. There was no trust—and, in rowing especially, if you don't have trust, you're fucked! When I look back, sure we had crazy-fast speed at times, but we were so inconsistent—we're lucky we even got into the final."

"What was it like to write about that?"

"Lots of emotions. Resentment, sadness, regret, but mainly anger—lots of fuckin' anger! Years and years of training for something that you think will end one way, and then...not even close. It still pisses me off when I think about it. All that time and effort—for what? Some shitty tracksuit? If we had just raced the way we were capable...at least if we had done that, and we'd still lost, it would've made losing easier. But we didn't even do that. DFL on the day it mattered most." Jason turned and looked directly at Robyn. "Dead-fuckin'-last, if you're wondering."

Robyn nodded her head and smiled cautiously.

I nudged my nose against Jason's leg. He reached down and stroked my neck. "Thanks, bud—sorry about all of the swearing." I had never felt him so upset. He had shared a lot with me on our runs, but never this. The more he talked with Robyn, the more I understood how he had acted during our first year together.

"Knowing you can't change that, how do you move on?"

"Change what?"

"That you had a poor race—how do you live with that?"

"A poor race? Ha, you and I have distinctly different language when it comes to describing shitty stuff!" Jason looked at me for a moment longer. "How do any of us just accept that, at some point, we all shit the bed..."

"Nice expression," said Robyn, clearly unimpressed with Jason's choice of descriptors.

"It's the perfect expression. Can you imagine anything worse?"

Robyn shook her head.

"What I'm realizing is that as much as I let our loss in Seoul define me for far too long, that loss is not who I am. 'I am not the result of that race,' is what I specifically wrote down in my journal."

"And how do you move forward knowing that?"

"Holy crap—my head's spinning." Jason laughed and put his head in his hands. "How many more questions do you have for me?"

"You don't have to answer them."

"I know, I know—and I appreciate you pushing me, I do. Well, mostly." Jason smiled at Robyn. "It's just, I've never talked about this with anyone before—not even Ike! Having to own this shit with someone else—that's new for me."

"And I feel honoured that you trust me enough to be this vulnerable. But—until you can understand what moving on actually feels like—you're going to run up against this time and again."

"I'm not trying to blow you off. I appreciate you want to talk about this." Jason took hold of Robyn's hand. "Thank you." Robyn gently smiled. "You know that expression, 'people come into our lives when we most need them'?" She nodded. "That's the only way I can make sense of this—of us. It's been more than a year now, and I feel like a different person—a better person—when I'm around you. Because of you, I like myself a whole lot more."

Robyn smiled. "Thank you for saying so, Jason."

"Ya, well, that's me—sensitive new age guy! Isn't that right, Ike?"

an old ring

That Christmas season, Jason wanted Robyn to meet his family. The plan was for her to spend Christmas at home in Nova Scotia and then join us in St. Catharines for New Years. With flights booked, luggage packed, and my plastic jail cell cleaned out, we were ready for our trip back east.

Jason and I arrived to an early snowfall and a house full of Christmas decorations. It was late when we pulled into the driveway. Despite that, Eleanor and Carl had a roaring fire to greet us. While Jason took his luggage upstairs, I hung out with his mom and dad and made myself comfortable by the fire—my home for the next two weeks.

I was keen for the usual family festivities to begin. Jason's siblings arrived a few days later with all of the nephews and nieces in tow. The house was bustling during the day, but things quieted down after dinner when I would curl up beside Carl right next to the fireplace.

Family meals included loud and playful banter, and, right on cue, morsels fell from above. Robyn, once more, became the topic of conversation. More specifically, his siblings playfully interrogated Jason about his intentions.

"When is the wedding planned for, Jase—this summer?" asked his sister Wendy. "Maybe you could do it at the cottage?"

Every night, someone managed to cycle Robyn back into the discussion. Jason just smiled and occasionally laughed. Especially when questions about a summer wedding came up. He wasn't biting.

On Christmas Eve, I lay stretched out on Jason's parents' bed amidst newspapers, crossword puzzles, and novels from Eleanor's book club. It's a wonder there was room for any of us. Jason sat at the foot of the bed, with his parents in their pyjamas under the covers, cozied up on either side of me.

"Your siblings are sure giving you the gears, son," said Carl.

"I've had worse, Dad."

"I wouldn't listen to them, dear," added Eleanor. "You do what's best for you and Robyn."

"I can't wait for you to meet her. She's quite something. Ike absolutely adores her."

"I'm not surprised," said Eleanor. "She sounds like a lovely gal."

Jason paused for a moment before continuing. "So if I was in the market for a ring—say, some fancy diamond ring, for example—is there any chance that you might happen to have an old family one just lying around?" Jason winced and waited for the response.

His dad's arms dropped to his legs, laying his newspaper across his lap. Eleanor immediately looked up from her book.

"What would you need that ring for, son?"

"Come on, Dad—what do you think?"

"That's wonderful news, Jason," said Eleanor. "Robyn is a lucky woman!"

"Well, I don't know if I'd go that far—but it's been well over a year, and she's still with me. So I must be doing something right!"

"Gosh, son—that's terrific news!"

"To answer your question—" Eleanor grinned— "I think I just might." She put down her book, got out of bed, and walked over to her bureau. Jason followed behind closely. She pulled out a large wooden box from one of her top drawers. "Your Grandma—Dad's mom—left me some old family jewellery when she died. I think there's a tiny little diamond ring in here that would do just fine."

Eleanor opened the box and removed another wooden box from inside. Then she pulled out several pieces of jewellery until she found what she was looking for. "I thought it was in here." Eleanor slowly raised the small diamond ring for Jason to see. "It's very old and needs to be cleaned and polished. But I think this would be a lovely engagement ring for Robyn. What do you think?"

Jason took the ring and turned it several times, examining it closely. "I think it's perfect, Mom. I love it. And I love that it's been in the family a while."

"A while—it's well over a hundred years old."

"Wow—I'm glad I asked," said Jason. "And—I'm not going to lie—it'll save me the money I don't have!"

Carl laughed. "When do you plan on asking her?"

"I was thinking of September, once her competitive season is over." Eleanor climbed back into bed and softly laid her hand on my back. "I don't want to distract her from her racing. So that means you have to keep this a secret until then—can you do that, Dad?"

"Do what?" he winked.

Robyn flew in from Halifax a few nights before New Year's Eve. Eleanor had a big family dinner waiting for her—nothing like easing into the family. Amazingly, Jason's mom squeezed in another place setting around the table, and for the next few hours, Robyn snuck in a few bites of food between the grilling she received.

"How's your training going?"

"Are you excited about the next Olympics?"

"What are your plans after running?" (Carl asked that one).

"What was it like growing up with eight siblings?"

And from Paul, "How on earth do you manage to live with Jason?" *Brothers will be brothers!*

No surprise, Robyn was a hit. Jason got the thumbs-up from everyone over the next few days, including his nephews and nieces.

With the ring securely packed, Jason and Robyn returned to our busy Vancouver home well-rested and ready to resume life as they knew it on the Coast. Robyn's training picked up right away. With her coach still in Victoria, they checked in regularly over the phone. I figured, with me as her training "rabbit," she'd be fine!

Robyn proved to be everything Jason had envisioned that first day they met. Don't ask me how he knew, but they had developed a close and trusting friendship where they truly supported one another. And, despite their limited financial resources, they made time for inexpensive fun in a city that had plenty to offer.

With Canadian grocery chains becoming interested in stocking Skeet & Ike's, Jason and Ian strategized their plans for growth in 1997. Ian was also interested in a small specialty food chain south of the border. Larry's Market was a Seattle-based grocery chain strategically located in some high-end neighbourhoods. He thought Skeet & Ike's would satisfy the intrigue of American shoppers looking for something deliciously new, so he secured a trial run in one of their stores. This meant more label designs for Jason—labels that didn't include French. Back to computer printouts and hand labelling. It didn't make sense to purchase a ton of labels until they were guaranteed a solid place on those American shelves.

A few days before heading south to debut their nut spreads, a young video-journalist from the CBC arrived to follow Ian and Jason around for a few days. Tracie worked for a network show called

Venture, which featured newly-minted entrepreneurs in their day-to-day adventures of chasing their business goals and dreams.

Jason had reached out to them wondering if they might be interested in a story about a guy and his dog that took a school project and made a go of it as a viable business. Turns out they were.

Having Tracie on site all day long didn't come without some trepidation. Especially from Ian. Venture had a reputation for catching its subjects making monumental mistakes in front of the camera. It all made for good television, but was it the kind of publicity they wanted or needed at this point in their journey?

As if on cue, and after almost a year of relatively easy going, the wheels came off for Jason. Mistake after mistake, all caught on film. Labelling issues mainly; misspelled ingredients, missing ingredients, not enough labels printed. The list was long; all discovered the day before they were supposed to leave for Seattle. Not only was Ian frustrated with Jason's untimely blunders, but having Tracie and her camera capture the tension in living colour didn't help.

After a long night of correcting his embarrassing mistakes, Jason and Ian, with Tracie onboard, drove off to Seattle to see what their American neighbours thought of Skeet & Ike's.

It was late when I heard Ian's truck pull into the driveway. Robyn, who was reading at the kitchen table, got up and kissed Jason. She retrieved his dinner from the oven, "Sorry, I couldn't wait."

Jason laughed. "I wouldn't expect you to wait, ever. But thanks, though—the border crossing was nuts. This smells delicious."

Jason got down on the floor and gave me an extra-long hug. Then he kissed me and sat while he rubbed my belly.

"How did it go?"

Jason moved his hand to my left ear and began to roll it in his fingers. "The store gave us prime real estate. We sold a bunch of jars, which Ian was happy about, obviously. Tracie got some good footage. So I guess it was a good day."

"So why do you seem flat?" Robyn was right. Something wasn't quite right. Jason's energy didn't match what he had just described.

He paused his hand that was rubbing my chest. "Something shifted today."

"What do you mean, 'shifted'?"

"It's hard to explain—when the first customer asked me the usual questions and I gave her my usual answers. She chose Butterscotch. No surprise, everybody loves that one. So Tracie's filming everything—our first sale in the US. All of it, caught on camera."

"Sounds perfect."

"No, you're right, it was good. The woman had some positive things to say. But, just before she walked away, I reached for her jar, took it from her hands, and told her that I wanted to sign the label because this was a 'big historic moment for us' or some bullshit like that. I signed it and gave it back to her."

"What did she say?"

"Nothing. She smiled, thanked me, and wished us good luck."

"I still don't understand what was wrong with that?"

"I signed it 'Skeet.' Not 'Ike.' Or not even 'Skeet & Ike.' I made it about me."

"I think you're being too critical."

"Nope, it may sound innocent enough—if not incredibly cheesy—but I recognized that it was important for me to be seen as the guy on the jar. That's a big shift from where I was when we first started. It's become about me and my reputation. I was thinking about it all the way home—my behaviour reminded me of rowing on the national team. It was all about me."

"I still think you're looking at this too closely, Jase."

Jason turned and looked at me. "All I know is that, any time I've made decisions based on me—as in what's in this for me—I've made some of the worst decisions of my life."

"It sounds like it was a good day for the business. Why don't you sit down and have something to eat, and we can talk some more?"

Jason got up off the floor and sat at the table. "You're right; it was a good day. But I know how I can get. And I don't want that for my future. For our future."

***

Robyn managed an injury-free spring season, which helped prepare her for some local tune-up meets in Victoria and Vancouver before heading south to Portland for the Prefontaine track meet. In July, she flew to France for some European races and the World Championships in Greece.

After two weeks of fine-tuning in Paris, Robyn was off to Athens for her first 1500 metre heat. A strong performance advanced her to the semi-final, where she had another solid race in preparation for the final two days later.

"Come on, come on, Robyn... Now, you gotta go now!" Given the chance, I bet Jason would've crawled through the television screen if that would have helped Robyn go faster. I had never seen him so animated. With just the two of us watching, he was safe to say and do whatever he wanted. "Yikes—tenth place, Ike. Mom's faster than that. Something must have happened."

The next day, Jason and I waited with flowers in hand at the international arrivals terminal. We were both keen to see Robyn. It was the longest she had been away since moving in with us in September.

Jason watched intently through the glass doors; I provided an easy distraction for the younger humans waiting for loved ones.

Soon, she appeared in the distance.

I began jiving back and forth excitedly as we made our way toward her. Jason dropped my leash as we got closer. I dropped to my back and began cooing while she rubbed my belly. Jason stood beside us, waiting patiently.

"Hello, you," Robyn looked up at Jason, her hands busily rubbing my wiggling body.

"Do I get a turn?" he asked, smiling.

Robyn laughed and looked at me. "Ike, I want to say hello to your dad, too—is that okay?"

Robyn stood up and hugged Jason. The two of them stood quietly holding one another for a long time. *I could wait!*

Once in the car, Robyn turned halfway in her seat so that she could reach me in the back. I sat up tall while she scratched my chest. "You're happy I'm home, eh, Ike? You missed me, didn't you?"

"Poor Pooh-Bear has been suffering with just me and the roommates—soooo hard done by." I reached forward and licked Jason's ear. "Sure, now you're showing me the love!"

Robyn stopped scratching me and put her hand on Jason's leg. "It's good to be home. I missed you." And then she looked at me. "Oh, and you, too, Ike."

"It's been strange not having you around."

With the sunroof and rear windows wide open, we drove along the busy streets as the cool ocean air swept through the back of the car, my fur dancing in the wind.

"Do you want to talk about your race?"

"Well, I had two really solid races heading into the final," said Robyn. "Then I woke up feeling flat and didn't have a great race. It happens." Robyn turned and looked out the window.

She could've used her special "rabbit!"

"Shitty," offered Jason. "Sorry, you couldn't put it together on the day it mattered most."

"Yes, and no—without those two good races, I wouldn't have made it to the final. It's just sports. Sometimes things line up. Sometimes they don't." Robyn rolled down her window and stuck her arm out to play with the breeze. "I was pleased with my training going into the meet. I'm still learning how to best work with my body. That's a good thing. So, overall, I'm excited for the upcoming year to see what more I can learn."

"We are so completely different," said Jason. "If I'd had a shitty race in the final at World Champs—I'd be pissed, first of all. And then my response would be... 'work harder, loser!'"

Robyn turned and looked at Jason with an inquiring gaze.

"What?" he said.

"Look how well that worked out for you!"

Ouch!

Jason had a fancy dinner waiting for Robyn back at the house. The two ate on the deck while Jason shared all of the goings-on with Skeet & Ike's. The city lights sparkled in the background as the last hint of orange hues hung over the Gulf Islands. They made plans to hike Black Mountain the next day. Naturally, I was good with that—it had been well over a year since we'd been up there.

Arriving at the parking lot, Jason seemed out of sorts. He spilled the entire contents of his backpack getting out of the car. Food, water bottle, and his camera—everything fell to the ground.

"You okay?" asked Robyn.

"I'm great. How could I not be?" he answered quickly as he gathered everything up. "There's not a cloud to be seen and I'm here with my two favourite...well, 'beings.'" Jason laughed and reached down to pat me. "Okay, you, lead the way, buddy!"

I took off. The ground was dry and crisp as we entered the trailhead. The smells were sharp with autumn closing in. Leaves were falling, and the ground was hard after another dry summer. The mountain was deserted—not another living creature anywhere. Jason was quiet on the way up. Robyn stopped multiple times to turn and appreciate the vista. "We have to do this more often. Every time I look back, it's like a postcard!"

"Yup—it's nice alright," answered Jason without even looking.

At the top, Jason pulled out some fruit and some energy bars. He tossed an apple my way. I caught it and found some grass to lay down and enjoy my well-earned snack. Then he got out his camera and started taking pictures of the spectacular view. After resting the camera on a rock, he called me over for a photo of the two of us using the timer.

"How about you and I, Robyn?" he called over to her while she ate her bar. "Do you want to get some shots?"

Robyn made her way over to join him. The camera beeped and snapped another photo.

"One more—okay?" asked Jason. "Ike, you get in here too."

Something was up; I had never seen him so nervous. Worse than his first Toastmasters speech. He was clearly flustered.

Jason knelt and looked through the viewfinder one more time. "Okay, it looks good. Stay put, Ike," instructed Jason. "Almost ready." Jason reached into his jacket pocket before gently pushing the shutter release button.

He made his way over to join us and sat down, he looked at Robyn and raised a small box in front of her. He nervously opened the box; his hands shook, and so did his voice. "I was wondering if you'd like to spend the rest of our lives together?"

With the camera beeping in the background, Robyn looked at the shiny ring in front of her. I felt her energy shift. Yes, she was surprised, but she felt serious in that moment too. I knew Jason loved being creative with everything he did. But Robyn wasn't swept up in the photo op. Instead, she looked deep in thought.

While the beeping quickened, Jason grew even more anxious. The moment the camera was destined to capture was imminent. Not knowing what else to do, he leaned forward and awkwardly kissed Robyn as the camera's shutter clicked loudly.

Robyn leaned back and looked at Jason. She took hold of the ring. "It's beautiful, Jason." Then she slowly looked up at him. "Yes. Yes, I would love to spend the rest of our lives together."

Boy-oh-boy, how on earth did you know? After so much time and so many moments having passed between them, Jason's prediction had come to fruition.

He leaned forward and kissed her again before jumping up and letting out a very loud and celebratory, "YES!"

I moved closer to Robyn and licked her face. "Oh, Pooh!" She said before laughing at Jason as he let out another huge nondescript yell—a massive release of his pent-up anxious energy. The veins in his neck protruded, and his fists clasped tightly as his voice echoed down the mountain. He returned to his camera and looked at me. "Okay, you and—now officially—your mom-to-be! You two—I want a picture of you two!" Jason raised his camera, his hands still shaking. "One more. Last one," said Jason, and he laid the camera down on its original perch and checked the viewfinder one more time. "Okay, family shot!"

Next, Jason reached into his backpack and pulled out the company cell phone. "Who do you want to call first? I think we should start with your mom and dad." I couldn't believe they were going to call other humans from the top of this mountain—how was that possible? Jason passed the phone to Robyn. She, too, now seemed giddy with excitement at the possibilities of the future life the two of them would share.

For the next few hours, they called family members and friends from the top of the mountain to announce their exciting news. Everyone was thrilled for them. Me, I spent the time searching the boulders and shrubs growing between them. Sure, I was excited, too—but I loved this place and I wanted to enjoy the sights and sniffs.

At some point, the positioning of the sun registered for Jason. "Holy crap—look where the sun is—it's at least two-and-half hours back to the car. I don't think we have two-and-half hours of sunlight left." With so many siblings and friends to call, they had been talking for a long, long time and hadn't noticed that daylight was running thin.

Robyn turned to look at the sun dipping low. "Well, we need to get going, then."

"Come on, Ike—we gotta hustle!"

Conversation during the return hike to the car was all about the wedding. It was hilarious to listen to Jason's ideas for the wedding versus Robyn's. Jason wanted a multi-day event. "Like a summer camp where people come for a few days and get to hang out and really spend some time together. We could organize a pub crawl, an afternoon of rowing or mountain biking or hiking. It's the West Coast, right? The majority of our friends and family are going to travel a long way for this. So let's make it worth their while!"

Robyn had a different version of an ideal wedding. "Or you and I—you're invited, too, Ike—could just go to a secluded beach or a place in the woods, exchange our vows, and just spend real quality time together in nature."

"What? Are you crazy? That's no fun!" answered Jason.

Apparently, they had some sorting out to do. And, for Jason, maybe even some compromising.

Two hours later, we were off the face of the mountain and into the thick forest at the base. The sun had long disappeared and it was completely dark. Robyn and Jason were having difficulty staying on the path because it was almost impossible for humans to see. On the other hand, I was well ahead of them and easily making my way to the trailhead. Finally, Jason called me back. "Ike, we can't see, buddy. And I didn't bring a flashlight. So you're going to have to be our eyes," Jason told me. "Here's your one and only chance to be a guide dog!" He laughed. "Come here, bud—give me your tail."

With Robyn holding Jason's hand, and Jason gently holding my tail, we began slowly navigating the trail that would eventually lead us to the car. It was a slow-going ordeal, but eventually we could hear the traffic from the highway and soon ventured out of the forest and into the parking area.

"Wow, there's a story for our grandkids, someday," said Jason.

"I'll say." Robyn sighed with relief. "Thank you, Ike. You would have made a wonderful guide dog—I just know it!"

I was well over the whole guide dog thing. Instead, these new wedding plans changed the game for me. Now I had something that I definitely wanted to stick around for. As much as we really didn't discuss the state of my health or my possible expiry date anymore, I was always consciously aware of its precarious and imminent arrival. At some point, I was going to check out. And based on the statistics that Allyson initially shared with us, it would likely be sooner rather than later. As far as I was concerned, Jason still had some more work to do—more honing, if you like. I couldn't leave now. If this guy was going to marry Robyn and be a human dad someday, I had to hang around as long as possible.

The routine that I had grown used to and enjoyed returned for the next several months. Robyn's training continued to progress and I enjoyed the perks of living with a world-class athlete. Our daily runs in the Endowment Lands and along Spanish Banks were a highlight. I always looked forward to running with, and even playfully racing, Robyn. We had an unspoken rhythm together. I would hang close by while she warmed up, but as soon as her workout began, I would come alongside and remain just a few strides ahead of her, gently trying to push the pace.

"You're the best training partner anyone could ever ask for, Ike. I sure appreciate the way you encourage me—thanks, Pooh Bear!"

Jason immersed himself in his work with Skeet & Ike's. Slowly and steadily, Ian placed their nut spreads into more stores. Although business was growing, Ian feared there was a change on the horizon. Peanut allergies were becoming more prominent, and peanuts and peanut butter sales were declining. Therefore, they needed to act quickly and find another product that could transition them away from being solely dependent on their nut spreads.

They wondered about soy nuts. There was a lot of buzz in the food industry at that time around the crunchy little nuggets. Ian and Jason spent several days trying to make a soy nut-based spread—to no avail. The results were unacceptable. It tasted okay, but it was too dry and wouldn't spread.

Ian wondered if seasoning the roasted nuts might be an option for a new snack. Jason brought home some test samples—delicious and crunchy! They were onto something.

During their demos in grocery stores, they both realized that almost everyone who came by to sample the nut spreads also had a snack item of some sort in their shopping carts. Jason saw a new snack item and its subsequent packaging as another avenue to share my story with more humans.

If the nut spreads were a success, the soy nut snacks were even more so. Ian successfully arranged to have little bags of Skeet & Ike's organic, naturally seasoned soy nuts into stores clear across the country within a few months. The newly minted entrepreneurs were now busier than they'd ever been. Skeet & Ike's had to hire their first manufacturing and sales human!

The downside for me was that the business had grown beyond its little office in our home. Ian and Jason moved to a much larger rented unit that could offer more office space and house the manufacturing equipment that packaged the soy nuts. This meant Jason was gone for hours at a time. Apparently, "No dogs allowed" in food processing places—a rule that made no sense to me. Thankfully, I had Robyn to keep me company. Between training sessions, she took courses at the Justice Institute. When she was home working on assignments, I cuddled beside her.

The next year, 1998, brought even more changes. Robyn was off to Australia to train with her coach and teammates in Adelaide. She'd be gone for four months.

Pat and Carolyn had moved out as well. We now had three new roommates, one of which had a cat, Prissy, who never came out of her room. And, given my introduction to Spook and Snow, I saw that as a good thing.

The night before Robyn was to leave for her training camp, Jason shared what had been on his mind. "I'm not sure how long this Skeet & Ike's thing is going to hold me."

"How do you mean?"

"I don't know how much longer I want to do this—the whole business thing. I don't know how long I can last."

"Last? I thought you were enjoying promoting the soy nuts?"

"I am. It's been fun. But, when I watch Ian at work, I can tell this is his thing—this is what he wants to do... forever! And, when I picture myself doing this work for twenty years, ten years, even five—I don't feel the same excitement. This is not going to sustain me forever. No way."

"What do you think's missing for you?"

"I love the graphic design work. I enjoy meeting people at food shows and having Ike there—that's all fun stuff. And I enjoy the demos most of the time too. But Ian could hire a designer. He could hire demo people. I don't see how or where my future is in this business moving forward. It's Ian's show. I mean, I asked him to be my business partner—and, clearly, I chose the right guy. But it's not for me. Not long term, anyway."

"So what are you thinking? What else would you like to do?"

"When I was training at Shawnigan Lake School back in the early nineties, I got invited into the art room to hang out with the kids and eventually taught some classes. I loved it. And, even though I grew up as the son of a teacher, I told myself I would never be one—when I was in that classroom or when I was coaching, I understood on a different level why Dad taught. I think I want to teach and coach."

Robyn sat beside Jason on their bed. "How much more school would you be looking at?"

"Well, UBC has a 12-month program—September to August. So if I started this coming fall, I'd be done next August."

"Whatever you think, Jason. We'll just make it work."

"I also phoned Peter at Shawnigan. He would let the administration know that I'd be looking for a job in a year's time. Coaching and teaching at Shawnigan? That'd be a pretty nice gig—Ike would love it!" Jason looked over at me. "Pooh-Bear, wait till you see the place. Miles of trails and open fields to run on. Not to mention a lake to swim in. You could even be in the classroom with me every day. Come out in the coach boat! Imagine living on that lake?"

"Sounds like a good life for Ike, alright!"

"For you too! For us. You'd have trails to run on. You could train with Wynn and your group in Victoria. We always talk about moving back to the Island. This is our chance—it would be perfect."

It did sound pretty good—the lake part, especially. But, at that moment, I was more concerned about losing Robyn for the four months.

***

Peter and his wife Joanne were dear friends of Jason's. During his comeback attempt for the 1992 Olympics, Peter had hired Jason as a junior rowing coach at Shawnigan. It allowed him the opportunity to train at the school, and coach and work in one of the boarding houses. It also afforded him room and board, along with some spending money, and an ideal place to row.

When things didn't work out with Jason's rowing career, he stayed on, fulfilling his coaching obligations. During that time, Peter became a Mentor to Jason. Peter, a competitive rower in his day, provided Jason with some real-life perspective—some of it difficult—that allowed him to see past his Olympic obsession and move on with his life. A good part of why Jason was now considering a teaching degree was because of conversations he'd had with Peter.

The next day, Robyn was off to Australia. It would be just Jason and me—me and my Clydesdale. Yes, naturally I missed my running partner, but, more so, I missed our little family. Jason was different without Robyn. He was quieter and didn't laugh as often. Although they shared emails back and forth and even had a few very long-distance phone calls, the separation was hard for him. Robyn had become a sounding board for Jason. He still got up every morning and wrote out his three pages, but not having Robyn around to share things with proved more challenging than he may have first considered.

He still unleashed his thoughts on me during our runs, but I could only listen. And listen, I did. Jason was keen to move on from the business. He had enjoyed his brief venture, but realized it was not for him. He applied to UBC and was accepted. He'd begin classes come September.

Springtime brought my annual checkup. Every year, I enjoyed a tremendous welcome from Allyson—cuddles and a belly rub on the floor while she filled me with compliments. Then she'd get down to business. A cold stethoscope listened to my heart and lungs, some pokes and prods along my spine, followed by blood work. I knew the drill by then.

A week later, Jason would get a call telling him to keep doing whatever he was doing. I was in good health, and my one kidney was managing the work of two. However, that spring, Allyson's receptionist called and asked Jason to bring me in again.

"Hello there, handsome," said Allyson while kneeling on the floor as I wiggled over to see her. "I want to speak with your dad about something we saw in your bloodwork," she continued as she rubbed my belly. "Hi Jason, thanks for coming in again."

"What seems to be the problem?"

"Well, there's no problem—either this silly dog has grown another kidney, or we messed up the test."

"What do you mean?" asked Jason. "What did you see?"

"Well, I've been doing this a long while, and I've never seen bloodwork from a dog with Ike's condition improve. You look at the last four years of tests, and you can see that his one kidney is doing a great job of cleaning his blood and keeping this beautiful boy healthy. And, at some point, we're going to see those numbers slide. Ike's kidney, no matter how healthy his diet, will begin to fatigue and struggle to do its job."

"Yup—I remember you warned me that there would come a day when his kidney would essentially run out of steam."

"Correct. So what makes this year so strange is that Ike's numbers have improved. Five years later, he's not sliding at all. Instead, he's getting better—and not just a little. We're talking a huge improvement!"

Allyson paused for a moment to let that sink in with Jason.

"Okay—how is that possible?"

"That's why we've asked you to come in again. I want to draw some more blood to make sure something didn't get mixed up in the test." Allyson put her face down to mine and kissed me between my eyes. "But, if the numbers come back the same, then I, for one, have never seen or heard of anything like it."

A week later, Allyson called with the test results. She told Jason that my numbers were indeed reflective of what two healthy functioning kidneys would produce. She couldn't explain it—Jason didn't care, he was over the moon.

The celebration, however, was short-lived. Robyn, now back from Australia, was struggling with her health. She had returned feeling fit and ready for her summer season of racing. Then, a week before she was scheduled to fly to Europe for some early track meets, she tested positive for mono. Her season was done without having even begun.

Robyn, ever trusting of the circumstances she was dealt with, took this as an opportunity to focus more on her health and explore ways to get stronger and support her training. That summer, long before veganism became common, Robyn completely eliminated animal products from her diet. Jason, who had long been a vegetarian who still ate fish and eggs once in a while, decided to join Robyn in her decision.

Me, I wasn't so sure. I loved the odd poached egg. And, when Jason barbecued salmon, there was nothing I enjoyed more than devouring the skin. Robyn had looked at me and said, "If I wouldn't eat you, why would I eat another animal?" How could I argue that?

Robyn, never one to sit around and mope, decided to embrace the time away from her racing and training by joining Jason and me for a few weeks at the cottage with his family; she was keen to go camping with us as well. Having never had a summer off from racing or training for more than a decade, Robyn seemed ready to enjoy a well-deserved break. Needless to say, Jason and I were ecstatic to have her along.

We travelled over to Vancouver Island and our favourite spot on Atluck Lake. Typically, the two of us hiked and swam and enjoyed the solitude. This time, Jason was as playful as a young pup. I could have done without his lily-white butt running around the campsite while the two of them skinny dipped, but I was heartened to see him so light and playful.

Given where the two of us had begun a few years before, this angry, bitter, and skinny young man had made some big strides. Now he looked like a Clydesdale—strong, muscular, and full of energy, joy, and life!

By September, Robyn was feeling ready to resume her running. She was rested and refreshed after some time away from her training, as well as feeling the benefits of a cleaner diet.

Jason was ready for school. He established a busy rhythm of classes during the day, while completing design work for Ian in the evenings. Robyn's days consisted of multiple training sessions while she continued her courses in victim reconciliation at the Justice Institute. Our weekends were about playing. We always made time to get out and enjoy some hikes in the woods.

As the spring term approached, Jason prepared for his final teaching practicum. He was nervous but excited to finally work independently with students. The requirement was for each student-teacher to spend three months at a local school.

One day Jason arrived home at noon.

"Why are you back so soon?" asked Robyn.

"Uhhh, I got kicked out!"

"What do you mean you 'got kicked out'?"

"What part of 'kicked-out' don't you understand?" Jason put his backpack on the kitchen floor and sat down at the table. "I was literally escorted to the front doors of the school and asked to leave."

"By whom?" Robyn looked shocked.

"The principal," explained Jason. "What an asshole! I should've told him to go fuck himself!"

"Okay, easy does it, why don't—"

"You know what he said to me?" interrupted Jason. "'Son, you'll look back on this someday and be grateful for what I did.' Fuck you!"

"Can you please take a breath, and then lead me through what exactly happened?"

"I'm teaching my class. My sponsor teacher's there. He's reading a magazine or something at the back of the class. Everything's going swimmingly until this kid throws a shoe at his friend from across the room. I look at the teacher. He does nothing. Then another shoe sails across the room from the other direction. Still, my sponsor teacher—whose fuckin' job it is to step in and make sure stuff like this doesn't happen—does nothing." Jason takes a sip from the glass of water that Robyn had got for him.

"So I ask these two little spoiled dickheads to leave. I get the class back on track and then go out to join them. As I approach, they're looking at me as if I'm the one who screwed up. So I ask them, 'Hey, what makes me the asshole here? You're the ones who threw the shoes!'" Jason pauses and shakes his head before continuing. "They say nothing. I tell them to go back in the classroom and see if we can try this again."

"Okay, I don't agree with your choice of words," said Robyn. "But how did that get you kicked out?"

"After class, these two little fuckers go to the principal and tell him I called them both *assholes*!"

Robyn gasped. "Oh, Jason—you've got to be kidding me!"

"Nope—about ten minutes after class, I'm called to the principal's office. He tells me what the kids said and has me escorted out."

"Jason, that's horrible—I'm so sorry."

"You know what he said to me as we're walking to the main doors? 'It's my last year as a Principal; I don't want the hassle of having to defend a student-teacher in front of a bunch of angry parents.'"

There was nothing that bothered Jason more than injustice. Especially when it landed at his own feet. Getting asked to leave mid-practicum because of someone's apathy—he was furious.

That evening he phoned Peter and told him what had happened. Peter said not to worry and that he would look into having Jason finish his practicum at Shawnigan. The school now had a vested interest in Jason. They were hoping to hire him for the upcoming school year beginning in September.

While Jason appreciated the gesture, he told Peter that he had a meeting scheduled the next day with the head of the education department at UBC. The University's policy was that if you got kicked out of your practicum, you were automatically removed from the education program as well. Things were not looking good.

Very early the next morning, I felt Jason's hand shaking me. "Hey, Pooh," he whispered. "I can't sleep. I need to move, buddy. Would you mind if we go for a run?"

Jason was no speed demon. And I was used to that—especially when we ran through the surrounding neighbourhood. But, that morning, we tore up those dark streets. I had never run at such a pace with him. Evidently, he had some steam that needed blowing off.

After a long shower, a good breakfast, and a calming pep talk from Robyn, Jason was off to learn of his fate. A few hours later, he returned, looking incredibly relieved. It turned out that a few dozen of the other students in the class had faxed letters in support of him saying that the two boys had purposefully set out to cause some trouble. He was reinstated at the university and would resume his practicum at another school. Catastrophe averted!

Jason was almost across the finish line. A summer of elective courses was all that remained. By September, he'd be ready to jump into a classroom.

Shawnigan Lake School offered him a full-time teaching and coaching position, which meant we'd be moving over to the Island a few months later. Robyn was over in Europe competing in early summer meets in preparation for the World Championships in Spain. Unable to watch this time, we waited for the phone call. Robyn didn't get past the heats in the 1500 metre. Although she'd had one of her best years of training, the heat in Seville, along with her allergies, combined to undermine her racing, yet again.

After well over a decade of high-level running, Jason was beginning to wonder when Robyn's athletic journey would end. Although he continued to defend her choice to pursue running during delicate conversations with family and friends, he also wanted to get married and have a family. Having little humans and running on the world stage didn't necessarily go hand in hand.

Adding fuel to Jason's impatience was a conversation he'd had with one of Robyn's teammates and her coach, who hadn't travelled overseas for this competition. "More than two-thirds of that field are dirty," the teammate said. "Robyn's going to have her hands full."

"What are you talking about?" asked Jason.

"What do you think she's talking about?" the coach said. "The level of cheating at the international level right now is off the charts."

Jason went on to share that he knew there were some athletes on the world stage in rowing that had cheated too. But it was never that many. Their conversation seemed to rattle Jason. The following day on our run, I listened to him vent. Yikes, he was mad. Like all of our previous runs together, he'd begin furious at something or someone, and eventually arrive at some sort of resolution.

Home from Spain, Robyn was disappointed enough; now was not the time for the 'how much longer' conversation. More immediately, they had to find us a home in Shawnigan.

Jason and Robyn decided to revisit our old haunts during our final week before moving. Kits Beach, Black Mountain, Lynn Canyon, and of course, the Endowment Lands. Halfway through our last run, I got a whiff of something—or someone—that I hadn't smelled in a long time. Iona was somewhere on the trails. I continued to smell her scent numerous times along our run.

Impossible. Iona had long finished her training and lived somewhere with her owner doing what we had all been born to do. But the scent was getting stronger. Until finally...

What? It can't be... Iona? "IONA," I called out.

She turned. *"Ike! Is that you?"*

We ran toward each other. *"Does your new family live nearby?"*

"My new family?" Iona asked. *"Oh, right—you wouldn't have heard."*

"Heard what?"

"We were all pulled from the program," she said, "Indie developed eye problems. Ian, hip problems. And, with your kidney issues, we all got pulled before they put any more time and money into us."

"Goodness," I said, *"I'm sorry to hear that. Are you with your original family?"*

"Yes, me and the girls!" She smiled and looked at me awkwardly. *"It's so good to see you, Ike. I have to be honest; I didn't think you'd still be alive. I mean, what I heard Roberta tell my human sounded serious."*

Iona stepped closer and licked my ear.

"That's okay, Iona. Every day with Jason and Robyn is a bonus. I don't get too fussed about what could be—I'm too busy having fun with these two," I said pointing my nose toward Jason and Robyn.

"My human showed me the nut spread with your face on it—she said she ran into Jason at the market, and he told her the whole story."

"Yes, Jason loves to tell everyone about me, and that nut spread," I replied. *"It's been kinda fun!"*

***

Finally, it was moving day. With the rented truck packed and the three of us squished into the front seat, we said goodbye to our home and made our way to the ferry. Heading up the Malahat—the highway that would lead us to Shawnigan Lake—Jason unexpectedly pulled off at the viewing station and parked. I sat up and looked out. We were far above the inlet below us. The view seemed to go on forever. After reaching into his backpack, Jason got out of the truck. He walked around to Robyn's door and opened it.

"Can you please step out?" he asked.

"What's going on?"

Jason reached up and took hold of Robyn's hand while she stepped out of the truck. He then directed her to the railing and asked her to step up onto the concrete part of the barrier. Robyn looked at Jason with an inquisitive gaze.

"What are you doing?"

Jason revealed what looked to be a homemade medal. He stepped closer to Robyn and held it up. "This gold medal has a dove on the front with the words, 'strength, courage, and integrity' surrounding it. And, if you flip it over, it has a small inscription. *Presented to Robyn Meagher, 1999, for embodying the truest values of sport.*"

Robyn smiled lovingly at Jason.

"Can you bend forward so that I can reach you?"

With a beautiful vista of Mount Baker and the Coastal Mountains behind her, Robyn bent forward for Jason to place his homemade medal around her neck. Then he grabbed both of her hands.

"Robyn, I've never met another athlete—another person—like you. It's not how I would've done it—I think you know that by now. But it's how you've done it. I was speaking with one of your teammates about some of the other competitors on the world stage. I had no idea. When I first found out about the level of cheating that goes on, I won't lie, I was pissed. Just ask Ike." Jason turned and looked at me watching through the open passenger window.

Yup, he went ballistic!

"And I know you've said this is a *journey* for you, and the medals don't matter to you, blah, blah, blah. And I've struggled to understand that. Holy fuck, have I struggled. The Sydney Olympics will likely be your last kick at the can, and I just want you to know that I'm—no, that Ike and I are behind you one-hundred percent. I want you to finish this ride on your terms. So if there's anything we can do to help, you just have to ask. Okay?"

Robyn let go of Jason's hands and took hold of the medal and turned it so that she could read it for herself. "This is the most beautiful medal I've ever received, Jason. I can't tell you how much this means to me."

She stepped down off of the concrete barrier and hugged Jason. I had to admit, he was learning.

island life

Peter's wife, Joanne, knew a lot of humans. As a public health nurse, she was closely connected with the surrounding community. Joanne introduced Jason and Robyn to an elderly woman looking for tenants to stay in her cottage during the winter months.

The large A-frame house was right on the lake, only a few hundred feet from the school gates. They agreed to the rental terms and, a week before school began, we showed up for the first time and walked into our new home.

Jason pushed open the door and I rushed in. A vaulted ceiling with enormous windows covered the entire front of the cottage. Out onto the deck, down onto the grass, there in front of me was the most incredible view of the lake. *I have a lake in my front yard!*

I ran down to the dock. Jason and Robyn were right behind me.

"Can you frickin believe this, Ike? Look what you have to play in, anytime you want." Jason turned to Robyn. "Joanne said it was pretty nice, but I wasn't expecting this! This is incredible—I can't believe we're going to be living here for the year!"

This was our new home. My days of "student-living" were over—no more cat roommates, no more shared furniture, no more strange humans coming and going; none of that. This was going to be good!

Even Robyn had come around. Originally, she was hesitant. She enjoyed her rhythm in Vancouver and all that the city had to offer. But, as the Olympic Games drew nearer, she could see the benefits of moving back to the Island in support of her preparation.

Sure enough, the picture Jason had described for my life at Shawnigan was coming true. We had a daily routine that was hard to beat. Every morning, after walking along the lake and onto the campus, we'd arrive at the art room where Jason taught. It was spacious and inspiring, with high ceilings, large windows, and workstations throughout the room. There was even a pretty-good-sounding stereo that Jason kept hopping during class time.

My favourite part was the students—young, energetic, mischievous high-school-aged humans who, surprisingly enough, were always friendly. Regardless of whether they were from Canada, the US, or some far-off country on the other side of the planet, they all welcomed me like I was their own. Many of them would tell me about their dogs at home and how much they missed them while they pet and hugged me. It was nice to feel so appreciated.

Jason's teaching style was similar to how he had raised me. He set some firm boundaries, then let the students play. The rebellious artist whom I was introduced to at Emily Carr lived on as a teacher wanting his classroom to be an escape from the structure and pressure of their other subjects.

In between classes, as we walked to and from the main building, I would meet some of the other dogs who, like me, came to class with their humans. Chico was a black lab who spent most of his days outside, staring at puddles, wondering who the other dog was staring back.

Some days I couldn't help myself. *"Who's in there today, Chico?"*

"Not sure, Ike—could be the same guy as yesterday!"

Rug, short for Rugby, was Peter and Joanne's golden. She was younger than me and, at times, full of unbridled energy—always keen to wrestle and chase.

After a few weeks of settling in, Jason's parents came for a visit. Without having to get into my travelling jail cell, I got to enjoy the perks of laying on the floor at the dining table below Carl, who had showed up with a special surprise for Jason—his old briefcase from when he was a teacher. Jason was touched by the gesture. Even more so when he read the note that Carl had placed inside; "Good luck, son. Be inspiring!"

After coaching volleyball practice Saturday morning, Jason joined us on the dock back at the cottage. Under blue skies, with a perfect air temperature and refreshingly cool water to swim in, Eleanor and Carl referred to our spot as a less-muggy version of Bobcaygeon.

"How do your students like having Ike in the class?" asked Eleanor.

"It's a reminder of home life for many of them—the ones that have dogs, especially. He gives everyone a big welcome at the beginning of class and then settles under my workstation. He's quite remarkable, this little guy."

"I would never have been able to take our dog, Tiger, to class," said Carl. "Gosh, could you imagine?"

"You should've seen what happened in the first week. One day, Ike spent the entire class curled up at the feet of a young boy from California. I didn't think anything of it until that morning at our daily staff meeting, when the headmaster told us that boy's grandpa had died the night before."

"Goodness, that is amazing," Eleanor said.

"We all like to think that we're perceptive of how others are feeling; Ike's on another level."

I appreciated Jason's acknowledgement. But I didn't see it as anything special. In fact, if humans weren't so caught up in thoughts and worries about trivial things, they, too, would be able to feel more. The pain and grief that young boy was experiencing were spilling out of him. It was impossible for me not to feel it. If Jason could've led more with his heart and less with his head, he would've felt it too.

For the rest of the visit, I spent my afternoons on the dock with Jason's parents while he coached volleyball and Robyn trained in Victoria. They couldn't throw my hockey balls as far as Jason could, but they never tired of my constant requests.

"Gosh, Ike," Carl would say. "You're going to empty the lake if you keep going in and out of there like that!"

A few weeks later, Robyn's parents, Gary and Adair, arrived with Erin and Kuz for Thanksgiving. Although both were quiet, they had a mischievous and playful side that showed when the stories began regarding growing up in their busy household. Like Carl, Gary was a reliable source of treats that continuously fell from above while I cozied up to him under the dinner table. *It must be a dad thing!*

Before living in that cottage, Jason and Robyn had never hosted so many humans. Now, on their own without roommates for the first time, it seemed like every weekend we had guests.

With Christmas came our first snowfall at Shawnigan. Not thinking the campus could be any more stunning, it was when covered in snow. The next morning, Jason, Robyn, and I took off on a long run through the trails that wove in and around the school's property. Enormous evergreens wrapped in blankets of white fluffy snow would at times come crashing down, dousing us in a cold shower. The cottage had a large pot-bellied stove that Jason kept well stocked with dry crackling wood. The heat emanating from the roaring fires was a welcome source of comfort after our playtime in the cold snow.

Jason's first term had been hectic. It was an intense pace he had grown used to from his work with Skeet & Ike's. But, along with a full week of classes, afternoon coaching, and evening duty in one of the boarding houses once a week, he was still managing Ian's packaging and design work. Despite his workload, Jason was happier than I had ever felt him. We spent a good portion of every day together. And, if I wasn't with him, I was running with Robyn in the surrounding trails or hanging out with her at the cottage. I loved our new life at Shawnigan.

Although Jason was earning a teacher's salary, they were still quite thrifty. Jason purchased the display Christmas tree at a Canadian Tire for half-price, along with all of the trimmings. After finding a prominent place for the glass ornament that he had painted for Robyn, he stood back and admired their first Christmas tree in their very own home. I had never seen Jason so excited for Christmas.

Erin and Kuz travelled over from Abbotsford with their new chocolate-lab cross, Cocoa, to celebrate the season with us. And they brought a cat! He was an orange cat, and his name was Chester. He was Snow and Spook's replacement. I remember being annoyed that a cat was coming for Christmas. But it turned out that Chester was the coolest cat I'd ever know.

It was always fun to hear humans express their appreciation for the cottage when they first walked in. "Woah! You get to look at this every day? I'd never get any work done!" said Erin.

Christmas morning brought more snow and a renewed sense of coziness to our cottage on the lake. With the fire roaring and Michael Bublé singing classic Christmas songs in the background, we gathered around the tree and Jason played Santa.

It was a magical day. After the gifts were opened, some blueberry-banana pancakes were served, including to Cocoa and me. After brunch, I returned to the fire to snooze on my Christmas gift from Robyn and Jason—a comfy new bed covered with a life-size picture of Winnie-the-Pooh. Robyn loved the print; no one enjoyed calling me Pooh-Bear more than her. After a nap, we were off to the trails for a hike. The thick blanket of snow absorbed the sound of Cocoa and me chasing one another up and down the trails while our humans walked and visited. He and I became fast friends too. He was about my size, fast, ball-obsessed like me, and he loved wrestling—what wasn't to like?

Far too quickly, the holidays came to an end. A new term began with Jason, and me at his feet, back in the classroom and now coaching rowing too. Peter thought Jason might be just the right coach to reinvigorate the junior girls' program.

After a few afternoons curled up in his coach boat atop two duffle bags stuffed with life jackets, I began to realize Jason was a different coach when it came to rowing. Gone was the playful leader I had seen interact with his volleyball team. Rowing Coach Jason was all business. He was never rude or disrespectful, but he had high expectations, and if the young athletes didn't meet them, he made it very clear.

Halfway through the winter season, while sitting in the living room after dinner one evening, Robyn asked Jason how things were going. "How many girls are you working with?"

Jason looked at the fire and pretended not to hear. I knew that he'd been dreading this conversation for a long while.

"Jason, how many girls do you have in rowing right now?"

"Umm, in total?"

"Yes, in total!"

"I have a coxed four. So, that's four plus...well, the coxie. So...five."

"That's it?" Robyn looked surprised. "How many did you start with?"

"Way back at the beginning of the second term?"

"Yes—way back at the beginning—how many signed up?"

"Ahhh, well, about forty-four. Yup, I think it was roughly..."

"Forty-four?" Robyn was shocked. "Are you joking? Thirty-nine have quit?"

"Well, I haven't done the math, but that would be a rough guess, I suppose." Jason fidgeted with the zipper on his sweater before getting up to adjust a log on the fire.

Robyn shook her head. "Why do you think all thirty-nine of those girls chose to leave?"

"Ahhh, well, now that you mention it—it does seem like a strange coincidence."

"Jason, come on—they didn't all just decide that it was time to try basketball or squash. They left because they weren't enjoying themselves." Robyn paused for a moment. "And I'm guessing that had something to do with how you were coaching them."

"Ouch!" Jason looked at Robyn. "Really? You think that I'm such a horrible coach that they all left?" Jason stared at Robyn defiantly. "And you're not even acknowledging the five that stayed! One's a coxie, but still..."

Robyn waited a moment. "Why do you think so many of them left?"

"That's easy—too soft," Jason snapped. "They couldn't handle the work."

Uh-oh, take cover, Jase!

"Oh, so girls can't handle hard work?"

Jason threw his hands in the air. "I didn't say that. I said *these* girls couldn't handle the work—not *all* girls."

Robyn got out of her chair immediately, crossed the room, and stood in front of Jason. I'd never seen her so—well—*mad*. She took a deep breath and continued. "What did Peter have to say?"

Jason looked at his feet. "Umm, that this would be my last year coaching junior girls. He doesn't want to decimate the program."

"Was he upset?"

"No. He kinda laughed when he said it." Jason settled his voice. "He said he accepted part of the responsibility for assigning the girls to me. And he also acknowledged that the season hasn't gone as well as he'd hoped."

"So why do you think it's different?" Robyn asked. "Why so much success with volleyball and not with rowing?"

"Volleyball was fun—I made it about having fun."

"And, rowing can't be fun because?"

"'Cause it's not. It's not a game. You don't play it. You endure it."

"Do you know how absurd that sounds?" Robyn returned to her chair.

"It's true! I mean, it's fun on some level. But kids don't generally sign up for rowing because they want to have fun."

"Wow, you're doing a great job selling your sport!" Robyn shook her head. "What if you made it fun?"

Jason scrunched up his face. "That's ridiculous!"

"Look, Jason, I'm not telling you how to coach. But my guess is that a little bit of *that guy* is showing up to your practices. You remember, *that guy*—the one you said you didn't want to become ever again? Well, I think you're becoming him—sounds like the big Olympic rower who only likes winning is worried about how these young girls will reflect his coaching!"

Robyn walked over to sit beside Jason. She took hold of his hands before continuing the conversation. "Look, you can be such a thoughtful person who has so much to offer these kids—you do. But maybe your ego is getting in the way?" Robyn looked at Jason with caring eyes.

"So what are you saying? I shouldn't train these girls as hard as I would train boys—I shouldn't prepare them to race? Or try to win?"

Robyn leaned back. "No, not at all," she replied. "If race preparation requires hard work, then that's how you train them. I guess I would just challenge you to make it more fun—more engaging. Perhaps find a bigger reason than just preparing them to race. Or win. What if they were motivated by something bigger?"

"Geezuz," uttered Jason rolling his eyes and head simultaneously. "I can't bring your self-help bullshit to my rowing practices, Robyn."

"Self-help bullshit? Says the guy who's been writing in a journal every morning for the past three years!"

"That's different."

"Oh, exactly how is it different?"

"Well, umm, it's work—it's hard work," answered Jason. "And I don't burn incense or chant or anything stupid like that."

"Please tell me you didn't just say that." She shook her head and looked over at me. "Ike, did your dad just say that—by not burning incense, journalling is not considered self-help?"

Oh, he said that alright. I definitely heard him say that!

"Jason, do you know how ridiculous you sound right now?"

"Okay, okay...the incense comment was stupid—I'll give you that."

Robyn took a deep breath. "First, would you please stop calling it flakey self-help stuff? It makes you sound like a redneck—it scares me! Second, if you opened up your mind a little, you'd discover that there's so much more to making boats go fast than just training harder than the other crews."

"Pfft—so what are you saying? I make this about discovering their untapped potential?" asked Jason with a sarcastic tone.

"You're the coach. But that sounds a whole lot more intriguing—and fun—than just slogging through practice day after day."

"I'm gonna have to think about it." Jason looked down at his feet and shook his head. "Fuck! I hate it when you're right all the time!"

Robyn put her hand on his back. "It's about doing what's best, not just what's right. Imagine if your high school coach had asked you if you wanted to find out what you were capable of. Do you think you might have been interested?"

"Of course."

"Then imagine coaching a crew of young girls where each member during the course of the season discovers what they're capable of—their absolute limits. Do you think that might produce a fast boat?"

Jason looked at Robyn and smiled. "Where did you learn all this shit?"

I could feel him lighten. Once more, Robyn had gently challenged Jason's old way of seeing the world and allowed him to arrive at a new perspective on his terms. From that night onward, Jason was different with his young crew. Not quite the playful coach she had invited, but he had heard Robyn, and he was doing his best to incorporate her perspective on how to work with this developing young crew.

After years running with Robyn, I had become accustomed to her different speeds. She had a recovery-run speed, a training-run speed, and a hill-run speed. Yes, as crazy as it sounds, there were days when she would head out with me at her side, and make her way over to Water Tower Hill. Then she'd run up as fast as she could and jog down, only to do it again and again and again. Me, I loved it. It was another chance to race Robyn. And the trail that led us to this hill was one of my favourites.

That year, something was different. Either I was getting older—which I was. Or Robyn was getting significantly faster. Not only was she staying with me for more extended periods on the incline, but she was running more of them in total than she had in previous years. As the early-season meets approached, I could feel that Robyn was ready. She had reached a new level of fitness and racing speed.

Jason had travelled to St. Catharines with his rowing crew for the Canadian High School Championships, so Robyn and I were on our own. The cottage was more peaceful when Jason was gone because Robyn didn't have the stereo blasting every waking moment of the day. She loved her solitude. And I enjoyed lying peacefully at her feet on the deck or the dock during the day, and later in the evening while she read inside. There was the odd motorboat or car that interrupted our silent retreat, but for the most part, the two of us enjoyed the company of another soul without having much to say.

By the time Jason returned, it was almost our moving day; we had agreed to vacate the cottage for July and August. There were still final reports to be written and the graduation ceremonies. But, for the most part, Jason's first year at Shawnigan had been a resounding success. He'd found a nice rhythm with his teaching and developed some good relationships with his students. Even his girls' crew had done well at the National Championship rowing regatta in St. Catharines, placing second among the top crews in the country in the junior girls' coxed four event. Jason had even mustered up the will to thank Robyn for her advice. As he put it, "I don't think they would've done as well as they did without you calling out my bullshit." Although rough around the edges, that was a solid compliment by Jason's standards.

Robyn, always modest, redirected the praise back to Jason. "You took the advice and worked with it. So I hope you can appreciate your part in their success too."

Peter and Joanne had a guest suite in their basement that we moved into for the summer. Jason spent his days working on packaging and design work for Ian while Robyn prepared for the Olympic trials in Victoria a few weeks later.

One morning, we decided to accompany Robyn to Victoria. The plan was to watch her practice and then go out for lunch afterwards. While Robyn warmed up with her teammates on the track, I chased hockey balls in the sunshine on the infield.

"Okay, Ike—time to head up into the stands and watch your mom rip up this track." As we walked over to the bleachers to find a seat, Jason stopped to see Robyn. She was speaking with her coach. They were discussing whether or not to continue with the morning workout.

Robyn explained that she felt her back tweak ever so slightly during the warm-up and was concerned about doing a hard training session with the Olympic trials only weeks away. She and her coach decided to proceed with caution and pull back at the first sign of any further discomfort.

We climbed the stairs and found a spot in the shade. Jason looked concerned as he settled himself into one of the hard plastic stadium chairs. I lay at his feet. I knew this year, in particular, was important for Robyn. She had managed her best spring training season ever and felt more prepared for the upcoming trials than she'd ever been.

While Jason watched Robyn's every lap, I dozed off in the cool breeze. Seeming as if I had just begun to sleep deeply, Jason woke me. "Okay, Ike, let's go down and see mom."

We walked down the stairs and onto the infield, where Robyn stood with her coach.

"How'd it go?" asked Jason.

"Pretty good."

"Pretty good?" said Robyn's coach. "Those were some of the fastest times you've ever run. I'd say it was more than *pretty good*. She's never been more ready!"

Jason smiled at Robyn. "How about your back—any pain?"

"No, it seems to have settled down. I'm just going to do my warm-down. I shouldn't be too long." Robyn turned to me. "Ike, do you want to join me?"

Do I?

"Come on—let's go for a little jog!"

We ran onto the track to join Robyn's teammates. This was going to be fun, running with a bunch of humans who looked like Robyn—greyhounds, all of them. And their idea of a jog was so not what I was used to. The other runners were playful and encouraging—they welcomed me into their pack.

Suddenly, Robyn gasped and grabbed her back. She stopped and stood erect. She grimaced. The other runners called for their coach. He and Jason ran over immediately.

"Where do you feel it?" Robyn's coach asked.

"It's my lower back. But it's shooting down my legs. I can't move."

Jason looked at her coach. Nobody spoke. There were four weeks to go until the trials.

Later that day, Robyn began treatment: acupuncture, massage, physiotherapy, chiropractic—every modality you could imagine, Robyn embraced it all. Her days were filled with rehabilitation. She had a short window to return to racing form and wasn't going to leave any stone unturned.

After a week of her strict recovery protocol, Robyn could walk without limping and jog slowly, but she still had a long way to go. After another week, she could run, but not fast enough to train. With two weeks until the Olympic Trials, Robyn had no choice but to announce her withdrawal from the event.

I curled up beside her on the deck every chance I got. I could feel her disappointment, but it was her sadness that was palpable. It covered her like a heavy blanket. Despite her injury, Robyn still did her best to remain optimistic, appreciative, and look for the opportunity in her unforeseen predicament.

Jason, however, was going to take more time; he was furious. I knew a very long run in the trails, complete with a lot of profanity and venting, was in our near future. Two days after Robyn's announcement, that run arrived. It didn't take long for him to begin sorting through Robyn's situation.

"You know what bothers me the most, Ike? Of all of the athletes who should be in Sydney, Robyn's at the top of that list. She epitomizes what the fuckin' Games stand for. Her last Olympic Games—in the best shape of her life. This is not fair—not one fuckin' bit."

We continued up Robyn's training hill; Jason paused to process. "But you know who will be on the track in Sydney? All of the fuckin' cheaters who blood dope and do whatever else they do to gain the upper hand. Tell me how that's fair, Ike? Eh—tell me how the fuck that's fair?"

I hadn't seen him this mad since he'd been kicked out of his teaching practicum. Something about Jason and his perception of injustice always pushed his emotions over the top. Through her hard work and commitment, Jason believed that Robyn had earned a better outcome. In his mind, she deserved to race in Sydney and finish her career at the top of her game. She had played by the rules and earned the best race of her life on the world stage. But, as Jason had painfully discovered for himself with his own Olympic experience, life wasn't always interested in what we deemed fair.

A few months earlier, Jason's friend Fiona had mentioned that she thought he still had some 'stuff to sort out.' Jason was taken aback at her suggestion.

"What are you talkin' about?" he objected. "I've done my work and then some." Fiona had disagreed and suggested that Jason attend a workshop, "The Heart of the Shaman," at some place called Hollyhock, on Cortes Island. It was a five-day course that helped participants delve into life's pressing challenges. Now, with Robyn's Olympic dream over, she expressed interest in joining Jason for the retreat.

I had to agree with Fiona—he did have more to sort out.

I stayed with Joanne, Peter, Rug, and their two girls, Ali and Lizzie. The week flew by. Before I knew it, my parents—as they referred to themselves—were home. Our reunion was exuberant and welcoming. I loved these two humans more than anything in my life.

Robyn received me as she always did—open and loving. Jason, although happy to see me, was quiet. After our initial greeting, he walked with Rug and me to the back of their property, where he silently threw a ball for us to chase.

After dinner, I lay at Jason's feet while he stood alone on the back deck. Peter came out to join him, carrying two beers. The days were getting shorter as the summer was winding down. The sky was brilliant red and the evening air was warm—not nearly as hot as it had been.

"So tell me about your experience?" Peter asked as he handed a beer to Jason.

"How late do you plan on staying up?"

Peter smiled. "The Coles Notes, perhaps? Whatever you want to share."

Jason paused for a moment. "Well, no surprise—it was a hippie-fest right from the get-go. The room—or the space, as they kept calling it—was full of feathers and bones and beads and drums and tie-dyed prints and all kinds of weird shit like that. There was incense burning all the time—full-on granolas!" Jason knelt beside me. He stroked my back and took a deep breath. "But, all that aside, the people—the facilitators and the participants—were incredible. Kind, thoughtful, caring, no surface bullshit—they were real. All of them were there to do some work."

"And what exactly did that entail?"

"Well, for me, it didn't get off to a good start. The first night, we stood around a large bonfire and paired off. Then we had to look at each other and say something like, 'I will hold you in my heart, honour your spirit, and live my life better for having known you.' Geezuz Murphy, I wanted to leave right then!"

Peter chuckled. "What kept you there?"

"Well, for one thing, it was expensive as hell—no way Mr. Thrifty was leaving. And, of course, Robyn was right into it—imagine that. So

I was stuck, whether I liked it or not. Besides, the food was out of this world."

"Did you take anything from it—other than the food?" Peter asked with a smile.

Jason laughed. "There was this guy named Doug—one of the facilitators. Ponytail, tanned leathery skin, smoked cigarettes that he rolled himself. He wore these old jeans with his Jesus sandals and a wrinkled linen shirt. He was quiet—hardly ever spoke. But, when he did, I heard him loud and clear. It was like he was speaking directly to my core."

"Say more about that," interrupted Peter.

"Well, on the first morning, we all sat in a circle and shared the reason that we had enrolled in the program. People talked about losing a child, having cancer, or struggling with childhood trauma—all big stuff, right? All things that one would consider worthy of *needing attention*. When it came to my turn to speak, I took a pass. I was thinking, 'Sorry to hear about your cancer, but I'm trying to come to terms with not winning a race!'"

"And this Doug—how did he make it safe for you to explore that?"

"I don't know. I mean, after the first morning session, I told him why I was silent, and he didn't flinch. He just listened. From there on, we just clicked. I talked. He listened. That, along with all of the group stuff—deep breathing exercises, meditation. Can you believe it? I fuckin' meditated!" Peter smiled. "And journalling—lots and lots of journalling. I came away having sorted out some of my shit."

"And what sort of shit would that be, Jase?"

"For the most part, it's about letting go. Letting go of my dream and the outcome of those Olympics. And all of the stories I wrote in my head that kept me stuck."

"Nice to hear," said Peter. "Can you give me an example?"

Jason turned and faced the sunset. "All this time, I thought that shiny medal would've changed how people saw me—how they treated me. That they would've respected me more, liked me more; hell, maybe even loved me more." Jason paused briefly. "Fuck, when I hear myself say it out loud—what a stupid-ass thing to believe."

Peter turned and slowly walked over to stand in front of Jason. "Do you think Ike would treat you differently if you had won that race?" Jason met Peter's eyes. "Tell me honestly, if you had an Olympic gold medal hanging on a wall somewhere, do you really believe Ike would be different with you?" Peter's tone was soft, but his intention was clear and firm.

"I never really thought of it that way."

They both stood quietly. Jason looked at his feet.

After a moment, Peter spurred the conversation again. "You haven't answered my question." A warm smile crossed Peter's face.

Jason looked up quickly. "What, it's obvious—isn't it?"

"I don't know. Is it?" Peter's smile slowly faded.

I could feel that Jason wasn't enjoying this. "No—no, he wouldn't care. He doesn't care," he replied sharply.

"I would agree," said Peter. "He doesn't care, Jason…about the things you've done, what you've accomplished, or, in this case, what you haven't. What he does care about is who you are—what's inside of you; that's what he sees."

Jason paused while he looked away and took a deep breath. "Sometimes, I think what he sees isn't all that pretty. Who I am inside isn't all that…good."

Peter put his hand on Jason's shoulder. "That's the beauty of dogs, isn't it? They see our potential—they feel it. They know what we're capable of—even if we don't. They feel our love, our care, and the service that's inside all of us. That, my friend, is what Ike feels from inside of you. And if Ike can feel it, then so can others."

a new direction

Moving back into the cottage that Fall was no less exciting than the first time. While Robyn and Jason unpacked their belongings, I spent the day at the dock doing what I do best. Every once in a while, Jason would step out onto the deck and throw two balls into the lake for me to retrieve. It was a great way to occupy my time. It could take a lot of swimming back and forth chasing one ball and then the next before I nabbed both of them. Then I'd run up to the deck and wait for Jason to come out and do it again.

Once more, we had visits from both Robyn and Jason's parents during September; two reliable sources of food scraps falling from the table, and many throwing arms to keep me amused down on the dock. With a year of teaching under his belt, Jason was more confident with his students. I could feel it. Once again, he ran his classroom like a business. The students had plenty of autonomy, but they were well-behaved young humans. Never once did I see a shoe sail across the classroom. Jason had boundaries, and made it clear there'd be repercussions when those boundaries were pushed. For the most part, he was strict, but he was also fair.

When I saw students occasionally testing those boundaries behind Jason's back, I wanted to warn them, *"Believe me when I say, you don't want to know what's on the other side of that poor choice."*

Invariably, when they didn't listen, they faced the consequences. Nothing too harsh, mind you. Just enough for them to realize he wasn't kidding.

With the focus still on fun, volleyball picked up where it had left off the season before. Some of the girls from the previous year's team returned, while others moved up to the senior squad. Once more, Jason's confidence was palpable on the court as he worked hard to establish a disciplined group of hard-working athletes, all the while making sure everyone was having fun.

I was the volleyball retriever. Unable to get the oversized balls into my mouth, I tackled them with my front legs and kicked them around the gymnasium. The girls laughed as did Jason. It was a fun way to pass the afternoons.

The end of September brought the Sydney Olympics and Robyn's event. To Jason's amazement, she not only watched her race but cheered on her teammates as well. To *my* amazement, Jason watched the men's eight event in rowing. It was the first time he'd watched any international rowing since his Olympic final.

This time, it wasn't just the rowing he was interested in; it was a young man sitting in the Canadian crew named Bryan. Jason had coached him at Shawnigan back in 1990. Ten years later, Bryan was representing Canada at the Olympics and Jason wanted to support him. He was quiet while he watched Robyn's event, but he cheered loudly when Bryan raced. I had never seen him so engaged and excited while watching sports on television.

Bryan's crew won the petite final, finishing seventh overall. Again, much to my surprise, Jason was happy for Bryan. "Seventh in the world—not bad at all, Ike!" A week after the Olympics, Jason reached out to Bryan, who had returned from Sydney, asking if he'd like to come up to Shawnigan and speak to the student body and staff during chapel. Bryan agreed.

Bryan stayed with us at the cottage. He was enormous—taller and broader than Jason; I had never met another human so large. He was also gentle and soft-spoken. The two of them sat by the fire and caught up. Bryan offered to share his speech with Jason in advance, "Just to make sure."

Jason assured him he'd be great. "Just keep it light, tell some funny stories. They'll love it!"

Robyn and I ran while Jason and Bryan were at chapel. After a refreshing swim, we headed back up to the cottage. When Jason stepped onto the deck, Robyn yelled to him, "You look handsome." He didn't respond—not even a smile.

"Where's Bryan?"

"He's visiting with some of the staff."

"And how did it go?"

Jason leaned on the railing looking out at the lake; his head fell forward between his shoulders. "Not good," he answered quietly.

Robyn re-wrapped her towel around herself and moved closer to Jason.

"Uh-oh, what happened?"

Jason lifted his head and looked out across the lake. "Well, it started okay. Bryan talked about staying in the Olympic Village, swimming at Bondi Beach, the energy of walking into the opening ceremonies—it was great! The students were spellbound."

"Then...?"

"Then...he started to talk about racing. He described the rowing venue and training beside the other countries. Racing the other countries and how much he hated them. He was getting fired up. Then, he drops this bomb—he says, 'It was like a war—like a goddamn war!'"

"Oh my, that's not good!"

"Not good? It was awful," confirmed Jason. "And Bryan just kept on going. 'I didn't go over there to lose—I went over there to win. And I was willing to do anything to win.'"

"Oh, Jase—I'm so sorry. How did the staff respond?"

"Well, amazingly, the padre didn't fall out of his chair. And the headmaster—I couldn't look at him. I just sunk into my chair and didn't move."

Jason turned and walked into the cottage.

"Where are you going?"

"Hold on a sec—I want to find something."

Jason returned with an old photo album. He opened it and flipped to the back. There he found a weathered envelope. He took hold of it, lifted the flap, and pulled out a photo. Jason briefly glanced at it before showing it to Robyn.

"You see this? This was on the front page of the sports section in the Globe and Mail the day after our final. 'Canadians Bomb Out in Seoul.'"

Robyn looked closely at the photo.

"I haven't looked at this photo since I retired. I still remember the shock, embarrassment, and rage pulsing through my veins at that moment. Listening to Bryan this morning, I heard—I felt—all of those same emotions coming from him. And, what makes it worse, is that I taught him that. I taught him that racing is a war. That losing is unacceptable. That hating your competitors is how you compete. Twelve years ago, if that had been me up there speaking, I would've shared the same bullshit."

Robyn put down the photo and took hold of Jason's hands. "That sounds like a painful reckoning."

"It's not me I'm worried about, Robyn. Look at the guy in this photo." There was Jason and his crewmates slumped over their oars at the finish of their Olympic final. "This is what I gave to a young boy. I taught Bryan everything he shared this morning."

Jason put the photo back in the envelope and laid it on the railing. Then he turned to face Robyn again. "My dad used to talk about legacy when he was a teacher at Ridley. 'How will you be remembered?' Now I get it. I understand why he talked about it so much. Well, if I died right now and people talked about what they remembered of me, it would be the bullshit from that photo."

Jason took a deep breath; his eyes scanned the lake. "That's it—I'm done. No more talk of war or hating your competitors—in fact, I'm never going to use the word 'win' ever again! From now on, I'm going to coach the way I've learned from you."

Robyn smiled softly.

"I mean, look at how you handled the Olympics this year. You cheered for your teammates! Christ, when Canada won at the '92 Olympics in Barcelona, I didn't cheer. I didn't even watch the race. But, if I had, I would've kicked in the fuckin' TV. If I couldn't win, nobody could!"

Jason turned to face Robyn and looked directly into her eyes. "So, right here, right now, I'm committing to you that I will never pass on the stuff I learned to another young athlete. Never. I'm going to change that story starting today."

Robyn stepped forward and held him tightly. Jason looked at me as I stared at them. In that moment, acknowledging the misgivings of his previous ways, he seemed determined...and lighter.

After another successful volleyball season, Jason looked forward to coaching rowing again. As promised, Peter had moved him to the junior boys' program. And, although he was still intense in his demeanour, his words reflected everything that he had committed to Robyn months earlier on the deck.

One of my favourite things about living at Shawnigan was the rhythm of teaching during the day and spending afternoons out on the lake in the coach boat with Jason and the junior boys. Despite the rainy winter months, I loved curling up on the soft lifejackets that Jason would place on the bottom of his boat for me. I could take in the view of the lake, hear the banter from the boys, and witness the monumental shift in Jason.

"You'd be proud of me." Jason and Robyn sat beside the fire after dinner.

"And why would that be?" asked Robyn with a playful grin.

"I'm two months into my coaching, and I'm doin' everything I said I would—no talk of war, hating competitors, and I haven't used the word 'win,' yet, either!" Jason smiled proudly as he awaited Robyn's acknowledgement.

"I'm glad you're feeling so good about your commitment."

Jason frowned in disappointment. "That's it? No, 'Way to go, Jase, I'm so proud of you! Keep up the great work!' You're just glad?"

"Jason, I'm thrilled that you've changed your coaching practice—I am. But those boys can feel you out there too. It's not just what you say to them or what you have them do that will determine their success."

"Now what are you talking about?" he scrunched up his face. "Is this more of your woo-woo stuff?

Robyn smiled and ignored Jason's comment. "How do you feel in Ike's presence?"

Jason looked away and shook his head. "I'm not coachin' dogs—they're teenage boys!"

"Humour me—answer the question."

"Ugh—like my grandma used to say, 'You're as stubborn as a bloodstain.'" Jason took a deep breath and thought for a moment. "Okay—I feel good. I feel safe. Umm, I feel happy?"

Robyn looked at Jason knowingly and waited. "Anything else?"

"Ahh, well, I guess he makes me feel..." Jason tilted his head back and closed his eyes. He took a deep breath and exhaled slowly; his shoulders dropped. "He makes me feel loved." He opened his eyes wide and glared at Robyn. "There, I said it! You happy?"

Robyn chuckled as she looked around. "Jason, you say that as if you're expecting your guy friends to magically appear and start making fun of you."

"It's just a big word—that's all. I don't use it much."

"I think it's beautiful that Ike makes you feel that way. It feels good to be loved." Robyn leaned forward. "What if your boys felt the same way you do in Ike's presence when they're with you? Just imagine that—what would they be capable of?"

Jason shook his head. "Where the hell do you come up with this stuff?"

Robyn leaned over to hug Jason.

"So not using the word 'win' wasn't enough for you? Now you want me to start loving these boys, too?"

Robyn smiled. "Yes, I want you to love them—like Ike loves you."

Jason let out a big sigh. "Geezuz—next you'll be asking me to meditate with them!"

Robyn gave Jason a mischievous grin.

"Don't even," replied Jason with a smile. "Not in a million years!"

***

Much to my enjoyment, Robyn maintained her fitness with trail runs behind the school. She had yet to begin training full-time and at full intensity. Her back injury had taken months to recover—she had to remain vigilant to not re-injure it.

Although they had identified the middle of August as a possible time to get married, Jason made it clear that he would support any decision she made moving forward. Given the circumstances surrounding her withdrawal from the 2000 Olympics, more than ever, he wanted Robyn to finish her career on her terms, with one more "kick at the can."

Robyn decided to give racing one more try. The 2001 World Championships in Edmonton, Alberta offered an added incentive to end her racing career in front of fellow Canadians, family, and friends. Although Robyn finished second at the World Championship Trials in early June, she missed the time standard. After two more unsuccessful tries, it was time to let go of her running dreams and begin another chapter in her life. Sadly, her body hadn't cooperated with her intentions.

At the end of June we moved into a permanent on-campus staff house well off the beaten path called The Outpost. Jason and Robyn were thrilled. They would no longer have to move twice a year. Me, I was happy too. We were surrounded by trees. It was a longer walk to the lake, but it was so peaceful at night. All we could hear was a choir of frogs.

Once the school year was complete, Jason kicked into his new role as wedding planner. From morning until evening, he was on the phone or in town, organizing arrangements.

No surprise, Jason's plan of a multi-day wedding won out. As he repeated during his convincing presentation to Robyn, "If friends and family are going to travel across the country for this, we're going to make it worthwhile!" Their wedding guests would stay in the students' residence; meals would be eaten in the dining hall; the ceremony and reception would happen in the front gardens—then dinner and dancing would move indoors.

The two days prior would include volleyball, hiking, mountain biking, swimming at the dock, with a pub-crawl in Victoria and a salmon barbecue at the rowing boathouse. And, of course, to top it off, Jason had planned a "learn to row" session complete with a regatta on the morning of the wedding. He'd finished brewing the homemade beer and wine. He'd ordered the flowers, the cake—which would be vegan, Robyn insisted. In fact, she had asked the school's chef to prepare a plant-based wedding dinner as well.

If it had to do with their wedding, Jason was on it—I had never seen this side of him. Lists were getting shorter. Projects became easier and Robyn was feeling less anxious about the one-hundred-and-twenty-five humans travelling to witness their vows.

With approximately three weeks to go, Jason was up early, looking over his tasks for the day, when the phone rang. "Hello?"

Robyn walked over to hear who had called. "It's Scott," whispered Jason.

"What's up? Why the early call?" Having his oldest brother call at this time of day had put him on high alert.

Jason lost all expression on his face. "Is he okay? When did it happen?"

Robyn signalled for Jason to put the phone on speaker.

"He's tired and resting," answered Scott. "It happened last night after dinner. Mom called nine-one-one, and, thankfully, the ambulance got there quickly. He's going to be in the hospital for a few days. The doctors are still waiting for some more results from his blood work this morning before they determine next-steps."

Carl? Carl had a heart attack?

"Can I call him?" asked Jason, now clearly shaken up.

"I'd give him a day or two, Jase. He's pretty groggy right now."

"What about the wedding?"

There was a pause on the other end of the phone. "I'd say it's probably too early to make that call," answered Scott.

Two weeks later, the campus was abuzz with family and friends. The only two who weren't here were Carl and Eleanor. The plan was to have them listen to the ceremony over the phone. Despite missing Jason's parents, the guests embraced the opportunity to celebrate Robyn and Jason. All of the events Jason had orchestrated went off without a hitch. It was nice to see Jason back in a rowing boat and smiling in the group picture on the dock after the race. The impromptu *regatta* was a huge success! He, his two brothers, and other high school rowing mates formed one crew, while the other crew had Bryan and other retired national team rowing friends mixed together.

Later that afternoon, after my bath, I joined Paul and walked behind the other wedding party members to the edge of the pond where the ceremony would take place. I was the ring boy and felt proud about my crucial role. The rings had been designed and made by a local jeweller. Robyn had asked the artisan to include symbols on their gold rings that were important to the two of them. There was a heart for love, an animal that represented each of them—Robyn was a butterfly and Jason a dolphin—a tree for the forests, planet earth, and even a symbol of me!

Robyn had designed her dress herself and had a local seamstress create it. I don't know how Jason was able to focus on his vows. Speaking of which, Robyn had written those too. And, in classic Jason fashion when it came time for him to recite, "There will be times when I might frustrate you," he paused and looked at the gathered guests, and laughed. "Will I ever!"

Finally, when told he could kiss the bride, he picked up Robyn like a feather, held her in his arms, and planted a big kiss on her lips for all to see. This was a first for Jason. Normally, public affection was not his thing. Although constantly holding Robyn's hand whenever they walked together, a kiss was unheard of. He was so light and playful that day, it made my heart happy.

If the activities were indicative of what was important to Jason, then the ceremony represented what was important to Robyn. Along with having written the vows, she had the children who were present come to the front of the gardens and read out a wish for the planet—more love, less hate, clean water and air, and a safe place for animals (my favourite one!). Not exactly Jason's style, but he had gotten pretty much everything on his list. My guess was, he was conceding to the "unique items" on Robyn's list as a compromise.

To cap it off, our business partner Ian, and his brother Dave, who was the best man, brought their guitars and performed the Larry Gowan song Jason has played for Robyn years before in the car, "When There's Time for Love." They did a fantastic job—I had no idea Ian could sing like that!

Watching the smile grow across Jason's face as he took in the moment was worth the six-year wait. Although I was nowhere near as sure as he was on that first date, I had come to love Robyn with the same depth I did Jason. They had been through so much together. Finally, it was definitely Robyn and Jason's time for love. If I were the crying type, I likely would have.

Given they had pulled off the wedding on a shoestring budget, there would be no honeymoon for these two. Instead, family stayed on for a few extra days, and Robyn and Jason were more than happy to host them.

I had to hand it to Jason, he had put together a remarkable wedding week. On the photo of the three of us that guests were asked to sign, someone had written, "Best Wedding Ever!" Although not having any other weddings to compare theirs with, I had to agree—it had been a fun few days and I could tell that the new bride and groom would treasure this gathering for their lifetime.

a change is coming

Before we knew it, Jason's third year at Shawnigan was underway. As much as I had enjoyed the quiet two weeks we had together at the end of August, I was excited for the return of the students.

Soon, we were well into our daily rhythm again. However, this year, Jason was coaching the senior girls' volleyball team because of his success with the junior program. Peter had asked him to continue working with the athletes he had helped develop over the last two years. Jason loved his time with these girls. They were fun and energetic, talented individuals who knew how to work *and* have fun. I resumed my established role chasing volleyballs.

Towards the end of term, Jason mentioned to Robyn that one of his students who lived up in northern British Columbia had some puppies that needed rehoming. Jason thought it would be good to adopt one of the pups as a playmate for me. I wasn't so sure. First of all, I didn't need a playmate; second, I was going to be nine years old. The last thing I wanted was some high-energy puppy demanding my attention.

Halloween evening, Jason arrived home with Benson in the back of the car. He was enormous! If that was a puppy, I couldn't imagine him full grown. He was part Akbash, part something else—they weren't sure.

Akbash, which meant *large white head* in Turkish, were used to protect livestock. They would live with cattle or sheep and protect them from predators. They had a reputation of being fearless in the face of danger. Loyalty was their trait.

Jason had me come outside to meet Benson, who was standing beside the car when I slowly walked down the porch stairs. "Benson, this is Ike. He's the boss around here—you understand that? The only way this works is if you let him run the show. If you ever challenge him—you're gone." Jason gave Benson a playful whack on his hind leg. "What do you think, Ike? He's a big boy, eh?" Jason grabbed the scruff around Benson's neck and gave it a playful shake. "Come on over and say hello, Ike. I don't think he's going to come to you. He seems a bit shy."

I walked over and gave him a sniff. *Boy-oh-boy—this big guy needs a bath!* As I continued to inspect him, he ducked his head lower.

"Hi, I'm not going to hurt you. You're twice my size, for goodness' sake. And, don't worry about Jason. He's just being protective of me. He and Robyn are wonderful humans. Believe me, you've just won the lottery!"

Benson continued to look down and avert his eyes.

"Hey, are you doing okay?"

"Hi. Thanks for letting me live here with you," said Benson quietly.

"Of course. You must be tired."

"I am. I was put in an old wooden crate early this morning, and I've been travelling in it all day long. All I know is, this isn't my home, and you're not my brother."

Benson almost seemed to be in shock. This was going to take some time.

The porch door opened and out came Robyn. "Oh my—he's huge!"

"I know—I was told he was big, but I wasn't expecting this."

Robyn stepped off the porch and walked over to Benson.

"Hello Benson, welcome to our little home," said Robyn. "I hope you'll be happy here. Can I give you a pet?"

In a few weeks, after Benson got used to our daily adventures to the classroom, the gymnasium, and the lake, he began to open up. The students were taken with him, and he with them. As an oversized country boy, he wasn't used to all the social interaction. Once the students got used to his size, they soon realized he was another kind and friendly pup just like me. He was about ten months old when he arrived. Although gangly, his favourite pastime was to sit on the porch and watch for deer. When one or two wandered into sight, he was off like a shot. I had never met a dog that could run as fast as Benson. Unfortunately, with his speed and lack of coordination, changing course often found him tumbling to an awkward stop.

Christmas followed shortly after our first snowfall. Waking up to a stocking filled with chewy treats and wrapped with a new collar made for a wonderful day. As we lay on the living room floor gnawing on our chewies, Benson looked up at me.

"If I was home right now—I mean, my old home—I'd be outside in the snow or laying on the dirty concrete floor in the shed. It was freezing cold where I came from! Living here with you and Jason and Robyn is so much cozier!"

"Do you miss your old home?"

"I miss my brothers and sisters—we were close. We would play and wrestle all day long. The humans who owned the farm were nice, but sometimes the men who came to work there were not."

"Is that how you broke your leg?"

"Kinda. A few months ago, I was riding in the back of a truck when the man driving it made a sharp turn. I fell out. When I got up, I couldn't stand

on my leg. The man stopped the truck and came back to get me. He tried to straighten the bone. It hurt, Ike. I yelled very loudly!"

I couldn't believe what I was hearing. Benson had a large bump on his right hind leg where the break had happened. His leg had twisted because it wasn't set correctly. It was incredible he could run as fast as he could.

"That's horrible! I'm sorry, Benson. Boy-oh-boy, wait until you meet Allyson. She's my vet. She'll take great care of you!"

"What's a vet?"

Although a massive dog, Benson had a gentle spirit—unless you were a deer! He began to trust Robyn and Jason more and more, and soon became a loving member of our little family.

With the new year came more cold weather, and the odd day when Jason couldn't get his crew out on the water because of the ice on the lake. On one particular occasion, Benson and I joined Jason and his crew for a run on the back trails. For big teenage boys, some of them were fast. Not Robyn-fast, but they could clip along at a decent pace. Benson and I ran with the fast runners at the front while Jason helped bring up the rear.

As we came over a hill, I caught the scent of a dead animal. A deer. A cougar had likely caught it and eaten its fill. Either we had scared it off, or it was planning on coming back later for another feed. It was likely the latter given neither Benson nor I could smell the big cat.

Both Benson and I approached the deer slowly. It smelled like a recent kill. Benson wasted little time grabbing sections of its lower belly and tearing away bite-sized chunks. I was more tentative. I'd had meat before, but never fresh like this.

As I sniffed around, trying to determine how I would enjoy a piece of this dead deer, Benson turned towards me and growled. I looked at him strangely.

"What's wrong...?"

I hadn't even finished my question when Benson lunged at me, knocking me to the ground. I lay on my back, looking up at him while he stood over me, snarling, teeth bared, with his front legs spread.

Before I could even register what to do next, Benson began to lift away from me into the air with a look of shock on his face. Jason had caught up with us and quickly thrown Benson to the ground, where he landed on his back with a thud. With a tight hold of Benson's neck scruff, Jason leaned forward until he was inches from his face. "What did I tell you? Don't you ever fuckin' challenge him, Benson—you got that?" Jason glared into Benson's eyes while the two of them took deep breaths.

The boys stood around us in silence. No one dared move.

"Is Ike okay?" one of the boys asked tentatively.

Jason released Benson and slowly stood up. Benson didn't move; he remained on his back, legs splayed.

Jason walked over to me. "You okay, Ike?" He bent forward and quickly ran his hands around my head and neck. I was fine. More surprised than anything. "He's okay. Come on, let's finish the run," answered Jason.

As we resumed running, I overheard one of the boys. "Holy shit, remind me never to piss off Dorland—did you see that? He threw Benson like he was a twig!"

Later that night, while Benson and I were curled up and dozing off to sleep, Benson explained what happened.

"Ike, are you awake?"

"What's on your mind?"

"I'd like to apologize for what I did earlier."

"Benson, it's okay—I'm fine."

"That doesn't matter, Ike. You see, on the farm, they'd feed us frozen pieces of lamb or cow. They'd toss it onto the ground and we'd grab what

we could. We had to protect our food, or go hungry. When I noticed you beside me by the deer, I just lost control—without even thinking."

"I appreciate you telling me, Benson. Really, I'll be okay."

"Can I ask another question?"

"Go ahead..."

"Is Jason always mean?"

"No. He was just protecting me. You see, Jason has this line. And, when it gets crossed, he'll stand up and defend whoever needs help. In this case, it was me. He would do the same for you."

***

Although Benson wasn't a fan of the water, he eventually got used to spending afternoons in Jason's coach boat. I would curl up and nap while Benson would stand at the front, waiting anxiously for when we returned to the safety of the docks.

Jason's coaching had evolved. He was different with the boys—softer somehow, while still holding his high standards. Although his rowers had raced well at the National Championships the previous year, they had been beaten by a faster crew.

This year, they had accepted Jason's challenge of discovering what they were truly capable of. In doing so, they worked hard—really hard. They were as committed to getting faster as Jason was. However, one day at the beginning of practice, they asked Jason for a team meeting in the change room. After everyone had found a seat, Jason got the conversation started. "What did you guys want to talk about?"

The boys looked at one another, but nobody answered.

"You called the meeting—what's on your mind?"

Finally, Max spoke up. "We were talking the other night. One of us said they're finding the training hard. Well, not just physically, but worrying about it all the time." The other boys nodded their heads.

"Like, waking up in the morning and the first thought being, 'How hard is rowing going to be today?'"

Jason looked confused. "Okay. And you're telling me this because...?"

"Because we want your advice," answered Nick.

"My advice?" Jason scrunched his face. "On what?"

"Being tougher," answered Nick. "You know—so that we don't have to worry about it all day long. So that we can push through the training when it gets hard."

Jason laughed. "Look, being tough—whatever the hell that means—isn't a switch you turn on in the morning."

"How did you do it? How did you manage this when you were rowing?" asked Max.

The other boys on the crew nodded their heads and leaned forward, encouraging Jason to share his wisdom.

"You don't want to know," laughed Jason. "Look, what I thought tough was when I was younger—you know, bravado, swagger—all of that bullshit macho stuff, that's not being tough. And it's definitely not what's going to help you change the way you see this training and push through the challenging days. Look, when I was your age, what my coaches taught me was a lie."

The boys looked deflated with Jason's answer.

"If you really want to know," Jason pointed at me, "he's the one who taught me what tough is and where it comes from."

"Ike?" all of the boys said in unison.

"Yes, Ike," Jason smiled. "When he was about ten months old, we were walking through the Endowment Lands in Vancouver one Sunday morning and we ran into this guy with his two huskies. Now, if you don't know Huskies, they can be a bit hyper, and sometimes they get in the face of other dogs. So these dogs, who are already pretty fired-up, come over to see Ike. Now, remember, Ike's not full-grown, and these two were both much bigger. And it wasn't clear to me if they wanted to play or if they were looking for trouble." The boys listened intently.

Jason paused and looked around the room. "What does Ike do? He drops to the ground and spreads his front paws, which signals, 'I'm not a threat—I just want to play.' Which, if you know goldens, is pretty much their MO."

"What did the huskies do?" asked one of the boys.

"Well, they do what most dogs do when they're invited to play; they reciprocate. After a moment or two of wrestling, things change. The huskies, who are now on top of Ike, have begun to ramp things up a bit and are growling as they hold Ike down. I look at the owner as if to say, 'Hey—get your frickin dogs, buddy!' But, if you can believe it, he's smiling as he looks on. So I take one step toward the dogs to break things up, and that's when Ike goes ballistic."

"Awesome—way to go, Ike! You kick some ass!" yells out one of the boys.

Jason laughs. "Ike managed to spin onto his stomach, then stood up with so much force that both dogs got thrown off. He turned and faced the dogs with his teeth bared and barked and growled like I had never heard this gentle little pup before. He was more intimidating than the Black Watch!"

The room went silent. "So how did that teach you what being tough was?" asked Nick quietly.

Jason smiled. "You tell me."

The boys considered the question.

"Ike didn't try to appear tough, but, when it mattered, he was," answered Max.

"Bingo, Max—that's exactly it. Ike didn't try to match the bravado of those two dogs. Instead, he tried to defuse the situation by being friendly and playful. But, when those dogs crossed the line, he stood up for himself. And what it took to stand up for himself didn't come from his head, or some thought or perception of what being tough was—it came from deep inside of him—from an inner knowing of what he was capable of. The strength and courage it took to defend himself came from his heart, not some tough-guy showmanship." Jason paused and looked around at each of the boys.

"And that's what I want you boys to discover. The strength and the courage it takes to simply show up for practice comes from inside you. When we get there, when all of you understand as a crew what I'm talking about, you will begin showing up to practice differently. And you'll discover that you have so much more to give when you're called upon to do so." The boys looked over at me. "Do you understand what we're trying to do here, fellas? It's so much more than just winning races."

One-by-one, each crew member came over and patted me on the head as they made their way quietly down to the dock for practice. As one of the boys was leaving by the door, he whispered to his friend, "What's the Black Watch?"

The friend replied, "Some scary-ass Scottish thing—I'll explain later."

Jason waited until they had all left before calling me over. He grabbed the scruff of my neck and playfully shook it. "See, I've been paying attention—to you and your mom! But don't tell her, okay? Thanks, buddy—you're a good teacher."

***

At the end of March, we had a freak snowstorm. Returning from rowing practice later that day, Jason decided it would be fun to go for a night run using his headlamp. Robyn took a pass, Benson was thrilled, and I agreed to go as well. But midway into the run, I began to feel tired—unusually tired. I found it difficult, not only to keep up with Benson but also to stay beside my Clydesdale, Jason.

After a mile or two of lagging behind, Jason stopped and waited for me to catch up. "You okay, bud? You're not getting soft in your old age, are you?" joked Jason. "You're usually kicking my butt at this point." He knelt down and hugged me. "Come on; we're almost there. I'll race you home!"

Benson circled back and checked on both of us. *"Everything okay, Ike? Did you two get lost?"*

"No, Benson, we're not lost, just having a rest. It's a race home. I'll bet I can beat you!"

"You're on!"

With that challenge, Benson was gone. At the best of times, he didn't need a reason to run fast. I rallied as much strength as possible and managed to arrive home before Jason.

Robyn came down to greet us in her snow-covered runners. "How was that?"

"It was absolutely beautiful in the woods."

"And you two?" Robyn looked at Benson and me.

"Something's up with Ike. He was hanging back for a while on the way home."

Robyn came over and knelt beside me. "Oh, Pooh-Bear. You weren't feelin' it out there tonight?" She kissed me on my forehead. "Maybe he got a stitch? Can dogs get stitches?"

"I'm not sure," answered Jason. "Either way, we want to keep an eye on that. Our boy's going to be nine this April!"

I wasn't sure either. I just knew I didn't feel like my usual self. The feeling didn't go away. I continued to struggle on runs, and, eventually, Jason and Robyn took me to see Allyson.

I was very happy to see her. Lucky for us, she had recently opened a new clinic in Victoria, just down the highway. She wasn't too worried. She simply said that I might have come to the end of my running career, and to transition me to walks and hikes and see how that went for a while. I had to admit, the walks were a welcome reprieve. Maybe all of our long runs through the mountains had worn me out. Allyson asked Jason and Robyn to keep an eye on my energy levels and report back in a month or so.

With April came my ninth birthday. It was remarkable that we were celebrating this day. Certainly not what the internal medicine specialist predicted. As usual, it was a celebration that I looked forward to every year. Jason cooked salmon for Benson and me. Benson was in shock.

"Wow—all of this because you were born nine years ago today? Glad I was here to help celebrate with you, Ike. Happy Birthday! Do you think I'll get a meal and gifts like this on my birthday?"

"I'll bet on it!"

As we sat on the porch enjoying the warm spring evening, Jason and Robyn began to share memories of past birthdays. "I remember the look on Allyson's face when I asked her if I could give Ike a point-five-percent beer for his first birthday—classic! Or when the managers at Granville Island let Ian and I bring Ike into the market and sing happy birthday to him with a big carrot cake. There had to be a hundred people who joined in!"

"Then there was *my* first birthday with Ike at Kits Beach," said Robyn. "How about the one with Erin and Kuz, when they had just got Cocoa? He was so tiny. He never left you alone, Ike; you were so patient with him."

"Yup—two birthdays at the cottage, and now number two here at The Outpost. What a gift you've been." Jason reached forward and ruffled the fur on the top of my head.

"And here's to many more, Pooh! Happy Birthday, beautiful boy!" Robyn got up from her chair, walked over, and sat down beside me. I stretched out and laid my head across her lap.

As the racing season began, Jason's crew continued their quest to find their best race at the National Championships. At the local regattas, his Shawnigan boys had won every race they'd entered. And, each time, they reflected to Jason, and each other, that they knew they could go faster.

Jason continued fine-tuning the crew with Robyn's reminders omnipresent. At the end of the last hard practice before they left for St. Catharines, Jason pulled his coach boat up beside theirs.

"How does that feel?"

"What do you mean?" Nick, the captain, spoke for his teammates.

"All of the hard work is done. There's nothing left but to rest up and execute your race. How does it feel to have arrived here?"

"Awesome," answered Nick. "We survived your workouts!"

The other boys laughed.

"Seriously," continued Jason, "I hope you all feel a sense of accomplishment having committed to what we set out to do and seeing it through. When I was your age, I loved the feeling of being fit and ready to race."

"But what if we lose?" asked another crew member. "What if we don't race the way we plan to in St. Catharines?"

"Great question," answered Jason. "You tell me—what if we do lose?"

Nick spoke up immediately. "It's our job to row the race we've trained for. If we meet a faster crew or have a lousy race, that's what sometimes happens—I can live with that."

"I can't tell you how good it feels to hear you say that," said Jason. He paused and looked out over the lake, "When I was your age, I never would've had that thought. That's why we don't talk about kicking the shit out of other crews or how much losing sucks. I don't want you guys to race the same way I did. You see, I was afraid of losing. I made losing mean some ugly things that you don't need to know—it wasn't healthy."

As sweat dripped from their chins, the boys stared at Jason and listened to his every word.

"In a little over a week's time, you're going to line up and race against five other schools. Regardless of the outcome, I want you to know that what you've accomplished out here with only yourselves to witness is enough for me. We could put the boat away today and I'd be good. What I've witnessed from each of you is enough! Now would I love to watch you win that race? I won't lie—I would. But I won't think any less of you if we don't."

I raised my head and turned to face Jason. *I wish Robyn had heard that!*

The night before Jason left for St. Catharines, he and Robyn sat at the table and discussed the upcoming regatta. "How are you feeling about the boys at this stage?" asked Robyn.

"Well, they've done the work. They've won every race so far this season, they've trained their hearts out—they're ready..."

"And? It sounds like there's an 'and' you're hesitating on."

"As much as I told the boys, I don't care what happens; there's a part of me that's terrified of what losing would mean."

Robyn smiled knowingly. "I can feel that, Jason. And I'm guessing your boys can too. I would suggest you watch how you hold the results. Our egos can be dangerous bedfellows. I invite you to consider your ego as part of what made Seoul so painful for you. Your ego was what made that loss mean so much— it wasn't just the loss that got you into trouble. It was the story you told yourself about it."

"Believe me, I'm trying. But I can feel this part of me that desperately wants to feel 'good enough' as a rowing coach, and I want others to see that too."

Robyn reached across the table and took hold of his hands. "Look at me." Jason looked up and stared into her clear blue eyes. His face softened. "I want you to know that I think you're more than good enough. You have so many remarkable talents. I see them. I see you. And I wish you could see them too."

Jason smiled slightly. "Thanks, Robyn—I'm tryin'."

"Go to St. Catharines. Love your boys. Have fun. The results will be what they are. It's that simple, Jase. Can you do that?"

***

Robyn ran to the phone and hit the speaker, "Hi Jase—how'd it go?"

"Well—they won."

"Terrific, and how are you with that?"

"I'm nowhere near as excited or relieved as I thought I'd be. I mean, I'm happy for the boys. They raced beautifully. But it's like what you said—the results will be what they are. They deserved to win. Now it's figuring out how that's landing for me."

"And the boys?"

Jason paused as he thought for a moment. "They did what they set out to do—find their best race on the day. I think they feel pretty good about that. Most of them are with their parents right now. So I'll get a better sense tonight at the dinner."

"Nice. I'm happy for you, Jason. Now go have some fun with your boys and their parents."

Jason sighed. "I will—love you, Robyn. And thanks—for everything. Give Ike and Benson a kiss from me."

Robyn bent down to kiss me on the forehead. "That's from your dad." Then she turned and did the same for Benson. Then she kissed Benson and me again. "That one's from me!" Robyn smiled and tilted her head in anticipation of her question. "Do you two want to head out on a walk?"

I certainly did. I always did, especially with Robyn. As much as I loved my time with Jason on the trails, I always felt like I was on guard.

Watching over him, listening to him, and, quite honestly, worrying about him. Not with Robyn. There was an ease to being with her. And not just the trails that she manoeuvred with grace—it was how she navigated life. Peaceful. Loving. Gentle. Open. My love for her had grown deep. She was perfect for Jason. And, in some hard-to-explain way, he was for her as well. What Robyn brought to our little home made my heart feel bigger.

As we made our way down the path leading from our backyard, Robyn stopped and looked at me. The sun shone brightly behind her. It created a brilliant white glowing silhouette that made her look like an angel. I knew she could feel what I was feeling.

She smiled and bent down beside me. "Oh, Pooh-Bear—I love you so much." Then she kissed me on the head. My ears went back as I began to wag my tail until my entire body was writhing back and forth. Then I rolled to the ground and splayed my legs, welcoming a belly scratch. "Awwww, Ike—you're amazing!" I let out a coo and a joyful cry that told Robyn I felt the exact same way about her.

After Jason returned, he focused his energy on finishing his teaching requirements. There were projects to mark and reports to write.

The fatigue that I had felt on our snowy run months earlier had progressed. I was feeling a heavy sense of lethargy. I no longer wanted to walk or swim. I spent most of my time curled up on the deck. Something was off. Jason and Robyn knew it too.

They arranged an appointment with Allyson. Despite her initial inspection, she found nothing unusual. Before we left, she decided to check my temperature just in case. It was high. I was running a fever, and, with that, blood tests were ordered.

The results indicated a high white blood cell count, meaning a possible infection. Now Allyson was concerned. At our follow-up visit, she asked Jason to let me stay at the clinic overnight while they kept an eye on me. Neither one of us was happy about that. Knowing I'd never spent a night alone in my life, Jason brought down my bed, some family photos, and even a get-well card that he taped to the wall of my kennel. He would come down every day after school and take me outside to a nearby park where he would read Winnie the Pooh to me while I lay in the cool grass.

As my condition worsened, I could sense that Allyson was becoming more noticeably upset. She was supposed to fly to Nova Scotia for a family reunion and was torn as to whether to leave me in my current state. After more tests indicated my white blood cell count was still rising, she ordered a plasma infusion at the local animal hospital.

My lungs had also begun filling with liquid and rattled and gurgled when I breathed. Using a large needle and syringe, Allyson drew as much of that liquid as possible. That, combined with the plasma treatment, helped me rebound slightly. I could breathe easier and felt more energetic. Allyson departed for her reunion. Claudia, Allyson's business partner, would assume my care while she was gone. I could tell Jason was hesitant—we'd only ever known Allyson.

Two days later, my condition began to worsen again. My lungs began refilling with fluid, and my white blood cell count was on the rise once more. I didn't need that information to know that my health was faltering again. My body was changing. I had lost weight. My joints were beginning to ache, and despite Jason's encouragement to keep fighting, I was growing tired. As a nine-year-old golden, I was three or four years from a typical lifespan. Given my circumstances, I remember thinking that was pretty good—I wasn't sure I had many more in me.

Claudia recommended that we travel to the mainland to see a Vancouver Animal Trauma Centre specialist. She called over and made an appointment for the next day.

the green human

The following morning, Jason, Robyn, and I were up early and on our way to Vancouver. Benson was not happy about us leaving him alone with our neighbour, Dean.

"You behave, Benson—we'll be back tomorrow."

Soon after we arrived at the centre, I was called into a small room with Jason and Robyn where an overzealous air-conditioning system blasted cold air. With Jason carefully holding my IV, we stood silent, waiting for the doctor. The dimly lit room was sparse, aside from a few fancy-looking machines on trolleys. There weren't even chairs to sit on.

A male human with green pants and a matching shirt walked in with his head down, reading the forms on his clipboard. "Can you pick him up and flip him over onto this gurney? Put his head at that end," he gestured with his hand.

Jason looked at Robyn. His eyes flared as he bent down to gather me off the floor. I'd seen that look before. Robyn took hold of the IV while Jason gently rolled me onto the canvas gurney between him and the green human.

As soon as Jason backed away, the doctor began to shave my stomach with electric clippers. He was fast. Soon I was furless from my ribs down. Next, he grabbed a plastic tube, shook it, popped off the cap and squeezed a jelly substance onto my bare stomach. My legs kicked as the cold liquid touched my sensitive skin.

"It's okay, Ike—just try to relax, buddy." Jason gently caressed my ear.

Rolling the nearby monitor closer, the green human put a shiny silver knob on the jellied part of my stomach and began to move it around. He watched the screen carefully, not saying a word.

"We were told to inform you that if you only see one kidney, that's because it's all he's got. He was born with two, but only one developed."

"You see that?" The doctor pointed at the monitor. "Those dark spots. That's cancer."

Jason looked at me and then at the doc, who had taken the shiny ball off my stomach, wiped it clean, and then quickly swiped across my stomach using the same rough paper towel. "Three to five days tops." He gathered his clipboard and moved to leave, then stopped. "Oh, and he won't need that IV anymore. A nurse will be in to remove it."

"Wait a minute," said Jason. The doc didn't respond. "HOLD ON A SECOND!"

Uh-oh. I haven't heard that tone in a long time.

The doc stopped and turned around. He didn't walk back to where Jason was standing. He just stood there waiting to hear what he had to say.

"You don't say hello to either one of us. You don't even say anything to Ike. Then you shave him like you're cutting your lawn, do a quick ultrasound and say, 'three to five days,' like we know what that means? What, he's going to die in three to five days? Is that what you're saying?"

After a long pause, the doctor answered quietly, "Yes. That is what I am saying."

Jason and Robyn were silent. He looked at me. His eyes welled up as he tried to hold back the stinging wave of emotion I could feel rising in him.

"How can that be?" Jason's voice was now quivering. "He walked in here on his own for Christ's sake—how is he going to be dead in five days?"

Robyn grabbed Jason's arm.

"I'm sorry about your dog, sir. Now if you'll excuse me." He turned and disappeared.

"How is Ike going to die in five days? Would someone please tell me that? This guy doesn't know a damn thing. What a fuckin' asshole."

"Jason, this isn't helping," whispered Robyn. She bent forward toward me.

Jason began to pace in a circle. With one hand on his head and the other on his hip, I could see he was trying to process the news that had just been delivered. "He didn't even acknowledge Ike. Can you imagine if Allyson were here? She'd be pissed too. That was bullshit!"

Robyn was standing beside me, stroking my ears. "Hello, my beautiful boy. Do you want to go visit with Auntie Erin and Uncle Kuz?" I looked into her glistening eyes. She knew. She knew what was coming. "You do? Okay, Pooh-Bear, let's have a visit. Dad's going to pick you up and we'll get going."

Jason carried me out of the clinic; he was stunned. I longed to be home sitting on our deck, listening to the birds and frogs on a cool summer evening and lying against him. I wanted to tell him that I was going to be okay. Everything was going to be okay.

Robyn ran ahead to get the back hatch open and my bed ready. Jason carefully laid me down.

"Gently," Robyn reminded him.

"Right here, Ike. Lay down, buddy." He patted my bed, encouraging me to face forward.

"Maybe we should've kept the IV in? Shouldn't he still be hydrated? Besides, it seems like we're quitting. Like we've given up." Jason stared at me. His eyes teared up again as he leaned in and put his forehead to mine.

I closed my eyes and felt him there. He was still mad, but his fear was now beginning to pour out of him.

"Is it true, Ike?" he whispered. Then he kissed my forehead and closed the back hatch. As he walked to the driver's side door, I moved my head so that I could see the two of them.

"I'll give Erin a call and let her know that we're on our way," said Robyn.

"I think we should stop at Skeet & Ike's. Ian'll want to see Ike. We're not that far from the plant, and it's sort of on the way out to Erin and Kuz's. Okay?"

"Sure, I think that's a good idea."

The radio started up as Jason turned the key. I didn't recognize the song, but they sure did. As the lyrics sang out, Jason and Robyn looked at each other, smiled, and began to cry.

A very good friend of mine told me something the other day.
I'd like to pass it on to you, because I believe what he said to be true.
Said we're here for a good time, not a long time.
So have a good time. The sun can't shine every day."

As Jason drove away, the two of them teetered back and forth from laughing to sobbing from one moment to the next, with the song playing in the background. Robyn, through her tears, began to clap and sing along with the chorus.

"So have a good time. The sun can't shine every day."

I knew there was no way on earth Jason would join in, but I was happy that the song had brought some perspective and levity to the situation. I was dying—plain and simple. We all do. Besides, it was part of the contract of being a dog—we usually check out before our humans. Now I was determined to hang on and help my dad prepare for the inevitable, as best I could.

Arriving at Skeet & Ike's, Jason and Robyn were quiet. The song had long ended, and the car ride had since turned silent.

"I'm going to use the washroom—back in a sec."

Robyn opened the back hatch to the car and leaned in to be with me. "How's my Pooh-Bear?" she said, softly stroking my forehead. Her hand felt warm and soothing. The sensation of her touch moving over my body was changing. I had become so thin, I could feel her hand touching every one of my bones as she gently stroked down my spine. It felt strange to me. I had seen my reflection in the glass door while walking into the clinic. This cancer wasn't wasting any time. Everything was beginning to hurt. I was just sore, everywhere. Feeling Robyn's loving touch was a nice reprieve.

Ian walked up to the car. "How's Ike doing?"

Robyn turned to meet him, got up on her toes, and hugged him. "Not great. We were just at the vet. He's got cancer. The vet said he only has a few days."

"Oh, Robyn, I'm so sorry."

"As I'm sure you can imagine, Jason's not taking the news well. He's not ready to let go. He's mad and lost. I think a part of him still believes Ike can beat this. He doesn't want to accept what's happening."

"Hi, Ian."

"Ah, Jase. Come here." Ian reached out to hug him. "I know what Ike means to you. I'm very sorry." Ian continued to hold Jason, and, after a moment, I could see Jason begin to shake as he sobbed in Ian's arms.

Some of the employees began to come out to see me. They came over to the car in small groups, gently patted me on the head, and said hello. Some were crying. I recognized most of them from when Jason and I had come over for meetings in the past. There was always food to be had at Skeet & Ike's; it seemed everyone had an open bag of dog treats at their desk. And they were only too willing to answer my wagging body with encouraging hellos and treats. They were good humans. I was going to miss visiting this place.

Once everyone had said goodbye to me, Jason spoke up. "We told Erin and Kuz we'd be there by 4:00. We should get going."

I knew he wasn't enjoying this procession. The display of emotion for me was more confirmation of what the doctor had shared. By saying goodbye, permission was being granted for me to go.

With final hugs, the back hatch got closed, and we were ready to leave. Ian came around to Jason's window. "I know it's hard. But, if you think about it, this is why you put Ike on that label way back at Emily Carr. Now he will truly be immortalized—forever. People will always know about Ike. That's a pretty cool thing, Jase. You did what you set out to do. I'm sure Ike appreciates that."

I sure did. Boy-oh-boy. I sure did.

Wanting to acknowledge his comment but unable to speak, Jason nodded and smiled.

We drove away.

I lay in the back, wide awake. This was a trip that I usually slept through. A good two-hour nap in rush-hour traffic. Just enough to recharge before an action-packed weekend in Abbotsford with Erin, Kuz, Cocoa, and Chester. Today, my body was too sore for napping, and my mind was too active.

"That was a good idea, Jase." Robyn placed her hand softly on Jason's leg as he drove. "Ian and the others would've appreciated that."

Robyn's comment went unacknowledged.

A while later, Jason reached forward and turned off the stereo. In my nine years of driving with him, that had never happened.

"I can't believe how many of them were crying," said Jason. "I mean, he's only been there...half-a-dozen times, maybe? And, they were crying. He's a dog."

Robyn waited quietly. Then she turned and faced him. "Many of them have known you for a long time, Jase. They know what Ike means to you...and to Ian. But, you're right, it is remarkable—the impact our little boy has on the people he meets." Robyn smiled.

"It's crazy how he makes people feel...I dunno, safe? That's the only word that comes to mind. Safe to be themselves. Safe to tell their truth. Just safe, period. Imagine being a person who had the same effect on others—the way Ike does?" Jason looked at Robyn. "Does that make any sense to you?"

"Perfect sense. Ike isn't capable of judging people, Jason. He has a way of letting us all know that we can be who we need to be without any fear of being rejected. He has a gift."

Erin and Kuz were waiting out front when we arrived. "Hello, Ike, you handsome boy, it's so nice to have you here for a visit." Erin stood by the open hatch and stroked my tender body.

"How did things go at the clinic?" asked Erin.

Robyn looked at Jason, who then looked at me. "It was rough. The doctor wasn't exactly gracious about the whole thing. We..."

"Gracious? He was a dickhead! He didn't even say hello to Ike. What an asshole"

"Jason, the man works in a critical-care clinic for animals. After years of having his heart broken, I would imagine he's developed a self-protecting strategy that sometimes shows up as cold and insensitive. Think about the trauma he's seen. He's doing the best he can."

I'd seen that look on Jason's face many times before. Robyn's voice of reason was not always what he wanted to hear. My guess—he just wanted to be mad for a while longer. Jason went into the house.

"What did the doctor have to say?" Erin asked.

"Ike has cancer."

"What? Robyn, I'm so sorry." Erin stepped forward and held Robyn in a long tight hug.

"He's given him three to five days."

"Three to five days? That seems awfully fast?" Erin placed one hand on my head and stroked my ears.

"Oh, Ike—you poor boy." Her eyes were sad. I stared back despite just wanting to sleep. "He looks exhausted."

***

I awoke to the aromas I associated with the comfort of being at Erin and Kuz's. I lay on my bed beside the dining room table as the four of them ate and caught up. Cocoa and Chester were snoozing nearby. The memories of this home were many, all of them good. I was going to miss this place.

"Do you remember the first time you left Ike with us? I think you were down east for Christmas? We were so nervous. We didn't want to screw up! Kuz and I would take Ike to the river. One day, he found this enormous dead salmon and rolled in it." They were all laughing. "He had clumps of rotten fish guts hanging from his fur." Erin's face was distorted as if she could still smell me.

I thought it smelled great. Why else would I have rolled in it?

"It took three days and probably six baths before we could stand having him in the house. Then—on the very next walk—he did the same thing!"

"How about the time Jason's parents were visiting, and we went to White Rock. Remember that dead seal Ike found?" More laughter. "You had to drive out here with the windows rolled down and Ike wrapped up in a tarp laying across your parent's laps in the back seat. I'll never forget the look on your dad's face!"

The memories continued to flow. I dozed in and out of the stories and the images of my time here with Erin and Kuz. It was a wonderful evening of special moments shared. Despite the continuous aches that throbbed throughout my body, hearing those stories felt calming.

Erin raised her glass toward me. "Ike, we will always be grateful for you coming into our lives. Without you, we would have never known what it is to love a dog the way we love Cocoa. Here's to Ike."

Jason slowly raised his glass and joined the others in acknowledging Erin's toast. He took a small sip of his beer. Robyn took me outside for my last pee before bed. I quickly returned to the backdoor. Even going to the bathroom was becoming an effort. My legs shook when I squatted. It seemed with every hour I could feel my strength leaving bit by bit.

Jason knelt beside my bed in the guest room and rubbed my ears gently. His touch was welcome.

Robyn joined us on the floor. "How are you doing, Jase?"

"Rough."

Robyn shared a warm smile. "We've certainly enjoyed some special times with Erin and Kuz. And Ike's played a big role in their lives."

"It's beautiful to hear how he's touched people."

Sleep was calling, but I wanted to lay there and enjoy how good it felt to have Robyn and Jason beside me. After a long period of silence,

Jason spoke. "Since the first day he showed up, Ike has relied on me to take care of him. Feed him. Walk him. Keep him safe. It's what I agreed to. I didn't need him. But he needed me." Jason paused for a moment. "When I was rowing—everything was about me. My training. My diet. My sleep. Everything was me first. I didn't care about anyone else except *me*. If someone or something interfered with my rowing, I stayed away. With Ike, I've had to care for someone other than me. Taking care of him has changed me."

Robyn gently smiled.

"Ike relied on my care and my love. As much, I guess, as I relied on his. There's been this interdependence." Robyn nodded. "But now I wonder...I mean, aside from food and a place to live, I don't know how much I gave him. I've never trusted anyone like I trust him. Even you. I hope you know what I mean by that." Robyn smiled and nodded. "Because of that trust, I've felt incredibly safe...to love him. To really love him. Like, 'do anything in the world to protect him' kind of love him."

Robyn slowly placed her palm on his cheek. "One of the things I love about you is that you cherish this little boy the way you do. And I know Ike feels that too. He feels that same level of safety and trust with you as well."

Silence returned to the room.

"What if I could love someone else the way I love Ike? What if I could love you that way?"

"I'm sorry I don't make you feel safe enough."

"No—it's not your fault. I just don't think you could! It's us. It's humans. We have too much shit in the way. Too many bullshit stories that we've concocted over our lifetime. But just think about it...what if we could love anything, including ourselves, without any fear of rejection. I mean, I know you've said this to me many times before, but I don't think I was ready to hear it. What if I could see in myself all of the good stuff that Ike does? Holy shit, what a different life that would be." Jason looked intensely at Robyn. "That would be pretty cool!"

Robyn nodded.

"Hmm, the day I picked up Ike from Roberta, she gave me this advice. She said, 'At the end of each day make sure you have more positive interactions with Ike than negative—make sure you say more nice things than not.'"

"That was good advice."

"Agreed. But I'm not so sure I've done that very well...with me."

"What do you mean?"

"I talk to myself the way my coaches did. I need to change that. I mean, when I was writing about this the other day, I realized one of the reasons Ike makes me so happy is because of the love that he pulls from me. Loving feels good, right? Loving Ike the way I do makes me happy. I want to feel that same happiness and safety when I love others too. And that probably starts with me." Jason paused for a moment and shook his head. Then he smiled at Robyn. "Geezuz, I sound like you!"

They both laughed.

It felt so good to hear what Jason had to share. I'd never heard him open up like this. My student was finally beginning to figure a few things out. I did love him. I loved everything about him. Even the rough parts—I could easily see past his stubbornness, brooding, and crazy obsessions, and embrace his tireless commitment to protecting those he cared for. Me, Robyn, his family and friends—we could always count on him.

Jason looked down at me. "I'm going to miss this little guy so much. I can't even begin to imagine life without him. He's been everything to me. I know it sounds kinda weird, but over the last nine years this dog saved me—he made me a better person."

Robyn leaned over and hugged Jason. "It doesn't sound weird at all."

going home

With the car packed and our goodbyes said, Jason began to pull out of Erin and Kuz's driveway.

"Jason, wait!" The car came to an abrupt stop. Erin ran to Jason's side and signalled him to lower his window. She reached in and grabbed his hand. "I just want to thank you one more time, Jason, for bringing Ike into our lives. He's taught us things we never imagined we'd learn from a dog. And brought us so much joy and laughter too."

Once again unable to speak, Jason got out of the car and wrapped his long arms around Erin.

Once the car hummed beneath me and the radio played softly, it wasn't long before I was fast asleep.

We found the perfect spot on the ferry's car deck for our return home. There wasn't a cloud to be seen. The sun's warmth felt soothing as I lay on my soft bed in between Jason and Robyn. In the few days since my diagnosis, I could feel the cancer taking over. It seemed any fat I had was now quickly disappearing, making the cool ocean breeze I would normally have appreciated feel cold.

"I'll call the clinic to ask if we can just go straight there and see Claudia. Okay?"

Jason nodded. With an open book on his lap, his hand hadn't stopped moving up and down my spine since we left the ferry terminal. I don't know how much reading he was doing, but the weight of his hand eased my aching back.

Robyn hit the end button. "Tracey says hello. She also said the clinic is normally closed at 6:00 pm, but they'll wait for us. They're such good people."

Jason looked at Robyn. "I'm curious to hear her plan."

The entrance to the clinic was only six steps, but it felt like a mountain. "Oh, Ike—how are you doing, sweetheart? You're such a good boy," said Tracey as I managed my way into the waiting room. She grabbed a bag of treats and tried to feed them to me. Normally, I would have devoured the entire bag; I could only manage one.

Claudia opened the door to the main treatment room. "Come on in, you guys." She tapped her hand on the large observation table in the middle of the room. "Can you bring Ike up here?"

Jason bent down to pick me up. "Okay, Ike—hold on."

"These tables are cold, and we want you to be cozy." Claudia spread a thick warm blanket under me. She warmed her stethoscope against her stomach and began listening to my heart and lungs. "Wow, that's quite a haircut, Ike." Claudia frowned and shook her head disapprovingly. "Ouch, he wasn't very gentle with you, was he?" After listening for a few moments, Claudia looked up at Robyn and Jason. "Surprisingly, his lungs don't sound too congested. His heart sounds pretty good too."

"Have you spoken with the vet from the clinic in Vancouver?"

Claudia looked at Jason. "I have. He called after he diagnosed Ike. He told me that he found several growths that he identified as carcinoma."

"He said Ike is going to die."

Claudia paused for a moment. "Jason, animals don't fear death the way humans often do. It's part of their life cycle, and they don't waste time thinking about it. Ike's not afraid of dying. What he's afraid of is leaving you. That's what worries him more than anything else right now."

Jason looked over at me. I could see his eyes welling up. Then his chin began to tremble. "So what are we supposed to do?"

Robyn came over to me and began to kiss my forehead while she stroked my back.

"Well, there are those who believe—and I would be one of them—that he's waiting for you to say it's okay for him to go, to say goodbye. You could help him by giving him that permission."

Jason stared intently at me. Tears streamed down his cheeks.

"When I've heard you talking to Ike; you've always encouraged him to be strong. To not quit. And to fight. I've heard you use those exact words." Claudia slowly took a deep breath. "After you left for Vancouver, the lab called with the results of Ike's last blood test. The pathologist asked if he was still alive? He had never seen a white blood cell count so high in a living dog—ever! He couldn't believe it when I told him that Ike had just walked out of our clinic and was on his way to Vancouver. That was three days ago. Goodness knows what that count would be now. Jason, Ike's been fighting—harder than any dog I've ever seen. His will to live is about you and only you. If you let him know that you're going to be okay—he'll be free to stop fighting."

Jason buried his face in my neck, laid his arms across me, and began to cry. Robyn held his hand and rubbed his back.

As we walked out to the waiting room, Claudia shared something else. "The vet in Vancouver also told me something quite surprising. At the end of our phone call, he asked, 'What's this about the dog having only one kidney?' I explained the x-rays from when he was a pup. 'Well, that dog's got two fully developed kidneys now!'"

Jason and Robyn were shocked. Me, not so much.

"So how do you explain that?" asked Robyn.

"Hmm. Good question." Claudia paused. "I went through Ike's records and found the results from his yearly blood work where Allyson was testing to see how his one kidney was holding up. In 1998, the results showed an improvement."

"Are you saying that somehow Ike grew a kidney five years after he was born?"

"Well, I can't say for certain. But that's what appears to have happened. I've been a vet for a long time and I've met countless dogs, but, I have to say, none of them have intrigued me the way this boy has. He's a remarkable soul—with a beautiful spirit."

Jason looked at me. "Pooh-bear—look at you, growin' body parts!"

Everyone laughed. It was a good note to end the discussion on.

Claudia let out a big sigh. "I would stop at the grocery store on the way home and buy the nicest piece of wild salmon you can find. Make that Ike's dinner tonight. Then, sometime before bed, have a heartfelt conversation with him."

"Thank you, Claudia," said Robyn. "For everything. You've stepped into a difficult situation, and you've handled it gracefully."

"It's been my pleasure, believe me—I've enjoyed getting to know Ike. Even under these circumstances."

Robyn hugged Claudia. And then Claudia walked over to Jason and grabbed both of his hands. "I'll be thinking of you this evening, Jason. I know it's not easy. But it's what's best for Ike."

Jason led me to the door.

"I'll have my cell phone with me all weekend. Call anytime."

***

"Wake up, Ike. We're home," Jason said as he opened the hatch. I could hear Benson barking as he jumped up with both front paws on the backdoor window.

"Hello, Benson! Hold on, I'm coming. How are you, big boy? Ohhh, it's good to see you too, fella." Jason opened the door and let Benson explode onto the deck. With his enormous tail enthusiastically propelling him from behind, he ran in circles before eventually making his way to the car.

"Where the heck have you guys been? I thought you said a few days?"

"Benson, we were only gone one night. That's a few days!"

"It seemed longer. Besides, I had to sleep all by myself last night. I missed you!"

"I missed you, too, Benson. But you can manage without me."

Benson sniffed my nose and the back of the car. *"You smell different, Ike!"*

"Bennie—were you a good boy?

"Well, if you call chasing me onto your kitchen counter good—then he was awesome!" Dean was walking up the driveway.

Benson turned and barked. "Benson! Easy buddy!" Yelled Jason as Dean welcomed Benson with some tentative pats on his head.

"Benson pinned you up on the counter?" Robyn was now walking toward Dean.

"Ahhh, ya!"

"I'm so sorry, Dean. How did you get down?"

"Lot's of cookies!"

"You have got to be kidding?" asked Jason.

"No, I spent a good while up there while this boy calmed down. He was fine for the first few visits. Ate his dinner. Came outside. Did his business. It was all going swimmingly. Until his night pee—that's when he was having nothing to do with me coming into his house!"

"Nice one, Benson."

"What? He scared me. It was dark! "

"So you pinned him on the counter?"

"Sorry, Ike." Benson lowered his head.

"Dean's the one you should be making amends with."

With that, Benson was on his feet wagging his tale and rubbing his head against Dean.

"Oh, sure, now you're lovin' uncle Dean," said our less-than-impressed neighbour.

"One thing's for sure, you don't ever have to worry about leaving the house with that guy at home!" Benson continued to lay on the charm with Dean. "So how's that handsome golden in the back of the car?"

While Robyn brought Dean up to speed on my condition, Jason grabbed the groceries and luggage and made his way into the house with Benson following close behind.

Dean came over to the car and began to pat my head. "Gryphon is going to miss you, Ike." He stared a while longer. His eyes were sad.

I wasn't very hungry, but I also wasn't going to let freshly cooked salmon sit in my bowl without trying to muster a bite or two. Benson's fish disappeared in no time. After one bite, I raised my head and paused. I couldn't eat. On any other day, this fish would be gone. But now everything just hurt.

"Benson. You can have the rest of this."

"Are you sure? I mean, that's nice of you to offer, but I don't..."

"It's okay. You finish what's left."

I stepped back. Slowly Benson made his way over to my bowl. With one mouthful, the fish was gone.

Jason and Robyn sat quietly at the dinner table; they had also finished eating. Neither was moving or saying a word.

"I can't believe Benson put Dean up on the kitchen counter? He's so gentle with us."

Jason sat still, not responding to Robyn.

"Dean said to say goodnight. He's around if we need anything. He's been so…"

"Can we walk around the backyard with the boys?"

Robyn reached across the table and put her hand on Jason's. "Of course, we can. Let me get these dishes first."

"Just put them in the sink. I'll get them later."

Jason stepped into the back room where Benson and I were resting on our beds. "Okay, boys, do you want to go for a walk?"

Benson was up immediately and waiting at the sliding screen door. I followed slowly behind him. As usual, Benson's wagging tail took up a lot of space. I stayed back to avoid having to make any quick movements.

"Come on, Ike. Let's see if the deer are out!" He bounded through the door as soon as Jason opened it.

"After you, Ike." I made my way onto the grass. "You coming, Robyn?"

I squatted to have a pee. My legs shook.

Benson stood motionless at the edge of the property. His head was pointing straight up, nose high in the air, trying to determine which deer, if any, were in the neighbourhood. I had never met a dog who enjoyed chasing deer as much as he did.

He turned and looked at me. *"Ike, there are a few deer in amongst the bush straight ahead. Are you ready?"*

"I think you're on your own tonight, Benson."

"What? Come on, Ike. I'll scare them up. You wait over here and see if I can get them to run right by you. Okay?"

"I'll wait here."

Benson stood still a while longer; his legs trembled with anticipation. He looked lean and strong in the evening's last light. I was going to miss my big goofy friend. His naive innocence. His playful spirit. His unwavering loyalty. Chasing deer with him on the trails behind the school. Even that huge windmilling tail of his. I would miss all of it.

With an explosive burst of speed, Benson was off, dirt shooting from under his paws as he bolted after the deer. I stood beside Robyn and Jason as we listened to him crash through the bushes. Within seconds we could hear the deer scatter. There was nothing stealthy about our boy, Benson. His strategy was the element of surprise, combined with hope—a lot of hope. To date, Benson's tactics had come up empty, every time.

What translated as barking to Jason and Robyn was actually Benson cursing as he chased after the fleeing deer. Knowing he had failed to catch his prey left him frustrated yet again.

Moments later, our brave hunter reappeared. Head down, tongue hanging from the side of his mouth, panting as he recovered from the chase.

"No luck again tonight, eh, Benson?" Jason laughed.

"Bennie, you leave those poor deer alone," added Robyn. "Hear me?"

"Next time, Benson. Next time."

"So close, Ike. Just a moment sooner, and I would've had one."

"I'm sure you'll get one tomorrow."

"You think? You really believe I can catch one?"

"Of course, I do. You'll get one!"

"Robyn, can you take Bennie inside, please? I want to sit out here with Ike."

"Of course. Come on, Benson. I'll get you some nice cold water before bed."

Jason stood still, looking out at where the sky met the trees. The sun had long disappeared. But there was still a soft blue light illuminating the horizon. I lay down beside him. The grass was cool and damp, normally a welcome sensation on a warm summer's night. Not this night, however; it was uncomfortable. It made the pain alive in me ache even more.

"Let's go sit on the porch."

I followed Jason to the front of the house, where he fluffed up my bed and then sat beside it. "Come here, bud. Curl up over here."

Jason slapped his hand on my bed. After one rotation to the left, I laid down. With my back against his leg and my head on his lap, Jason's body heat provided an escape from the chilly night air.

The buzzing porch light above us strained to hold back the blackness spilling in from the evening sky. I could see enough of Jason's face to know that he was off somewhere, trying to make sense of our unwelcome circumstances. I knew him better than anyone—even Robyn. The last few days had shoved him, too fast, up against a moment in time that he hadn't prepared for.

"How are you doing, Ike?" Jason stroked my forehead. "It's been a crazy few days, my friend."

It had been. As much as I knew something was wrong, even before the green human, now the life I had known was quickly disappearing.

The front door creaked open as Robyn came out to join us. "I just want to say goodnight to Ike. Okay?"

"You bet." Jason rubbed my ears.

Robyn bent down and kissed me on my forehead. "Goodnight, Pooh-Bear." She rubbed my belly where my fur had been shaved away. Her touch felt warm. "You sleep tight, Ike. I'll see you tomorrow." Robyn stood up and walked back to the door. "You okay?"

"I'm good. Just saying goodnight—I'll be up in a sec."

Robyn smiled as she closed the door behind her.

It was late, and I was tired, but I willed myself to stay awake. Typically, our time on the porch before bed would have me dozing off.

Jason paused and took in a long breath. His eyes began to well up. "I don't want you to hurt, Ike. That's the last thing I want." His voice cracked as he began to speak. But, as he continued, he found his words and felt stronger beside me. "I know you hear me—I know you do." He paused and looked straight into my eyes. "Oh, those eyes of yours—I could look in your eyes forever." Jason smiled as we stared at one another for a moment longer before he continued. "So if you want to go, you can go. I'll be okay. I mean—I'll miss you more than anyone or anything I ever lost. But, if this is it—if you're too tired for this—I want you to let go." Then another long breath. "And if you want me to help you—if you want me to phone Claudia tomorrow or the next day and have her come up here—then you need to tell me that. Show me that. You understand? I need a sign."

Jason grabbed the scruff of my neck and gave it a loving tug. "Hey—I love you, Ike." He stared at me again. "Do you remember the first time we met? All you wanted to do was beat the crap out of your siblings."

I do. You were so nervous.

"Man, I was so nervous—I had no idea what I was getting into. It's been a beautiful ride, though. Thanks for choosing me all those years ago, buddy. I'm not sure what my life would've been like without you."

I could feel him shift. He had heard Claudia earlier in the day, and he was gradually getting there. He understood it was time for me to go. "Okay, Pooh—bedtime, my friend."

Jason helped me to my feet and then followed me inside, where Benson had already curled up his long body and nodded off.

"Right here, Ike." Jason laid my bed on the floor beside Benson's and gently patted his hand on the top. Once I was settled, he bent down and kissed my nose. "Love you, Pooh. Have a good sleep. I'll see you in the morning."

He then leaned over to Benson. "You, too, Benson. Love you, big boy. Sleep tight." Benson raised his head and wagged his tail as Jason kissed him on his ear.

"You guys were out there a long time. I was worried."

"Benson, you fell asleep."

"Ya, but I was worried right up until I fell asleep. Are you okay, Ike? You smell so different. I'm not telling you that you stink or anything. I mean, I would tell you...that you stink. If you did..."

"I'm fine. Just go to sleep, Benson."

"Okay. Night, Ike."

I was cooler without Jason beside me. It was going to be harder to stay warm through the night. My insulation had almost all disappeared.

"Benson? You still awake?"

He stretched before responding. *"Yup. I'm awake. What's on your mind?"*

"Um, it's cold. Can I... Would you mind if I slept beside you? I could sure use some of your body heat."

Benson raised his head and looked at me sideways. It was one of many things that I loved about him. There was no hiding his thought process. If he was thinking—and he was—you could read it on his face.

"Well, I suppose you could. Why are you so cold?"

"Not sure. Would you mind?"

"No, not at all, Ike." Benson got up and made room for me on his bed.

I curled up and leaned into him. The warmth emanating from where he had been lying felt comforting. As did the heat coming from his large frame.

I could tell by his silence that his head was still raised, and he was looking at me. *"Do you need me to put my front leg over you, Ike?"*

"No, Benson. This is perfect. Goodnight, buddy."

a day like no other

I awoke to Benson having a running dream. When you're as big as he is, it's not subtle.

"Benson. Benson. BENSON!"

"What? What's up? What do you need, Ike?"

"I need you to stop chasing deer while you're sleeping!"

"What? How did you know? That's incredible! Do you always know what I'm dreaming about?"

"Just a lucky guess. Did you at least catch him this time?"

"I was just about to! That's when you woke me up."

"Sorry,"

"I think it's time to get up anyway. I'm hungry; do you think we'll get salmon again?"

The morning sunlight spilled into our room from the kitchen—the birds outside announced the day's beginning. The air was still cool, but the rising sun did its best to provide some warmth.

"Are they up?"

"I don't think so. I haven't heard anyone moving around."

"Did I keep you warm last night?"

"Yes, thanks. You'd make a good furnace!"

Benson was proud of himself. I was still curled up against him, enjoying a few more moments of his body heat, when we heard the first signs of life from upstairs. The toilet flushed, and, moments later, Jason was coming down to join us.

Benson stood waiting with his head hanging over the gate. His tail did its usual dance as Jason got closer.

"Hello, Bennie—how are you, big fella?" Benson was now standing with his front paws on top of the gate, sniffing and licking Jason. "I missed you, too, buddy!"

Jason opened the gate so that he could kneel beside me. "Good morning, Ike—how's my little boy?"

I raised my head and met his eyes. He looked worried as he searched my face and body. He ran his hands along my spine and then back up along my stomach and ribcage. His touch wasn't soothing anymore. Everything now hurt. "Oh, Pooh—you're too thin. Here, let me get you something to eat. Come on into the kitchen. I have some more wild salmon."

As he walked over to the fridge, Benson close behind him, I made my way to the backdoor. I could hear him fumbling with our bowls as he cut up the fish and added some extra kibble to Benson's dish. With a bit of added water, breakfast was ready. He turned to face us and place our dishes on the floor.

"Ike? Where'd you go?" I continued to face the door. "What are you doing? Oh—do you have to go to the bathroom that badly? Let me open that for you." I carefully made my way down the steps to the driveway. "Okay, you go busy, and then come back in here when you're done."

Jason returned to the kitchen to take care of Benson. I stood on the gravel with my eyes closed, soaking up the healing rays from the morning sun. I relaxed and, without squatting, let a few trickles of urine fall to the ground. Then I turned and looked at the house. But, instead of climbing the steps and walking back inside the kitchen to that fragrant salmon, I crawled under the deck behind the stairs and laid down. The ground was warm from the sun striking it at the perfect angle. This would be my spot. I was ready.

Moments later, Benson came bouncing down the stairs and went over the grass to do his morning business. Returning to the house, he stopped, lowered his head, and peered through the steps at me.

"Ike? What are you doing under there?"

"I'm tired, Benson. I just want to sleep."

"That's a strange place to sleep. I mean, we both have beds, you know! Why don't you come out here and sleep on the deck? I'll even lie beside you and help keep you warm if you want."

"It's okay—the sun feels good under here."

"Benson, what are you looking at?"

Jason leapt off the deck, crouched down and peered in at me. "Ike? What the hell are you doing?" He got down on his knees and tried to crawl under the deck with me. He was too big. "Ike—get out here!" Although his voice was insistent, I didn't move. He reached for me and grabbed my front paw. "Come on, bud. Come out from under there," he encouraged me as he began to tug on my leg.

"Ahhhhhhhhhh, that hurts."

"Jason, what are you doing?" asked Robyn.

"It's Ike. I guess he crawled under the deck, I'm trying to get him out."

Jason tugged on my leg some more. "Come on, Ike. What the hell?" He was getting frustrated, but I had no intention of moving. I was too tired. Too sore.

"Be gentle with him, Jase."

"Well, I can't leave him here!" Jason re-gripped my leg and pulled me out in one motion.

"Ahhhhhhh!" I lay still while Jason and Robyn stared at me.

I took a deep breath and gathered my strength. Jason and Robyn stood beside me without a word spoken. Then I struggled to my feet and walked over to a thick shrub growing on the edge of the lawn. I carefully manoeuvred myself under it and lay down again.

"Good morning, everyone," announced Dean as he appeared in the driveway. "The vet tech in me had to know how our handsome patient was doing."

"Good morning, Dean," answered Robyn. "You're standing right beside him."

Dean turned and looked back at the shrub. "Ike! What are you doing in there, silly?"

"I can't figure it out." Jason was now standing beside Dean, looking in at me.

"Is this one of his favourite spots?" asked, Dean.

"No—not at all."

They all stood quietly.

"Hmm, I think he's ready, Jason."

"What do you mean?"

"Well, when animals are ready to die, they'll often find a spot where no predators can get at them, and they'll wait there to die."

Jason squatted down beside the shrubs, lifted up a branch, and stared at me. "Thanks for letting me know, buddy." Jason took a deep breath.

Benson slowly walked over to me. His head was low and his tail motionless. His head tilted sideways as he was trying hard to make sense of this. As we stared at one another, his eyes began to glisten.

"I don't want you to leave me. I don't want you to die. You're like my big brother—I need you."

"Awww, Benson. I know it's hard for you to understand this, but I wouldn't leave you if I didn't believe that you would be okay without me. Jason and Robyn will continue to love you like they always have."

He stared a little longer, tilting his head the other way. *"Is this why you smell so funny?"*

"Yes, Benson. I'm sick. And the sickness makes me smell funny."

"Is there anything I can do for you?"

"Take care of Jason and Robyn. Love them with all your heart. That's it. That's what you can do."

"I can do that, Ike. I will do that!"

"Benson—come on." Jason called. "We have to get some things ready for your brother. Let's go!"

The two of them disappeared around the side of the house.

Robyn walked over and crouched down close to me. "Oh, Ike. I'm going to miss you so much. But, if you're ready to go, we'll help you." She stared at me through the thick shrub that stood between us. "You know, I bet your bed is a lot more comfortable than those broken twigs you're laying on."

I knew it was, but I was going to stay put for now.

saying goodbye

"Ike. Ike! Wake up, buddy."

I opened my eyes to see Jason crawling toward me. "Look, I get it—we understand what you want. But you don't have to spend the rest of the day in here, lying on these prickly sticks. Let's get you on your bed so you can rest more comfortably." Jason reached under me and gently picked me up. Using his feet to snap branches and push them out the way, he carefully brought me out from under the bush and placed me on my bed on the porch. "Here, this is much better. You keep sleeping. Claudia's on her way."

Benson came over and sat beside me.

"Hi, Benson."

"We've made a bed for you up on the rock face behind the house. Jason cut a bunch of cedar bows and then stacked them one on top of the other. It'll be quite soft, and it'll sure smell nice for you."

"That's where you guys went?"

"Yup. I think Jason wants to make this a real celebration of you. That's what he told Robyn. There are photos of you all around the bed. And, all

kinds of other stuff. Cookies. Orange hockey balls. Your collar and leash from when you were a puppy. Some candles."

"Thank you, Benson."

"It doesn't mean I'm okay with you leaving."

In the distance, I could hear a car coming up the gravel driveway and turning in front of the house. It was Fiona. I could see Brodie in the back seat. Jason and Robyn greeted her with a hug.

"Thanks for calling me." I could see Fiona struggling with the news. Brodie jumped out of the car and came straight over to see me.

"I heard Fiona talking on the phone with Jason earlier. Fiona wanted to see you. We're not staying for...you know, later. But at least I got to see you."

"I'm glad."

"We had a lot of fun together. Do you remember that first night I met you? When Jason and Robyn took us for a walk in the snow?"

"I do."

"I kept chasing after you for the entire walk. You were so patient with me. We shared some great times together—running, wrestling, swimming, eating. I won't forget any of it."

"Neither will I, Brodie."

"Hello, Ike." Fiona sat down beside me. "I heard the sad news and wanted to say goodbye." She avoided my gaze while she stroked my ears. "Thank you for being so good to Brodie—so patient."

"Told ya!" added Brodie.

"He was always happiest when you came to visit, and then missed you terribly when you left."

"Brodie?"

"Okay, so I missed you a little!"

Fiona leaned down and kissed my forehead. "Goodbye, Ike. You be good, wherever you're going, okay?" After one more kiss, she got up and made her way to the car.

Are you kidding me? Thanks, for introducing Robyn to Jason!

"Thanks for coming up." Jason hugged her goodbye.

"Travel safe, Ike. I'll see you again sometime, old friend."

After Fiona left, Jason put Benson inside and then helped me into the car. Robyn joined us, and we drove over to the cottage. Jason carried me to the lake, where he gently placed me in the water. With the sand beneath my feet and the water gently touching my chest, I felt invigorated once more.

Jason and Robyn were silent as they stood there with me. I looked up at the cottage and remembered the hours I spent chasing balls thrown from the deck and into the lake. My young legs would carry me back and forth and back and forth, tirelessly, all day long. I remembered when Cocoa would visit and we would wrestle in the shallow water. He was a good friend.

I carefully walked to the dock, climbed on with Jason's help, and slowly made my way to the edge, where I lay down and looked out over the lake. I remembered the many afternoons I spent travelling up and down this lake with Jason while he coached his young rowers. The number of times I launched myself off of this dock and into the dark blue water.

My humans sat on either side of me, dangling their legs in the water, each with one hand on my back. "A lot of good times in this lake, eh, Ike?" said Jason.

I looked up at him—he smiled.

"Even some late night swims—you were always keen no matter the time of day," added Robyn.

I turned and looked at her—she smiled too.

Then I leaned my head forward to get a drink. The cool water was soothing going down my parched throat.

This was it. I had lived the life that was meant for me. I had chosen my student, and he had provided me with adventures I couldn't have imagined when we first met. I had lived more years than I had been promised, with the two humans I would choose again in a heartbeat.

I'd leave behind the excruciating pain that had consumed me these last few weeks and take with me the beautiful memories of my fortunate life with Jason and Robyn. I loved these two, and I knew they loved me as well. It was time to go.

Later that afternoon, the clouds closed in, covered up the sun, and began to spit rain. As a few close humans began to arrive, Jason and Robyn greeted them while Benson took Rug and Gryphon around the side of the house to see the cedar bed he had helped build earlier in the day.

"Hello, Ike." Peter knelt beside me and stroked the fur along my spine. "Thanks for being a good friend to Rug. She's going to miss you. Hell, we're all going to miss you."

"I don't know, Jase—I would only do this for you and Ike. Not sure if I'll make it through," shared Joanne.

"You do what you have to do, Joanne. Just know it means a lot to Ike and Robyn and me that you're here."

Moments later, Claudia arrived. "How are you two doing?"

"It's been a strange day," Jason said.

"Thank you for coming up here on such short notice, Claudia. We appreciate your support," added Robyn.

"I'm honoured to be here. These moments are the hardest part of my job and the best—it's a gift to help these creatures along."

The three of them made their way over to my bed.

"Hello, Ike. I'm here to help you." Claudia knelt and stroked my ears and the top of my head. "I'm going to get a few things ready."

Robyn stayed with me while the two of them disappeared around to the back of the house. She sat down on half of my bed and stroked my back.

A few moments later, Jason returned. "Okay, Claudia's ready. She wants us to bring Ike around."

Robyn quickly grabbed Jason's hand. "What if today isn't the day? What if Ike just happened to go under the porch for no good reason? I mean, you never know, we might be able to keep him going. To nurse him back to health. What if we just focused on..."

"Where is this coming from? We've talked about this, Robyn. There's no way some good food and lots of love will bring Ike back to full health. We're going to put Ike through another day of pain? No way!"

"But what if we're wrong? What if Ike isn't that sick?"

"Come on, Ike; let's go, buddy."

I struggled to my feet and followed Jason around the side of the house where everyone was gathered. It was hard just walking.

"Jason, wait. Let's really think about this first."

"I've done more thinking about this than anything I've ever had to consider. We're not turning back. It's not fair to Ike."

"Jason—grab Ike! I'll get some towels," yelled Dean.

Jason turned to see me squatting as if having a bowel movement, with blood running from my rear.

"Oh, Ike, buddy," Jason dropped to his knee beside me and put one arm under my chest for support while Dean wiped the blood from the fur on the back of my legs. Then Jason swung his other arm behind my back legs and picked me up. "Robyn, it's time."

She took a long slow breath and comforted me. "I'm sorry, Ike. I just needed to be sure. I didn't want to get this wrong. Of all things, this has to feel right." I understood. Robyn, ever the optimist, was holding onto the faintest hope that I could pull through this.

Jason carried me onto the rock face and gently laid me down on the cedar bed. Benson was right. It smelled incredible—rich and green and lush, like the many days we spent running through many forests.

The photos were perfect—I recognized all of them. The cookies smelled tempting—the orange hockey balls, perhaps even more so. And my tiny puppy collar—a wonderful reminder of the day I came home with Jason and we began our life together. The candles? That had to be Robyn.

Claudia gave me a shot of something to relax me and help relieve the throbbing ache that was pulsing throughout my entire body. Jason called for everyone to come up and join us.

"Thanks, to all of you, for being here today. As you well know, Ike is an important part of our family. I can't imagine what life will be like without him. As I was thinking about what to say earlier today while Benson and I were gathering all of these cedar bows, I remembered a speech I gave years ago at Toastmasters. I went searching through some old files and found it. I'd like to reread it today, if you don't mind. It still applies. Maybe even more. But before I do that, we would like to give everyone who would like to say something a chance to speak." He looked over at Peter. "Peter, or Joanne, did either of you want to say something?"

Peter smiled and looked at their daughter Ali. "Actually, Ali asked if she could share a poem."

"Of course, Ali—anytime you're ready."

Ali stood up and brushed her hair out of her eyes. I had spent many hours with her and Rug, chasing balls in their backyard. She was a thinker like her dad. I was happy to know she had something to share.

She pulled out a neatly folded piece of paper from her pocket. "This is a poem that I like. And I think it would be good for Ike to hear. It's called Rainbow Bridge."

Jason and Robyn smiled at Ali. She took one final look at her dad and began.

"Just this side of heaven is a place called Rainbow Bridge.
When an animal dies that has been especially close to someone
here, that pet goes to Rainbow Bridge.
There are meadows and hills for..."

Listening to Ali read her poem, I remember being reassured, if only through the voice of a young human, that I would one day be with Jason and Robyn again. What a wonderful thought to leave with.

Ali smiled and looked up at Robyn.

"Oh, Ali—how beautiful. Thank you so much. I'll look forward to meeting Ike at that bridge someday."

Ali looked at her dad before putting the piece of paper back in her pocket.

Several other humans spoke about all the fun, adventures, and mishaps we'd had. Then Jason stood. He had taken his Toastmaster's speech about his friendship with me and altered it a little. He pulled the folded papers out of his pocket and held them in his shaking hands.

"A true friend is described as someone you can reveal your genuine colours to with no hesitation. Where two beings establish a relationship based upon complete trust and honesty—sounds pretty special, doesn't it? How many of us can say we have a friendship like this?

"You see, I have a friend with whom I don't censor my actions or thoughts, or moods, or anything... I am completely myself in his presence. I trust him with my most personal insights. There isn't anything I don't feel comfortable discussing with him. He makes it quite easy, though—he's a great guy!"

The last time I had heard this speech—the first time I heard it—Jason had read it perfectly. Today, his delivery was different. He spoke the same words...this time, however, from his heart. It was his truth—from deep inside of his core, because that's where he had learned it. Jason had finally grasped the purpose of life he'd been searching for and the true meaning of love. It was, indeed, the perfect time for me to go.

> "I can't imagine the term 'unconditional love' having more relevance. I screw things up far more often than he does, and yet he's always there when I need him. Someday he'll leave me."

Jason paused as a rush of emotion rendered him unable to speak.

Robyn squeezed his hand, "Breathe." He lowered the paper and turned to Robyn. His forehead was creased, his eyes were red, and tears streamed down his face. "Just take a deep breath. We can wait."

Jason paused, following Robyn's advice, and then let go of her hand, collected himself, raised his folded piece of paper, and continued.

> "...But he will have left with me the memories of our time together. And his teachings will never get old. When I think of him, I'll smile when I imagine that look he'd give me when it was time to play. And, if I want him by my side again, I'll just whistle like I used to—and he'll be there."

Robyn reached for Jason's hand. The rain continued to spit, and the wet ground smelled ripe and earthy as Robyn and Jason braced themselves for what they knew came next.

"Are you two ready?" Claudia asked.

They looked at one another before turning to face Claudia and nodding in unison.

Robyn bent forward and put her lips close to my ear. "Thank you, Ike. Safe travels, my love. I will forever be grateful for what you have brought into our lives. Goodbye, my little Pooh-Bear."

With one more kiss, she returned to her kneeling position.

Jason stroked my head and leaned in. He paused and took a deep breath. "I'll hold you in my heart, honour your spirit, and live my life better off for having known you." He managed a knowing smile before continuing. "Thanks for everything. I don't know what I would've done or who I would be if you hadn't come into my life. You were my perfect little guide dog. Thank you, Ike." He kissed me on my forehead before leaning back and looking at Claudia. "Okay," he said quietly with a subtle nod.

I had been his guide dog. It had filled my days with purpose. For that, I was incredibly grateful. With trust and faith, Jason, too, was beginning to find his.

Claudia, with tears in her eyes, struggled to see the needle. "Once the drug takes hold—it happens quickly." Claudia held onto my back leg and inserted the needle into a vein. She pulled the tourniquet loose and squeezed her thumb to empty its contents. "Uh-oh—the vein just ruptured. This rarely happens. I'll have to move to his front leg. Okay?"

"Of course, Claudia. Whatever you need to do."

Benson stood up and moved close. He knew something was wrong.

"He's okay, Benson—he's okay." Rug tried to console him.

"Sorry, Ike. I'm going to have to move into your space a little more." I could feel her knees against my back as she moved further up my spine. It's what I wanted—the ruptured vein was no accident. She had been a loving presence these last few days, supporting Jason, Robyn, and me. For these, my final moments, I wanted to feel her closer.

“Give me your hand, Jason.” Claudia took Jason’s hand and put it on my heart. “Can you feel it beating?”

He nodded.

Claudia searched for another vein in my front leg. “Here’s a good one. It won’t be long, Ike. Sorry about this, little fella.” I could feel the needle once more enter my leg, and the pressure building as the cold liquid was released into my vein. Within moments, a rushing sound grew louder in my ears. Soon a sensation of floating came over me. Like I was in the lake, but I wasn’t swimming. Finally, a soothing warmth travelled up my core and, in an instant, the pain that had consumed me disappeared.

“It’s stopped,” said Jason quietly. “His heart—it’s stopped beating. He’s gone.” He leaned down and kissed my ear. “I’ll love you forever, buddy.”

It was over. I had left my tattered and ravaged body behind. The cancer’s relentless aggression had taken its toll on me physically, as well as emotionally. What I had endured was far beyond what I had expected. Yes, I remained committed to Jason and delayed my departure for as long as possible. But the searing stabs that burned intensely with every move, every breath, had left me beaten. Set free, I felt nothing. And, with that freedom, my spirit chose to stay longer. I wanted to keep an eye on Jason and Robyn, but first, there was one human that I had to see.

Travel was no longer a physical expression; it was a thought. I could be wherever, with whomever, whenever.

In Nova Scotia it was early evening; Allyson and her husband, Rob, sat at a long table surrounded by her East Coast family—aunts, uncles and cousins. They were just finishing dessert when I came to her.

She stopped eating, put down her fork and leaned into Rob. “Something’s happened to Ike,” she whispered.

“Ike? You mean the dog?”

"Yes, I mean the dog—something's happened! I can't explain it—I've got this strange feeling. It's as though he's just walked in front of me." She paused and looked directly at Rob. "Look—I have goose-bumps," she pulled up her sweater and showed him her arm. "Something's happened to him!"

"Allyson, that's impossible—Ike is thousands of miles from here!""

For nine years, she had been my loving and tireless doctor, more than just someone Jason took me to for blood work, meds, or stitches. Allyson had cared for me like I was her own. She had let me into her heart and walked into mine too. She had shown Jason how to be with me. I wanted her to know I was okay, I was at peace.

Rob grabbed Allyson's hand and put his arm around her. "It's okay. I'm sure Ike's fine."

***

"Whoa—hold onto your hats!" yelled Dean. Everyone covered their eyes and braced themselves as an enormous gust of wind came roaring up from the open field behind them. Then the clouds broke open, and the sun shone brightly down upon the group.

Although slightly nervous at first, our friends' laughter grew louder as they looked at one another in amazement while holding onto jackets and other clothing items as the wind whipped powerfully around them.

Joanne smiled at her two girls, Ali and Lizzie; the two of them were wide-eyed in wonderment.

"I've never seen anything like that!" said Dean.

The wind subsided and the sun continued to shine. Everyone made their way off the rock and onto the lawn below.

"If you want to come inside, we've got some refreshments and some nibblies." Jason quickly made his way into the kitchen to set out the food and drinks. Robyn remained outside, hugging and thanking everyone for being there. The tone had changed to that of a celebration. Even Benson, Rug, and Gryphon were back to wrestling and playing on the lawn just below my body—as they should. It was exactly as I'd hoped.

"If everyone could please grab something for a toast and gather around, that'd be great." When the guests turned to face Jason with drinks in hand, he began. "First of all, Robyn and I want to thank all of you for being here today. We know it's not every day that you get asked to come and be with a family dog while they take their last breath. As you've heard us reference many times before, Ike was like our firstborn. He was our little boy—we loved him very, very much. We want to thank you for being an important part of his life. Dean, your care for Ike has been invaluable. Peter and Joanne, you've played such an important role in Ike's life. You've welcomed him countless times into your home and your family. We know he's always felt like your home was his second home. We've appreciated your generosity tremendously."

Next, Jason turned and faced Claudia. "I don't know how you did what you did, but the way you've shown up for Ike these last few days has been remarkable. When Allyson left for the East Coast, I was nervous. Now I know why she entrusted Ike to you—thank you, Claudia, for loving Ike the way Allyson would have. We'll never forget that."

With tears streaming down her smiling cheeks, Claudia brought her hands together in front of her face and bowed slightly to acknowledge Jason.

Joanne spoke up. "The reason we loved Ike so much was because of how much you loved Ike—it was infectious. Thank you, Jason and Robyn, for including us today, and for so many other special times, with that beautiful dog of yours. We're sure going to miss him!"

Jason smiled. "Okay, if you want to raise your glasses, we'd like to toast the reason we're all here today. To one of the most extraordinary souls that I've ever had the pleasure of knowing." Jason turned to face my body, now alone on the rock face. "Here's to you, Ike."

"To Ike!" everyone echoed in unison.

"You know, Jason," said Peter, "the mystics say that it takes a big wind to lift a big spirit. Given what just happened here this afternoon, I'm relieved we didn't all blow away!"

The stories and visiting continued for a while longer. Lots of laughs, a few more tears; all of it, a good sign of a life well-lived.

After the guests had left, Jason, Robyn, and Claudia sat beside my body and continued sharing stories. Benson sat close beside them while keeping an eye out for any wandering deer in the field out back.

All those years ago I had made the right choice in choosing Jason. The journey we shared had proven more than I could've asked for. I felt content listening to the two humans I adored sharing their recollections of our time together.

"So tell me about that first day when you met Ike." Claudia asked.

Jason paused, looked at Robyn and then shrugged his shoulders. "I dunno... Ike was different—that's for sure. And it wasn't just that he was handsome as hell. He was present. He was strong and independent. He was kind. He was thoughtful. I know it sounds strange—like I'm describing the Buddha or something. But he wasn't just a dog who loved to play and have fun—it also seemed like, all along, he was sort of looking out for me. It's hard to explain. It was just a feeling I had—that he was with me for a reason."

"But why did you choose him? Surely you didn't pick up on that the first time you met him?"

"Well, truthfully, I let him pick me. But afterwards, when all of his siblings were wrestling. One by one, they all lay down and fell asleep—all except for this one guy. He didn't. He wanted to keep going at it. I knew at that moment that he was going to be the perfect dog."

Claudia put her hand on my head. "So Ike was a fighter right from the beginning."

Jason smiled. "I guess so. It certainly seems that way, doesn't it?"

"One last question. What is it you think he taught you, Jason?"

"How long do you plan on staying?"

Claudia laughed and smiled up at the sky.

"I was thinking about that while I was gathering these cedar bows earlier today with Benson. Plain and simple—this beautiful boy taught me the meaning of love." Jason paused again and then laughed. "I guess it took a long time, though. Like, nine-years-a-long-time! But I finally got it."

The three of them all sat quietly a moment longer and took in the early evening sounds and smells. The birds were still singing while the resident frogs began to warm up their voices for their evening concert.

Finally, Claudia stood up, took a deep breath while looking out at the field one last time, and then smiled and turned to face Jason. "That was a beautiful answer. And—that was a beautiful day for a beautiful dog." Claudia looked at my body and smiled. "I'm so grateful that you included me. I can't tell you how profound the experience was for me. Thank you."

Jason and Robyn got up and acknowledged Claudia's comments with a hug.

All three of them took one last look at my body resting motionless on the cedar bed. "Jason, will you please carry Ike's body over to my car?"

Jason crouched down and gently slid his hands under my ribs and head.

When we got to her car, Claudia popped the hatch. "Right in here, Jason. Just lay him down here."

As Jason moved to place my body in the back of Claudia's car, he whacked my head against its side. "Oh shit—sorry, Ike," he said, embarrassed.

Claudia laughed. "No apologies needed, Ike's long gone. That's just his tired old body laying there. Technically, it's just a sack of worn-out bones and water at this stage."

"Really?" Jason was taken aback by Claudia's seemingly clinical response. "You think?"

"This old body wasn't Ike, Jason. It was the container he inhabited—kinda like the vehicle that he used to go through life—and he sucked every last ounce of life out of it. The spirit that lived in this old body—that was Ike. That's what you and so many others loved so much—his spirit. That's the part of him that crawled inside of your heart and touched you."

Jason turned and looked at my sack of worn-out bones and water.

Robyn stepped forward to give Claudia another hug. "We're so grateful for all that you've done."

"It's been my pleasure—truly. His ashes will be ready in about a week. Take care, you two. And, you, too, Benson—take care of your mom and dad!"

without me

The next morning, I watched Jason awaken to a shaking bed. "Benson. BENSON! Wake up!" Benson raised his head. "Can you please stop chasing deer in your sleep! You keep waking us up!"

What? How does everyone know what I'm dreaming about? I don't know what you were dreaming about!

"Pretty nice bed, eh, Bennie?" Robyn stretched herself awake and scratched Benson's stomach while his tail began to whirl in appreciation. Robyn had convinced Jason that Benson deserved to sleep in their big bed last night, given he would be all alone with me now gone—*poor baby!*

Jason gave Benson a loving whack on his side before climbing out of bed and opening the blinds to the small balcony attached to their bedroom. Looking down at the rock face below, he quietly whispered, "Would you look at that!"

"What?" said Robyn, still laying in bed beside a delighted dog.

"There are two fawns with their mother standing right beside where Ike was laying yesterday."

Benson sat up. *Did somebody say fawn?*

Jason gently slid the door open. The two of them slowly stepped onto the balcony, careful not to scare the deer below. The mother deer looked up, sensing the spectators. Unaware, the fawns continued munching on the sweet dewy grass. Feeling no threat, the mom returned to feeding beside her babes.

"I've never seen deer this close to the house." Jason looked back at Benson, who was still sitting on the bed, head cocked sideways. "Benson, you won't believe who's right outside the dining room door below us."

Who?

"Shhh. Don't encourage him," said Robyn, intent on enjoying their morning visitors a while longer. "Oh, look, white butterflies! One, two, three—four of them. And they're all fluttering around just above Ike's cedar bed."

"Holy shit—look up there! Two eagles circling above the house." Robyn followed Jason's pointing arm until she found them. "What the hell is going on?"

With heavy hearts, both of them standing in their pyjamas, they took in the mystical scene that played out before them.

"How are you doing?"

"Not great," answered Jason. "Peter was right."

"What do you mean?"

"He sent me an email last night, thanking us for including them yesterday. It was nice what he had to say. At the end, he wrote something about grieving. Something like, 'They say, the greater the love, the greater the hurt—if that's true, hold on, you two could be in for a rough ride.'"

Robyn put her arm around Jason and pulled him closer.

the end

Acknowledgments

I want to extend a heartfelt thank you to all who, on some level—direct or otherwise—helped make this book happen! John Sarsfield for planting the idea of sharing Ike's story back in 2000. Melva McLean who, in 2015, upon completing the edit of my last book, Pulling Together, remarked, "Okay, is that it for your rowing books, because it's time to tell that story about your dog, Ike!" To my early readers, who managed through the 150,000 word manuscript—thank you for your time, feedback, encouragement, and support. Tara McGuire who, as my editor, invited me, pushed me, encouraged me, and kid-gloved this book across the finish line. Elise Volkman for proofreading; somebody had to clean up the mess. Kristy Hill, the graphic designer who made this book look as good as it possibly could. Megan Williams who, along with her incredible team at The Self Publishing Agency, coached me through the process of taking my manuscript to a finished novel. To the members of RUSH: Alex Lifeson, Geddy Lee, and the late Neil Peart, for expressing sounds and words that made life better. Ra McGuire and Brian Smith, members of the band Trooper, who wrote "We're Here For a Good Time" and allowed me to print some of the lyrics in this book. The author(s) of “Rainbow Bridge,” a beautiful poem that has soothed many a heartbroken human through the days, weeks, and months following the loss of a pet. Pat and Trev, for your patience, guidance, encouragement, humour, and, well... love! Erin and Kuz for opening your home and hearts to Ike and me. Ian Walker for going on that first hike up Black Mountain! If you want to see the inspiring things Ian is up to now, check out leftcoastnaturals.com. Allyson and Claudia for a lifetime of care and love for our pups! To Robyn and Mataya for your patience, support, and love throughout this process. Benson, Katie, Oakley, and Bella, for your playful, mischievous, wise, and loving spirits. And, to all my friends and roommates who made life lighter, easier, and more fun!

Finally, I want to acknowledge Kevin Neufeld, or Neuf as he was affectionately known. As a member of the 1984 Canadian Men's Eight at the Los Angeles Olympics he won a Gold Medal—he was my hero. In 1988 he sat behind me in our Canadian crew at the Seoul Olympics—he was my teammate. Ten years later, we reconnected and delevoped a meaningful friendship—he became a Mentor. Sadly, at the beginning of 2022, Kevin died of pancreatic cancer. As a son, sibling, husband, dad and friend to so many—Kevin was love. Rest in peace, my friend.

Jason Dorland is an Olympian, father, partner, coach, entrepreneur, and storyteller who dedicates his life to pursuing excellence in himself and those he supports. He is the author of "Chariots and Horses: Life Lessons from an Olympic Rower" and "Pulling Together: A Coaches Journey to Uncover the Mindset of True Potential." When Jason is not running with his dogs Oakley and Bella on the trails or swimming at nearby Thetis Lake near his home on Vancouver Island, he's sharing experiences and life lessons through keynotes and workshops with his wife, business partner, and fellow Olympian, Robyn Meagher. To find out more about their work, visit yourheartspace.ca.

If you'd like to support Ike's growing community and spread the word, please post a photo on your social media platforms of you reading "IKE: the dog who saved a human," and tell everyone what you thought—what made you laugh, what made you think, or what may have touched you.

And, please include #LoveReadingIke when you post so that others can follow along.

Thanks for your help—very much appreciated!